CONTENTS

PART III   FRAMING THE APPLIED LEVEL: THEMES,
ISSUE AREAS, AND CASES

ACKNOWLEDGMENTS

This book summarizes the first stage of a project the authors developed under the aegis of the F. A. Hayek Program for Advanced Study in Philosophy, Politics, and Economics of the Mercatus Center at George Mason University. The volume synthesizes, draws on, and uses the following materials:

Aligica, Paul Dragos. "Public Administration and the Classical Liberal Perspective: Criticism, Clarifications, and Reconstruction." *Administration and Society* 47 (2015). (We thank Sage Journals for permission to reprint material from this paper.)

———. "Public Administration, Public Choice and the Ostroms: The Achievements, the Failure, the Promise." *Public Choice* 163, no. 1 (2015): 111–27. (We thank Springer for permission to reprint material from this paper.)

Aligica, Paul Dragos, and Peter J. Boettke. "The Two Social Philosophies of Ostroms' Institutionalism." *Policy Studies Journal* 39, no. 1 (2010): 29–49. (We thank John Wiley and Sons for permission to use material from this paper.)

———. "Institutional Design and Ideas-Driven Social Change: Notes from an Ostromian Perspective." *Good Society Journal* 20, no. 1 (2011): 50–66. (We thank Pennsylvania State University Press for permission to reprint material from this paper.)

Aligica, Paul Dragos, and Vlad Tarko. "Co-production, Polycentricity, and Value Heterogeneity: The Ostroms' Public Choice Institutionalism Revisited." *American Political Science Review* 107, no. 4 (2013): 726–41. (We thank Cambridge University Press for permission to reprint material from this paper.)

Boettke, Peter J., Vlad Tarko, and Paul Dragos Aligica. "Why Hayek Matters? The Epistemic Dimension of Comparative Institutional Analysis." In *Revisiting Hayek's Political Economy*. Vol. 21 of *Advances in Austrian Economics*, edited by Peter J. Boettke and Virgil Henry Storr, 163–185. Bingley, UK: Emerald Group, 2016. (We thank Emerald Insight for permission to reprint material from this book chapter.)

Tarko, Vlad. "Against Gargantua: The Study of Local Public Economies." In *Elinor Ostrom: An Intellectual Biography*. London: Rowman and Littlefield, 2016. (We thank Rowman and Littlefield for permission to use material adapted from this chapter.)

Our special gratitude goes to the Mercatus Center and our colleagues at George Mason University. The list of those who offered us invaluable feedback and supported our efforts in multiple ways is large: Richard Wagner, Virgil Storr, Tyler Cowen, Dan Rothschid, Bobbi Herzberg, Stefanie Haeffele, Larry White, Don Boudreaux, Chris Coyne, Peter Leeson, Jayme Lemke, Ion Sterpan, Rosolino Candela, Arielle John, Solomon Stein, Jerry Ellig, Adam Thierer, Matt Mitchell, Dan Butler, Jennifer Zambone, and Eileen Norcross. Paul Lewis, Filippo Sabetti, Jerry Gaus, Peter Levine, Jim Johnson, Joshua A. Miller, and Jeremy Janow have been constructive critics of some of the key arguments advanced in this book. Many sincere thanks to all of them.

A draft of this book was the beneficiary of a book manuscript review conference held by the Mercatus Center in May 2016. We thank the Mercatus Center and the workshop's participants: Sebastiano Bavetta, Roberta Herzberg, Bill Blomquist, Aurelian Craiutu, Charles M. Gray, Stephen Miller, Patrick Overeem, Hilton Root, Erwin Dekker, Arjo Klamer, Claire Morgan, Karol Soltan, Aris Trantidis, and Richard Wagner. A second manuscript review workshop was organized by the Mercatus Center in August 2018. We are grateful for the comments received then from: Brian Knight, Patrick McLaughlin, James Broughel, Jennifer Huddleston Skees, Oliver Sherouse, Brent Skorup, Adam White, Adam Theirer, Anne Hobson, Walter Valdavia, Jerry Ellig, Eileen Norcross, and Veronique de Rugy.

We gratefully acknowledge the help of our assistants, Eric Celler, McKenzie Robey, and Jessica Carges for helping us prepare the final version of the manuscript. Macey Fairchild and Preetham Raj have coordinated and managed with great care and professionalism the production process. We are thankful for all their efforts.

Our special thanks go to David Pervin at Oxford University Press. His patient and professional support for this project is gratefully acknowledged and appreciated.

All these colleagues, project partners, and friends are absolved from responsibility for anything imprecise, flawed, or controversial in this work.

Introduction

Pro-market ideas and skepticism toward the role of the state have had an undeniable influence on contemporary political debates. Sometimes on the offensive, sometimes on the defensive, they are a constant presence and a major point of contention in contemporary public discourse and public policy. How much should we trust the invisible hand of the market to produce socially desirable outcomes as opposed to trusting the political and bureaucratic apparatus of modern democracies?

Critics and supporters alike associate the origins of pro-market ideas and skepticism about government with the intellectual tradition of nineteenth-century classical liberalism. Rooted in the Continental and Scottish Enlightenment, classical liberalism used to be associated with labels such as "laissez-faire" and the "minimal state." But these labels don't do justice to and don't accurately represent the views of prominent twentieth-century classical liberals like Friedrich Hayek or James Buchanan. A label like "laissez-faire" came to imply a mere faith in markets based on no analysis or understanding of the institutional and social environment of the market forces. However, classical liberals like Hayek and Buchanan have actually spent most of their intellectual energies trying to understand (a) the economic and political institutional framework that makes a society work well and (b) the social choice processes by which we can hope to constantly improve this institutional environment in the face of technological changes and other new challenges.

In one area in particular, the classical-liberal doctrine has lingered in semi-obscurity and underdevelopment. Its perspective on public governance, both its theory and its practical recommendations, is far from clear. Does classical liberalism entail a systematic framework of principles regarding public governance? If so, what are its broad recommendations and how does this perspective differ from other, more well-known perspectives on public administration? The answer seems elusive. Classical liberalism ascribes a larger scope to markets and a smaller one to government, but this is far from embracing an anarchist political philosophy. The evidence in this respect is overwhelming. Classical liberalism accepts a wide range of collective arrangements and activities ranging from certain types of regulation to the provision of specific public goods and even to specific welfare policies. As such, the question arises, within the range of government activities that classical liberalism accepts as legitimate, or at least not entirely beyond the pale, what are the particular classical-liberal views on the instruments and procedures of the administration of collective affairs? Does classical liberalism entail a distinctive point of view not only about *what* government should do, but also about *how* government should work? What kind of doctrine of govern-ance and public administration does classical liberalism inspire? Is it possible to re-construct or piece together such a position using the existing literature and practice?

This book is a pioneering attempt to answer these questions. This volume presents a fresh analytical and historical perspective on the theory of governance embedded in the classical-liberal tradition. We articulate the elements of the classical-liberal posi-tion on public governance that recognizes and confronts the problems of collective co-ordination and administration in the public arena, as opposed to either circumventing those problems or imposing institutional designs and policy standards that are not in full accordance with the nature and structure of the relevant collective phenomena. This book thus fills a large gap in the academic literature, the public discourse, and de-cision makers' and administrators' understanding of the nature and management of the public sector. Our main objective is to overview, clarify, and elaborate the elements of a distinctive perspective on the problem of collective choice and public govern-ance. Proponents of this perspective may call it "classical liberalism" and opponents may call it "neoliberalism," but the label matters less than the distinctiveness of its conceptual system, its features, and the demonstrated or potential feasibility of its implementation.

To better situate this book in its intellectual context and to better illuminate its sig-nificance we need to note that, as explained in the following pages, the field of public administration—as a systematic approach to the problem of public governance—emerged as a distinct field at the end of the nineteenth century, when the demise of classical liberalism as a reigning political and economic paradigm made room for the modern developments that led to the emergence of the administrative state, the wel-fare state, and the totalitarian state.[1] Hence, classical liberals did not participate in substantive ways in the intellectual development of public administration as a field. Later, in the second half of the twentieth century, when the revival of classical liber-alism redefined the parameters of many public debates and public policies, the focus was overwhelmingly on criticism of the existing policies and administrative structures and less on the reconstruction of governance doctrines and institutional designs. Only limited attention was dedicated to the development of a positive doctrine of public governance.

In many ways the early development of public administration was an explicit rejection of classical liberalism. For example, Woodrow Wilson's *Congressional Government* included an explicit rejection of the American constitution under the view that, in order to have a coherent public administration, the system of checks-and-balances needed to be replaced by a hierarchical system with a single center of power and "will" at the top.[2] This view became the underlining background assump-tion in the field of public administration, and led Vincent Ostrom to write *The Crisis in American Administration* and *The Political Theory of the Compound Republic*, partly as a defense of the constitutional vision of a polycentric system with countervailing powers. Furthermore, as we elaborate in the second and third parts of the book, more or less independently of the influence of Vincent Ostrom, the contemporary mainstream accounts of public administration are slowly, and thus far incompletely and inconsistently, rediscovering the importance, benefits, and challenges of a polycentric system of governance. Within this intellectual context, it is useful to articulate a full-blown, self-aware, and coherent classical-liberal position on public administration.

This book is an attempt to respond to this challenge. The task is facilitated by the fact that, although a fully fledged classical-liberal doctrine of public governance has not been articulated and presented as such in the literature, several important scholars in the fields of economics, political science, and social philosophy have elaborated the key building blocks of such a doctrine. Our task here is hence more of a synthesis. At the same time, in the field of public administration, especially under its more recent avatars labeled "governance theory" and "public management," a normative ethos focused on individuals, rather than predefined collectivities and classes, continued to be influential, with the practical challenges and constraints acting in many cases as a reality check at the applied level, reinforcing elements of this individualist ethos. All these influences had to be reflected sooner or later in both the practice and the theory of public governance. Our argument builds around all those contributions and elements, operating in the overlapping area of political theory, the field of public administration, and economics, an area that has been roughly associated with the idea of political economy, broadly defined. Hence the subtitle of the book.

The first part of the book identifies and presents the basic elements of a contemporary rendering of the classical-liberal take on public governance. These basic building blocks, heuristics, and principles lead to a distinctive intellectual system, with an underlying logic and specific properties. The objective of the first three chapters is to outline the logic, structure, and properties of this mode of thinking about public governance. This perspective differs in important ways from other possible modes of viewing, conceptualizing, and approaching the challenges of collective choice and collective action.

Chapter 1 introduces the basic egalitarian and individualist foundation to public governance in the classical-liberal tradition. At the most elementary level, the analysis is based on the repudiation of what Adam Smith called the "vanity of the philosopher"—the vanity of the elitist intellectual who believes that their own preferences take precedence over those of the "common" people. The "vanity of the philosopher" is associated with what others refer to as the "high-modernist," "seeing-like-a-state" "synoptic vision" of social order and governance, according to which the state apparatus should be used to implement a privileged elite vision upon the rest of society. In contrast to this progressive, high-modernist approach, the classical-liberal position embraces normative individualism and its twin corollaries—freedom of choice and freedom of association.

Can we have a less elitist "synoptic vision"? The social choice critique of the use of a social welfare function as a presumably objective method for aggregating everyone's preferences, which could then be used as a guideline for public policy, answers in the negative. As highlighted by William Riker in his classic, *Liberalism against Populism*, or, more recently, by Achen and Bartels in their critique of the "folk theory of democracy" in *Democracy for Realists*, there is no objective method for aggregating and centralizing individual preferences into a unique vision of the "common good." At first glance, the "folk theory of democracy" seems to provide a way to avoid the elitist "vanity of the philosopher," but the social choice critique shows it to be a naive and unsuccessful attempt. *There is no way to avoid having to deal with the complex problems*

of how heterogeneous associations form and try to influence policy. As such, the recognition of the insights brought by the public choice revolution in social and policy sciences becomes essential, as are the public choice caveats regarding the capacity of the
modern state's mechanisms to successfully generate the outcomes that many progres-
sives want it to deliver.

To understand how modern states can be built in a way that allows people with
diverse and contradictory views to coexist peacefully we need a more consistent use
of the comparative institutional analysis approach in assessing institutional performance and failure. Markets, states, and "third-sector" institutional arrangements are
all judged comparatively—and based on similar standards—in the context of how
they actually function in the real world (as opposed to how they should function ideally in our utopian imagination).

These basic ideas are intimately connected and form a logically consistent package.
They are: (a) normative individualism, (b) social choice concerns about preference aggregation and the public choice approach to these concerns, and (c) comparative institutional analysis.

For instance, once normative individualism is assumed, the social choice concerns
and the public choice approach follow naturally. Once a public choice stance is taken
regarding the institutional performance of a certain governance arrangement, comparative institutional analysis automatically becomes the default analytical benchmark. Once comparative institutional analysis is used, normative individualistic
assumptions inevitably re-enter the scene, as one needs to avoid assessment criteria
that arbitrarily privilege one point of view above others. In conjunction, these building
blocks and the underlying logic connecting them define a distinctive and consistent
position on public governance. Critics of our position should bear in mind those
connections and the difficulty of picking and choosing among them. The elements
come as a relatively tight package deal, and it is conceptually difficult to adopt only
some elements of this package.

Chapter 2 builds on these foundational insights and takes a step closer to a more
applied discussion. The preeminence of normative individualism and of the principles
of voluntary exchange and association, as well as the institutional aspects implied
in the intellectual system outlined in the first chapter, suggest caution in claiming
the primacy of one particular governance or institutional form in a complex world
of multiple trade-offs. A governance doctrine trapped in a search for pure forms of
private organization or public organization, transfixed on ideal types of private and
public, would be deficient both normatively and empirically. Chapter 2 shows how
it instead makes sense to take an approach that focuses on the following: (a) the variety of real and possible institutional and governance arrangements at the interface
between public and private, with areas of overlap and tension, as defined in various
circumstances by the relevant social actors involved; and (b) the comparison of the
feasibility and efficacy of those arrangements in delivering a variety of outcomes, out
of which the preservation of life, liberty, and property are essential.

The most important shift in perspective that follows from this is emphasizing the
dynamic nature of the relationship between the private and the public. *To understand
institutions and evaluate governance structures one needs to pay attention to the processes
of their emergence and to possible obstacles hampering their adjustment and evolution.*

Chapter 2 charts this dynamic territory, identifying a set of factors at work in shaping the public-private interface and the governance architecture that deals with it: the nature of the (collective) good or service; the technology available for producing the good or service and the mechanisms available for monitoring and enforcement; and the social context in which the good or service is provided, involving people's preferences and beliefs. The logic of the classical-liberal theory of governance leads to a focus on process and constant adjustment, a philosophical orientation that is fully consistent with the realities of governance, as shaped by the nature of services, goods, technologies, and social context.

Chapter 3 is grounded in awareness of human fallibility, structural uncertainty, and historical contingency and proceeds on the assumption that both markets and governments may fail in their roles as social coordination mechanisms. Given the factors and processes discussed in Chapter 2, the question becomes: What conditions encourage the emergence of efficient public choice structures for the management of the private-public interface? To put it differently, *how can we best encourage and help individuals to self-organize and associate at different levels, in ways that they see as most effective for realizing their individual and collective goals?* This is not only a matter of normative individualism but also one of adaptability and resilience. An adaptive institutional system is needed for ever-changing circumstances: decentralized, flexible, and structured for learning and coordination, for the collective management of continuous change in communities in which heterogeneous and dynamic individual preferences and beliefs play a major role as drivers of change. This means a switch of focus is needed from formal institutional design to a better appreciation of heuristics. It is necessary to limit excessive concern with specific policies that target specific end states and focus instead on the institutional frameworks that shape the processes of learning and action in response to various challenges. Chapter 3 presents a set of key notions for framing and understanding this dynamic process and the phenomena associated with it in ways that are particularly relevant for governance analysis and design: the focus on process and dynamic governance reinforces the core idea of the voluntary action principle. The notions of countervailing powers, voluntary sector, and nonstate governance lead to the overarching and encapsulating idea of polycentricity, the governance keystone of the normative individualist system of classical-liberal inspiration. Along the epistemic dimension, we emphasize the role of discovery, aggregation, and distribution of knowledge in society, and the fact that these concerns are natural complements of the notion of polycentricity.

The first three chapters thus demonstrate that there is a distinctive intellectual approach that consistently converts a normative individualistic vision into a model of governance that materializes and safeguards that normative ideal. Using the relevant political economy and especially public choice insights generated by more than one hundred years of intellectual history, Part I thus outlines the theoretical building blocks and the applied-level parameters of the classical-liberal theory of governance. It is true that many of the elements that define this position may be found either separately or as subsets in different and other (more or less consistent) combinations associated with other perspectives. Yet when combined together, the entire set creates a uniquely coherent configuration. That configuration gives the distinctive perspective on governance that we associate with the classical-liberal tradition.

It should be noted that, although we are trying to articulate a classical-liberal position, traditionally considered as opposed to the public sphere and very skeptical to public administration, the argument has placed us at the core of the idea of public administration. We are talking about institutional arrangements through which societies structure and govern the public domain, about the portfolio of organizational instruments that people use to create and manage the public sphere. However, our approach is not one of going through the standard steps of building a theory of bureaucracy with models of hierarchy, authority, and social control. This does not mean that authority, hierarchy, and control do not have a role. They do indeed, but they are no longer the defining background. We now approach public administration from the perspective of choice, association, adaptability, learning, and resilience, focusing on the processes that take place at the private-public interface. The background framework has changed.

Part II turns to the public administration literature and its evolution. We look at the field, as it has evolved in its intellectual history, in an attempt to locate the relationship between the mainstream of governance and public administration scholarship and the classical-liberal theory of governance. The main objective is to show how the fields of public administration and public choice (who was the main carrier of the classical-liberal ethos in the social sciences at that time) converged in their evolution, in the 1960s, with the burst of the public choice movement in the larger arena. The focus is on the intellectual junction point and the developments at that confluence. The contributions of Elinor and Vincent Ostrom emerge as uniquely important. Working in both traditions—public administration and public choice—the Ostroms created an entire program aimed at their integration.

Chapter 4 documents those developments, charts the conceptual territory, and puts the Ostroms' contributions in the context of the intellectual history of public administration. Identifying areas of convergence and affinities between the two intellectual domains, the chapter presents the Ostroms' ambitious attempt to blend the two traditions into a distinctive type of public administration: democratic public administration. The "seeing-like-a-state" perspective in public administration is openly challenged by the "seeing-like-a-citizen" alternative in a field that, by the time the Ostroms started their program, was trying to unshackle itself from the inherent statism of its Wilsonian legacy.

Chapter 5 illuminates the specific nature of the synthesis attempted by the Ostroms and their associates and discusses the successes and the failures of their endeavors. Their efforts to promote the public choice perspective in public administration and the public administration perspective in public choice were aimed at engendering a paradigm change from bureaucratic public administration to democratic public administration. These efforts are presented here as a reference point, a model, and a case study entailing several lessons about the nature and limits of such endeavors. We also build upon the work of Michael Spicer, a remarkable author who has kept alive this type of approach in the field of public administration by combining public choice and knowledge process theory, long after the initial effect of the Ostroms' efforts faded.

Chapter 6 further elaborates the conceptual apparatus emerging from those efforts, especially the pivotal notion of polycentricity, as a unifying and organizing framework for governance theorizing. The Ostroms crafted the basics of a systematic approach to institutional hybridity, diversity, quasi-markets, and quasi-governments, and they spelled out the logic that unites those ideas into a comprehensive theoretical system. Recognizing that their system is still a work in progress, Chapter 6 tries to reinforce the emerging theoretical framework in three major ways: first, by explicitly articulating the elements of a theory of value heterogeneity as a foundational component of the entire approach; second, by clarifying a technical ambiguity in the construction of the co-production model that connects the domain of individual subjective values with the domain of institutions and social order and elaborating the implications; and third, by reconsidering the issue of polycentricity, the capstone of the Ostromian system, in light of the first two points.

The chapter advances a fresh elaboration of the notion of polycentricity, seen as a solution to both the co-production problem and the problems of social choice in conditions of deep heterogeneity. We emphasize several critical features that pertain to both its positive-analytical dimension and the normative one. The relevance of polycentricity as the key framework of the classical-liberal theory of governance is thus reasserted and reinforced.

Part III is an attempt to illustrate more concrete applications of the concepts, principles, and theories that define the distinctive governance theory described and elaborated in this book. This part takes another step in the applied direction. Seen in conjunction, the cases explored in Chapters 7–9 show how governance problems can be thought of using the intellectual instruments introduced in the first two parts of the book. The three issue areas discussed—metropolitan governance, independent regulatory agencies, and corporate social responsibility—are positioned at the sensitive interface between the private and the public, and each illustrates a different facet and challenge of governance in conditions of complexity and hybridity.

Chapter 7 focuses on the problems of metropolitan governance, one of the first domains in which the polycentric theoretical lens has been applied. The example of police services is used as an overture, as the chapter revisits the field and the literature fifty years after the Ostroms were involved in the metropolitan reform debate and launched their program. Further elaborations and new insights are presented. The public choice institutionalist polycentricity-based perspective is applied, illustrated, and expounded at a concrete level.

Chapter 8 explores the issue of independent regulatory agencies. Independent regulatory agencies are a serious challenge to democratic administration. They are government organizations of unelected officials who often resist even mild attempts to conduct an audit, and they are vulnerable to corruption, rent-seeking, regulatory capture, and revolving-door problems. The chapter first notes why independent regulatory agencies may nonetheless respond to genuine needs. Namely, they are a way of addressing controversial problems that are hard to decentralize. The common solution proposed by most critics of the regulatory state, namely to return to the legislature the rule-creation responsibilities now ascribed to independent regulatory agencies, seems to be not very promising in most cases. Legislatures lack the relevant knowledge and bringing such matters into the realm of everyday political swings would create too much regime uncertainty. But, although the critics of the regulatory state may have provided few viable alternatives so far, their arguments are still powerful and not easily dismissed. The chapter uses classical-liberal governance theory and the institutional imagination associated with it to offer a better understanding of the operations of independent regulatory agencies and their possible improvement. An in-depth look questions the conventional wisdom regarding independent regulatory agencies and their functioning in the larger architecture of contemporary governance systems. Imagining alternative arrangements that may reduce deficiencies and improve performance illustrates the classical-liberal approach at work in one of the most complex and difficult areas of public governance.

Chapter 9 pushes the frontier of the discussion into a new, growing, and controversial governance debate area: corporate social responsibility. One of the most sensitive issues in polycentric governance systems, with their hybrid institutional arrangements at the dynamic interface between the private and the public, is that of specifying what are, and what are not, the responsibilities of the private sector— business firms and enterprises—with respect to the public domain. The chapter offers an exploratory attempt to address this challenge. Corporate social responsibility has emerged in the past several decades as a preeminent concept and an issue area that engages the problem of the public role of private businesses. The literature has grown around the notions of social responsibility and stakeholders and thus presents both a challenge and an opportunity for the governance perspective articulated in our book. Chapter 9 demonstrates how the ideas and theories discussed combine, complement, and bolster the literature and the associated applied-level insights.

Each of the three chapters in Part III challenges aspects of the conventional wisdom while putting to work the concepts of polycentricity, public choice, knowledge processes, countervailing powers, and freedom of association. In conjunction, they show that the classical-liberal perspective articulated here is able to offer a coherent, imaginative, and constructive approach to a set of tangible governance challenges.

We conclude the book by documenting an intriguing phenomenon. It turns out that the clearer the articulation of the classical-liberal perspective on governance, the more we discover that there are parallel and independently developed attempts to define and implement akin approaches already out there. Those similar approaches do not identify themselves as "classical liberal" and do not follow from the traditional classical-liberal conceptual underpinnings or intellectual genealogy. Such convergence from different and quite distinct ideological directions gives credibility to the claim that these proposals are not merely ideological wishful thinking but capture possible areas of consensus rooted in a realistic scientific understanding of the problems at hand. We conclude our argument with the observation that contemporary governance theory and practice seem to have moved increasingly closer to some of the core ideas of the classical-liberal perspective on governance; therefore, it is fully justified to contemplate this perspective as a coherent intellectual package based on a specific set of normative assumptions.

Three potentially controversial matters must be addressed before moving ahead to the more substantive discussion. The first is related to use of the term *classical liberalism* and the idea of associating our intellectual effort with the stance designated by the term. As some reviewers and commentators of our manuscript have argued, the use of the term *classical liberalism* may be detrimental because it introduces unwanted and unneeded ideological luggage. In fact, our book, they say, is an argument that shows how a combination of normative assumptions and institutional design and empirical insights leads to a distinctive view about the nature of effective and desirable governance principles and practices. Why do we not simply stick to that, in itself a noteworthy contribution? Why do we need the ideological tangent? One may argue that the label is irrelevant. Why do we not simply label it in a neutral way ("Governance Theory X," for instance) and move ahead without looking back?

This may indeed be a convenient approach, especially given the current ideological climate in academia. Yet, there is value in recognizing the existence of a long intellectual history and an already established tradition. The programmatic normative individualism and the associated intellectual and institutional apparatus meant to reflect and protect it are not something new. As noted, there is an internal coherence in this tradition—an underlying logic connecting its parts. Once normative individualism is accepted as a political axiom—the preferences of the individual members of a society should be the ultimate legitimizing force and the driver of governance systems—and once there is an understanding of the profound problems posed by the aggregation of those preferences into social welfare functions, then a particular governance theory and a certain set of political practices must be accepted. The history of the classical-liberal tradition is the history of this logic unfolding and becoming clearer and more explicit in time. It is not our invention. We are participants and contributors to this development, and we are not interested in pretending to be more original than we actually are. There is an entire intellectual history behind the insights we elaborate in our book, and it needs to be acknowledged as such.

Moreover, because we are not concerned here primarily with the history of thought, we do not do justice to the rich elaborations that exist in this long tradition. If readers are intrigued by our account, they may want to delve further into that rich history of ideas, which in many ways provides neglected insights. We cannot and do not want to obscure this long tradition. On the contrary, we want readers to engage more with it. The specific history of ideas, which sometimes progresses and other times leads to dead ends and detours, matters. The evolution of those ideas, their ups and downs in the public arena, their mutations, are part and parcel of the governance process we try to chart and elaborate. Some of these ideas have emerged from or have been applied to governance practice. The interplay of ideas and institutions and the learning from different events and from different environments and historical circumstances have shaped the classical-liberal thinking about governance. In the end, history matters. Separating current governance ideas and doctrines from their roots—for epistemological or ideological reasons—would lead to a diminished and impoverished understanding. At a minimum, we have the obligation to evoke and remind our readers of the existence and relevance of this history. The simplest way to do so is to use the label that comes closest to evoking it. Therefore, although we understand and appreciate the concern that using the term *classical liberalism* so saliently in our arguments may distract or even repel some readers, we think that intellectual probity and intellectual effectiveness make its use inescapable for the type of scholarly enterprise we engage in this book.

The second potentially controversial element is related to the place that the Ostroms' work has in the argument, narrative, and conceptual reconstruction attempted here. We anticipate the following question: To what extent is there justification to associate the classical-liberal label to the Ostroms' work or to aspects of their work?

A discussion about public governance today, in the aftermath of the public choice and institutionalist revolutions, must deal sooner or later with Ostroms' contributions, as both of them were past presidents of the Public Choice Society and a constant presence there, for a long time and from its very beginning. Their contributions were pivotal to the intellectual history of governance in the twentieth century, and our own project is significantly indebted to their perspective. The Ostroms' democratic administration, as an alternative to both bureaucratic administration and the radical new public administration, stands, with its Madisonian and federalist reverberations, at the confluence between the fields of public choice and public administration as a bearer of a deeper and broader social philosophy encapsulating both positive and normative elements.[3] It is also impossible to avoid noticing the general normative orientation and genealogy of the public choice program out of which the polycentricity and public economy research agenda of the Ostroms has emerged. Normative and methodological individualism and the self-governance ideal are some of the key features.[4] Notwithstanding some recent dubious claims, it is not difficult to document (as we do in Chapters 4 and 5) the ways in which the Ostroms' work was received, as well as the ways in which the underlying social philosophy of their message was perceived and branded by mainstream scholars in the field of public administration. This all points toward a certain profile. The clustering of features goes preponderantly in one direction. All we do here is to recognize this reality and take the argument from there to where its logic leads.

We do not even want to claim that this social philosophy should be seen as *exclusively* classical liberal, and we do not insist on calling the Ostroms classical liberals. It is true that, especially in the work of Elinor Ostrom, a certain communitarian sensibility is also present. Hence, we do not deny the hypothetical possibility that someone might attempt to reconstruct the Ostromian theory of polycentricism and self-governance as part of a different system, with different assumptions, different implications, and a different ideological flavor. We have not seen that done so far, and we are hard pressed to imagine how a system predicated on normative and methodological individualism and on the importance of social and institutional diversity could have an orientation very different from the one identified in the pages of the present book. Yet, we keep an open mind and want to leave the issue open for investigation. It is undoubtedly the case that the Ostroms have been far more interested in descriptive and scientific accuracy than in fitting into a predefined ideological position. At this point, all we claim is that the Ostroms' contributions are fully compatible with the classical-liberal tradition and obviously overwhelmingly rooted in it. In addition, we claim that the Ostroms' contributions provide an excellent vehicle or basic structure for updating and advancing a contemporary version of a governance theory in the classical-liberal tradition. We are confident that the Ostroms would not have opposed the use of their work as a source of inspiration, benchmark, vehicle, or building block for the development of governance theories and approaches in any tradition compatible with the ideals and values of self-governance.

Consider the following account by Vincent Ostrom in a letter to James M. Buchanan dated October 10, 1977:

We are . . . confronted with the puzzle that the market may derive solutions where no one is concerned with maintaining the institutional integrity of a market, including the security of property rights, enforcement of contracts, and the community of interest which market participants share in common. The institutional provision of a market as such is of the nature of a public good (i.e., subject to joint use where exclusion does not apply) even though market participants engage in the exchange of private goods as they make use of that joint facility. . . . The cross pressures affecting market transactions and moral communities may mean that each is subject to serious weaknesses implied by the operation of the other. Perhaps one way out of the puzzle is to follow the federalist approach and recognize the potential for multiple communities sharing diverse sets of values. Unless we get the appropriate mix we may be in trouble.[5]

Thus, the big picture is concerned with a combination of the following difficult issues: (a) the fact that the institutions that underpin markets, and hence secure long-term development, appear to have some aspects of a public good and thus can be vulnerable to the typical free-rider problem; (b) the tension between the market's amoral nature—which delivers anything for which there is enough demand and hence caters to a wide variety of conflicting preferences—and people's conflicting moral judgments—which allow them to condemn various things that markets amorally deliver; and (c) the tension between the benefits of self-governing decentralization that allows people the freedom to associate with others who have similar moral views and hence allows small communities to regulate markets according to a variety of moral beliefs and the benefits of creating large-scale unrestricted markets that tend to undermine the capacity of local communities to preserve their moral and aesthetic idiosyncrasies.

In the same letter, Vincent Ostrom notes that survival of the system ultimately depends on people maintaining a broad understanding and appreciation of the liberal principles that justify the system. Unfortunately, that understanding has come under heavy attack from both Keynesian progressivism and nationalist neomercantilism:

Constitutional principles do not work by themselves but depend upon the shared beliefs and shared values held by the members of a community that has recourse to particular types of political settlements. The instruments don't work unless activated by people who know how to make proper use of them and who appreciate their limits. It is precisely this set of beliefs that has eroded under the force of logical positivism where political phenomena are treated as though they were natural phenomena rather than artifacts created to serve human purposes. Thus, the political theory of the Founding Fathers had important normative components: justice was an important value to be realized and if essential characteristics of the human animal were not taken into account, justice could not be realized. The neo-mercantilism inherent in Keynes and the new Leviathan inherent in the assumption that the President knows best, simply leave us morally defenseless. . . . To the

extent that we feel that we can contribute to a revival of constitutional understanding, it seems to me that we also shall be contributing to a moral re-
generation of a society that begins to appreciate that we can never have the
best of all possible worlds.[6]

As such quotes show, affinity to the classical-liberal philosophy is hard to deny. And,
needless to say, Vincent Ostrom's concern is still with us today and is perhaps even
more acute than it was forty years ago. As noted in his letter to Buchanan, Ostrom
placed his hopes in preservation of the "federalist approach," according to which we
"recognize the potential for multiple communities sharing diverse sets of values."[7]

This leads us to the third and last potential controversial issue, one related to the
concept of polycentricity, a concept first used programmatically by Michael Polanyi
and one that has come to play a key role in our argument. The theory of governance
that we develop in this book as part of the classical-liberal tradition gravitates around
it. However, polycentricity and the associated epistemic processes are studied today
from multiple scholarly perspectives and ideological angles. Again, the question is to
what extent it is justified to associate polycentricity with the classical-liberal perspective and tradition. Governance in the classical-liberal tradition is strongly based on
diversity, heterogeneity, and complex division of power and knowledge. The emphasis
is on a process that depends on social learning and adaptation in a pluralistic society.
Just as Friedrich A. Hayek argued with respect to the order-inducing and learning
capacity of the market in radically heterogeneous and uncertain conditions, the
classical-liberal theory of polity similarly emphasizes how individuals come to learn
how to cooperate and adapt by building evolving communities. Polycentricity is in
many ways a technical concept designed to address these very concerns. As such, it is
indeed steeped in the classical-liberal tradition. However, these concerns are not ideological per se—they are related to general concerns about avoiding public policy errors
and building an institutional system capable of responding to unexpected shocks and
adapting to new challenges. Consequently, although the intellectual history of the
idea of polycentricity is classical liberal, its relevance is far broader and more ideologically neutral.

A closer look at the intellectual strategies and challenges used to approach
polycentricity reveals how they suggestively resonate with the pattern of investigation and conceptualization that the founding figures of the classical-liberal tradition
applied initially to the economic order. Polycentric systems, explains Elinor Ostrom,
are "complex, adaptive systems without one central authority dominating all of the
others."[8] And by providing an overarching concept, the theory of polycentricity may
help draw analogies from the study of one type of adaptive self-organizing system
upon another. This, according to Vincent Ostrom, is not always a simple task because

penetrating an illusion of chaos and discerning regularities that appear to
be created by an "invisible hand" [implies] that the tasks of scholarship . . .
will be presented with serious difficulties. . . . Patterns and regularities which
occur under an illusion of chaos may involve an order of complexity that is
counterintuitive.[9]

In his overview of different types of polycentric systems, Vincent Ostrom[10] lays out several challenging examples apart from market economies. They all have the same features: they are decentralized systems in which coordination happens without hierarchical command and control, and they lack market prices for a coordination mechanism. How does coordination happen then? Such are the hard cases of emergent social orders, and the concept of polycentricity aims to provide a framework for analyzing under what conditions such emergent orders can be expected to coordinate in a productive fashion. What is at stake in the attempt to build a theory of polycentricity, according to Vincent Ostrom, is "nothing less than a theory of hidden order, a theory of an 'invisible hand' directing the 'social mechanism.'"[11]

In brief, polycentricity is, first, a mere description of the complexity of social reality; second, a heuristic-analytical device for beginning to understand how order emerges in complex social systems; and, finally, a normative framework for discussing how to improve institutions. Exploring these dimensions and trying to use the insights thus gained to improve private and public governance, tellingly reveals significant patterns of similarity and convergence with the intellectual tradition whose defining moment was the search for, and the identification of, the hidden order of market processes. Again, we do not claim that the polycentricity theme belongs exclusively to the classical-liberal tradition. After all, it is a social science idea whose normative interpretation could vary in different political philosophy frameworks. All we claim is that its features match well with the classical-liberal perspective and that it could be used in a natural way as a central concept in the construction of a modern, up-to-date theory of public governance in that tradition. Overall, in this case, as in the case of all other considerations, arguments, and investigations we advance in this book, we try to follow as close as possible the spirit and the logic induced by a question asked by the Ostroms, a crucial question that motivates and defines their lifework:

> If citizens are to be first their own governors and active participants in the governance of their affairs as they relate to one another in diverse communities of relationships, can such societies be constituted by some single center of Supreme Authority exercising governmental prerogatives for Societies as a Whole? Or do democratic societies get constituted by using ideas to pool, rearrange and compromise existing interests in relevant communities of relationships applicable to the scope and domain of activities that take account of what needs to be accomplished?[12]

PART 1

A DISTINCTIVE PERSPECTIVE ON GOVERNANCE

The Building Blocks

The first part of the book introduces a distinctive theoretical position that may be called—for good intellectual and historical reasons—a "classical-liberal perspective" on governance. This theoretical position also leads to a unique applied-level perspective, reframing many familiar debates in a new light. Using the relevant political economy and especially public choice insights generated by more than one hundred years of intellectual history, we outline the theoretical building blocks and applied-level parameters of this point of view.

Chapter 1 articulates in public choice and political economy terms what we mean by "classical liberalism." We explain the connections and the differences from both the libertarian position and the left-liberal position. We emphasize that the classical-liberal position combines a number of mutually enforcing ideas in a consistent "package." These ideas include freedom of choice and freedom of association as the normative individualist grounded guidelines, skepticism toward the possibility of aggregating individual preferences into a unique social welfare function as a supposed objective and uncontroversial guideline for public policy, and a consistent employment of the comparative institutional analysis approach in which government solutions are compared to both market and civil society alternatives.

Chapter 2 delves deeper into the analysis of the public-private distinction. Unlike the axiomatic property-rights version of libertarianism (employed by authors like Rothbard or Ayn Rand), the classical-liberal position is built upon the recognition of the complexity of property-rights arrangements, and on the fact that these arrangements evolve in time depending on new technological and social developments. We explain how to think about this crucial matter by focusing on the process of property-rights creation and redefinition.

Chapter 3 expands our perspective beyond the issue of property rights into the complex matter of institutional change in general. We introduce the concept of polycentricity as a fundamental conceptual tool for thinking about how to facilitate social-institutional experimentation and the discovery of new institutional solutions to social-economic problems in a resilient manner. Polycentric structures facilitate knowledge aggregation and experimentation while also providing a system of checks and balances that reduces abuses of power and incentive problems more generally.

1

The Classical-Liberal Theory
of Governance

This chapter maps out the foundations for a classical-liberal position on the theory and practice of public governance. Although such a task inevitably touches on traditional themes of political philosophy and political theory, the discussion here is not meant to be a systematic outline of the philosophical or doctrinal "essence" of classical liberalism. The emphasis is only on a restricted set of elements that are highly relevant due to their *governance* theory implications. For an extended and up-to-date discussion of the nature of classical liberalism and its philosophical neighbors or competitors, the excellent works of several scholars provide the essential bibliographical background.[1]

Any modern economic and political theory of governance is defined by a particular stance regarding the proper scope of collective action and a preferred set of methods for dealing with public goods and externalities problems. How should we decide what problems fall within the public sphere and require collective decision-making? What are the best institutions for governing the public sphere? A standard misunderstanding perpetrated by many critics and friends of classical liberalism is to assume that it simply denies the domain of collective action altogether and that it is a doctrine inflexibly adverse to the "public," in the name of the "private."

This misinterpretation leads to a failure to grasp one of the most distinctive features of this tradition: the programmatic effort to approach the problem of the "public" and its relationship with the "private" using the fundamental normative benchmark of *voluntary consent*, while at the same time acknowledging the limits of the utopian or romantic anarchist dreams of a purely voluntary society. The dream of rendering the government entirely obsolete has been kept alive from the romantic utopia of William Godwin's *Enquiry Concerning Political Justice*, to Peter Kropotkin's *Mutual Aid*, and to twentieth-century anarchists like Murray Rothbard and David Friedman. By contrast, we are building here upon a non-utopian vision that acknowledges some "limits to liberty," to use James Buchanan's words, while at the same time still aiming to discover which institutions can most effectively maximize individual freedom and which intellectual outlook on politics and society best keeps alive an ongoing gradual reform process that ever expands freedom.

As such, we start with an exploration into the problem of public choice, collective action, and the scope of public domain. From an economic point of view, the most fundamental issue about our topic is that *public administration begins where economic calculation ends.* "Economic calculation" refers to the basic challenge be-hind the overall social problem of allocating available resources to alternative pos-sible ends. In the realm of private goods and services this problem is solved in a bottom-up emergent fashion as a side effect of the profit-maximizing actions of individuals and firms (figure 1.1). The typical model of economic decision-making in terms of maximizing expected profits embeds a cost-benefit analysis on the part of individuals and organizations, and brings societal constraints into the individual decision-making. As long as the institutions of a market economy (i.e., reliable contracts, property protection, and a predictable purchasing power of money) are in place, such individual-level economic calculation leads to roughly efficient social outcomes, meaning that resources tend to end up allocated to their most-valued uses. A firm calculates its profits as revenues minus costs. In turn, revenues and costs are measured using *market prices* for the resources used in the production pro-cess (including labor) and the *market price* for the product/service created. Each of these market prices reflects broader societal supply and demand for the resources used and for the products/services created respectively. In other words, in com-petitive markets, a firm's revenues indicate the social benefits created by the firm to consumers, while its costs indicate the opportunity costs for society as the re-sources used by the firm could have been used for other purposes. In a nutshell, this means that profits embed both *information* about whether a firm is creating something that is more valuable (as far as the broader society is concerned) than the resources it is consuming, and an *incentive* to act upon this information. A neg-ative profit means that the firm is wasting valuable resources in order to produce a relatively less valued product/service, and the negative profit itself also generates

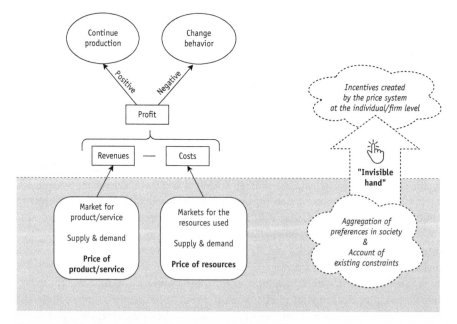

Figure 1.1 The "invisible hand" mechanism of the market.

an incentive to change such behavior. By contrast, a positive profit means that society at large values the product/service more than it values the resources used in the production process, and the positive profit encourages the firm to continue such productive and socially beneficial behavior.

Importantly, the above logic of the "invisible hand" of the market does not hold in the public realm. For instance, if one firm's activity has large negative externalities upon third parties (e.g., pollution), and there are no effective public institutions to address this problem, the harm caused to those third parties is not included in the market prices—as the third parties are not included in the exchange process that gives rise to the market prices. One conceivable solution to negative externalities is to establish Pigouvian taxes, which will increase the costs faced by the firms. Enacting a Pigouvian tax is an attempt to (monetarily) quantify the harms suffered by the third parties. With the tax in place, the firm's profit maximization calculation changes as its costs side of the equation changes; for example, the firm will now have incentives to find ways of reducing the negative externality. However, importantly, there is no market mechanism by which to discover the *efficient level* of a Pigouvian tax. The government establishing such a tax may either set it too low, hence not fully addressing the negative externality problem, or too high, therefore overreacting to a relatively small problem. It is entirely possible even for the government to establish a Pigouvian tax that makes matters worse, for instance, severely curbing a useful economic activity (highly valued by many) for the purpose of reducing a relatively minor problem. It is important to be aware of the deep conceptual difficulties involved in the attempt of discovering the efficient level of even something as simple as a Pigouvian tax. This gives us a simple example of the *type of problem* that challenges public administration in virtually all of its activities.

Generally speaking, public administration faces a serious intrinsic problem in that it operates only indirectly or mediated with the market prices to guide its activities. That is why even *evaluating* whether the activities of a public administration are efficient is a very difficult task, let alone the task of *designing* a public administration that incentivizes its members to act in accordance with efficiency considerations. The public administration cannot act as a profit-maximizing firm because it uses resources not priced via markets and because it has revenues from taxation rather than voluntary exchanges. If the markets for the product/service or the inputs or both are missing, the connection between, on one hand, the aggregation of preferences in society and the existing production constraints and, on the other hand, the incentives to act in ways consistent with those preferences and constraints breaks down (see figure 1.1). Other types of mechanisms need to be introduced to substitute for the absence of the market's invisible hand mechanism. Some of these mechanisms may work better than others, but one should bear in mind that even the problem of how to *evaluate* and *compare* them lacks an obvious solution.

Thinking critically about public administration implies taking this problem of economic calculation seriously and carefully evaluating alternative mechanisms for resource allocation. How can public administration best decide how to influence the ways in which scarce resources are allocated in society, given that, in many regards, it cannot rely on the market system in most of its decisions? The classical-liberal perspective on public administration has a distinctive answer to this question, and tries to find alternative mechanisms to the market by taking inspiration from the reasons why the market's invisible hand works. This is why concepts like *polycentricity* will play an important role in our account.

In the realm of the "public"—in the absence of private property, market prices, and the profit-and-loss mechanism—we do not have recourse to the "benefits-minus-costs" method of evaluating efficiency. We can do a few things in response: attempt to develop processes that mimic the private sector (the Wicksellian-Musgrave move and the polycentricity perspective) or we can consider the questions of scale and scope of governmental services under the assumption that those areas that don't meet a certain definitional test would be left to the private or independent sector. The question about how the independent sector can fill in gaps is also important because it affects our expectations about what would happen in the absence of government control in various areas. This leads us to consider not just how local or decentralized a government should be, but also to understand its relationships to private governance or communal governance operations.

In contrast to this, the bureaucratic administration approach argues that we can organize affairs economically outside the context of the market. Proponents of this view either have to assume that the cost-benefit analysis need not and in fact should not apply—because "economists know the price of everything and the value of nothing," and sometimes we just "ought to do the right thing" regardless of cost considerations—or they think they have discovered the appropriate methods and processes for revealing citizens' demands in the production and distribution of public goods and can mimic the private sector in the public sector.

In this book we are both challenging the paradigm associated to the rise of the bureaucratic administration in the twentieth century and contributing to the alternative perspectives proposed within the public administration literature by bringing in considerations developed in the public finance, public choice, and new institutional economics literatures.

Our approach may sometimes seem akin to "new public management," but, as the emphasis on the importance of the economic calculation problem should make clear, we are in several ways disagreeing with that approach. For example, one needs to stay guarded on the issue of "public-private partnerships" precisely on the grounds that such partnerships do not actually create markets in inputs and outputs. Having something produced by a "private firm" while both inputs and outputs continue to be priced by government fiat in no way addresses the issue. Efficiency is assured by having market prices as constraints on both ends, not by simply having the management in private hands. Similarly, there's no inherent merit in "running the government like a business." Actual businesses tend to be efficient because both their revenues and their costs are determined by market prices, set by actual supply and demand. For example, a decentralized system in which local governments are producers of public services but are forced to engage in Tiebout competition, and where tax rates are determined by the workings of this competitive quasi-market, may very well be more efficient than a centralized government that runs everything through public-private partnerships.

The Distinctiveness of the Classical-Liberal Position

We identify the following ideas as the foundation of the classical-liberal governance theory:

1. A bottom-up perspective to understanding social order and evaluating governance structures. This has two important corollaries:
   a. Freedom of choice and freedom of association as the main normative guidelines, rather than top-down stipulation of specific "social goals"; and
   b. Skepticism toward the possibility of aggregating individual preferences into a unique social welfare function as a supposed objective and uncontroversial guideline for public policy.

2. Consistent employment of the comparative institutional analysis approach. This has an important public policy corollary. A government solution to market failures is acceptable only if
   a. The government failures associated with that solution can be made smaller than the market failure it is trying to address; and
   b. Civil society ("third-sector") institutional arrangements are also less efficient than the government solution.

The above principles undoubtedly create somewhat of an antigovernment stance. However, far from neglecting or being hostile toward the public and collective dimensions, the classical-liberal intellectual tradition in fact articulates a profound and nuanced approach to those dimensions. But, to see this, one needs to bear in mind the distinction between society and government and accept that there are many consensual ways in which we can deal with collective matters. Furthermore, there are many possible ways of organizing governments and assigning them various responsibilities, especially in a federal system. The classical-liberal literature is built around the analysis of the public space in its relationship to the private space. We are not going to engage in a comprehensive or systematic elaboration of the rich philosophical classical-liberal tradition. Our emphasis here is only on the practical elements relevant to understanding the classical-liberal perspective on governance and public administration. In this respect, the gist of classical liberalism, in its practical dimension, is succinctly captured by Kukathas, who notes that classical liberalism is

> a political outlook which responds to human diversity by advocating institutions that permit different beliefs and ways of life to coexist; it accepts the fact of the plurality of ways of life—of the multiplicity of religious and moral values in the modern world—and favors toleration. . . . It rejects the idea of an organic and spiritually unified social order in which the interests of the individual are brought into perfect harmony with the interests of the community. Individuals have different ends; there is no single, common goal that all must share; and, necessarily, these ends come into conflict. The problem, from a liberal point of view, is to regulate rather than eradicate these conflicts.[2]

As such, the main question that classical-liberal governance deals with is how to organize public governance such that this multiplicity of values, interests, and preferences can best coexist and that as many people as possible can thus live as part of society without feeling they are forced into an institutional structure with which they disagree. When it comes to governance systems in general, the main challenge according to the political theorist Robert Dahl is that "to live in association with others necessarily requires that [one] must sometimes obey collective decisions that are binding on all members of the association. The problem, then, is to discover a way by which the members of an association may make decisions binding on all and still govern themselves."[3]

The ultimate classical-liberal ideal is a society of maximally free individuals—that is, a society in which, as long as one is peaceful, one is never forced to do or be any-thing that one does not want. As James Buchanan notes, such a society must fun-damentally engender and incorporate a market economy: "Under regimes where individual rights to do things are well defined and recognized, the free market offers maximal scope for private, personal eccentricity, for individual freedom in its most elementary meaning."[4] However, as any overview of the literature reveals, all major thinkers in the classical-liberal tradition take seriously the institutional and opera-tional challenges implied by the existence and administration of the complex domain of collective choice and collective action in which social aggregation of individual preferences and coordination of individual actors pose many profound challenges. Accepting these challenges, while worrying about the dangers of centralized power and of legitimizing coercive governance methods, gives classical liberalism its distinc-tiveness. As we discuss in more detail in the next chapter, classical-liberal thinkers go beyond mere criticism and deconstruction of the idea of a public collective realm, and propose a different constructive approach. The internal tensions the public-private dyad induces are unavoidable and there is no reason to pretend there is an easy way out. Classical liberalism rejects the mirage of the intellectual constructions that try to reduce the public to the private or vice versa.

This stance has deep normative and moral implications. To use Vincent Ostrom's terms, a "Faustian bargain [exists] in which human beings are required to have po-tential recourse to instruments of evil to advance their joint or common good."[5] By acknowledging the complex reality of the human condition, with both its private and public facets, classical liberalism takes the messy road of ambiguities, complexities, and contradictions as opposed to the simple one of axiomatic and a-priori consistency that comes from siding with ideal-type extremes.

Authors like Hayek and Buchanan keep alive the radically libertarian ideal of a purely voluntary and contractual society. Yet, it is important to note that they are skeptical of the idea that the details can rationally be constructed regarding how that end state of affairs would actually look. As Buchanan notes, "We make no attempt to generate specific predictions as to what might emerge from the prospective agree-ment among contractors who choose behind the veil of ignorance." The reality is too complex to allow for a single general solution to all problems, and thus "no single decision rule was likely to be chosen for general applicability over the whole range of political action[s]."[6] Moreover, there are numerous property-rights arrangements that are compatible with the idea of voluntary organization and self-governance. As illustrated by Elinor Ostrom's work on how communities manage common property by devising rules and norms, sometimes the property arrangement that works best is neither one of individual property rights nor one of state property.[7] Instead of imagining an ideal end state of affairs, the focus must be on conceptualizing the institutional arrangements and the mechanisms and processes of institutional change that tend to move society in the direction of the contractualist ideal: voluntary agreement, voluntary exchange, and voluntary association. Whether society will ever get there, or how exactly that end state of affairs would look, is anyone's guess. But no matter how exciting it is to engage in such speculation about the optimal end state and how important it is to keep alive the normative ideal, it serves no purpose to conflate the normative ideal with applied theory.

In dealing with the governance challenges in a classical-liberal paradigm, we thus need to keep in mind the institutional regimes and arrangements and their functional role in a universe guided by normative individualism and constrained empirically by the heterogeneity of preferences, beliefs, endowments, and capabilities. It is a system of competing, incommensurate values, seeking a modus vivendi, a system of value pluralism and conflicting claims of human flourishing. At the most basic level, its aim is peaceful coexistence. At the most advanced level, it is a system of pluralist forms of flourishing and the appropriate institutional regimes associated with them. The challenge is to create—given real-life, historical, and empirical circumstances—a governance structure for partially conflicting and partially complementary interests or goals.

In brief, classical liberalism has as a defining feature a concern for the implications of governance arrangements of collective action, public choices, and collective goods under assumptions of normative individualism and circumstances of deep heterogeneity. Hence, it must struggle in uneasy ways with intrinsic theoretical and practical tensions. It tries to work out a compromise between the simplicity, clarity, and consistency of the conceptual apparatus on the one hand, and the realism and practical relevance of its constructs on the other hand. At a closer look, the classical-liberal tradition ranging from Adam Smith in the eighteenth century to Buchanan and Hayek in the twentieth century is precisely about the public realm and the ways it could be structured to accommodate the diversity and freedom of the private realm. Once the confusion regarding the place of the public or collective dimensions and phenomena in the classical-liberal perspective is clarified, the ground is cleared for further elaboration.

"Seeing Like a State" and the "Synoptic Delusion"

In the practice of construing institutions and governance arrangements, one could take either of two stances, on the basis of two distinct views. On the one hand, implicitly or explicitly, consciously or not, situations may be imagined and assessed from a privileged, commanding-heights position. Ideally, this would be the perspective of a benevolent and omniscient ruler, or perhaps a hypothetical impartial observer who is the bearer of an objective, unique, and well-defined "public interest." This hypothetical actor would define what should be done, and the state is conceptualized as an imperfect implementation of this observer and ruler. From this "seeing-like-a-state" perspective, all social problems are observed, analyzed, and potentially solved by an external force ("the state") acting upon society.

By contrast, the classical-liberal perspective focuses on individuals living together and being understood in their various capacities as producers, consumers, citizens, and self-governing beings. According to this perspective, all that exists is a society of normal human beings, without an overarching knowledge, who live and operate in local conditions, in domains that are more often than not in the fuzzy area between the public and the private, in conditions of relative uncertainty, having a mixture of selfish and generous motives. There is no hypothetical impartial observer, and the state is not an outside force but a complex organization embedded within society and entangled with markets and various pressure groups in complex ways. This perspective provides an escape from the temptation of seeing like a state. When we think about governance, we need to start "seeing like a citizen" and wonder what kind of institutions people would create if they were truly allowed to live under conditions of political freedom and equality.

Under the seeing-like-a-state perspective, there is a strong social engineering presumption: Economic and technological efficiency, social justice, and social equality could and should be achieved through top-down manipulations, interventions, and constraints on the basis of superior motives and expert, privileged knowledge, all mobilized and rendered practical by the state. Interestingly, even when the state is assumed to be democratic, the rhetoric and knowledge production is meant for a special audience or social group—those who are in charge of running the state. As noted by Abram Bergson in his discussion of the theoretical articulation of a democratic version of statism:

> According to this view the problem is to counsel not citizens generally but public officials. Furthermore, the values to be taken as data are not those which would guide the official if he were a private citizen. The official is envisaged instead as more or less neutral ethically. His one aim in life is to implement the values of other citizens as given by some rule of collectivist decision making.[8]

James Scott notes as well that seeing like a state is linked to a social engineering mentality associated with the ethos of "high modernity" with its faith in science and predictive control. The object is to "arrange the population in ways that simplified the classic state functions of taxation, conscription, and prevention of rebellion."[9] That type of objective requires a perspective that "implies a viewer whose place is central and whose vision is synoptic."[10] Scott shows why and how "state simplifications" work to "provide authorities with a schematic view of their society, a view not afforded to those without authority." According to this perspective,

> the authorities enjoy a quasi-monopolistic picture of selected aspects of the whole society. This privileged vantage point is typical of all institutional settings where command and control of complex human activities is

paramount. The monastery, the barracks, the factory floor, and the administrative bureaucracy (private or public) exercise many state-like functions and often mimic its information structure as well.[11]

We are now at the core of what Hayek calls the "synoptic delusion." This delusion, writes Hayek, has at its core "the fiction that all the relevant facts are known to some mind, and that it is possible to construct from this knowledge of the particulars a desirable social order." The enthusiasts of a deliberately planned society, explains Hayek, imagine an "art of simultaneous thinking," that is to say, "an ability to think at different phenomena at the same time and compose in a single picture both the quantitative and qualitative attributes of those phenomena." In doing so, they simply assume away "the central problem which any effort towards the understanding or shaping of the order of society raises: our incapacity to assemble as a surveyable whole all the data which enter into the social order."[12] The synoptic delusion reveals the pivotal role of knowledge in social order and especially the importance of correctly understanding the implication of the limits of knowledge in designing and running a governance system. The main challenge for those engaged in designing and running governance systems is

> the fact that knowledge of the circumstances of which we must make use never exists in concentrated or integrated form, but solely as the dispersed bits of incomplete and frequently contradictory knowledge which all the separate individuals possess. . . . It is rather a problem of how to secure the best use of resources known to any of the members of society, for ends whose relative importance only these individuals know. Or, to put it briefly, it is a problem of the utilization of knowledge.[13]

One could further elaborate Hayek's position, but at this specific juncture it is more important to just point out the differences between the various perspectives (seeing like a state vs. seeing like a citizen) and to observe the significant implications for our major theme: governance and public administration. The high modernist bias is to think in terms of the state, to define the problems and their solutions as if the state had a "point of view," and to assume a special idealized set of capabilities on behalf of the state.

Normative Individualism: Freedom of Choice and Freedom of Association as Normative Guidelines

There are two directions on the path toward the applied-level implications of the classical vision presented above. The first is mainly normative and pivots on the problem of the individual as the ultimate bearer of the normative weight of social order. The other combines problems of conceptual coherence and practical feasibility and concentrates on such issues as preference aggregation, social welfare functions, and goal effectiveness in collective decision-making and collective choice settings. Let us start with the purely normative dimension.

The key question is this: What is the ultimate justification for social orders or regimes that allow individuals, their members, to choose separately on an entire range of issues, including occupation, location, associations, lifestyle, production, and consumption? In other words, what is the source of the normative power behind a regime that allows individuals to decide among alternatives on personal, individual, case-by-case bases?

The classical-liberal response is that individuals are the ultimate sovereigns in matters of governance and social organization—normative individualism. Individuals have the right to choose the institutional and governance systems under which they live. Classical liberalism, without denying the reality of coercion and of the Faustian bargain,[14] affirms unequivocally the primacy of the voluntary. Hence, classical liberalism, by nature, questions the legitimacy of organizational forms and regimes that restrict or deny the primacy of voluntarism, even if they do so using the "commanding heights" of the state and invoking the name of science, progress, and social justice.[15]

It is important at this point to insist that the principle of voluntarism and agreement, seen as a heuristic benchmark of governance doctrine, is far from denying the existence or even the necessity of constraints and coercion in governance. But coercion comes as part of an extended process associated with an entire institutional apparatus that has its normative basis in individuals and their system of agreement. As Buchanan put it, in such regimes, "legitimacy is extended to choice restricting institutions as long as participating individuals voluntar[ily] choose to live under such regimes."[16] Or as the legal theorist Randy Barnett elaborates, a classical-liberal system of governance must combine both freedom and constraints on action:

> Liberty has a structure and this structure implies both freedom and constraint of action. . . . Like a building, every society has a structure that, by constraining the actions of its members, permits them at the same time to act to accomplish their ends. Without such structure chaos will reign and the current population could not be sustained. But not all "social structures" are the same. Like poorly designed buildings, some impose constraints on action that inhibit rather than facilitate the ability of persons to survive and flourish. Others are better able to tailor the nature of these constraints to facilitate their inhabitants' pursuit of happiness.[17]

Vincent Ostrom makes similar arguments from a different angle:

> I cannot imagine that human societies can exist without the exercise of some coercive capabilities. A question, however, remains of whether, in the presence of common knowledge, shared communities of understanding, and mutual trust, modest coercive capabilities might be sufficiently diffused through a system of social and political order so that a monopoly of rulership prerogatives can be foreclosed. Principles of self-governance might then be applied to the diverse patterns of associated relationships existing in societies. . . . As long as a culture of inquiry can be maintained and

open discussions of interrelated interests can be pursued, a way is available to achieve enlightenment and resolution consistent with standards of fairness.[18]

It can thus be seen how the conceptual and normative elements of the classical-liberal approach to public administration become clearer and begin to crystalize into a system. They combine a normative individualist stance with an institutionalist understanding of human behavior while trying to escape the synoptic delusion. Such an approach realistically recognizes the essential role of structure and constraints in the architecture of governance systems. It also recognizes and respects the scientific ethos that has fueled the progressive movement. Yet it does so in a manner tempered by an awareness of the limits of knowledge and control in society and of that dimension of institutional order that is not the direct result of planning and structure-inducing top-down approaches. Thus, as Hayek writes, "the fundamental attitude of true individualism is one of humility toward the processes by which mankind has achieved things which have not been designed or understood by any individual and are indeed greater than individual minds."[19]

All these elements are synthesized and pushed to a new theoretical level in a more technical and philosophically sophisticated way in the analysis and criticism of crucial issues of the aggregation of preferences toward collective decision-making—the social welfare function problem, which is the second direction of the articulation of the classical-liberal vision into a public governance doctrine.

Skepticism regarding Social Welfare Function Aggregation and Its Objectification, Used as Public Policy Guideline

The most important alternative to the elitism criticized above is the theory of social choice formalized by economist Ken Arrow in the early 1950s, but dating back to at least the eighteenth century in the works of the Marquis de Condorcet. We should see this as the progressive attempt to adopt normative individualism. What if it was possible to preserve the seeing-like-a-state perspective while at the same time adopting the democratic ethos that puts individuals' values and views in charge of policy? To do so, one would need a democratic procedure to aggregate individuals' values and views, hence creating a "social welfare function" that would then set the goals of the state. A planner or social engineer firmly planted on the commanding heights of the state will thus still be able to claim democratic legitimacy for their top-down designs if such a process for the aggregation of individual preferences or values into collective preferences was possible and put into place.

The democratic progressive solution thus seems simple: a hypothetical, stylized social planner uses information about what individuals want and gets a correct assessment of what society, as a whole, wants in the aggregate. Then the state, once instructed with this information, acts to implement the objective, perhaps calibrated by some additional expert (neutral and objective) knowledge. Hence, it could still be claimed that, despite the top-down social engineering approach, individuals are the basic unit and the foundation and source of the governance system. They continue to count in the system. What the social planner does is simply use a social expertise to execute the transition from the realm of the private to that of the public, which otherwise might not be possible. Understanding the dual problem implicit in this straightforward approach is key to understanding the challenges and dilemmas of modern governance theory.

Outlined above is what Achen and Bartels call the "folk theory of democracy,"[20] and it is probably the most common view among experts and decision makers of the democratic progressive persuasion. The problem with this proposed solution is that it turns out not to be practically or technically feasible. A vast literature has emerged in recent decades on such themes as K. Arrow's aggregation problems[21] and A. Sen's liberal Paretian impossibility, which challenges the consistency and feasibility of such approaches. As noted by Achen and Bartels in their recent overview of this large literature, "Arrow's theorem demonstrated with mathematical rigor that what many people seemed to want—a reliable 'democratic' procedure for aggregating coherent individual preferences to arrive at a coherent collective choice—was simply, logically, unattainable."[22]

These and similar insights indicate that, as long as we take the problem of intersubjective utility comparisons seriously, group incoherence is a problem for *all* methods of group decision-making that aim to transform individual options into collective options. This means that *any* attempt to aggregate the opinions or values of participants, by *any* means, must be highly problematic. As Achen and Bartels put it, "that result raised fundamental logical problems for the populist ideal by calling into question how *any* sort of electoral process could reliably aggregate potentially complex individual preferences into a coherent 'will of the people.'"[23] Furthermore, such an attempt implies that in order to reach decisions that satisfy conditions of rationality, a "dominant member" is needed in the group whose members' preferences or options are aggregated. The especially noteworthy corollary for our discussion is that group decision-making must take place under the shadow of a basic trade-off between social rationality and power concentration. Fairness and consistency seem to be in tension structurally when it comes to collective social decision-making.

Buchanan's critique of the social welfare function uses such observations as a starting point to question the aggregation of preferences to the level of government via a social welfare function. For Buchanan, "the economy and the government are parallel sets of institutions, similar in many respects, and, of course, intersecting at many separate points."[24] On the one hand, the economy is "that complex of institutions that emerges as the result of the behavior of individual persons who organize themselves to satisfy their various objectives privately, as opposed to collectively."[25] On the other hand, government "is simply that complex of institutions through which individuals make collective decisions, and through which they carry out collective as opposed to private activities."[26]

From this perspective, which refuses to model government as a single, unitary goal-driven entity, the concept of a social welfare function becomes even more problematic. In the standard benefit-cost analysis, once the expert "has defined his social welfare function, his public interest, he can advance solutions to all of society's economic ills, solutions that government, as deus ex machina, is, of course, expected to implement."[27] We should note how important the role of the expert is in this conceptualization of the government or the state. When a social welfare function is defined, government is by necessity understood as a goal-driven entity, which obscures by assumption all the processes by which policies are actually created and implemented. Government becomes a deus-ex-machina fantasy that fulfills its assigned purpose. By contrast, focusing on the political and public administration mechanisms at work leads to a conceptualization of government as a complex polycentric structure comprised of many decision-making centers rather than a single entity with one goal. As Buchanan and his associates repeatedly note, government is instead an emergent phenomenon akin to the market.[28] But if so, the role of the economist also changes: "It is wholly beyond his task for the economist to define goals or objectives of the economy or of the government and then to propose measures designed to implement these goals."[29]

This kind of restricted role does not sit well with the desires of most experts. This issue touches the core of expert-driven governance and introduces another important nuance in defining the classical-liberal position. Buchanan notes that "most economists, and, I suspect, most political scientists, view government as a potentially benevolent despot, making decisions in the 'general' or the 'public' interest, and they deem it their own social function to advise and counsel this despot on, first, the definition of this general interest, and, second, the means of furthering it."[30] By contrast, Buchanan's advice is quite different:

> The role of the social scientist who adopts broadly democratic models of government process [is] to explain and to understand how people do, in fact, govern themselves. . . . The social function is not of improving anything directly; instead, it is that of explaining behavior of a certain sort which, only remotely and indirectly, can lead to improvements in the political process itself.[31]

As Vincent and Elinor Ostrom write, public choice grew out of the frustration of public finance economists that politicians did not implement the policies generally accepted in the economics profession as welfare enhancing.[32] Why not? Asking such a question moves us slowly from the territory of social choice to that of public choice. To explain, public choice assumes that, on average, politicians are at least as self-interested as anyone else. However, ironically, the theory assumes that the economist (including the public-choice theorist) is a soft-hearted altruist who cares only about the public interest. While this might have well been true for one particular economist or another, it cannot be assumed that such altruism holds for all economists. By contrast, Frank Knight, a scholar associated with the classical-liberal ethos and Buchanan's professor at Chicago University, clearly sees that such an assumption is highly problematic and understands that, in order to form a correct expectation about the behavior of the "economist as advisor," the economist needs to be modeled as a self-interested party as well. As Buchanan explains:

> Some might go on to suggest that basic choices on macroeconomic policy be taken from the decision-making power of ordinary politicians and placed in the hands of a small group of "experts", "economic technocrats", [and]

"planners", who would, presumably, be able to "fine tune" the national economy in accordance with true "public interest", and wholly free of political interference. This somewhat naïve approach ignores the question concerning the proper incentives for the "experts", along with the demonstrated difficulties in forecasting.[33]

It may thus be seen how the problem of expert advice and preference aggregation in democratic governance are intertwined. This perspective has been continued by the Virginia School of Political Economy to this day. David Levy and Sandra Peart summarize the problem by noting that "while it is in the interests of society at large to obtain the truth, it is by no means clear that any one advice-giver has the incentive to seek the truth."[34] And Richard Wagner notes that "what is commonly described as 'public policy' turns out to be a form of shell game because there is no outside position from which some purported 'policy maker' can intervene into a human population system."[35] This is because "reformers are just as much a part of the system about which they refer in their calls for reform as is everyone else in the system. The typical posture of those who advance calls for reform is that they stand apart from that system . . . That posture is an illusion that hides the reality that their calls are but one of the outputs or activities of the system in which they are but one element."[36]

The classical-liberal political economy and, by implication, its governance theory start by acknowledging the significance and implications of all these problems. One cannot engage in a theory of governance by simply assuming them away. While acknowledging the heuristic and analytical usefulness of the thought experiments and of the theoretical apparatus used to run them, they draw attention to the limits and the applied-level lessons and implications to be derived from them. They recommend that we note how the social mythology of the state, the synoptic delusion, coupled with the mirage of the technical apparatus of preference aggregation and the models of scarcity, allocation, and choice, may entice us to imagine and think in terms of a collective decision maker or "chooser," even though such a being is nonexistent. Moving from there to conceptualizing such a supra-individual entity as the decision maker of choices that are effective and that maximize an objective function, subject to a set of specifically defined constraints, is a small step. The vulnerability of this position is obvious.

As Buchanan summarizes, there are two ways in which misleading analysis and practical irrelevance are induced. The first is that the logic of choice, maximization, or allocative efficiency based on the model of an individual chooser is applied to a situation where no such entity, person, or collective person exists.[37] To assume that such a unified, singular, synoptic mind and sovereign decision maker exists may be an intriguing and (perhaps in some cases) a useful thought experiment. Yet to build an entire approach to the design and governance of social-political systems on such an experiment—in many cases pushed to its logical limits or even beyond—is simply mistaken.

Second, as noted, the costs and benefits of alternative directions of action and different decisions are hardly something objective, easy to identify, assess, or compute. Setting aside formal paradoxes of aggregation, individual decision makers have many shifting subjective views and preferences on multiple issues. To create a "social preference" and "national social function," those views and preferences must be homogenized and objectified. Objectifying while aggregating a set of subjective preferences into a social, collective, objective preference raises problems of both a theoretical and a practical nature and are formidable indeed. In brief, as useful as it may be as a thought experiment of heuristic intention, the social welfare function of a social system modeled as a decision maker is of limited usefulness as the basis for an applied-level governance and public administration doctrine. In an interesting way, it is nonetheless an important heuristic and analysis device, important in drawing attention to the limits and pitfalls of an approach that embraces indiscriminately the "viewing like a state" perspective.

Public Choice Caveats regarding the Capacity of the Modern State's Mechanisms to Successfully Generate the Outcomes It Is Supposed to Deliver

Even if decision makers assume that the social welfare function aggregation and objectification would be feasible, other problems would persist. These problems include the practical capabilities of state institutions (and of governance systems in general) to execute the specified goals or to successfully generate the outcomes they are supposed to deliver. This is both a structural and an empirical problem. As such, it suggests a cautious approach to governance and public policy, one that relies not on ideal theory, abstract models, or a hypothetical future perfectibility of human nature and institutional performance, but on historical and empirical data and evidence.

In the contemporary social sciences, this type of intellectual attitude has manifested most saliently and intensely in the field of public choice, the research program that has made its main object of inquiry the nature of collective decisions and the institutions that shape and implement them. Hence, the dual significance of the term *public choice*, a phenomenon of pivotal interest for public governance and a research field dedicated to its study. In this respect, the field of public choice has generated, starting in the 1960s, the most substantial set of insights relevant for the classical-liberal approach to public administration. By methodically examining—beyond romantic and utopian wishful thinking and using a method concentrated on individuals' actions and interests—how collective choices are made and put into practice in various contexts, the field of public choice has revamped the study of modern governance systems in all facets—bureaucracies, states, parties, elections, and interest groups. Public choice has thus become the preeminent intellectual and social scientific source for the revamped classical-liberal take on governance and public administration. Its program is not only a criticism of the social-engineering assumptions and approaches of mainstream economics but also the foundation of an alternative perspective with roots in the classical-liberal ethos. As Buchanan explains:

> Public choice did not emerge from some profoundly new insight, some new discovery, some social science miracle. Public choice, in its basic insights into the workings of politics, incorporates an understanding of human nature that differs little, if at all, from that of James Madison and his colleagues at

the time of the American Founding. The essential wisdom of the 18th century, of Adam Smith and classical political economy and of the American Founders, was lost through two centuries of intellectual folly. Public choice does little more than incorporate a rediscovery of this wisdom and its implications into economic analyses of modern politics.[38]

At the core of all public choice theories, explains Anthony Downs, stands the commonsense observation that an official at any level in the public or the private sector "acts at least partly in his own self-interest."[39] Statistically speaking, the altruistic, purely public interest-driven behavior cannot depart in the public-sector arena so significantly from the average of pro-social behavior in other normal circumstances of social life. The behavior of public-sector bureaucrats that is at the heart of the analysis of an important part of public-choice institutions, processes, and phenomena should be treated both for normative and analytical purposes in the most realistic way possible, overcoming the romantic and naive assumptions that infuse high modernism. William Niskanen, another founding figure of public choice, convincingly explains this thesis: public decision makers and administrators indeed work in the public interest, as efficiently and effectively as possible, given the incentives and information they have, but it would be naive to think that their behavior and performance have nothing to do with self-interest or the motivation induced by such factors as "salary, prerequisites of the office, public reputation, power, patronage . . . and the ease of managing the bureau."[40]

The crucial idea is to systematically use the same behavioral assumptions, the same model of man, and the same motivational structure when studying, assessing, or designing the public sector as when studying and assessing the private sector. In other words, there is an attempt to create a common theoretical foundation for the analysis of both public and private sectors. In doing so, the conditions are created for genuine comparative analysis of the structure, functioning, and performance of public and private governance, the market, and the state.

A common assumption before the public choice revolution was that the government would try to benevolently implement policies assumed to best serve the public good. However, such an assumption of altruism would actually eliminate the need for coercive government altogether. Market failures—the main economic argument for government intervention—only occur because people are assumed to act in their narrow self-interest. If, by contrast, we assume them to act benevolently, people will *voluntarily* pay for public goods, refrain from causing negative externalities, refrain from making use of asymmetric information at the expense of others, and so on. Hence, the need for government only arises because people indeed often act selfishly and, if the gains are large enough, antisocially. But, such selfish and potentially antisocial people cannot be blindly trusted to suddenly act altruistically when given great powers over others. If anything, they can be expected to act even worse than usual. Consequently, the realistic picture that emerges is that we need some government to correct some market failures, but we also need strong constraints upon this government to prevent the people involved in its operation from abusing their positions and making the existing problems even worse.

The observation that the state or governance units or entities are just complexes of institutions—arrangements of rules and incentives through which collective decisions are made and implemented—leads to a number of methodologically significant conclusions. If the state is not seen as a supra-individual entity separate from the individuals who run it, then the state's operations and components should be analyzed piece by piece and analytically deconstructed, with a focus on the relevant individuals' actions and interests. If the government is not a benevolent despot making optimizing decisions on behalf of and for the public or collective interest, then we need to understand what is going on in reality and the sole way to do that is by accounting for the interests and decisions of individuals acting in different social and institutional circumstances and arenas. In other words, this is a truly social scientific research program that builds methodically as a corollary and an extension of a series of observations and assumptions regarding human nature and social institutions.

In order for us to get a better sense of its applied-level implications as well as its potential to serve as a conceptual defining feature of the classical-liberal perspective on governance, we must place this research program in the context of the two hundred years of intellectual and social science historical evolutions that define the underlying logic that anchors the problem of governance—that is, the twin themes of "market failure" and "government failure" and the implications for the way in which public institutions and public governance are understood.

Comparative Institutional Analysis: Markets, States, and "Third Sector"

In the modern political economy, the problem of governance is seen ultimately as the problem of managing the performance of two key institutions: the market and the state. Hence, the problem of the failures of these institutions has become essential for the ways in which we define and describe the governance doctrines and positions.

Market idealization has been criticized almost from its inception, and the shortcomings, failures, and unintended consequences have been constantly evoked as arguments for the state's role. It was Adam Smith, not Karl Marx, who pointed out that extreme refinements of the division of labor can result in an atrophying of human development as people become appendages of machines rather than creative creatures who should be accorded dignity and respect. Adam Smith also pointed out that businessmen of the same trade seldom meet other than to conspire to fix the price of their products.

But Smith also provided caveats after each such indictment. First, the famous quote about price-fixing is followed by noting that, if we accept the principle of freedom of association, "it is impossible indeed to prevent such meetings, by any law which either could be executed, or would be consistent with liberty and justice." However, importantly, he continues by noting that "though the law cannot hinder people of the same trade from sometimes assembling together, it ought to do nothing to facilitate such assemblies; much less to render them necessary."[41] This is, indeed, the fundamental issue underlying the public choice critique of rent-seeking and regulatory capture.

Second, his analysis does not end with his initial observation but rather continues with an examination of how the system evolves. The identified negative consequences are often, although not always, mitigated through expanded trade and technological innovations. This expansion often leads to the development of substitutes that undermine attempts to create rents, either by private collusion or government grants. Smith sees economic progress as a great correction. He argues that politics all too often acts as a hindrance to this progress, and it is nowhere as dangerous as it is in the hands of those who believe they should rule over others. Furthermore, interestingly, for Smith these caveats are a matter of more than purely positive economics. Smith advances a "system of natural liberty" that is based on guarded optimism regarding the working of self-interest for public interest (invisible hand) and skepticism regarding government's intervention (visible hand). That was in many respects the quintessential classical-liberal position.

From Adam Smith onward, the argument for the market was always a comparative institutional one, not an absolute claim. But critics—whether technical, such as Karl Marx, John Keynes, and John Galbraith, or literary, such as Charles Dickens and John Steinbeck—want to paint defenders of markets as making absolute claims about the superiority of the free market. In their view, to defend capitalism means not only to defend the material improvements afforded to mankind but also to defend, or deny, the existence of any negative aspect accompanying these improvements. Thus, the existence of mass unemployment, poverty, discrimination, exploitation, and political patronage as features of the system have been and still are offered as arguments of market failure.

The evolution of political economy thus came to be increasingly seen through the "market failure" and the "government failure" paradigm. In the transition from classical to neoclassical economics, arguments in favor of the role of the state were increasingly based on a theory of market failure. The economist Arthur Pigou was central in this evolution, and yet Pigou was still cautious in comparison to his followers and intellectual heirs: "The case cannot be made more than a *prima facie* one, until we consider the qualifications which governmental agencies may be expected to possess for intervening advantageously."[42] His point was straightforward: "It is not sufficient to contrast the imperfect adjustments of unfettered private enterprise with the best adjustment that economists in their studies imagine. For we cannot expect that any public authority will attain, or will even wholeheartedly seek, that ideal."[43]

Thus, even with Pigou, there are vestiges of the same guarded attitude toward the government and its abilities. It is only with the next generation of neoclassical economists that the qualms and caution are swept away and the high-modernist mindset with its faith in social control, planning, and the state's abilities takes over. For governance purposes, the theory of the market becomes the basis of the "failure theory" that justifies and gives free rein to government schemes, intervention, and planning. This is the moment when the climate of opinion dominated by the enthusiasm for centralization, state, and bureaucratic management becomes dominant.[44] And this is the context in which can be seen the work of the scholars who paved the way for the public choice revolution in understanding comparative institutional performance and failure, and thus revamped the foundations of the classical-liberal perspective of public governance.

As a precursor, Ronald Coase's work deserves a special note as an excellent illustration of the institutionalist turn introduced by the insights of these political economy and instituonal theories. There are at least two readings of Coase's basic idea. The first states that, in a world of zero transaction costs, the initial distribution of rights does not matter because individuals will negotiate away any social conflicts through bargaining. The second reading states that, in a world of positive transaction costs, institutions determine the pattern of outcomes. What gets forgotten in this discussion is that the primary purpose of the first point is to critically engage the conventional wisdom of mid-twentieth-century public choice economists and to use that criticism to highlight the second point and thus push the debate at a new level.[45] The standard neoclassical model of market failure was by design an institutionally antiseptic theory. It was grounded in the standard assumptions of perfect competition and sought to demonstrate that, with respect to certain activities, the market economy alone would fail to produce optimal results because of the external economies associated with certain goods. The proposed remedy was for the public sector to establish the exact tax or subsidy scheme that would bring social marginal costs and benefits in line with the social optima.

Authors such as Coase and Buchanan pointed out that, under standard assumptions, Pigou's remedy was either redundant because, in that environment, actors would negotiate away the conflict, or it would be nonoperational because, if the assumptions about knowledge are changed, public actors will not be able to bring into alignment the social marginal costs and benefits. Coase points out that, in a move away from the shifting of property rights via market exchange with a substitution of public-sector allocations, the costs of this alternative approach must be acknowledged. Specifically, society will have to do without the ability to calculate monetary costs and benefits; society will have to do without the ability to mobilize the dispersed information of time and place that exists in the system as a result of the suppression of prices and profit and loss; and society will have to deal with the play of various special interest groups in the process of political allocations.[46] Coase refers to this as his "novel" theory—novel, he adds, if you have not read Adam Smith. In *Cost and Choice: An Inquiry in Economic Theory*, Buchanan[47] develops a similar argument; taken together, the frameworks that Buchanan and Coase developed in the early 1960s were key components of the Virginia school of political economy.[48]

In the mid-1960s, the Coase theorem, as it came to be known, took on an intellectual life of its own[49] and came to be identified with the Chicago school of economics, providing the basis for its optimism about the behavior of markets (see table 1.1). The first reading came to dominate and—to Coase's own regret—moved the discussion from comparative institutional analysis to the abstract efficiency of the market mechanism and its universal applicability across institutional environments. Rather than an empirical examination of the variety of bargains and the details of contractual arrangements that individuals engage in to turn situations of social conflict into opportunities for social cooperation, the Coase theorem became symbolic of a "whatever is, is efficient" style of reasoning.

Thus, strict dichotomization became embedded in the discussion, and insights about institutional diversity were neglected. It was that neglect that set the stage

Table 1.1 **The debate over market and state failure**

Stages of debate	Market	Government	Judgmwent	Who?
Pre–Great Depression	Perfect	Perfect	Limited government, laissez faire	Mainstream economics
Great Depression to 1970s stagflation	Imperfect	Perfect	Intervention and command and control	Keynesian economics
Great Depression to present	Almost perfect	Imperfect	Limited government, laissez faire	Chicago school (Austrian economics)
1970s to present	Imperfect	Almost perfect	Intervention but less command and control	New Keynesian economics
1950s to present	Imperfect	Imperfect	Agnostic— cost–benefit calculation	Virginia and Bloomington schools of public choice

for the debate between the Chicago school of economics (almost perfect markets, imperfect governments) and the New Keynesian economics (imperfect markets, almost perfect governments). The forceful criticisms of the market economy that emerged in the 1980s and 1990s from the work of the Joseph Stiglitz framed this debate. If markets are always efficient with zero transaction costs, perhaps they are always inefficient in the face of positive transaction costs. Stiglitz demonstrates the intellectual fragility of the Walrasian system by examining the sensitivity of general welfare theorems to assumptions concerning information and market structure. With slight deviations from those core assumptions, the welfare results flip. A similar dichotomization emerged that is related to unemployment under the strict assumptions of rational expectations. In the new classical rendering of rational expectations macroeconomics, where actors do not suffer from money illusion, involuntary unemployment is not possible, only voluntary unemployment—in other words, vacation. Again, Stiglitz's new Keynesian macroeconomics challenged that result by showing that slight deviations, including such phenomena as long-term contracting and the payment of efficiency wages, could result in unemployment. From this strict dichotomization, an indictment of failure results. Yes, in the comparative analysis, there are erring entrepreneurs juxtaposed with the inconsistencies of collective choice and bumbling bureaucrats, but somehow "faith" in the markets is only possible if the theorists assume perfect foresight. Lost in even the most sophisticated discussion of market failure and the economic analysis of the shortcomings of the "invisible hand" is recognition of the institutionally contingent nature of market outcomes.

The stage is now set for the contribution brought by the public choice revolution in this respect: The comparative institutional analysis, on methodological individualist marginal analysis and normative individualist assumptions, of the interface between the public and private as defined by the state failure–market failure dyad. With it comes a renewed emphasis on the limits of the state as a governance instrument and an interest in the diversity of institutional arrangements that are neither markets nor states but that could provide critical governance functions, the so-called "third sector."

From the evolution of the perception of the issue of market failure versus government failure and its implications for the ways in which public institutions and public administration are understood, we can now better define the nature of the contemporary classical-liberal stance. Buchanan and Congleton[50] note that toward the end of the twentieth century the vision of politics started to change back to a more skeptical and realist position. Developments worldwide, including the 1989 collapse of the Soviet bloc, the crisis of the welfare state, and the evolution of scholarly inquiry on public policy and practitioners' lessons and experiences, all created conditions for change (or at least an adjustment) in the climate of opinion: "Both in the academy and on the street, politics and politicians are now exposed to a skepticism that is reminiscent of the late eighteenth century"—the period during which the constitutional principles for the politics of classical liberalism were forged. Thus, at the closing of a historical cycle, we seem to be again somewhat more favorable to the cautious attitude regarding the potential and promise of public governance systems. In its light, we may see the classical liberal position reviewed and reconsidered: in a sense it looks indeed like closing a cycle, an invitation to return to a more realistic and institutionally grounded understanding of the operations of market and the state, and of governance systems in general. Following the logic of the methodological individualist social science approach—marginalizing the market, marginalizing the government,[51] and marginalizing the variety of institutions that are "neither markets nor states"— and its extensive application over time to a variety of phenomena and institutional settings, we are now also more aware of the perils and pitfalls of the excessive enthusiasm placed in the formal models of either the market or the state. We have a more nuanced understanding of the comparative theory of institutional success and failure guiding our governance systems.

Conclusions

Our overview of an updated classical-liberal perspective on public governance reveals an underlying logic that connects its underlining elements in multiple ways. Together they constitute a system that is more than the sum of its parts. Normative individualism, dismissal of the synoptic view, and doubts about the social welfare function are all facets of the same conceptual system. They lead in a natural way to the public choice and the comparative institutional analysis methods for analyzing governance systems. In a similar way, adopting a public choice and comparative institutional analysis approach will lead, sooner or later, to the rediscovery of the unavoidable relevance of the normative individualist principle via a recognition of the centrality of social choice and preference aggregation problems in any governance system.

This cluster of ideas, with its underlying coherence and distinctive liberal identity, has stood the test of time, but it has also flourished in response to the historical economic, political, and ideological developments of the past hundred years or so. This set of ideas integrates major insights gained during this period, especially the more recent criticism and assessment of the top-down governance model and its track record. If that is the case, it may be reasonable to claim that the current classical-liberal position on governance and the relationship between the state and the voluntary sector (the market and civil society) could be considered a fusion of the lessons of two hundred years of intellectual, political, and administrative history.

Classical liberalism emerges as an approach informed by theory and history, scholarship and practical experience, while avoiding the extremes of utopianism and romanticism. It reasserts itself as a perspective open to learning from new empirical discoveries, as well as from the arguments and evidence brought to the fore in intellectual and social scientific debates. It recognizes the inescapable reality of the collective domain, its distinctiveness and irreducible nature, as well as the intricate challenges, trade-offs, and limits of collective decision-making and action in this inter-individual space. In practice, classical liberalism's application takes to the applied level an awareness of the challenges and opportunities presented by normative individualism and institutional diversity, and the dangers and dead ends of dogmatic and easy, one-size-fits-all solutions. Last but not least, on the basis of an evolving and nuanced view of the role and nature of the social scientific knowledge needed for the governance and design of the artefactual universe of social institutions, classical liberalism acknowledges the limits of knowledge and social control when it comes to human beings and their actions.

This introductory overview leads to (a) a clearer articulation of the distinctiveness of the classical-liberal position regarding the grounding of its applied—governance and public administration—dimension; (b) a perspective that anchors that position in the intellectual history of the debates and evolutions that took place in the relevant social sciences and political philosophy during the past hundred years or so; and (c) an insight that brings some support to the controversial thesis that, once seen in this light, the classical-liberal position may very well be considered an underlying intellectual force that shapes and influences, even when not directly acknowledged as such, modern thinking on the problem of the governance, institutional, and political-economic order. In other words, the classical-liberal position may well be an intellectual center of gravity toward which, in the long run, both empirical developments and analytical logic pull our thinking on governance issues. The objective of this chapter is not to engage in discussion surrounding this last thesis. As mentioned, the goals are more modest: to establish the distinctiveness and individuality of classical liberalism as a perspective on public governance problems and solutions. While doing so, it may be useful to keep in mind Ludwig von Mises's intriguing viewpoint:

> Liberalism is not a completed doctrine or a fixed dogma. On the contrary, it
> is the application of the teaching of science to the social life of man. And just

as economics, sociology and philosophy have not stood still since the days of David Hume, Adam Smith, David Ricardo, Jeremy Bentham and Wilhelm Humboldt, so the doctrine of liberalism is different today from what it was in their day, even though its fundamental principles have remained unchanged.[52]

The classical-liberal approach is geared toward change, deliberation, and choice in a world of ongoing ideas and beliefs in systems-driven transformation. Classical liberalism's response to that reality is a governance structure that is organized for resilience and adaptability; for learning and coordination; and for the collective management of continuity and change in societies and communities in which the heterogeneous and dynamic individual preferences, knowledge, and beliefs play a major role as drivers of social transformation. As the rest of this book will make increasingly clear, this aspect of intellectual dynamism, adaptability, and flexibility has a major role to play at different levels and in multiple ways in the classical-liberal universe of governance theory and practice in which the discovery, production, and dissemination of knowledge are essential.

2

Function, Structure, and Process at the Private-Public Interface

Chapter 1 presents the building blocks of an updated classical-liberal approach to public governance based on more than a century of political economy debates and political-administrative history. Recognizing that both market and state may fail in their roles of social coordination mechanisms, the updated classical-liberal approach starts from realistic assumptions and expectations regarding the capabilities and performance of collective action initiatives, public institutions, and bureaucratic organizations. The governance structure it favors is based on normative individualism and is geared toward change, deliberation, and choice in a world of ongoing uncertainty and transformation, driven by myriad volatile and uncertain contextual variables that determine the success and failure of both private and public actions.

The present chapter moves from basic governance theory to applied theory, focusing on the interface between the private and the public. To understand the anatomy, physiology, and pathology of public governance, we must look at the private-public polar concepts and at the phenomena that are defined and modeled through each concept and their dichotomy. One of the main challenges to a classical-liberal applied theory of governance and public administration—that is, a consistent system of governance based on and supportive of normative individualism and voluntary association—is the collective setup and management of the processes that take place in that interface domain. This chapter takes another step forward in the applied-level direction by taking a closer look at the crucial private-public interface. First, we examine the problem of the interface as a major underlying theme throughout the entire history of modern political economy. Then we take a closer look at the private-public interface domain, analyzing a set of essential factors and mechanisms that explain the interface processes and their governance architecture: (a) the nature of the goods or services; (b) the technologies available for producing the goods or services and the mechanisms available for monitoring and enforcement; and (c) the institutional arrangements and social contexts in which the goods or services are provided, including people's preferences and beliefs.

The Private-Public Dichotomy Interface

As a matter of intellectual history, the discussion regarding the boundary between the private and the public is a decisive component of the ways in which various approaches to governance have defined their positions. We go further here. Our working thesis is that in an applied-level approach based on normative individualist principles—as a recognition of problems of both social choice aggregation and public choice implementation—the focus cannot be on the ideal types of private and public or on a search for pure forms of private organization or public organization and their firm and pristine boundaries. To be sure, a large part of the traditional literature is dedicated exclusively to creating pure, ideal models and to contriving strategies to convert anything else that seems to deviate from the mold of the favorite model. Such an approach, however, is not the optimal path in light of public choice theory and the theories that reflect classical-liberal principles.

The path that grows logically from both public choice theory and normative individualism is that of being very cautious in claiming the absolute superiority of a particular governance or institutional form irrespective of context, functions, and circumstances. There is a prima facie preeminence to the principles of freedom, autonomy, and liberty. But that preeminence is a matter of ideal theory, and it is introduced as such by all major classical-liberal authors, not as a dogmatic benchmark in the real world of multiple trade-offs. Instead, precisely because individuals are endowed with freedom of choice and association, the sensible approach with governance structures is to (a) focus on the variety of both real and possible institutional and governance arrangements that emerge at the interface between the private and the public as defined in various contractarian and voluntarist circumstances by the relevant social actors; and (b) compare their efficacy in delivering institutional performance functions out of which the preservation of life, liberty, and property is essential. A good governance system creates the conditions for both institutional emergence and institutional assessment.

That is indeed the trademark of the applied-level approach. The key point that is hard to overemphasize, especially because it often goes unnoticed, is that the focus is on the interface between the private and the public. To be more precise, the focus is on the large and dynamic domain resulting from the overlap and friction of the private and public. Most of the time, human beings act at that interface. Their actions, preferences, beliefs, and interests combine various degrees of "privateness" and "publicness," however defined. The institutions and social structures that shape or emerge from that combination display a similar mix of characteristics, however they may be defined in various times, circumstances, societies, or cultures. That territory is where the interesting and important things happen when it comes to governance. An applied-level approach must start there. Ideal types—the models and theories of the pure forms—are used as instruments and benchmarks. They provide normative standards and analytical and heuristic tools. Exploring the interface territory with the use of political economy concepts and theories provides a clearer and more concrete grasp of the nature of classical-liberal, applied-level governance theory and public administration. When engaging in this exercise, we should keep in mind that this is an applied perspective and avoid confusing these ideal types or models (used to illuminate and capture what is relevant in the overlapping gray areas) with institutional blueprints or with reality.

The literature on market failures offers probably the best window to the problem of the interface. It is noteworthy that all authors relevant to the discussion of market failure (and later state failure also), a discussion defining the core of modern political economy, agree that the pertinent distinctions are fuzzy and relative. The more elaborate and nuanced the approaches are, the clearer the complexity and vast nature of the interface territory in which the private and the public coexist in various proportions.

John Stuart Mill is obviously a major figure of political economy in this respect. The role of the state is basically determined as a function of a set of criteria emerging from the market's failures. But paradigmatic in this respect for the point we want to make is J. S. Mill's discussion of the very sensitive issue of the tension between private opinion and public opinion. It is an extreme case, giving sharp insights into the issues at stake, even if it is not a market failure situation. Mill's credentials as a classical liberal may be questioned in some respects, but when it comes to freedom of speech, his take is to this day very close to the gold standard. Yet Mill acknowledges that there is an interference of the public in the domain of the private when it comes to opinion and its expression, and that intrusion is legitimate. The implications for individual independence are fully recognized. He analyzes the problem of freedom of speech and the role of the state, using a model of two domains, or two spheres, that overlap. The area of overlap where public concerns put some limits on private expression is a reality of life. Regulation and enforcement start from that reality.

But the most important point for our discussion and the reason that Mill is so important here as a case study and an illustrative vehicle is not so much this otherwise commonsensical reality. The key is the manner in which Mill thinks about the borderlines, about how the limits between private and public are drawn. Although not arbitrary, those limits are something that must be discovered, something that must be constructed in various circumstances and cannot be defined a priori by a utilitarian calculus or an alternative principle.[1] The boundaries of the state's action are a dynamic phenomenon. Intervention in the name of the public "does not . . . admit of any universal solution."[2] The boundaries are not defined in a universal way but rather as a matter of "expediency," which is determined by an ongoing discovery process in which the public and the private interact. That notion is essential, for if the solution to securing freedom of speech and shaping the proper sphere of public authority is a process, then the question becomes what that process will look like. Are there any ways to make sure the process is not arbitrary and that it will satisfy minimal normative standards? It can be noted that the institutional and governance dimensions gain shape around this process, bridging the political-institutional system with normative ideal theory.

As overviewed and analyzed by the economist Steven G. Medema,[3] Henry Sidgwick, a significant author in the market failure tradition, continues Mill's line and argues for a more empirical approach at the interface area. He insists that modern scientific investigation should have a say in defining the frontier and interface of the private and public domains. His emphasis on the role of the epistemic element (in this case, scientific knowledge) in defining the boundary and the territory is well taken. Yet he fails to note the problem of institutions, which operate with local, personal, and tacit knowledge and facilitate a discovery process in real life. Moreover, he ignores the fact that applying scientific knowledge to governance requires a particular institutional apparatus and raises huge moral and political challenges. Sidgwick (again, following in the steps of Mill) is also concerned with a pivotal issue that is outside ideal theory and that relates to the applied level: the problem of costs. Institutionalization and implementation of governance solutions are not free. Definition and enforcement on the private-public frontier and the political and bureaucratic processes by which "public" is defined and reinforced come with price tags. The fact that the ideal or the desirable, no matter how minimalistically defined, may not be sustainable as an investment of resources and energy is a major issue. Sidgwick's point is straightforward: like it or not, the position and dynamics of the private-public boundary are shaped by the resources available. Hence, the various costs involved are an additional element to consider.

Another major figure in the market failure tradition of studying the private-public interface takes a similar approach. Medema[4] notes that the economist Arthur Cecil Pigou is not so much in favor of state action against market failure as he is in favor of a contextualized approach that involves comparative institutional analysis:

> There are many forms and many different degrees in its failure. Inquiring how far Government is fitted to take action against these failures, we find that its fitness to do this varies, not only in different places and different times but also as between interventions directed against different kinds of failure.[5]

Hence, the sphere of the public—the sphere deemed to be part of the state's domain of intervention—varies. Medema synthesizes Pigou's view as follows: "There is no definitive answer that one can give, a priori, about the magnitude of the problems associated with state intervention."[6] That is, "generalizations are of no help" in dealing with these issues because "particular conditions of time and place render sweeping generalizations inappropriate."[7]

As may be expected, the clearest and most sophisticated treatment of the issue is found in the public choice tradition. The fact that the theme is essential to this tradition, and not a peripheral corollary, is revealed by its salience in the literature of the continental tradition, which is the precursor to public choice. The economist Antonio de Viti de Marco[8] is emblematic. If responsibility for the provision of public goods is taken as a proxy or an indicator of the private-public boundary, something important is revealed about the nature and dynamics of the private-public frontier:

> It does not follow logically that the State is or must be the exclusive producer of the goods destined to satisfy all collective wants, nor that private enterprise is or should be the exclusive producer of the goods destined to satisfy all individual wants. No such clear-cut division of labor exists in reality, since at times the State produces goods destined to satisfy individual wants, and at times private enterprise produces goods destined to satisfy collective wants. Indeed, it may be pointed out that there scarcely exists a public service the germ of which one does not find in private enterprise, ready to develop, if only as a complementary agency, whenever the State proves itself insufficient. . . . Even more numerous, however, are the examples . . . of public services . . . which are on the way to assuming a permanent place in the business

of the State, . . . and still more numerous are those that are found in the group of public services which are at the margin and which, at the present stage in history, are sometimes produced by the State and sometimes by private enterprise.[9]

Similar insights are supported by Knut Wicksell's work. By introducing a strong emphasis on the voluntary element and on the processes of collective decision-making in the production and financing of public goods, he illuminates individuals' preferences, agreements, and exchanges. Wicksell's analysis—which is developed as a mental experiment—deals with different preference aggregation alternatives through voting as informed by subjective estimation of the price of public goods. Wicksell thus illuminates the range of possible alternatives and clarifies the blurred and dynamic lines between private and public.

Let us add to this list Coase's work, discussed in Chapter 1, which supports similar insights from a different angle. Market failure as a boundary condition that defines the proper space of the private is not so much the result of something pertaining to the essence of the market itself but rather is the consequence of government failure to establish well-defined property rights that will facilitate transactions. The territory of the private-public frontier may be seen as a function of multiple failures. With real-life situations (not "blackboard economics"), the choice is not between optimal markets and optimal government but rather among various social arrangements, none optimal and all more or less a failure. Externality problems, as a factor shaping the private-public frontier, may be solved through a negotiation process if the appropriate institutional structure is in place to facilitate such a process. The a priori boundary between private and public is constantly renegotiated by a social process of discovery, tinkering, and muddling through. Goods and services can be produced and provided in a variety of settings, and each setting induces different outcomes. The applied-level challenge, as opposed to the theoretical one, is to construe conditions for the appropriate institutional structure to operate and emerge in a given context.

How is this boundary renegotiated? Following in the footsteps of Wicksell, James Buchanan analyzes the logic behind individuals' exchanging rights of access and develops a contractarian solution to determining when the government should produce public goods. In *The Demand and Supply of Public Goods*,[10] Buchanan arranges private and public services on a continuum. Units of a good typically include both divisible and indivisible elements; thus, the definition of a unit becomes an empirical matter that also depends on the range of people over which indivisibility extends and the existing structure of property rights. It follows that the question of under what circumstances the collective governmental supply will be more efficient than the private or noncollective supply requires case-by-case evaluations of the goods in question, together with similar comparisons of how various noncollective and collective organized supply arrangements can perform the functions of financing, allocating, and distributing the goods.[11] There is nothing formulaic or dogmatic about this. Buchanan's entire work is dedicated to the systematic study of public choice, collective action, and decision-making, and to nonmarket institutional arrangements and processes. While assuming explicitly the mantle of the classical-liberal tradition, Buchanan was at the same time one of the most profound students of the public realm and its governance.

In a similar way, Hayek's work is predicated on the challenges posed by the existence of common concerns, collective purposes, and collective action and the interface between, on the one hand, the public domain that they define and, on the other, the private domains. For instance, he opens volume 2 of *Law, Legislation and Liberty: The Mirage of Social Justice*[12] with a concern regarding the imprecise borders of certain concepts, such as "general interest," evoked to motivate large-scale collective action. Circumscribing correctly the collective action levels and domains is a central task. One can see how Hayek tries to deal in a constructive way with the slippery and complex interface between the public and the private, the collective and the individual.

This effort is fraught with tensions. It is easy to note a vacillation in Hayek's thought between skepticism regarding the state—its role and capabilities—and arguments according to which "there is little reason why the government should not also play some role, or even take the initiative in such areas as social insurance and education or temporar[ily] subsidiz[e] certain experimental developments."[13] Arguably against his own spirit,[14] Hayek admits to compulsory provision of standards of cooperation with strangers applying uniformly over an open or a great society.[15] Moreover, when large numbers of consumers are involved, the free-rider problem may require compulsory provision of certain transportation and communication infrastructures; statistics; and standards of measurement and services of protection against violence, epidemics, and natural disasters.[16] The contractarian justification that Hayek offers—namely, that individuals would rationally agree to a coercive basic scheme knowing that all others are similarly coerced—is obviously different from the libertarian ad hoc joint contracts whereby each contribution is contingent on the contributions of others. It is worth mentioning, though, that once the level and target of coercion are decided at a stage of a large collective, both the provision and the levying activity could be administered privately and competitively, possibly through a voucher scheme.[17] Moreover, Hayek favors actions "outside the market" to "assist people who for one reason or another cannot through the market earn a minimum income," and he endorses universal education.[18] Yet Hayek does not offer a theory or an institutional design on how these public actions could be organized or should take place. All in all, tensions subside. Working out a way of dealing with the technical, institutional, and moral problems posed by the public sphere is at the core of his intellectual enterprise.

The conclusion of this survey of select milestones of ways in which the private-public interface has been dealt with in the history of political economy is that the most important and interesting problem seems to be the overlapping interface domain and its governance. The insights in the public choice tradition, starting with its continental precursors, are clear in this respect, thus being the astute observation of political reality and of the evolution of the relevant political economy thought. As Medema, whose thorough analysis we use here, notes, public choice authors incorporate "the political process in their theoretical analysis of public sector activity," creating a framework for developing "a parallel between private and public sector activities that [leads] them to model the political process like a market or exchange process."[19] As a result of this deft analytical move, the appropriate functions of the state, and their extent, were not something to be taken as given or gleaned from history, philosophy, jurisprudence, or even causal empiricism, nor were they to be determined by working out instances of market failure, devising associated remedies and asserting the ability of government to undertake corrective actions. . . . Rather the appropriate functions of the state were seen as something that is or ought to be worked out and continually determined over time through the political process.[20]

Our discussion leads to a more complex and more relevant applied-level understanding of the private-public dichotomy as a governance principle:

> The distinction between private and public good provision lay in the institutional processes through which their provision was worked out—the market in one case and the political process, through which demands are registered and tax prices are established in the other.[21]

That, as we shall see, is critical for the classical-liberal theory of governance and is a starting point for a more elaborate and complex approach that goes beyond basic dichotomies.

Conceptual Framing of the Frontier Domain of the Private-Public Interface

Let us now put together more methodically the conceptual and theoretical map of the private-public interface domain. The clearer a view we get of it and the better we understand the nature of this dynamic process, the better we will understand the task of creating or managing governance arrangements to deal with the problems and opportunities the interface domain poses.

The private-public distinction is determined by several important dimensions. Let us group them by (a) the nature of the good or service; (b) the technology, including the institutional technology, available for producing the good or service and the available mechanisms for monitoring and enforcement; and (c) the social context in which the good or service is provided, involving people's preferences and beliefs. Let us take them one by one.

The Nature of the Good or Service

At first glance, goods and services are more or less public because of their inherent nature (see table 2.1). The standard economic approach is to highlight two characteristics. The first is negative consumption externalities—that is, the harm caused to others when one person consumes a good. For example, if one person consumes the good, less may be left for others—what is known as rivalry of consumption. The second characteristic is excludability—that is, the ease of establishing property rights over the good so as to prevent free riders (nonpayers) from consuming the good.

If the negative consumption externalities are small, the good is a communal good; it is something that can be enjoyed simultaneously by many without being depleted. Depending on its excludability, a communal good may be produced and provided in a club (which can exclude nonpaying consumers and, hence, finance the production of the good by requiring a membership fee) or, if excludability is very hard, a communal good is a genuine public good. It is usually assumed that, without compulsory taxation, genuine public goods will be underproduced because the producers of the good cannot secure voluntary payment from all consumers of the good. This problem does not occur if excludability is easy because membership in the club is voluntary.

This common assumption about public goods is not valid in general, although it may be valid from case to case. Under imperfect competition with a positive entry cost—for example, under the Cournot competition model—the quantity provided on the market is lower than the perfect competition quantity, and hence the price can be higher than the marginal cost. With public goods, the marginal cost is very small (near zero); because of small consumption externalities, there is little cost to add another consumer. Therefore, even if only a relatively small number of consumers pay voluntarily, the difference between the small marginal cost and the imperfect competition price can be high enough to cover the initial fixed costs and entry costs and hence make production of the public good profitable (see figure 2.1). A typical example is the production of music under the constraints created by widespread internet piracy. The fixed costs of producing a new song are relatively large, whereas the marginal costs of selling the song online to an additional person are very close to zero. However, the music industry is not perfectly competitive, and so it can still ask for a nonzero price for each song or album. In figure 2.1, P^* is the average between the price asked for by the music industry and the price (often zero) asked for by pirates. Despite widespread piracy, paying consumers still exist, and they are numerous enough that music production is still a very profitable enterprise. Music in the internet era is thus a public good (in the technical sense defined above) and yet still profitably produced by private enterprise.

Even so, it can be argued that although public goods can sometimes be produced profitably by the private sector, they will still probably be underproduced relative to the hypothetical perfectly efficient level. That said, the most relevant comparison is not with such a hypothetical perfectly efficient level. The relevant comparison is across institutions. Would the public good be produced more efficiently or less efficiently under other arrangements—for example, by a democratic government's monopoly—with

Table 2.1 **Types of goods**

	Easy to exclude	*Hard to exclude*
Large negative externalities	Private goods	Common pool resources
Small negative externalities	Club goods	Public goods

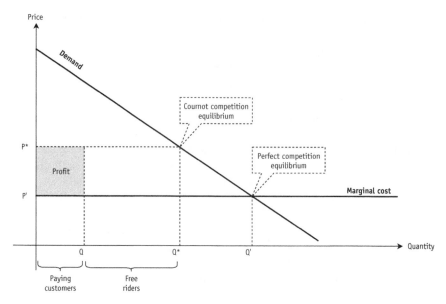

Figure 2.1 Profits from providing a public good under imperfect competition.

all the problems and inefficiencies associated with alternative arrangements? The bottom line is that all institutional systems are rife with inefficiencies,[22] and hence the proper comparison is always among real-world alternative institutions not between one real-world institution (real markets, real governments) and a utopian perfect system (perfect government, perfectly competitive markets).

The most difficult case is that of common pool resources, which involve both high-consumption externalities and low excludability (table 2.1). Typical examples include communally owned pastures, which may be overgrazed; fish in the ocean, which may be overfished; overuse of antibiotics, which may lead to antibiotic resistance; air pollution; and traffic congestion. Unlike the case of public goods, where free riders can be more easily tolerated, in the case of common pool resources, free riders actively cause damage. In other words, the more free riders there are, the less the paying consumers can receive the goods they are paying for.

The problem associated with common pool resources is referred to as a tragedy of the commons and is usually modeled with the help of a prisoners' dilemma (see table 2.2). If participants cooperate, they avoid the tragedy of the commons, such as overgrazing the pasture, overpolluting, or causing antibiotic resistance. However, if one person defects (e.g., by bringing too many sheep to graze the pasture, by using cheaper but dirtier technology, or by using antibiotics carelessly), that person gets an even bigger personal benefit. Hence, the temptation exists to cheat, and it is difficult to achieve credible commitment to cooperation, given that everyone faces the same incentives. The equilibrium (shown in gray in table 2.2) is for everyone to defect and, hence, for the tragedy to occur.

People can escape the tragedy if they manage to change the game.[23] For example, if people successfully enforce the punishment of defectors, the game can be changed

Table 2.2 **Engineering cooperation by punishing defectors**

Prisoners' dilemma	Person 2			Stag Hunt	Person 2	
	Cooperates	*Defects*	→		*Cooperates*	*Defects*
Person 1 Cooperates	(3, 3)	(0, **5**)		Person 1 Cooperates	(3, 3)	(0, **2**)
Defects	(**5**, 0)	(1, 1)		Defects	(**2**, 0)	(1, 1)

Note: Nash equilibria in gray. Payoffs in bold are changed.

to a stag hunt, which has two equilibria, one of them cooperative. (In table 2.2, thanks to the creation of a sanction, the payoff for unilateral defection is changed from 5 to 2.) In the stag hunt, people cooperate if they trust that others will cooperate.[24] Repeated interactions in the prisoners' dilemma, combined with reputation mechanisms, can also overcome this problem. In this case, the discounted stream of payoffs for a long series of plays makes it advantageous to choose to cooperate.[25] Taking the long-term perspective is thus another way to reduce the payoff from unilateral defection.

As Elinor Ostrom points out, a common error in analyzing the tragedy of the commons is that "the constraints that are assumed to be fixed for the purpose of analysis are taken on faith as being fixed in empirical settings."[26] Researchers mistakenly assume that "prisoners in the famous dilemma cannot change the constraints imposed on them by the district attorney." In fact, people are rarely prisoners in a fixed institutional environment. At least to some extent, they are free and self-governing. They are entrepreneurial, in socially productive or destructive directions, not only within a given set of rules[27] but also in changing the rules.[28] As such, "the question [should be addressed] of how to enhance the capabilities of those involved to change the constraining rules of the game to lead to outcomes other than remorseless tragedies."[29] Elinor Ostrom uncovers numerous examples in which people escaped the tragedy of the commons by creating, monitoring, and enforcing various kinds of rules for punishing free riders.

Technology and Institutions

Technology can affect both the excludability and the rivalry aspects of goods and services. In other words, to see these dimensions as inherent properties of goods is mistaken. They depend on the interaction between their nature and the technological context.

As noted earlier, internet technology has made the excludability of songs much more difficult and has virtually eliminated the rivalry of consumption. Before the internet age, music was a private good in that its informational content was relatively hard to detach from its material substrate—vinyl records, CDs, and tapes. As a result, consumption was rivalrous (if one person owned a given record, another could not), and exclusion was easy (standard rules against material theft worked well). By making information easily transmissible, apart from its material substrate, the internet has undermined both aspects of the good and has transformed music into a public good.

The reverse phenomenon also occurs.[30] For example, E-ZPass technology has made the excludability of roads much easier.[31] It used to be relatively difficult to exclude drivers from roads because there can be only so many toll stops without causing traffic jams. Even such a solution as levying a road tax to the price of gas is not well targeted; for example, a driver buys gas in one state and travels through another. With E-ZPass, it is easy to collects funds for roads without slowing traffic. Hence, what used to be a common pool resource is turning into a private good. New technologies also make it easy to apply congestion pricing in cities and to privatize roads. In line with the comparative institutional analysis idea mentioned earlier, we would have to compare, for example, whether the deadweight losses of private roads owing to imperfect competition in transportation are greater or smaller than the government inefficiencies in providing roads.

Foldvary and Klein argue that public policy changes concerning public goods or common pool resources are always outpaced by technological innovations that affect excludability and rivalry.[32] In other words, policy is always behind the times. Even with well-meaning policymaking, there will be highly inefficient policies because of the adaptability problem. Bureaucracies change slowly, and they are rife with knowledge and incentive problems. For example, Maryland Route 200 uses E-ZPass technology to turn the road into a club good, but even if it would be more efficient to privatize it or for it to have been built privately. Bureaucratic incentives work against reform and, given the climate of ideas in the United States, policymakers and voters may not even be aware of the possibility of privatization. This brings us to the important topic of social context, which economists usually neglect. Although first, we will discuss institutional context.

Institutional Context and the Calculus of Consent

Another way to view the private-public dyad is to ask why certain issues are left to markets and others are addressed by political means. Buchanan and Tullock offer a simple yet deep answer.[33] Their approach generalizes the logic of Coasian bargaining with positive transaction costs to the case of agreements among many actors, rather than between only two. The importance of their approach can hardly be underestimated. In the words of the Ostroms, Buchanan and Tullock's "principle of conceptual unanimity gave meaning to what [we] had observed and what was accomplished"[34] throughout a large set of empirical examples in which people created and enforced rules to deal with collective issues.

The logic of Coasian bargaining between two parties shows that, when transaction costs are low, the parties will eventually reach an agreement about how to assign property rights and hence eliminate deadweight losses by setting up compensation mechanisms. For example, if a shepherd's sheep trample a farmer's land and damage the crops, the damage counts as a deadweight loss; to put it differently, the actions are inefficient. But if the two parties come to an agreement for, say, either the shepherd to pay the farmer to build and maintain a passage across his land or for the farmer to invest in building the passage on his own or for the farmer and shepherd to share the cost of building the passage, the deadweight loss disappears because the cost of the damage has now been included in both actors' decisions. When transaction costs become too large, such agreements are impractical, and other institutional arrangements are devised. As Coase and the economist Oliver E. Williamson point out, when the transaction costs involved in bilateral repeated dealings are too large, firms and organizations emerge.[35] For example, when General Motors faced a large enough uncertainty about its supply and price of car body styles, it ended up buying a manufacturer of car bodies, hence including that activity in the firm instead of continuing to rely on the market for car bodies.[36]

Buchanan and Tullock push this logic beyond bilateral agreements to cover social contracts.[37] They note that, even when rational ignorance problems are ignored, any collective decision-making harms a part of the population, namely those who disagree with the decision but must obey it. Buchanan and Tullock refer to this as "external costs," meaning that the decision-making group creates this type of externality for those who disagree. They note that, in line with the Coasian bargaining logic, these external costs decrease as a move is made toward unanimous decision-making, which is essentially a large-scale bargaining process among many people.[38] However, in practice, unanimous decision-making is not possible because the transaction costs are too large (e.g., it would take too much time). Hence, if transaction costs are included in the calculations, unanimity is not efficient. To account for this, Buchanan and Tullock include transaction costs under the name of "decision-making costs" and note that, contrary to external costs, these costs increase as more and more people are included. Assuming these are the only costs involved in collective decision-making (which is not entirely correct; for example, enforcement costs are important), the efficient level of consensus can be found by finding the minimum of the total costs (external costs plus decision costs).

This optimal level of consensus may be larger or smaller than the majority rule (see figure 2.2). The optimal level is determined by the shape of the two cost functions. For example, when there is a fire, the optimal level of consensus for calling the firefighters is very low, basically one. That is because the external costs function is basically flat— everyone has the same interest in this matter. In other contexts, the optimal level of consensus can be very high. For example, a jury must reach a unanimous verdict to convict someone accused of a crime. The decision costs in a group of twelve people are small, and the external costs (i.e., the cost of convicting an innocent person) are large. In other cases, the optimal level of consensus is more than a simple majority even if the decision costs are high. For example, constitutional changes require larger levels of consensus than the passage of regular laws because the consequences of constitutional changes (i.e., their external costs) are much larger.

This perspective gives us a way to think about the total costs of collective decision-making, which, in the context of democratic politics, can be identified with the cost of government. Buchanan and Tullock use this perspective to provide an institutional perspective over private-public distinctions. If, in a given area, the cost of government is lower than the cost created by market failures—that is, by the unregulated behavior of private actors—the issue under consideration is a legitimate government concern (see figure 2.3, panel a). If, by contrast, the cost of government is higher than the cost of market failures in that area, government should not concern itself with that issue (see figure 2.3, panel b).

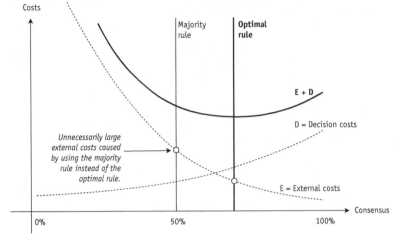

(a) Majority rule under optimal rule creates unnecessarily large externalities

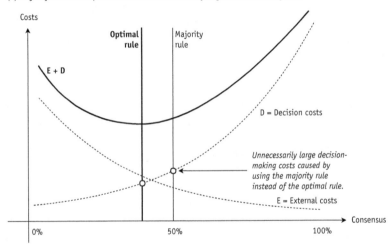

(b) Majority rule above optimal rule creates unnecessarily large decision-making costs

Figure 2.2 Calculus-of-consent explanation of the inefficiency of majority rule. (a) Cost of government > market failure. (b) Market failure > cost of government.

On the one hand, this logic allows evaluation of the scope of government, such as which issues should be left unregulated and which should be brought into the realm of collective decision-making. On the other hand, this logic provides a striking perspective on federalism by also permitting evaluation of different scopes of governments at different levels. Buchanan and Tullock briefly explore this idea,[39] but it is Vincent Ostrom who does the most investigation.[40] Interestingly, Vincent Ostrom, Charles Mills Tiebout, and Robert Warren also famously anticipate much of the calculus of consent logic.[41]

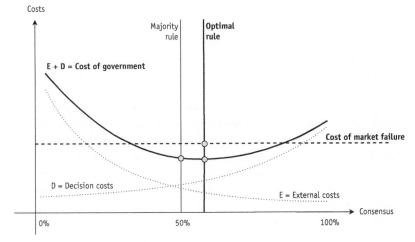

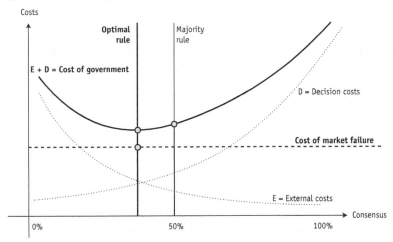

Figure 2.3 Calculus- of- consent approach to the private- public distinction. (a) Cost of government < market failure. (b) Market failure < cost of government.

As a simple illustration, consider again panel a and panel b in figure 2.3. The only difference between them is that in one the decision costs increase far more than in the other. As a result, in panel b, even the minimal possible cost of government (under the optimal rule, rather than under majority rule) is higher than the cost of market failure. In panel a, even the slightly inefficient majority rule is of lower cost than the cost of market failure. Panel b describes the federal government and panel a indicates the local government. Because local government involves fewer people, and perhaps a more homogeneous population, collective decision-making is easier. Consequently, the problem created by market failure can be efficiently addressed by local government but not by the federal government.

As mentioned, and as Buchanan and Tullock are the first to acknowledge,[42] the calculus of consent ignores many important factors. For instance, it is not obvious how to include economies of scale in the analysis. But the point we try to make here does not require a complete theory. The point is only that institutional factors, which influence decision-making transaction costs, can have a dramatic impact on whether an issue should be considered private or public. As we switch from panel a to panel b in figure 2.3, what changes is not the nature of the issue—the market failure does not change—but the institutional apparatus available for making collective decisions.

Many other factors can have a similar effect. For example, consider the growing centralization of the United States—that is, the fact that the scope of the federal government has gradually increased. From a calculus-of-consent perspective, we need to understand the underlying factors that have changed the two cost curves. Perhaps the importance of mass media in the twentieth century, for example, made it easier to reach national consensus on a wider variety of issues, hence decreasing the decision costs curve, as in the transition from panel b to panel a in figure 2.3 Many other factors could be proposed. Our point is only that not all factors involved are inherent to the issues. Many were technological, cultural, or institutional. Hence, the private-public distinction requires attention to those other factors. To understand the institutional changes in the real world that affect the private-public interface, such as the expansion of the scope of the federal government in United States, we need to look at additional factors.

Social and Cultural Contexts

When analyzing the private-public distinction from the perspectives in the previous section, political economists draw one common conclusion: public policy rarely fits economists' concerns regarding the efficient provision of public goods or common pool resources. As pointed out by the Ostroms,[43] this disconnect provided the impetus for the birth of public choice. But, even today, public choice struggles to include ideas, ideology, and beliefs in the analysis.[44] Standard public choice, such as analysis of rent-seeking or of bureaucracy, usually focuses on incentives problems, highlighting that individual actors in the public sector often face personal incentives that are at odds with general welfare and efficiency considerations. Although such analyses are, of course, highly relevant and important, they do not offer a way to analyze changes, particularly because all the models are equilibrium models. In those models, the determinants of change are thus exogenous. To understand institutional changes in general, and changes of the private-public interface in particular, we must understand ideas.[45]

For this purpose, the proper framework of analysis must be grounded in subjective preferences and beliefs about what constitutes a common good. The standard theoretical apparatus of microeconomics deals well with preferences about private goods. The reason that such preferences do not pose great theoretical difficulties is that people with different preferences can easily coexist. If one person likes vanilla ice cream and another prefers chocolate ice cream, nothing stops the two from both having their way. We can expand the microeconomic analysis to deal with the creation of institutions by thinking about people's preferences for other people's behaviors. Thus, rather than thinking about preferences over public goods or common pool resources, which, as we have seen, have shifting domains depending on technologies and institutions, we should instead think of individuals coping with other individuals. To put it differently, what constitutes a public good is a consequence of how people have managed to deal with one another and with their conflicting preferences about each other's behaviors: it is not something that is determined by the inherent nature of the good. The standard approach assumes that the inherent nature of the good, as a public good or a common pool resource, creates social dilemmas with which people deal more or less efficiently by creating institutions. In our approach, people have conflicting preferences about other people's behaviors, which creates a very different perspective on social dilemmas; as a result of the institutions people build to cope with each other, certain goods end up being defined as public goods. The public nature of a good is a consequence of preferences, conflicts, and institutions and is not a starting point of analysis.

It is possible to deal with some preferences about other people's behaviors by means of contracts. For example, when a firm contracts with its suppliers or with labor, it is expressing a preference about behaviors. This example may be slightly more complex than preferences about private goods such as ice cream, but the situation is still relatively easy to resolve. What makes contractual situations easy is that if someone does not want to agree to a contract, no one is forced to interact with that person. In other words, a selection process is possible such that people with mutually agreeable preferences about each other's behaviors can end up together and people who cannot agree can continue to coexist peacefully because no one is obligated to be part of the contract. This type of contractual selection process gives rise to clubs in the general sense of the word.[46] Voluntary clubs appear not because that is how goods that are inherently club goods get produced; rather, they are a byproduct of the contractual mechanism for harmonizing preferences about other people's behaviors. Clubs, in fact, often produce a wide range of goods, which are not "club goods" in the sense defined by table 2.1. For example, apartment buildings are clubs that provide club goods, such as protection or illumination of the residents' parking lot, but also many private goods, such as elevators, air conditioning, and electricity. Strictly speaking, it is possible to charge each tenant individually for use of the elevators, air conditioning, and electricity, but it is often the case that these goods are kept collective. It is not because of the inherent nature of the goods that they are kept collective, but because people can and do agree about each other's behaviors.

Next, we present a paradigmatic example of how institutional innovation can diminish conflicts by transforming what previously was a single public good into a set of coexisting club goods. When state and church are not separated, the underlying religious diversity must be funneled at the collective level into a single acceptable religion. All citizens must be members of the state church. The separation of church and state, allowing a multitude of churches to coexist on the same territory, radically changes the issue. It eliminates the necessity of the debates and processes that lead to homogenization. It preserves, rather than solves, the heterogeneity of religious beliefs and values.[47]

Our example also highlights the fundamental difficulty of achieving the liberal utopia of a perfectly consensual society, associated with the normative individualist assumptions and systems. The main problem is that one person may have objections not only to other people's behaviors but also to their preferences. To give an obvious example: (a) *I don't like to kill people*; and (b) *I prefer to associate only with others who have the same preference*; but (c) *I also want no one, regardless of whether they agree with me, to be allowed to kill people*. The first two steps are the basis for the creation of voluntary clubs, but the third step makes them insufficient. This example is obvious, as are the rules against theft and fraud. With respect to such preferences, the consensus is so large that there is no controversy in imposing the rules on everyone. The situation gets trickier with a move toward more controversial issues, such as the various aspects of social justice, but the analytical structure does not change. In general, it looks like this: (a) *I prefer X*, and (b) *I prefer to associate with people who fulfill X*, but (c) *I prefer that everyone must fulfill X*. It is the third step, when X is deemed a moral issue, that makes voluntary clubs insufficient. In the religious freedom example, the reform was possible only because enough people agreed to give up on the third step. This type of change is a cultural, ideological, and moral change that is a logical prerequisite to institutional change.

If administrative units are seen as nothing but gigantic homeowners' associations,[48] that is, clubs, then the same problem is at the root of the debate about centralization or decentralization. If X occurs in all but a few states, and X is deemed a moral issue, strong pressure will develop in favor of centralizing X. This is a very different factor from the institutional factors highlighted in our earlier discussion of the calculus of consent. Similarly, if not many but some firms do X, and X is deemed a moral issue, there will be strong pressure for government control and regulation. To understand this logic is to also understand why private arrangements will be deemed insufficient. Private and club arrangements, by definition, cannot impose the same thing on everyone.

What all of the above show, once again, is that it is naive to think that the private-public distinction is simply a consequence of the inherent nature of the goods, and that it is also naive to try to reduce this complex set of issues to dichotomist ideal theorizing. Beyond the relatively trivial remark that technology affects rivalry and excludability and the subtler calculus of consent institutional logic, we need to acknowledge and focus on people's beliefs about what constitutes a moral issue, which will prevent them from accepting pluralism as a viable arrangement. The private-public distinction is more than just a technical matter in economics. To understand it, we must ultimately understand the cultural processes that expand or contract the set of moral issues (figure 2.4), hence making it harder or easier for pluralistic solutions to be accepted.

In addition, we must understand the intellectual arrangements and political processes associated with the dynamic interface. The framing and the administration of this very interface are the key arena and function of the governance process. That said, the question of interest from the perspective of our discussion is to continue to identify, articulate, and present the consequence of all of the above in practical terms. The next step in the applied-level direction of public administration is to note that in practical terms all of the above mean one thing: governance in a classical-liberal

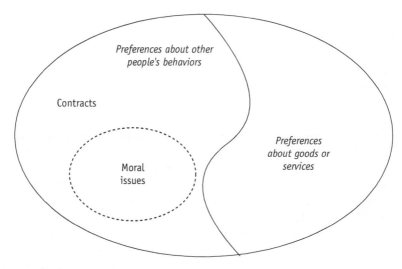

Figure 2.4 Moral issues in the universe of preferences.

perspective means taking seriously the ambiguity, uncertainty, complexity, and continuous change of social order. By necessity, that means a flexible approach is needed that accommodates, and even encourages, institutional diversity that is both the result and a condition of the diversity of human values, interests, and preferences manifest in different and dynamic environments. In this respect, the sole answer is to create the conditions for the ongoing emergence or adaptation of the institutional arrangements most adequate to deal with changing and diverse circumstances, be they environmental and technological parameters or social preferences.

Now it can be seen how the pieces of the classical-liberal governance puzzle fit together. Freedom of exchange and freedom of association are fundamental to the applied-level theory of classical liberalism. These freedoms are the logical extension of—they are intrinsically required by—the underlying normative individualist principle. At the same time, they are drivers of the governance process. Another major implication and corollary of the line of arguments outlined above is the emergence to salience for the applied level of the institutional diversity problem. The diversity of institutional forms is robustly correlated to the diversity of circumstances, problems, and preferences of the social actors. Freedom of exchange and freedom of association are intrinsically sources of pluralism. At the same time, pluralism generates a diversity of experiments in social solutions. The variety of institutions and the freedom to experiment, adapt, and adjust at the complex frontier between private and public leads to an increased overall resilience of the system. The case for the advantages of institutional pluralism and the case for resilience through innovation and adaptive change together are the case for institutional performance in general. As the political scientist and anthropologist James C. Scott puts it,

> Radically simplified designs for social organization seem to court the same risks of failure courted by radically simplified designs for natural environments. The failures and vulnerability of monocrop commercial

forests and genetically engineered, mechanized monocropping mimic the failures of collective farms and planned cities. At this level, I am making a case for the resilience of both social and natural diversity and a strong case about the limits, in principle, of what we are likely to know about complex, functioning order.[49]

A view of the process is also a view of intuitional diversity. Human diversity, normative individualism, process, freedom of choice, freedom of association, and institutional diversity are intrinsically connected and are part and parcel of the same governance model or system. Governance in such a system means taking seriously the diversity of human values, beliefs, and preferences, as well as the ambiguity, uncertainty, complexity, and continuous change of social order. That, as is shown here, means by necessity adopting a flexible approach that accommodates, and even encourages, institutional diversity that is both the result of and a condition of the diversity of human values, interests, and preferences. In this respect, the answer to governance philosophy is to create the conditions for the ongoing emergence or adaptation of institutional arrangements. Those institutional arrangements should be the ones that are most adequate to deal with changing and diverse circumstances, be they environmental and technological parameters or social preferences. It is essential (a) to encourage institutions and organizations to be flexible and adaptable to inputs and signals coming from the environment, groups, and individuals, and (b) to encourage the freedom to choose and organize. Market-based private solutions are favored, but not because of some commitment to metaphysical entities called markets. They are favored because the processes taking place in the markets are more often than not closer to the normative and efficiency conditions intrinsic to normative individualism and freedom of exchange and association.

Now it is clearer why rigid adherence to a single formula or model creates problems. Far from being a mere doctrinal position, this point is well supported by contemporary research in institutional theory. There is no single, unique, universal, or centralized solution for public governance. Social order "is not presided by a government," a notion used, significantly, instead of governments,[50] and there is no single external agent, the government, an "amorphous, fictitious and omnicompetent entity," exogenous to the various situations of social life requiring governance.[51] When it comes to organizing people to solve public governance problems, there is no reason to expect less heterogeneity and freedom of association than in the private sector.[52] The classical-liberal perspective simply builds on these realities.

Conclusions

By exploring the functions and processes at the interface of the private and the public, we take another step toward defining the parameters of the normative individualist, classical-liberal perspective on governance. Thus, what may be seen growing are the contours of an approach whose goal is not a rigidly predefined governance structure but rather a creation of the conditions of an adaptive institutional system, flexible and able to incorporate and use governance-relevant signals that emerge either spontaneously in social practice or deliberately in social analysis. That approach slowly leads to a distinctive mode of viewing and conceptualizing governance as a process organized around learning and adaptation, both considered pivotal elements in the constellation of governance functions. The goal is to create conditions that facilitate the emergence, growth, and evolution on a contractarian and voluntary basis of a structure of public choice and public administration. In fact, entrance is from a different angle to the territory of the complex set of institutional arrangements that combine rules and incentives to give operational content to the idea of an open society (Popper) evolving by way of a complex knowledge process (Hayek) of institutionally framed procedural tinkering (Hayek, Popper, Ostrom, Buchanan).[53]

3

Dynamic Governance

Polycentricity and Knowledge Processes

The preceding chapters show that the logic of normative individualism, bolstered by skepticism regarding preference aggregation processes that assume human and institutional fallibility and by a realist stance on the feasibility and efficacy of collective action, leads to a view of governance in which the key area becomes the dynamic interface between the public and the private. Governance is revealed to be mainly about the collective management of an ongoing process happening at the interface between the two spheres. It is a process in which (a) technology affects rivalry and excludability, (b) different institutions induce different decision-making transaction costs, and (c) culture matters in determining the range of acceptability of diverse solutions. If that is the case, the focus of governance as a social function and its institutional apparatus must be on that dynamic, on the ways by which a social group deals with that challenges a collective problem. But, if the nature of the challenge is to shape and manage a process, the questions are these: How do we frame, understand, and approach this dynamic process and the phenomena associated with it? Are there broad underlying ways to frame the process and the associated phenomena which are particularly relevant for governance analysis and design? What are the conceptual and intellectual frameworks mapping this process that are relevant for the applied theory of governance?

Surveying the existing relevant literature and the history of governance doctrines in that light, a number of themes and approaches may be identified that satisfy three key conditions: (a) they are theoretically and normatively consistent with the aforementioned principles and vision; (b) they assume explicitly a connection with the core classical-liberal tradition represented by the Scottish Enlightenment, by American Federalists, and the Tocquevillian perspective; and (c) they are present (albeit implicitly, mostly unconsciously, and in fragmentary forms) in the public discourse and policy standpoints of advocates of classical-liberalism-inspired solutions to contemporary public governance problems.

This chapter presents a set of key notions, grouped as follows: (a) the idea of process-focused, dynamic governance having at its core the voluntary action principle; (b) the notions of countervailing powers, including the importance of a voluntary-sector, nonstate governance; (c) polycentricity, the governance keystone of the normative individualist system of classical-liberal inspiration; and (d) the concern with learning processes and the institutions that best allow societies to gain, preserve, and use knowledge, another key feature and framing principle of this tradition. The focus on the role of knowledge in society is a natural counterpart of polycentricity. Interestingly, the concern about creating a resilient and adaptive social system, which is able to quickly and reliably learn from past mistakes, leads to the *same* institutional arrangement as the focus on voluntary agreement and the concern about abuses of power. A priori, the concern about incentives and the concern about information need not point in the same direction—one could have imagined that a trade-off between the two is in play. Interestingly, it is not so. In conjunction, these notions shape the distinctive classical-liberal perspective on governance and the applied-level solutions inspired by it.

Process versus End State

In light of the public choice analysis and the normative individualist principle, the most important consequence of the complex, contextual, and dynamic nature of the public-private interface is that it is impossible to advance an a priori, universal, operational governance formula for the public domain. This applies to the general formula of a "minimal state" as well—an expression of ingrained skepticism regarding governmental performance but which lacks substantive content as a prescription of organizing and operating public administration arrangements. The question of whether an issue will be managed through private or public arrangements is a matter that must be decided by the circumstances of each given case within a broader constitutional agreement about how such a policy-level decision-making process is to be performed (including constraints regarding which individual rights cannot be undermined). Such a decision includes the specific configurations called for by either private or public arrangements as well as the preferences and decisions of the individuals involved in the circumstances.

This approach has a double anchor in the classical-liberal tradition. First, there is the logic of collective action and decision-making—based on the same methodological and normative individualist principles that define the theory of the market, including market failure theory. Second, the classical-liberal ethos of freedom of choice is extended into the public arena. The idea of self-governance comes with a strong presupposition in favor of people being able to associate and organize freely in ways they find best. But this presupposition assumes they do not infringe on the rights of other individuals and groups that do not want to be part of the collective-associative enterprise: principles of voluntary association and freedom of exchange.

The logic of the argument, followed to its end, induces a spectacular change of perspective. The focal points are no longer predetermined ends but rather the processes that lead to various desired outcomes and the institutional arrangements that frame those processes. In the clash between the end-state (or final-outcome) approach and the process (a chain of causes and consequences) approach, classical liberalism leans robustly toward the latter. This observation is crucial and requires an elaboration.

The end-state or final-outcome perspective, writes Norman Barry, attempts "a description of the features of a society at a specified point in time" and attaches to it a normative claim. For instance, it may describe "the features predetermining the society's distribution of income, wealth, power, prestige, status and the structures of the economic and political systems." Thus, normatively speaking, this perspective "creates an ideal, a final state or goal, and declares its implementation the final purpose of politics."[1] Process theory does not focus on various snapshots more or less arbitrarily selected on the complex continuum of social life, but instead tries to look at the chain of causes and consequences and, even more importantly, the rules of the game generating that chain. Social actors interact in a setting that defines their calculations and preferences and that constrains or enhances certain behaviors. What are the rules that frame and shape the process? What configuration of rules generates the type of behaviors and processes that best satisfy specific normative standards? In brief, normatively speaking, a "decentralized activity, interaction and co-ordination of social action" is suggested, not a particular predetermined state.[2] The end states are obviously considered, but the approach goes beyond the end state: the focus is on the procedural rules.

A change of emphasis from thinking mainly of end states to thinking also of process has important practical consequences. Rather than being fixated with a particular unchangeable configuration of institutional arrangements, the change process itself becomes as important as the favored arrangement. Instead of unfreezing an institutional arrangement only to refreeze it in a new configuration, the goal is to make the system flexible and adaptable, resonating closely with the preferences of individuals on the ground. In the end, this process can be seen as an extension of Hayek's argument regarding the generality of rules and regulations that aim to create "favorable circumstances" even if it is not possible to "control the outcome":

> Such activities in which we are guided by a knowledge merely of the principle of the thing should perhaps better be described by the term "cultivation" than by the familiar term "control"—cultivation in the sense in which the farmer or gardener cultivates his plants, where he knows and can control only some of the determining circumstances, and in which the wise legislature or statesman will probably attempt to cultivate rather than control the forces of the social process.[3]

Extending this logic to public governance means that public administration is not so much about control and especially control of outcomes. It is about cultivation by shaping the circumstances of collective choices and actions. It is about prudently and pragmatically operating in a dynamic area of deep ambiguity and uncertainty, guided by a general knowledge of principles, leaving room for as many forms and levels as possible of "publics" and "collectives," with their values, preferences, information, and incentives to manifest themselves. That means limiting the concern about specific policies that target specific end states and focusing instead on the institutional frameworks that shape the processes that lead to various states. It also means allowing individuals to organize at different levels, in the ways they see as most effective for realizing their individual or collective objectives while giving society resilience through adaptability. Let us focus now on the structural conditions that engender and facilitate that ability to organize.

Toward Polycentrism: Countervailing Mechanisms and Voluntary Governance

Two focal points emerge that bring together the themes and issues of countervailing mechanisms and voluntary governance as frameworks to convert the classical-liberal vision into applied approaches: (a) the notion of polycentricity and (b) the idea of an epistemic or a knowledge process as an underlying dimension of polycentric institutional order.

From a structural-functional perspective, classical-liberal governance may be seen as compounding three stances projected on a process background. The first stance is a reactive or defensive approach focusing on the mechanisms aiming at coping with the "administrative state." It is an extension of the checks-and-balances, separation-of-powers doctrine that, in the realm of public administration, is put to work as a mechanism reining in the "administrative state." The second stance is a proactive position to the social and governance role of the neither-market-nor-state domain of civic society and self-governance that is seen as an alternative and sometimes as a complement to the state. The third stance is an extension of governance theory in the direction of pluralism by putting together the first two approaches under an overarching principle. The idea is to not only look for governance solutions inside the state's organization and administration, but also (and mainly) to look at the broader picture of governance arrangements a society generates outside the sphere of the state. With this lens it becomes clearer that there are many legitimate governance alternatives at various levels, and that they all have a variety of functional domains and roles. But to see the larger picture requires us to shift focus from the modern administrative state as the unique and preeminent form of public administration to a polycentric perspective that sees the state's administrative apparatus as part of a broader and more complex social governance system. Polycentricity becomes the dominant principle that captures those and related aspects.

All three areas require extensive separate discussion. The standard literature on public administration, which does not claim a classical-liberal lineage, dedicates much attention to them. Those areas are now so much a part of the institutional luggage of modern democratic systems that they are taken for granted and are considered universal, implicitly assumed elements of modern governance, with their lineage forgotten. But their full dimensions and capacities are revealed and understood only when they are seen not in the hybrid forms of real-life, mixed-governance arrangements. Instead, they need to be seen as part and parcel of a system and tradition based on normative individualist assumptions and on agnosticism regarding social aggregation and welfare functions. For the purpose of our argument, it is important only to outline those three areas while also noting relevant authors grounded in and advancing the classical-liberal tradition.

Let us start by restating the general challenge: how society creates the conditions for the emergence, growth, and evolution of a public choice and public administration structure whose function is the collective setup and management of the private-public interface. To do so in the classical-liberal tradition, the first task is to control and tame the monocentric, power-accumulation tendencies intrinsic to political systems. In this respect, the most salient solution in the classical-liberal tradition—and in the history of political thought in general—has been an appeal to institutionalize the control of power through the separation-of-powers doctrine and a dynamic process of checks and balances. As the economist Scott Gordon[4] explains in his study of constitutional doctrines aimed at controlling the state from ancient times to the present, the principle of countervailing power in which power is dispersed and controlled by power is considered by the classical-liberal tradition to be a necessary condition for the preservation of liberty and a central and necessary element of the architecture of the modern liberal-democratic state.[5] For our purposes, it is not necessary to reintroduce or discuss that tradition. We confine ourselves to the current challenge: how we can adapt the application of this institutional design principle to the historical and political evolutions of the past hundred years or so. In that respect, the growth of what has been called the administrative state is the most important phenomenon to be considered.

A vast literature exists that addresses the problems associated with the rise of the administrative state. As an illustration of a consistent articulation in constitutional theory terms of a classical-liberal response to the challenge, M. J. C. Vile's work on the separation of powers provides an excellent vehicle.[6] Vile notes that the administrative state "has taken an autonomy of its own."[7] In many respects, he argues, "it is only marginally under the control of its political masters."[8] The other branches of the government are under pressure: "The administration sits like a great cuckoo in the nest, elbowing out the historic actors in the drama of government."[9] The idea that we have an executive branch consisting of civil servants who, guided and monitored by appointed leaders, execute what the legislature has decided is no longer valid. The reality has evolved. The distinction between political leaders and bureaucrats or, more precisely, between their functions in the system has become very complex. That complexity has a significant impact on the system's functioning: "Political leaders spend a great deal of their time attempting to manage the administrative machinery for which they are ostensibly responsible but which they are invariably unable to control."[10] Yet, notes Vile,

> it is important that opponents of the administrative state should not assume that it can be abolished. There is no way to predict how large or how important administration will be in five or fifty years' time: it may be larger, or it may be smaller, but it will be there. The priority, therefore, is to control it.[11]

In such circumstances, it is necessary to revisit and update the institutional-constitutional arrangements. The key seems to be in revisiting the traditional theory of separation of powers. Instead of the classic three branches, now there are four de facto branches: legislative, executive, judicial, and administrative machine. Vile states: "The logic of the present situation therefore is to accept that there are now four branches of government and to provide the control mechanisms necessary to prevent the abuse of power by any of them."[12] Any attempt to work with a conceptual scheme that has only three branches of government and to distribute functions among them fails on purely pragmatic grounds because that scheme does not provide a realistic framework for action. This attempt leads not only to the question of the appropriate methods by which to control the increasing power of the administrative branch but also to questions regarding how to control and guide each branch and the balance among them in view of the rise of administrative power. The problem is a recurring theme in modern constitutional history: How does society achieve a balance across the branches of government that will both safeguard individual freedom and ensure that government delivers the services it is responsible for, given ongoing changes in the system.

In other words, increasingly complex means of control are needed to safeguard the rights of individuals so as to prevent abuse of power by bureaucrats and administrators. Various instruments, from legal and judicial review to scientific advice and evaluation, are available and may be put in place (as they increasingly are) in the current framework. Yet the ultimate challenge is bigger: there is absolutely no reason to treat the administrative branch as either an exceptional or a transitory phenomenon of marginal relevance. It is necessary to apply to it the same logic and treatment applied to the other branches. The challenge is to address the problem at its roots and beyond its surface manifestations. To address the problem at its core, it is necessary to revisit the separation of powers and to examine the logic of countervailing powers in a broader context of society. The very logic of countervailing checks and balances leads to nonstate governance structures, and from there the notion of polycentricism is only a small step.

We stress again that the idea is not that preoccupation with the emergence of the administrative state and the functional differentiation of the administrative branch of government is the classical-liberal position on public administration and public governance. The point of our argument and of the reference to Vile's take on the classical-liberal response to the administrative state is to note that the approach based on the logic of checks and balances is a prime classical-liberal mode of dealing with the problem of public administration. The liberal tradition looks at the problem of power, and the various political-institutional ways to contain, disperse, and control it, as a means to create an efficient governance arrangement that preserves liberty. The applied-level public administration corollary is that, under the conditions of a growing administrative apparatus of national states, "there needs to be a new approach to the way government is articulated and that entails a quite different approach to the mechanisms by which control is exercised over administration."[13] Vile illustrates a profound mode of engaging the issue through his questioning of the traditional threefold doctrine of government branches and powers. But with an approach from that angle, the logic of countervailing powers in the divisions of governance tasks must extend outside the narrow confines of the state's apparatus. This logic leads in an inescapable path toward the polycentric vision.

On its logical development toward the notion of polycentrism, the functional analysis of governance structures and their countervailing powers discussed above moves smoothly to the domain of the voluntary association and civil society. To make the normative individualist, non-statist perspective on public governance operational, the focus needs to shift outside the confines of the state and its administrative-bureaucratic apparatus. More precisely, the focus needs to be in the domain of community, civil society, nongovernment, and nonprofit forms of organization. That institutional interest in social arrangements outside the state comes (a) as an extension of the principle of checks and balances (which is extended to the entire social system, with the countervailing powers of civil society keeping the state under control) and (b) from the classical-liberal assumption that society works best if the state is limited to a narrow and well-defined set of functions. Behind all this is the idea that there is an inherent distribution of responsibilities among institutions in a society. Each sector—state, market, voluntary, nonprofit—has its strengths and weaknesses. Therefore, responsibilities must be allocated following each institution's capabilities. Under normal social circumstances, civic society—the third sector—could cover a large range of governance and functions of social service. Hence, a classical-liberal approach to public administration is intrinsically connected to public governance that is carried out through the third sector, with the voluntary sector as a competitor or a complement to state-based, state-executed governance. Even more challenging is that this applies not only to normal social circumstances. As the research line advanced by Virgil Storr et al.[14] has demonstrated—both through theoretical arguments and case studies and empirical analysis—the "third sector" may operate effectively in this function in exceptional social situations of disaster and crisis as well.

From the relevant literature redefining and relaunching this line of argument in the second half of the twentieth century, we note the insightful contribution of Richard Cornuelle, fully conversant with contemporary developments. Cornuelle starts with the observation that, in the second half of the twentieth century, the balance between the three sectors was profoundly altered.[15] He notes that in the United States (and in advanced industrial democracies in general), "we have assigned social responsibility on the basis of estimates of the capacities of various institutions that history is proving to have been tragically mistaken."[16] Hence, there has been an increasing asymmetry that has important governance implications: "America's most ambitious institutions tend to be the least effective, while its most effective institutions tend to be the least ambitious. The federal government has an incomplete sense of its limitations; the independent sector has an incomplete sense of its strengths."[17] In the United States, beginning in the 1930s, when American society began to centralize, the civil society or independent sector "had been pushed off out of sight, into small, unimportant reservations of responsibility."[18] America "continues to sing the praises of pluralism but the nation has become a society with two important sectors and the vestige of the third."[19]

The logic invoked by Cornuelle rejects a division of responsibility between two sectors: the public (by which is meant the government) and the private (by which is meant business). In such dualist systems, there are no limits to the potential scope or size of government and the public business can no longer be defined de facto. Because the third sector is an ineffective contender for public responsibility, it appears that there is no alternative to the state. Government continues to grow by default. Against dualism works the social pluralism manifested in the institutions of the independent sector. They are part of the governance system of a democratic society. In fact, this pluralism is essential to the proper functioning and even the survival of the other two: state and market. The logic regarding this aspect is straightforward: the third sector must compete for social responsibility with the state and must do so programmatically, systematically, and aggressively. As a result of the growth of the state, the process of competing and rationally deciding between the state and the third sector as alternative vehicles of public governance has been distorted. Moreover, the government is on the verge of having a monopoly on the power of both (a) to define what is public and what is not, what is public business and what is not, and (b) to judge what the adequate and inadequate nongovernment approaches are to dealing with that monopoly.[20]

Based on all of the above, a classical-liberal approach is thus forced sooner or later to challenge three views or suppositions that became popular and influential in the twentieth century. The first is that the third sector is something of the past, a relic of premodern times. The second view is that the third sector does not function because it does not know how or is structurally unable to. The third view is that the third sector is secondary and subordinate to the state. Because of their unwillingness or incapacity to fully articulate these challenges and advance a working alternative, current movements inspired by classical liberalism fail to make a convincing case for the powerful idea that public governance and public administration are vaster and far more complex than the state-focused approach suggests, which implies a collective choice area that may be national in scope but outside the domain of government.

Again, it is important to note the general parameters of the approach and the ensuing logic of making the classical-liberal foundational view operational. The details may vary. Some may insist that the classical-liberal position requires a doctrine of separation of civil society from the state. The third sector is not an instrument of the state but a contender and an alternative to the state. Or as the economist Kenneth E. Boulding puts it, "The private grants economy may be justified primarily in terms of being a check or countervailing power on the public grants economy."[21] Others may consider that the two sectors are complementary and should work in tandem to solve the failures of the other, thus accepting a formula that may be close to the lines defined by the idea of a third-party government by Lester M. Salamon and Helmut K. Anheier.[22] Irrespective of the specific approach taken, the core idea is that classical liberalism invites a reconsideration of the function of self-governance based on civil society and the voluntary sector, in the broader scheme of the governance of a social system. Governance goes beyond the formal apparatus of politics and administration as grown and operated around the modern state. A viable and successful system of public administration should have both a structure and an operating area that involve a variety of institutional arrangements and forms at multiple levels competing and cooperating in overlapping jurisdictions. This is precisely what polycentrism tries to capture.

Polycentricity and Competitive Governance

Following the logic of countervailing powers and voluntary-sector governance leads to polycentricity, the principle that incorporates and reinforces those ideas to new levels. The idea of polycentricity was introduced and theorized in the field of public administration by Vincent Ostrom, who developed it along the line of argument first advanced by the classical-liberal author Michael Polanyi.[23] Polanyi distinguished between two kinds of order. The first order is directed by an ultimate authority exercising control through a unified command structure. The second kind of order is a relatively spontaneous one of overlapping, competing, and cooperating centers of power and decision-making that make mutual adjustments to each other in a general system of rules.[24] As V. Ostrom explains in developing a federalist Tocquevillian theory of public governance, a monocentric political system has a monopoly over the legitimate exercise of coercive capabilities and the prerogatives for deciding on and enforcing the rules vested in a single decision structure. However, a polycentric political system is one in which "many officials and decision structures are assigned limited and relatively autonomous prerogatives to determine, enforce and alter legal relationships."[25] In a polycentric political system, there is no ultimate center having a monopoly over all governance domains, areas, and issues. All actors, including the rulers, are constrained by both countervailing powers and an overarching system of rules. Thus, polycentricity emerges as the main candidate for the position of the preeminent framework and conceptual focal point in the theory of governance inspired by the classical-liberal tradition.

V. Ostrom's book contains a powerful narrative of a series of paradigm changes in political and governance doctrines.[26] The growth of a "science of politics" along the lines defined by Thomas Hobbes, David Hume, Adam Smith, and Alexis de Tocqueville, argues Ostrom, was derailed by twentieth-century views about the nature of political inquiry. Political science had adopted the wrong paradigm. A different paradigm, an alternative way of looking at the social and political worlds, was needed. The problem was a practical one, not just theoretical and academic. Thus, urban issues, environmental crises, and race problems seemed without solution, or at least it seemed that administrative and policy theory had no solutions to offer. The cause, Ostrom argues, was the fact that political science and administrative theory were excessively shaped by a state-centric, monocentric vision. That view assumed a bureaucratic paradigm, centralized control, homogeneity of administrative structures, and separation of the political from the administrative. As such, it neglected two important aspects of public organization. First, different circumstances require different decision-making structures. Second, multiorganizational arrangements might be possible in the same administrative systems. The bureaucratic paradigm was framing both the analytical and the practical approaches in ways that were not only unable to offer solutions but also unable to even identify problems. Seeking an alternative was a vital task.

The monocentric vision, focusing on the state and "seeing like a state," as well as assuming the existence of a unique center of power and authority, was so deeply rooted in the practice of social sciences that by the time Vincent and Elinor Ostrom began their intellectual assault, it seemed commonsensical. The Ostroms, working at the core of the field of public administration, challenge the conventional wisdom and, while criticizing it, demonstrate what an alternative may look like.[27] In the process, the idea of polycentricity starts to emerge as a central concept in the architecture of the alternative paradigm. The reference point in the Ostroms' endeavor is, interestingly enough, Woodrow Wilson. Their decision to identify the paradigmatic case of the monocentric philosophy in Wilson's work may seem idiosyncratic. But with more understanding of the nature of the Ostroms' criticism of Wilson's assumptions comes the realization of how inspired and appropriate their choice was. Of course, between the lines of this criticism is a revisionist intellectual history of political and policy sciences in the twentieth century.

As V. Ostrom explains,[28] Wilson's analysis marks an important paradigm shift in American political science. One of the main dimensions of that shift was in understanding the US political system, a dimension that went beyond the idea of efficient government administration through the rule of experts—the better-known "Wilsonian stance." Wilson's assumption that "there is always a single center of power in any political system" was accepted as a basic postulate by many, even if that gave an obviously distorted perspective. Therefore, attention was obsessively concentrated on the central level. All other levels and forms of governance and association were neglected or considered marginal if they were not directly linked or associated with the system of government and its center of power. The insights given by such authors as Tocqueville, whose work was a source of inspiration for the Ostroms, were lost. Features that were considered of such salience and importance in Tocqueville's classical analysis were ignored. "The incommensurabilities between Tocqueville's portrayal of democracy in America and Wilson's portrayal were of radical proportions even though only fifty years intervened between those two presentations."[29]

Vision frames the perception of reality, and different visions imply different analytical approaches. Because the Wilsonian approach is based on the idea that "there is always a centre of power . . . within any system of government,"[30] the issue of the location and application of power shapes the focus and vocabulary of the monocentric approach. The entire exercise is power centered in ways that may become extreme and limiting. Choices, decisions, rules, preferences, ideas, and values are secondary. They are only inputs or outputs in the power process or, worse, a veil that clouds reality—that is, power and its workings.[31]

These analytical implications of the monocentric approach constituted a major concern. The fear was that even when not explicitly dealing with the issue of power, this vision had deeply penetrated and shaped the language of political science. Most political analysis was infused or defined by its hidden assumptions, its implicit social philosophy, and its language. Hence, there was a concern not only for the limits and dangers of the mainstream approach but also for the fact that, once the monocentric presumption was abandoned, difficulties would arise from a new horizon of complexities that evade the mainstream vocabulary. It was obvious that an approach from a polycentric vision could not rely on the research agenda's convenient definition of power or of using government or the state as the key unit of analysis. An alternative had to be constructed, "suggesting that a system of ordered relationships underlies the fragmentation of authority and overlapping jurisdictions that had frequently been identified as chaotic"—a polycentric political system viewed as "a set of ordered relationships that persists through time" and that has "many centers of decision making that are formally independent of each other."[32]

Before and after becoming operational and subject to an empirical agenda, polycentricity belongs to the realm of what Joseph Schumpeter calls preanalytical vision: "In order to be able to posit to ourselves any problems at all, we should first have to visualize a distinct set of coherent phenomena as a worthwhile object of our analytic effort."[33] In the alternative paradigm, the government as a basic unit becomes secondary and the individuals and their action areas take the forefront of the analysis.[34] This approach combines a theory of human action with a theory of social organization that draws on "a substantial structure of inferential reasoning about the consequences that will follow when individuals pursue strategies consistent with their interests in light of different types of decision structures in order to realize opportunities inherent in differently structured sets of events."[35] In other words, polycentricity suggests a different vision that implies and fuels a different analytical approach—that of reframing the issues from one center to many and from there on to concrete actions by the social actors.

In summary, the polycentric perspective is more than a challenge; it is, by all standards, the pivot of an entirely novel viewpoint and an alternative conceptual construction. Criticism of the Wilsonian approach, and its analytical and methodological implications, amounts to sketching an alternative. The emerging conceptualization has important implications for analysis. Multiple centers of power overlap in competition and cooperation as individuals act in specifically defined social and institutional settings. This ecological rationality—with an emphasis on the dynamics that take place between ideas, rules, decisions, and learning—is part of an effort to reject the vision behind the Wilsonian mainstream approach and to contribute to the growth of an alternative.

While advancing polycentricism as an alternative public administration paradigm to what he identifies as the monocentric Wilsonian doctrine of the mainstream, V. Ostrom simultaneously creates an up-to-date framework for a classical-liberal approach to public governance. An intuitive way to describe a polycentric system is that it combines elements of the centralized governance of current national states with federalism-based arrangements (defined by a certain division of responsibilities across levels of government) and with self-governance or third-sector arrangements that differ from formal government and operate on a circumscribed set of functions with limited ability to exercise coercion. Polycentrism, write Bickers and Williams, is a governance structure "composed of nested and partially overlapping public organizations, from narrowly local organizations up through the national level (and potentially even the international level) each with jurisdiction for a circumscribed set of public functions."[36] Defined in this way, the idea becomes an effective way to think about and analyze the operations and performance of institutions in the public sphere:

> A system that has multiple centers of power at differing scales provides more opportunity for citizens and their officials to innovate and to intervene so as to correct maldistributions of authority and outcomes. Thus, polycentric systems are more likely than monocentric systems to provide incentives leading to self-organized, self-corrective institutional change.[37]

In other words, polycentrism has a series of features that meet the classical-liberal standards for attributes and principles of good governance reflecting normative individualist principles. "Because of their nested and overlapping structures," explain Bickers and Williams, "polycentric systems can respond to the preferences of publics that may vary enormously in scope."[38] In such a system, "it is possible to structure governance mechanisms that correspond to each of the publics that confront particular policy problems." In brief, irrespective of the label, an institutional framework that (a) is based on freedom of choice and movement of citizens; (b) encourages competition and multiple institutional alternatives; and (c) engenders institutional and organizational experimentation, learning, and flexibility in the public sphere seems to be an outstanding illustration of classical-liberal principles applied to public governance.[39]

An additional element in Ostrom's analysis deserves special attention: the problem of knowledge processes and the role of ideas. Ostrom sees in Wilson's work an indication of a turning point in the history of modern political thinking, the moment when the move toward dismissing and marginalizing the role of ideas gained real strength. Ostrom is convinced of its paradigm-changing nature, not only because of its radical and aggressive monocentrism but also because of its stance on the role of ideas regarding the nature and role of knowledge processes and epistemic choices in social order and change (see Chapter 4 for a more detailed look at Wilson's position).

The two issues, monocentrism and rejection of the role of institutional design ideas (and ideas in general), are related. Ordinarily they may not be, but in this case they are intrinsically connected. They are the basic elements of the historic intellectual shift that was challenged by Ostrom's "new" vision of democratic public administration. As a result of this shift, the distinction between "institutional facts," with their knowledge and ideational content, and "natural" or "brute facts" was lost. Also lost was the intricate dynamics among the ideas, rules, information, knowledge, decisions, and learning that drive social change. Treating ideas as "paper pictures" concealed the reality of politics. Because ideas, learning, and knowledge were not taken seriously, the entire set of epistemic processes pertaining to the role of ideas and learning was not seriously considered.[40] To fully understand polycentricity as a governance idea, it is necessary to understand the epistemic problem—the role of knowledge and ideas in governance and their relationships to institutional structures and processes.

Epistemic Processes in Markets and Nonmarket Settings

V. Ostrom notes that, notwithstanding the positivist rage dominating social and policy sciences at the time of his writing, ideas, knowable regularities, and informed practices must be treated as political realities. It is hard to conceive political order without assuming that people "create their own social realities by reference to some shared community of understanding (pictures in their minds) and live their lives within those realities as artifactual creations."[41] Human society, or social order, is ultimately a system of communication and coordination in which symbols and language are essential. There was no doubt that the most serious mistake in the social sciences was to ignore epistemic processes spontaneously associated with the production, aggregation, discovery, diffusion, and uses of knowledge in society—the role of "ideas, conjectures about regularities, and the careful use of informed practices that are constitutive of that reality."[42]

Indeed, the most basic and typical approach to governance systems is to examine individuals' choices in light of their constraints. Actors must weigh the costs and benefits of each decision. In light of this conundrum of choice within constraints, the talk tends to be about incentives. Institutional structures are seen, more or less, as incentive structures. Yet any discussion of incentives—their nature, structure, function, and dynamics—implies a discussion of information, knowledge, and learning processes. For people to learn through time how best to cope with their constraints, they must have the incentives to get the decisions right. But they also must have access to the correct and relevant information for the contexts in which they decide and to be able to evaluate past decisions. They should be operating in an environment that facilitates their learning—from nature, from others, and from their own and others' mistakes. Both incentives and information are byproducts of the institutions in which individuals make choices and learn from the past. Analysis that seeks to understand the social world must therefore account for the institutional environment in which individuals are acting so as to understand how information is produced, evaluated, and changed. Political economy at its finest must therefore combine analysis that pivots on incentives with analysis that emphasizes the epistemic processes in place.

It is in this context that Hayek's contribution should be viewed. Hayek is the scholar who has done the most to draw attention to the issues and their implications. His work converges with and bolsters, from an economics direction, the line of argument advanced by V. Ostrom, who comes from the direction of public administration and governance theory. The major merit of Hayek's work in this respect is that he (a) disentangles the epistemic dimension from the incentive one, drawing attention to its specific features and relevance; (b) develops a set of insights about the facets and operations of that dimension in the context of market processes; and (c) creates the foundations for an extension of the knowledge process analysis from market settings to political and governance settings through both institutional and constitutional analysis. In doing so, Hayek articulates a perspective that avoids the traps and temptations of scientism and social engineering, two enticing directions for any theorizing that emphasizes the role of knowledge and ideas in society. The classical political economy tradition revived by Hayek recognizes the role of knowledge in society but also that people are not highly rational beings. Instead, they are highly fallible creatures "whose individual errors are corrected only in the course of a social process, and which aims at making the best of a very imperfect material."[43] As such, his work is the preeminent illustration of the approach that claims its roots in the tradition of moral philosophers, fallibilism philosophy, and the political economy of classical-liberal inspiration. Let us take a closer look at how the knowledge problem intertwines with the classical-liberal stance on coordination in both market and nonmarket settings.

Hayek argues that theorists had been misled by the assumption of perfect knowledge on at least two levels.[44] First, he says, if the assumptions are taken seriously as first-level assumptions in a model, the model itself will be stuck in a radical indeterminacy. The I-know-that-you-know-that-I-know puzzle is actually very serious in that a profit opportunity known to everyone is realized by no one. So Hayek seeks to redirect theoretical attention. Perfect knowledge rather than an assumption is the defining characterization of a competitive equilibrium. To illustrate Hayek's point in a different way, consider that the optimality conditions of price equal marginal cost and that production at the minimum of the average cost of production is not an assumption of the model but a byproduct of the competitive process. Optimality results from the filters of the price system—freely adjusting relative prices and accurate profit-and-loss accounting—working to guide the production plans of some to mesh with the consumption demands of others. Prices guide production, and calculation enables coordination.

Second, Hayek argues that theorists were wrong to highlight behavioral assumptions, such as perfect knowledge, rather than the institutional conditions that enabled the price system to adapt and accommodate the ceaseless change of a dynamic economic system and that steered economic actors to learn what they needed to learn and when so as to coordinate their plans with those of others and to do so in a way that resulted in an equilibrium state of affairs. Markets, in Hayek's rendering, become learning mechanisms, and how effective they are at teaching is a function of the institutional environment in which they operate.[45]

Hayek's basic insight is that context—both that in which economic activity takes place and that of decision makers and their knowledge of unique times and places—matters. The importance of context was lost with the assumption of perfect knowledge, and the theoretical apparatus of the perfectly competitive model de-emphasized the learning by economic actors in response to changing circumstances. As Hayek believes, the economic problem that society must address is not the allocation of "given" resources among competing ends.[46] The "data" of the market are never given to a single mind or even a collection of minds. Rather, the problem is "the utilization of knowledge which is not given to anyone in its totality."[47] Furthermore, discovery and use of relevant knowledge emerge only in the market process itself, as economic actors react and adapt to changing circumstances. "It is," Hayek writes, "perhaps, worth stressing that economic problems arise always and only in consequence of change."[48]

Hayek's key argument is that knowledge communicated and acted on in the process of adaptation to changing tastes, technologies, and resource availability is not the sort of knowledge that can be entered into statistics. The knowledge used in society is that of the "circumstances of time and place." Thus, one must reconceive that "the economic problem of society is mainly one of rapid adaptation to changes in the particular circumstances of time and place"[49] and the price system and see the price system as the solution that guides production plans and coordinates those plans with the consumption demands of willing buyers in the marketplace. It is the "higgling and bargaining" of the market economy, as Adam Smith taught, that brings about the coordination of economic activity through time.

Hayek comes to focus on the issue of the acquisition of knowledge because the misunderstanding among economists about the limitations of the pure logic of choice and the nature of equilibrium resulted in theoretical and practical confusion. As he would put it, there must be something fundamentally wrong with an approach—no matter how strong its merits—when it leads to disregard of the fundamental problem under investigation. People are, Hayek stresses, imperfect creatures who interact with other imperfect creatures in an imperfect world, and thus the central mystery of social cooperation under the division of labor is how certain institutional patterns will engender a pattern of human interaction where the necessary knowledge for plan coordination is constantly communicated and utilized by the actors in the economic system. "Any approach," Hayek states, "such as that of much of mathematical economics with its simultaneous equations, which in effect starts from the assumption that people's *knowledge* corresponds with the objective *facts* of the situation, systematically leaves out what is our main task to explain" (emphasis in original).[50] The prereconciliation of plans does little to explain the process by which disparate, often divergent, plans come to be reconciled. Again, the process by which the knowledge necessary for this reconciliation of plans comes about is completely ignored in the analysis. As Hayek concludes,

> I am far from denying that in our system equilibrium analysis has a useful function to perform. But when it comes to the point where it misleads some of our leading thinkers into believing that the situation which it describes has direct relevance to the solution of practical problems, it is high time that we remember that it does not deal with the social process at all and that it is no more than a useful preliminary to the study of the main problem.[51]

Hayek's "epistemic turn" was due precisely to the tendency among his contemporaries in economics to evade critical questions about the process and its institutional infrastructure, or what more recently has been dubbed the ecology by which human decisions and economic activity transpire.[52] Economic science emerges, Hayek argues, from observation of the tendency of the subjective plans of economic actors to dovetail over time with the objective facts of the economic situation. To clarify, objective facts of the situation can be referred to as the existing state of tastes, technology, and resource availability. Market process guided by relative prices, and the lure of profit and the penalty of loss, will tend to produce a situation where the pattern of exchange and production corresponds with the external facts. Rather than solve this central mystery of economics through the assumptions of perfect knowledge and perfect markets, Hayek argues that we must explore (a) the institutional conditions under which the pattern exists and (b) how individuals acquire knowledge and use changes to dovetail economic plans through time. This line of argument has implications that obviously go beyond the problem of markets.

Such was the state of the argument when public choice economics emerged in the 1960s, redefining and rethinking governance theory.[53] In developing the theory of government failure, public choice economists relied on consistent and persistent application of neoclassical economics to examine the area of politics. What incentives, public choice economists asked, do public officials face in making and implementing public policy? By systemically examining the incentives in the political process, public choice economists were able to identify sources of systemic government failure associated with the vote motive, special interest politics, rent-seeking, and bureaucratic red tape.[54] The result was a theory that tended to emphasize interests rather than ideas in understanding political outcomes.[55] Yet the epistemic problem was looming in the background, and sooner or later it had to come into the limelight. In short, public choice reproduced the same tensions in the analysis of politics that Hayek identifies in the neoclassical model of the market. Rational choice theory morphed into a closed-end model of decision science, and the examination of politics as exchange morphed into a single-exit model of a structure-induced political equilibrium. However, whereas the neoclassical logic was leading more or less automatically in that direction, the insights of key public choice scholars were pointing in different directions.

Interestingly enough, James M. Buchanan sought to resist the "conceptual closure" of public choice. His own development of the constitutional level of analysis was one such attempt to offer an alternative that accounted for human decision makers engaged in bargaining activity and transforming situations of conflict into opportunities for cooperation through constitutional craftsmanship.[56] Buchanan was joined in that effort from different angles by Elinor and Vincent Ostrom, who argue that to truly grasp the importance of constitutional craftsmanship, the neoclassical constraints have to be relaxed and that knowledge and the idea of learning-based change in the rules of the game have to be introduced into the picture.[57] We have seen that Hayek suggests precisely that with respect to market theory. A critical part of the Ostroms' work is rejection of the assumption of omniscience and of the belief that there is a one-size-fits-all solution to social dysfunctions. The Ostroms also introduce an interest in adaptability, resilience, and learning in conditions of change and uncertainty. That is done on a background in which beliefs, values, and language matter as basic parameters of action situations and action areas.[58]

In a sense, the epistemic perspective in public choice and nonmarket settings may be simply and straightforwardly seen as a natural evolution of its game theory apparatus. Once game theory becomes a basic tool of the public choice paradigm, the epistemic turn claimed by V. Ostrom is no longer surprising to anyone familiar with the evolution of applied game theory in the past fifty years—from classical game theory through evolutionary game theory and behavioral game theory toward epistemic game theory. Epistemic game theory focuses on the cognitive dimensions of strategic interactions and on the problems of knowledge, expectations, and shared understanding. That focus clarifies any methodological or foundational formal misunderstanding regarding epistemic processes, including epistemic choices and meta-level decision-making regarding knowledge and information. Yet probably the epistemic dimension as framed in public choice is best understood in the context of the constitutional political economy of which Buchanan and the Ostroms are prominent practitioners. In both cases, the appeal to the epistemic element through a formulaic and formal invocation of game theory models would seem, as in Hayek's case, an easy and not very constructive way to avoid a difficult intellectual challenge. Hence, such authors as Buchanan and the Ostroms grapple with these problems in institutional and political economy frameworks.

As Buchanan puts it, the pattern of outcomes in an economic system "emerge[s] from the whole set of interdependent choices made by individuals as these choices are constrained by the *structure* of the economy."[59] One individual's choice in a given structure can exert only negligible effects on the overall aggregated pattern of outcomes. As such, to the extent that "the pattern of results is subject to deliberative change," this can happen only "through effective changes in structure, i.e. in the set of rules that constrain the exercise of individual choices within the rules."[60] But once again, assuming, especially in a democratic context, that "the individual can exercise no influence on the structure of the economy as he chooses separately and independently among the options that he confronts," it follows that "any choice among alternative sets of rules must be, and can only be, collective."[61] That collective choice process requires, however, an information and knowledge base. Choice presumes a minimal understanding, an evaluation of alternatives. Incentives-based analysis must incorporate, sooner or later, the epistemic element. V. Ostrom's emphasis on the importance of "shared communities of understanding" for the emergence of productive social orders focuses on a deeper "constitutive" level but follows the same logic.[62] Meta-constitutional beliefs and values shape the very nature by which incentives are seen and operate. Ideas come into the picture both with a framing and a normative function. Once this function is established, questions about knowledge and incentives move to the level of the collective. Under what institutional system does the collective most effectively use available information and learn from past mistakes? Under alternative institutions, what incentives do individuals have to search for new ideas about how to change the structure of the economy such that the aggregate pattern of outcomes is improved according to the preferences of the members of the community? The interplay of incentives and knowledge processes in constitutional-institutional analysis becomes salient.

In the same way that Hayek's theory of competition as a discovery procedure combines knowledge and incentive problems in an inseparable whole, so would an epistemic-entrepreneurial theory of public choice and public governance. With such a theory, institutions may be seen as facilitators and shapers of decisions at different levels (operational public choice, constitutional) through knowledge processes. Knowledge generation, aggregation, distribution, and uses become both dependent and independent variables in relation to institutional structures and change. In brief, the epistemic dimension manifests and materializes itself in multiple ways in governance research both at the level of its theoretical hard core and at its applied-level peripheries for the older and the more recent generations of scholars.

V. Ostrom's challenge to fellow public choice theorists to move beyond envisioning public choice theory as little more than an appendage to neoclassical price theory is a plea to make more explicit and systematic that which is already present in various forms and degrees.[63] Ostrom insists it is necessary to go beyond simple price theory because, at the most elemental level of relevant neoclassical theory applications, individual choices within rules do not much affect the structure of the economy, and price theory only describes choices within the given rules. The key is the nature and change of rules, and epistemic processes are heavily significant for that. Knowledge matters, as do the discovery and diffusion of ideas. As argued by Ostrom, if in the end all public choice theory amounts to is an appendage to price theory, ignoring the essential problem of knowledge discovery, future progress in governance analysis is bound to be minuscule at best.[64] But if the future of scholarship is found not in the closed-end model of choice and the single-exit equilibrium models but in puzzling over the complexities of social dilemmas and agonizing over anomalies, progress will indeed be possible. Only by taking the epistemic perspective seriously in research contexts driven by questions and issues, Ostrom argues, can movement ahead be realized in understanding the real dimensions of governance processes in complex, dynamic polycentric systems.

What precisely does the perspective of epistemic choice mean in the context of a political economy, institutional analysis, and governance theory? The existing literature reveals four major areas to examine:

1. The first area is the recognition of the implications of the knowledge problem for the evolution of social norms and institutions. The intricate web of mutual expectations at the foundation of social institutions evolves over time and generates specific institutional configurations. The most basic direction of epistemic analysis is the evolutionary and process analysis of the nature, structure, and change of nonmarket institutions in light of knowledge problems and their solutions.

2. The second area is the awareness of epistemic properties of specific institutions and the comparative analysis of the structure and performance of different institutions in light of knowledge problems. Comparative analysis of epistemic properties and of the performance of markets and democracy is a salient and easy example. Recent interest in "epistemic democracy" problems and the claim that "the rule of the many" outperforms as a public decision mechanism is another example, one that in this case is more strictly focused on a governance and public choice domain.

3. The third area calls for looking beyond the complex emergent processes to see the institutional design—its capabilities and limits as well as the role of knowledge production and specialization in social systems. At its core, this approach explores the epistemic division of labor and the relationship between codified and general knowledge and the informal, local, and dispersed knowledge in social change, social design, and social control. As Buchanan explains, the task is to explore "the room left for the political economist or anyone else who seeks to reform social structures to change laws and rules with the aim of securing increased efficiency in the large."[65]

4. The fourth area includes problems related to the so-called meta-constitutional level: (a) the system of beliefs, values, and ideas; and (b) the knowledge accumulated in a cultural, historical, and evolutionary manner that frame the constitutional, institutional, and public governance arrangements at a deeper level.

The key to further elaborating the perspective that focuses on the epistemic dimension of social order is the parallelism between the pioneering analyses of epistemic processes that define the market and the extension of that type of analysis to nonmarket settings. Through his studies of market processes, Hayek creates a model and a benchmark for a similar approach in nonmarket settings. The question is this: How far can Hayek's market-based insights be taken into nonmarket territory? Thus, the problem for public choice and institutionalism is not whether the epistemic choice challenge is to be acknowledged and taken seriously. Rather, the problem is how to better tailor the epistemic approach when applying it to the entire range of diverse institutional structures of modern society—economic, political, and social.

Illustration: A Public Administration Analysis

The viability and relevance of the knowledge process approach in traditional public administration and their link to the better-established polycentricity are amply illustrated by Michael W. Spicer's remarkable but insufficiently recognized contribution.

Spicer[66] uses the works of Hayek to add another layer to his public choice–based argument about bureaucratic "constrained discretion."[67] While acknowledging that Hayek views the "public administration movement" with some suspicion, Spicer argues that Hayek's writings—particularly the emphasis on dispersed knowledge, the rule of law, and the critique of democracy—offer a fresh perspective on existing debates in public administration. In particular, Spicer notes the affinity between Hayek's account and the so-called new public administration group and also the Blacksburg school,[68] although both place less emphasis than Hayek on the importance of rules to constrain administrative discretion, preferring to rely on the ethical values of public administrators."[69]

Spicer[70] reuses Hayek's arguments about the use of knowledge in society[71] in his analysis of federalism. He first notes that "Hayek argued that much of the particular knowledge that individuals possess can only be used to the extent that they use it in their own decisions. Such knowledge is not given but can only be discovered as individuals work on the particular tasks that they have undertaken." Furthermore, because all data need interpretation and different people interpret data in different ways, the problem of aggregating information for the purpose of taking collective decisions is even more difficult than in the private sphere. In markets, different interpretations lead to divergent entrepreneurial decisions,[72] but in the public sphere consensus needs to be built. As Spicer says, "The problem for a society becomes then not a problem of ascertaining facts in the sense that they might be known to some expert observer, but rather how to use and reconcile different subjective views on the facts as held by different individuals."[73]

This leads to a knowledge-based argument in favor of decentralization, which is very different from the preference and incentive-based standard arguments: "Some decentralization of decision making or discretion is desirable on the grounds that only individuals at lower levels of the hierarchy can have the relevant information, particularly the knowledge of circumstances of time and place to make certain decisions."[74] Moreover, "decentralization provides an incentive for individuals at lower levels to acquire relevant information, which might otherwise never come to light. Decentralization then facilitates both the acquisition and use of practical knowledge and experience that exist within the organization."[75] Spicer notes that this argument puts Hayek in the company of Michael Harmon's "interpretative public administration"[76] and mirrors the arguments of the political scientist and economist Herbert A. Simon about decentralization rooted in his account of bounded rationality.[77]

The decentralization argument raises the following dilemma: How decentralized should public administration be? Spicer argues that Hayek's emphasis on the importance of the rule of law—the idea that the same rules should apply to everyone—offers a stopping procedure.[78] When decentralization is only a pretext for discrimination rather than being genuinely useful for discovering relevant knowledge, it becomes a problem. "The key to effective decentralization, in Hayek's view, is the presence of a system of rules that govern the interaction of individuals and that limit the harm that individual actions can create for others."[79] A typical example is when jurisdictions impose import tariffs against one another.[80] To Hayek, the benefits of decentralization come from more efficient use of local knowledge, whereas the costs are due to more difficult coordination for eliminating such mutual harms. To put it differently, the benefits of centralization are that, under proper democratic procedures, it forces people with divergent viewpoints to find common ground, whereas the cost of centralization is the potential loss of relevant local knowledge.

Spicer[81] discusses Hayek's critique of majoritarian democracy, which, he argues, lends support for his own view about bureaucratic constrained discretion.[82] According to Hayek, by abandoning the ideal of the rule of law, current democracies have undermined their capacity to engender what V. Ostrom refers to as "shared communities of understanding."[83] As Spicer writes, "Hayek argued that the degeneration of majority rule into a process of simply buying votes makes impossible majority decisions based on general principles."[84] That is a consequence of how modern democracies make budget decisions:

> Modern legislative bodies are free to establish both the rules by which the tax burden is to be shared among individuals and the level and composition of government expenditures. As a result, the majority in the legislature can use the budget to obtain goods and services that benefit their supporters and at the same time shift the costs of financing such programs and services to others.[85]

In other words, rather than being a process of consensus building and knowledge aggregation, as Hayek envisions the ideal,[86] democracy becomes an area for special interest conflicts. This development is highly relevant to understanding the relationship between public administration and politics because, according to Spicer,

> it weakens the case for simply following the dictates of majority rule. If majority rule has largely become a tool by which some groups exploit others, then the moral claim by elected leaders for complete obedience on the part of public administrators is eroded. A system of public administration that is totally compliant with the wishes of a majority simply becomes a more effective instrument of exploitation of citizens by majority coalitions. If this is correct, public administrators should not blindly follow the will of the majority but rather should be permitted to exercise some level of discretion in a lawful manner.[87]

In other words, once majority rule has become a tool for exploitation, as a consequence of the erosion of the ideal of the rule of law, bureaucratic discretion can operate as a constraint on political power. That will be effective depending on the limits of the bureaucratic discretion, such that the opposite problem is avoided—that of too much bureaucratic discretion when "public administrators . . . become an object of influence from various groups seeking relief from the coercive actions of government."[88] Ideally, "the power of public administrators to discriminate between citizens is limited by general rules providing equality of treatment."[89] More realistically, a picture appears of an imperfect polycentric system in which different decision centers constrain each other and none of them act in full accordance with the ideal of rule of law, but, nonetheless, their mutual constraints prevent full-blown decay into a completely exploitative system.

Conclusions

By revisiting process-oriented governance, polycentrism, and knowledge, we have a better sense of what is more precisely entailed in what we have identified as classical-liberal principles of governance. And that understanding shows why the operationalization and institutionalization of these principles in concrete arrangements and structures must diverge from the social engineering model. Moreover, although those principles are traditionally considered to be opposed to the public sphere, a closer look at their application reveals that they are at the core of the very idea of effective public administration, reflecting the preferences and values of the citizens. Indeed, both sets of issues—those brought under polycentrism and those under epistemic processes—are in multiple ways at the core of public governance, irrespective of the ideology that frames an understanding of it. Those two sets are essential in helping us understand and chart the institutional arrangements through which human societies structure and govern the public domain. In addition, the two shed light on the portfolio of organizational instruments that humans use to fashion and manage the public sphere. They illustrate that it is possible to approach these issues from an angle different from the theories of hierarchy, authority, and social control. Whereas recognizing that authority, hierarchy, and control each have a role, the classical-liberal tradition approaches public administration from the perspective of adaptability, social knowledge and learning, pluralism, and voluntary organization in polycentric, dynamic systems. In doing so, the classical-liberal tradition follows consistently the applied-level logic induced by its normative individualist foundation.

PART II

PUBLIC CHOICE AND PUBLIC ADMINISTRATION

The Confluence

There are multiple ways in which the classical-liberal position, as described in part I, may be pictured in relationship to, or as part of, the field of public administration, broadly defined. It is important, however, to go beyond conceptual speculation and look at the field as it has evolved over time and describe this relationship in more specific terms. This part of the book is dedicated to that task. The development of the disciplinary domains of public administration and public choice may be seen as two distinctive streams or two evolving traditions. Yet in their evolution in the 1960s, with the burst of the public choice movement, a convergence took place.

Part II focuses more precisely on the intellectual junction where public choice meets public administration. The developments at the confluence are of special interest here, and Elinor and Vincent Ostrom's work, defining the quintessence of that confluence, emerge as uniquely important. Working on both traditions—public administration and public choice—the Ostroms create an entire program aimed at an integration of the two traditions. Chapter 4 takes the vantage point of the field of public administration and maps the disciplinary context of those developments. It charts public administration as a field, and identifies the subdomains that are most amenable to the classical-liberal ethos and conceptualization. The convergence area is identified thematically and conceptually, as well as a moment of disciplinary intellectual history.

Chapter 5 illuminates the specific nature of the Ostroms' program and of the synthesis they and their Bloomington school associates attempted. The chapter discusses the successes and failures of their efforts and, more precisely, explores the public administration roots and facets of the Bloomington school of public choice and institutional theory, thus revisiting the problem of the applied dimension of public choice. The chapter investigates the nature, significance, and reception of the Ostroms' work, seen as a pioneering attempt to promote a double agenda: on the one hand, to advance public choice theory as a paradigm shift in public administration, and on the other hand, to advance public administration as the preeminent applied domain of public choice theory.

Chapter 6 focuses on the conceptual framework and apparatus of those efforts. The underlying theme is the pivotal notion of polycentricity as a unifying and organizing framework or principle. The chapter revisits the theory of institutional hybridity and diversity behind polycentricity, with a view toward further elaborating it. The Ostroms' system is reconstructed, along with the value heterogeneity-coproduction-polycentricity axis. This chapter articulates the theory of value heterogeneity and the fuzzy boundaries between the private and the public. It also rebuilds the model of coproduction, thereby clarifying the ambiguity surrounding a key technical assumption of public choice theory, and demonstrates why it should not be confused with the Alchian-Demsetz team production model and how coproduction engenders a type of institutional failure that is neglected elsewhere. In light of this analysis, the chapter reconsiders polycentricity, the capstone of the Ostroms' system, explaining why polycentricity may be seen as a solution to both the coproduction market failure problem and the problems of social choice in conditions of deep heterogeneity. The relevance of polycentricity as the key framework of the classical-liberal approach to governance is thus reasserted and reinforced.

4

Public Administration and Public Choice

Charting the Field

To understand the distinctiveness of the classical-liberal perspective on governance we need to place it in the context of the mainstream line of intellectual developments in governance studies and doctrines. More precisely, the task is to set the stage for an analysis of how public choice and comparative institutional analysis ideas have interacted over time with the field of public administration and with what consequences. The notion of public administration inevitably evokes the idea of building specialized institutions for public or collective action: the organization and management of people and resources in governance. Public administration is about the technology of human cooperation taking place through various arrangements of social coordination, cooperation, command, monitoring, and control. For a long time, "public administration" was the main label used to designate governance themes. More recently, labels like "governance" and "public management" have entered the stage.

The terms *public* and *administration* come packed with a set of questions and significant theoretical baggage. For our purposes, we note two themes.

First, for the idea of *administration*, the most important and sensitive element is the dividing line between politics and administration. Wilson famously declared that "the field of administration is a field of business. It is removed from the hurry and strife of politics; it at most points stands apart even from the debatable ground of constitutional study."[1] But to what extent is this separation possible? What phenomena take place at their interface? How large and how relevant—theoretically and practically— is the overlapping gray area? How should this overlap area be conceptualized? What practical ways are there to implement the separation? Wilson was adamant that "administration lies outside the proper sphere of politics. Administrative questions are not political questions. Although politics sets the tasks for administration, it should not be suffered to manipulate its offices."[2] But is it really advisable to insist on this separation, or under which contexts is this more reasonable or less so? Insisting too much on this separation unavoidably makes public administration less democratically accountable. But eliminating the distinction entirely would undermine the goal of building a competent and professional public administration. How much politics is involved analytically and in practice when engaging in public administration projects?

Second, when it comes to *public*, the issue, again, is one of delimitation. What is public and what is private? What are the demarcation criteria? How can we delineate the "proper" sphere of collective, common affairs? How can we make the conceptual criteria operational in practice? What is the relationship between public administration and private administration?

Based on these two criteria we can map out a variety of theoretical positions with respect to public administration, as table 4.1 illustrates (in practice, the two variables can of course be seen as continuous). The extent to which the public administration is supposed to be controlled by politics determines the distinction between bureaucratic and democratic administration. By contrast, the scope of government (whether large or small) determines the distinction between progressive and liberal administration. Consider the following analogy made by Wilson:

> Our success is made doubtful by that besetting error of ours, the error of trying to do too much by vote. Self-government does not consist in having a hand in everything, any more than housekeeping consists necessarily in cooking dinner with one's own hands. The cook must be trusted with a large discretion as to the management of the fires and the ovens.[3]

A liberal would agree with the first two sentences, but notice that Wilson is *not* arguing about the scope of government but about the scope of politics. He wants a large scope of government, but he also thinks that most public affairs should be managed by a professional, politically independent, public administration. By contrast, a liberal would insist, to use Wilson's analogy, not on having an excellent professional cook but on having many restaurants to choose from.

The same two themes rest at the foundation of public choice as a domain of inquiry. The "public" in the name of both fields requires systematic and ongoing demarcation efforts, not only at the level of principles, but also in case-by-case investigations. Similarly, the tension between strategic rationality in political behavior with its stratagems and spoils, on the one hand, and the rule-guided behavior implied by bureaucracy and constitutional arrangements, on the other hand, is an inherent feature in the foundation of public choice.

Such similarity between the two intellectual domains is not an accident, and it requires us to consider the tensions between the two approaches. There is an inevitable confluence between them and we consider here the intellectual developments set in motion by this confluence. The public administration–public choice junction is overwhelmingly defined by the Vincent Ostrom's work, which is an ambitious attempt to blend the two traditions and create a conceptual framework for a distinctive type

Table 4.1 **Different visions for public administration**

	Large scope of government	Small scope of government
Politically independent public administration	Progressive bureaucratic administration (Wilson)	Liberal bureaucratic administration
Strict political control of public administration	Progressive democratic administration	Liberal democratic administration

of public administration, which he labeled "democratic public administration" in contrast to "bureaucratic administration."

Public Administration, Political Science, and Public Choice

The practice or activity of public administration existed long before full awareness of its existence made it an abstract theme and an object of systematic inquiry. Civilization and government administration, writes Dwight Waldo, one of the most influential public administration scholars of the twentieth century, "have had a close, mutually stimulating and supporting relationship."[4] In fact, "most of the six thousand years of what we regard as the history of civilization, government administration and not private or business administration has been center stage."[5] This is "the First Fact about government administration, the proper foundation for a science, an art, a craft, a technology, a theory, an ethic, or a philosophy of government administration."[6]

As self-awareness and scientific theorizing in this respect emerged, public administration focused on the hierarchical, command-and-control, bureaucratic aspects of public organization and coincided with the gradual emergence of ever-larger and more complex administrative systems. Those systems were associated, first, with the modern state and its apparatus and then with parallel developments in the business world, starting in the nineteenth century. The bureaucratic, administrative, or managerial revolutions, both in practice and in thinking, led to the advent of two related fields—public administration and business administration—and to their emergence as academic disciplines. Hence, one of the best ways to get a clearer sense of the nature of public administration as a discipline is to consider it in parallel with business administration.

Evoking or using the better-known field—business administration—as a foil is one of the most effective ways to introduce the second and to get a general sense of its nature: they have the same mixture of theory and practice, the same interdisciplinarity (opportunistically using results and instruments from different disciplines), and the same portfolio of subfields that are organized around core functions of management and governance (personnel, finance, budgetary control, motivation, and so forth). At the same time, we need to bear in mind one of the key ideas emphasized in Chapter 1: public administration begins where economic calculation ends. This sets a fundamental difference between public administration and business administration, and the analogy between the two cannot be pushed too far.

Given the fact that the administrative apparatus is essential to government and a defining characteristic of governance and given its crucial position in modern societies, a question arises naturally: Why does the field specifically dedicated to the study of the apparatus for managing public affairs have such a limited recognition and visibility in the usual discussions of public affairs? This explains to some extent why public choice scholars are neglecting public administration. In this they share the company of most other social scientists, journalists, and the public at large. Why do we tend to always think about public affairs in the terms dictated by political science or the economics of public policy when most practice-relevant ideas from these disciplines pivot on the assumption of the existence of at least a partially functional system of public administration? Why, for instance, has political science "paid essentially no attention to the historical development of administrative technology, despite its close relationship to the development of government; and little attention to contemporary public administration, despite its impressive magnitude and manifest importance"?[7] To treat political theory as being opposed to government theory is "prejudicial and misleading," writes Waldo, and it is "rather similar to the study of anatomy without physiology or physiology without anatomy."[8] And yet that is what happened. This question raised by Waldo[9] has puzzled public administration scholars for a long time. Taking a closer look at how Waldo—a friend, collaborator, and critic of Vincent Ostrom—tries to deal with it offers a useful angle in the attempt to get a clearer sense of the nature and relevance of public administration and, by implication, of Vincent and Elinor Ostrom's work.

Part of the answer, explains Waldo, is found in accidents of history. From its inception, political science was fascinated by and paid "more attention to the Greek literature of politics than to the Roman experience of government and its consequences for the contemporary world."[10] The Greeks "brought 'the political' to self-awareness, and their concepts, values, and theories became the basis of Western political thought."[11] But "city-states (as against ancient empires) required relatively little administration,"[12] and in them administration was regarded as a part-time or short-term, honorific, amateur endeavor. To that, we add "the propensity of the Romans, to whom much administration owes a debt, toward the practical rather than the philosophical."[13] It is true that the Romans created an administrative apparatus that governed an empire extending over three continents, yet "while they 'rationalized' it in law, they did not 'philosophize' about it."[14] All those actions were decisive for much that followed. "There are weighty tomes that treat the development of political theory through two and a half millennia without so much as a mention of administration."[15] In fact, the "language, terminology, is indicative: political theory, not government theory; political is derived from the Greek polis, government from the Latin *gubernare*."[16] The political "reached self-awareness with the Greeks," whereas administration "did not reach self-awareness until the late nineteenth and early twentieth centuries."[17] Governments had always had corps of functionaries and even training schools for them; nonetheless, "only within the last century has the idea of administration as such arisen."[18]

The rise of the field was thus long and delayed, and it took place only in the twentieth century and came to full fruition in the 1970s, a final stage in a process of self-awareness and independent institutionalization. That was precisely when two scholars—Vincent and Elinor Ostrom—operating at the boundary between public administration, political science, and public choice—came to the fore to advance a fresh perspective on public governance. It is only when seen in this broader picture that the real dimensions and significance of their agenda can be appreciated for our discussion. The intellectual context and the genealogy of their approach create a bridge for our effort to disentangle and articulate a classical-liberal perspective on public governance through the public choice revolution in political economy to which the Ostroms were a part from the very beginning, and which Vincent Ostrom tried, but largely failed, to bring into public administration as well.

To fully understand the features of the classical-liberal perspective on governance and public management, we need to place this view in the context of the field of public administration compared to the fields of political economy and political theory. In the public administration literature, instances of explicit reference to and identification with traditional schools of doctrinal political thought are limited, evasive, indirect, and clouded in ambiguities. That ideological emasculation applies to all political doctrines, not only classical liberalism. Public Administration scholars may have ideological priors, some of them obvious, yet the ideological stance is not dealt with explicitly as part of the process of definition or articulation of the various emerging and evolving thematic or general positions. Hence, to even more precisely locate the problem of the classical-liberal perspective (or at least its possibility) in the big picture of public administration thinking, additional effort is necessary. We need to get a sense of the domain, its intellectual territory, and the diversity of themes and approaches that define the relevant literature. Also, we need to get a sense of its evolution in time.

Only in that way can we appreciate how the classical-liberal ethos and the theoretical construct that reflects it fit or contrast with various themes, domains, and approaches of the field. Also, it is only then that we can understand where and how the classical-liberal perspective has relevance and affinities; and where it converges or diverges from various public administration domains, themes, and founding ideas, as well as some of their avatars over time. One may imagine, indeed, many ways in which the type of doctrinal and theoretical construct sketched in part I could be pictured as part of the field of public administration, broadly defined. However, one must see how the field in real life—or as it has evolved in its intellectual history, with all its themes, subdomains, and approaches—accommodates or could accommodate this construct. Let us start with that task and then move to the moment when the public choice movement entered the stage.

Public Administration as a Constitutional Problem

The task of charting a field that is "diverse, eclectic and pragmatic"[19] is far from easy and straightforward. Yet certain patterns emerge from a survey of the works that try to map the intellectual landscape, as part of either an intellectual history of the field or an introduction to it. The clusters and patterns of themes, approaches, and perspectives identified by scholars of public administration will help us place the classical-liberal approach more precisely in its suitable context. Before attempting to give a brief overview of the field, let us start by highlighting an area of deep consensus that exists between even the most diametrically opposed perspectives, such as that of Woodrow Wilson and Vincent Ostrom.

Vincent Ostrom can be seen as the quintessential anti-Wilsonian theorist,[20] and yet they agreed on a fundamental matter: thinking about public administration ultimately and unavoidably leads one to consider *how the constitution deals with the problem of authority*. As Wilson put it,

The study of administration, philosophically viewed, is closely connected with the study of the proper distribution of constitutional authority. To be efficient it must discover the simplest arrangements by which responsibility can be unmistakably fixed upon officials; the best way of dividing authority without hampering it, and responsibility without obscuring it. And this question of the distribution of authority, when taken into the sphere of the higher, the originating functions of government, is obviously a central constitutional question. If administrative study can discover the best principles upon which to base such distribution, it will have done constitutional study an invaluable service.[21]

The theory of polycentricity developed by Vincent and Elinor Ostrom and their collaborators, which we delve into in chapters 3 and 6, is indeed precisely an answer to Wilson's call to find "the best principles upon which to base such distribution" of authority. As Wilson noted, "To discover the best principle for the distribution of authority is of greater importance, possibly, under a democratic system, where officials serve many masters, than under others where they serve but a few."[22]

This being said, the agreement ends when we get to the specific question of how to distribute authority. On one hand, Wilson argues that authority should be centralized and organized hierarchically in order to facilitate accountability. Wilson anticipates the public choice concept of voters' rational ignorance and notes that, especially in a democratic system, where voters cannot be expected to pay too much attention to politics, it is important for accountability to be clearly and easily visible. Otherwise voters will not be able to exert the proper pressure on the political system, and their trust in the system will falter.

Trust is strength in all relations of life; and, as it is the office of the constitutional reformer to create conditions of trustfulness, so it is the office of the administrative organizer to fit administration with conditions of clear-cut responsibility which shall insure trustworthiness. And let me say that *large powers and unhampered discretion seem to me the indispensable conditions of responsibility*. Public attention must be easily directed, in each case of good or bad administration, to just the man deserving of praise or blame. *There is no danger in power, if only it be not irresponsible. If it be divided, dealt out in shares to many, it is obscured; and if it be obscured, it is made irresponsible*. But if it be centered in heads of the service and in heads of branches of the service, it is easily watched and brought to book. If to keep his office a man must achieve open and honest success, and if at the same time he feels himself intrusted with large freedom of discretion, *the greater his power the less likely is he to abuse it, the more is he nerved and sobered and elevated by it*. The less his power, the more safely obscure and unnoticed does he feel his position to be, and the more readily does he relapse into remissnes.[23]

As is clear in the passage just quoted, Wilson indeed recognizes that some tradeoffs may be at play, in particular the fact that a hierarchical system eliminates checks and balances and the separation of powers. However, he dismisses the concern. In his view, "our peculiar American difficulty in organizing administration is not the danger of losing liberty, but the danger of not being able or willing to separate its essentials from its accidents."[24] Indeed, there is nothing more at odds with classical liberalism than Wilson's claim that "the greater his power the less likely is he to abuse it, the more is he nerved and sobered and elevated by it."

By contrast, both the public choice and the new institutional economics approaches to constitutional analysis focus primarily on the issue of preventing abuses of power.[25] According to these perspectives, trust is a consequence of making abuses of power difficult and of governments establishing credible commitments to protect property, contracts, and the rule of law. Wilson was writing before the rise of twentieth-century totalitarian governments and, hence, had fewer concrete and dramatic examples at hand about what actually happens when institutional positions of large unchecked discretionary power are created. No one can still claim such naiveté today.

Vincent Ostrom's claim about the "intellectual crisis in public administration" was based on the observation that, although by 1970s we moved beyond the Wilsonian naiveté about the dangers of unchecked discretionary power, the field of public administration was still largely based on the Wilsonian conceptual background, as highlighted above. Furthermore, Vincent Ostrom looked at public choice theory as an alternative foundation to public administration precisely because public choice theory, and the Virginia school in particular, was based on the concern about abuses of power. And yet, as we highlight in our brief summary below, the public administration field seems to have slowly moved away from the Wilsonian foundations not by suddenly embracing Vincent Ostrom's alternative proposal but in a more gradual and cautious fashion. Vincent Ostrom's book has become a classic of the field, and yet one with little direct influence. We are arguing that the field is in fact converging on Ostrom's position, and that an awareness of the conceptual background provided by public choice and institutional economics is of great benefit.

Public Administration: Charting the Field

In *Mastering Public Administration: From Max Weber to Dwight Waldo*, Brian Fry and Jos Raadschelders[26] present one of the most intuitively clear and recognizable modes of framing and introducing the field and its evolution. They start with the classical approach defined by Woodrow Wilson's 1887 *The Study of Administration*, the book that introduced and promoted the idea of a science of administration and that launched a search for general principles leading to improvement in organizing and managing the public domain. By the beginning of the twentieth century, that trend was morphing into scientific management, influenced by F. W. Taylor and the rationalization movement, with its ideas about "the one best way" of performing a task. The objective of being more efficient in the division of labor—of taking advantage of large-scale institutional specialization—was further extended and applied to organizations themselves. The departmentalism approach, which concentrates on the efficacy-inducing features of formal organization structures and which focuses hence on organization principles, had already been used in the military and private business. The new and

increasingly vigorous public administration perspective wanted to apply the principles systematically to public organization and management. The literature studying
this perspective looked at issues such as (a) grouping like activities in distinct units on
the basis of common or closely related objectives; (b) linking responsibility with authority; (c) safeguarding unity of command; (d) having operations structured around
a clear-cut chain of command going down and a chain of responsibility going up; and
(e) having a line that differentiates operating or end-purpose activities from staff activities such as advisory, consultative, or support services.

The classical period was followed after World War II by a period of rethinking,
relaunching, and expansion, dominated by a militant scientific spirit induced by
behaviorism, positivism, and reactions to both. It was a rich and complex period in
which the multifaceted and pluralist nature of the field of public administration was
further consolidated. The political scientist and economist Herbert Simon's work on
administrative behavior and his criticism of the classical perspective—that is, the
tenets of most prewar literature—was a defining moment. His programmatic focus
on the analysis of decision-making, in an enthusiastic positivist paradigm and the
counterreactions from Waldo and Peter F. Drucker, remain to this day a defining debate
about the nature, methodology, epistemology, and applied dimension of public administration as an intellectual field and practice. In the end, a plurality of perspectives
entered the stage. The human relations movement challenged managerial practices.
Taylorism and organization specialization, the movement's proponents argued, offer
a too-limiting approach, and a range of social and psychological aspects and needs
must be accounted for in an organization. On parallel lines of research, the works of
sociologist Robert K. Merton, the sociologist and legal scholar Philip Selznick, and the
sociologist and theorist Peter Blau explore bureaucracies and organization processes,
as well as their pathologies. Those scholars also explore the psychological aspects of
organizational behavior in social-psychological settings, with the insights applied to
organizational development.

Of special interest is the emergence of the contingency perspective, a reaction
against the "one best way" approach to organization design and management solutions.
The contingency perspective argues that management is relative, since it is at its core
an "adaptive process in response to environmental stimuli," and that "the appropriate
style is contingent on a number of organizational considerations."[27] Hence, the object
of the contingency approach is not to build generalizations or identify social or organizational laws but "to stipulate the conditions under which a particular approach is
likely to be successful."[28] Finally, by building on the work of the psychologist Abraham
Maslow and the human relations school of management, organizational humanism
drew attention to the ethics and personal-individual dimension. That attention was
a response to the presumed fixation on efficiency and productivity issues, as well as
expression of the concern that management was becoming a sophisticated form of
manipulation. Organizations, be they private or public, should not be seen as mere
instruments to increase productivity; they are also places that express and facilitate
human values and aspirations.

The line that emphasized pluralism of values and objectives along with efficiency
resonated in many respects with different lines of arguments and perspectives that
evolved in parallel. Increasingly salient in the 1960s was the "administration as

politics" and/or "administration and politics" approach. The stance taken by Waldo, who uses and engages political theory in framing and analyzing public administration, was becoming increasingly influential. Waldo and his followers introduced into the field unprecedented intellectual sophistication and a nuanced understanding of the historical context of both the theory and the practice of public administration, as well as the trade-offs and tensions between different objectives and values in public governance. Waldo was insistent that public administration, as a social science, was not and could not be value free. Taking the physical sciences as a model in public administration would be theoretically misleading and might foster massive applied-level errors. Moreover, public administration is deeply embedded in its social-political context. To Waldo, the link with politics is crucial:

> Nothing is more central in thinking about public administration than the nature and interrelations of politics and administration. Nor are the nature and interrelations of politics and administration only of academic theorizing. What is more important in the day-to-day, year-to-year, decade-to-decade operation of government than the ways in which politics and administration are conceptualized, rationalized, and related one to the other?[29]

At the threshold of the 1970s, the ideas expressed by Waldo and reinforced by the turbulent 1960s led to a deep and multifaceted soul-searching in the field. Diverse efforts in reconstruction followed. One of the most visible expressions was the new public administration movement, a rather radical expansion of the humanist perspective with special concern for participation and social and democratic values. Notable on the technocratic side was the emergence of analytical interest in the problem of public policy: policy process, policy formulation, implementation, and evaluation. As exemplified by the work of the political scientist and economist Charles Lindblom and the political scientist Aaron Wildavsky, analytical interest leads to increased institutionalization through departments and schools of public policy, an extension of but also an alternative to traditional takes on public administration.

By the beginning of the 1970s, the stage was thus set for the developments defined and at least partly motivated by the thought of an acute intellectual crisis in public administration. The debates around the nature of the crisis and the way out led to the more recent evolutions in the direction of governance and new public management. Consequently, they are a key point in our argument and a critical juncture in the history of the field, as the rest of the chapter points out.

All of the above could be further nuanced. A couple of examples from the literature illustrate both the diversity of the field and the relative confluence of the different frameworks and periodization used by scholars. Raadschelders takes the effort to methodically chart the intellectual territory of public administration to a new level.[30] He aims to provide an entire set of conceptual maps, an extended and sophisticated attempt to intellectually assess and organize from different angles the efforts made. Thus, different approaches to conceptual mapping are identified in function of knowledge sources, theories, schools of thought, intellectual debates, and main topics of interest. Clusters of concepts and themes illuminate the variety in the field, reconsidered for different angles. His analysis of the literature confirms what previous surveys identify. Setting aside slight variations and personal interpretations, most authors dealing with the issue note the same pattern. Between 1900 and 1940, there was a focus on efficiency and rationalization of activities related to public administration. The dominant concern was with management and a Taylorist rationalization of activity and organizational structures regarding the extension of the logic of specialization. A change took place after World War II with the emergence of decision-making and behavioral approaches, humanist psychology, and social scientific methods aimed at organization design and behavior. Next came rethinking and a soul-searching moment, which led to a reconfiguration that introduced more saliently issues of power, legitimacy, ethics, and justice.

Similarly, the public affairs scholar Howard McCurdy[31] looks at the dominant intellectual disciplines influencing public administration at different points in time. He gives a sense of the variation that comes from introducing different accents and angles of interpretation. In the beginning, the first half of the twentieth century, the main intellectual influences were scientific management and business management models, plus philosophy and political approaches radiating from the still-lingering Wilsonian impetus. Then between 1945 and 1965, the behavioral school and the political school were dominant. The years from 1965 to 1980 marked the era of applications and the rational school, which included management policy analysis, comparative institutional analysis, and organizational development. After 1980 came a period of reconsideration of ethics, values, and pluralist politics. In brief, the diverse interpretations of the nature and evolution of the discipline of public administration offer a relatively stable and clear perspective of the field, its texture, and its evolution.

In looking at the big picture, we can note a certain clustering of themes. Setting aside the intellectual history and evolution of the field of public administration, the literature generally uses a rough but useful mode of illuminating the division of interest and focus in the study of public administration. On the one hand, there are authors and approaches that focus on the relationship between administration and its sociopolitical-economic environment as a condition of its operation. On the other hand, there are authors and approaches that focus on the issues and dynamics internal to an organization and its management.

Herbert Simon advanced the idea that there are three domains of interest in public administration: (a) the problem of the organization of the levels of government, (b) the behavior of individuals as social agents operating the machine of government, and (c) the relationship between politics and administration.

James P. Pfiffner[32] describes three schools of thought. First, there is the legal historical approach, which focuses on normative and philosophical views on the formal relations among branches of government. Second, there is the structural descriptive approach, which operates with scientific management assumptions and applies business models to public administration. And third is the behavioral approach study of human behavior in organizational context. The management and public policy scholar Grover Starling[33] organizes the domain into three classes: (a) public or political management, which deals with the political and legal environment, intergovernmental relations, and administrative responsibilities; (b) program management, which deals with decision-making, planning, organizational structure, and execution; and

(c) resources management, which deals with human, financial, and other resources and their use.

The public administration scholar Gary Wamsley and the sociologist Mayer Zald[34] develop a framework that is constructed around two dimensions. On the one dimension is the environment—the structure and processes related to external factors that shape the operations and evolution of the organization unit. On the second dimension are the internal aspects—the structure and process that take place in the operating units. The two dimensions could be approached from a political or an economic perspective that defines the second dimension. The result is a two-by-two matrix that not only allows the creation of a typology but could also function as an analytical framework.

Continuing our survey, let us note that Frederickson et al.[35] introduce, review, and discuss a range of theories that are currently part of the theoretical portfolio of the field, from the theory of political control and bureaucratic politics to postmodernism and decision theory. A close look at their work reveals the same clusters of contours. The first cluster contains theories that deal with the politics-administration interface. In that category are theories of political control of bureaucracies, such as exploring the appropriate range of discretion for bureaucrats in democratic policy, capture theory, and agency theory, as well as theories of bureaucratic politics, such as the policymaking roles of bureaucracies and administration. The issues at stake are the interplay between the administrative process and the democratic process in determining public decision-making and public policy, the reciprocal control and influence of elected officials' control and administration, and the role of organized interests in relationship to administration and political process. The second cluster consists of theories that focus on the organization and management of bounded public institutions. They are based on the "description of organizations as [a] unit of analysis"[36] and discuss the design and evolution of structural arrangements for the conduct of public administration—organizational design, institutionalism, structural theory, hierarchy, alternatives to hierarchy, and high-reliability systems. The third cluster contains theories that explain human behavior in public management and the implications for effectively running public organizations in accordance with different ethical and organizational performance criteria: organizational behavior theory; group theory; human relations; Theory X and Theory Y; and an entire range of approaches that deal with motivation, routine and tasks, control, regulation and communication, and oversight and evaluation in organizations.

In addition, Frederickson et al.[37] dedicate special attention to the micro-level decision-making that is seen as a privileged locus in the study of administrative behavior. Hence they have separated chapters on decision theory and rational choice theory and the problems of rationality, irrationality, and optimality in public decision-making. Finally, their work extensively covers the topic of "governance." They treat it as a term associated with a "repositioning of public administration,"[38] a recurring event, taking place in the past several decades, and thus dedicate attention to ways in which the governance-focused approach transgresses, undermines, and challenges traditional themes and disciplinary boundaries. The chapters on decision-making, rationality, and the governance paradigm take a transversal look at the foundational assumptions and applied implications of the approaches and themes in earlier chapters. Overall, the familiar clustering of themes and approaches resurfaces from the authors' extensive and nuanced overview of the field of public administration.

Our tentative review of some of the most salient attempts to survey or frame the field of public administration literature leads to a double observation. First, there are focal points that are relatively stable ways of grouping the approaches and the themes. There are some natural configurations of thematic, analytic, and interpretive perspectives that resurface and that help provide a sense of the nature and landscape of the diverse, pragmatic, and eclectic field of public administration. Second, the field is a dynamic one of shifting accents and variable contours. It has an ongoing ability to absorb themes and approaches—to integrate them—and thus "to transform itself into new shapes and purposes each generation, or on twenty year cycles, to respond to particular needs of the times."[39] Or as Raadschelders explains, the evolution of which topics and approaches are relevant at a given point in time "suggests that the study has responded to changing environmental circumstances."[40] The conjecture that public administration has constantly responded both to changes in the real-life environment of governance and its practices and to the relevant public and intellectual debates thus seems warranted.

The Interface Revisited

Out of the many developments surveyed in this chapter, developments that took place during the past twenty years or so, one has important significance for discussion here. It is the influential recurrence of the older theme of seeing public administration as inherently embedded in the sociopolitical environment. It is an approach that conceptualizes administrative practices and structures as part of a complex relationship with the environment, mediated by the political process. An entire family of approaches has gained salience, gravitating around the idea of governance, an idea that both incorporates the standard functions of the modern state and goes further to explore the ways in which people organize and manage collective action and public space.

Governance, Raadschelders explains, "includes attention for collective actors outside the public realm who influence to [a] smaller or larger exten[t] what happens in the public realm (such as NGOs [nongovernment organizations], interest groups, lobbyists, private corporations, media)."[41] Hence, public administration as both a practice and an intellectual discipline must take that aspect of governance into account. That aspect, as we shall see, is a useful anchor in our attempt to delineate the coordinates of the classical-liberal perspective's potential location in the broader picture of the field of public administration.

As noted, public administration can be thought of roughly as dealing with (a) the inner structures and operations of government organizations and (b) the relationship between social and political context and government organizations. Once that distinction is introduced, it is evident that a normative individualist, classical-liberal approach is relevant for both distinctions, but its major effect is on the second, the connection between administration and its sociopolitical environment. That is to say, an attempt to chart the field and to locate the convergence area of the public choice, classical-liberal perspective and the public administration field has a prima facie reason to look at the issue.

An additional way of approaching it is to consider public administration as a study of public organizations and the policy process, with a strong emphasis on the legal aspects of public action. Or the allocation of resources and values may be considered as a form of competition in the struggles associated with the policy process. Or the management of organization forms and the resources involved in collective processes may be considered. Yet, while recognizing the validity and incorporating the insights of all of those considerations, it is possible to go beyond the public sector and look at the nonprofit sector and self-governing institutions.[42] This point is essential. That stance opens a distinctive perspective toward a distinctive tradition of public administration thought. Sometimes more visible, and other times more submerged by other more salient perspectives, it always signals a distinctiveness of focus, interpretation, and normative stance. Its key element is self-government, the idea "that people are able to associate for and organize collective action on a voluntary basis," explains Raadschelders.[43]

Indeed, it is a bold move to put the voluntarist individualistic principle and its self-governance corollaries at the foundation of public administration. In the mainstream view, as expressed by Raadschelders, it is debatable that such an approach is even possible, beyond small groups, on a large social or institutional scale. Yet Raadschelders notes that, in the eyes of scholars such as V. Ostrom, not only is scalability a possibility but also public administration itself should be a science of associations. Such a science of associations must include "all associations (nongovernmental organizations, homeowners associations, church organizations, labor unions, etc.) and not just public organizations."[44] Without being against the normative goals at stake, Raadschelders is skeptical of public administration as the theory and practice of association.[45] However, this Tocquevillian interpretation of governance as the science and art of the association is on the table, and cannot be ignored.

For the current argument, we need only note that, with a Tocquevillian theme, we have reached a key point in exploring the classical-liberal perspective in public administration. At this juncture, it is important to note the existence and increasing visibility of this perspective, given V. Ostrom's bold move to advance it to the front stage. That move should be seen as a notable evolution in the history of public administration. In the 1970s and 1980s, key assumptions of this type of approach were already challenging the entire field. In conjunction with the realities of bureaucratic failure and government dysfunctions, those challenges induced a disciplinary refocus. Reassessing and rethinking the interface between the traditional administrative and bureaucratic structures and the rest of the sociopolitical system became pivotal. In many respects, this reassessment brought about a profound paradigmatic change of perspectives. Evolutions that were only partially driven by intellectual and scientific debates created the favorable condition. As we will see, the challenge was indeed responded to in the literature, and the emergence of the governance perspective was one of the main responses. The dimensions of this distinctive take on the nature and function of public administration are noteworthy. Even if the radical interpretation of governance as self-governance is toned down, the implications are still significant.

The public administration scholar Robert Denhardt gives a sense[46] of what his own plea, made during those same years, to move beyond the restrictions of past definitions may mean in this context. An alternative definition of the field, he explains, should have the following characteristics: "It should identify public administration as a process, rather than as something that occurs within a particular type of structure (hierarchy, for example); and it should emphasize the public nature of that process rather than its connection to formal systems of government."[47] To be even more precise, a modern public administration theory should combine two distinct approaches. On the one hand, there is a democratic approach "concerned with the ways in which public institutions promote social values that have been defined and applied with a high degree of citizen involvement and with a high degree of responsiveness to the needs and interests of the citizenry."[48] In that case, the focus is on issues of freedom, justice, and equality. On the other hand, public institutions should support an organizational approach "concerned with how individuals can manage change processes to their own or to corporate advantage, especially in large systems."[49] In that case, the focus is on issues of power and authority, leadership and motivation, and the dynamics of groups in action.

The emerging conclusion of our overview of the domains and facets of public administration is now clearer. In our attempt to locate the proper place of the classical-liberal perspective on public administration, the type of logic and approach behind the broadly defined governance agenda seems to be a prima facie candidate for potential affinities with what we call the classical-liberal perspective.

It is true that such a perspective has relevance for all aspects and dimensions of public administration and its study. There are some elements of normativity or some types of solutions that may satisfy criteria defined as classical liberal, irrespective of the level, the form, or even the organization aspect of governance. Yet, it would be both a conceptual overstretch and normatively dogmatic to do that. There is a natural alignment between (a) the perspective of political economy and public choice, and (b) the specific facets, domains, and approaches. It is natural to think that classical-liberal ideas and assumptions must be applicable and sometimes unavoidable when discussing issues that pertain to the politics-administration, democracy-bureaucracy, rules-versus-discretion interface. Whether one likes it or not, the very nature of the phenomena in case implies it.

We now have a better sense of where to look, as a starting point, in our attempt to identify the intellectual and practical issues that may be most accommodating to a classical-liberal perspective of the public administration tradition. It may be no surprise that the best way to locate this perspective is at the interface between the political and administrative process. As we know, the volatile, complex, and confusing areas of interference are key to understanding the problems of governance. Waldo repeatedly warns that "nothing is more central in thinking about public administration than the nature and interrelations of politics and administration."[50] That is not something of mere academic-theorizing interest. Waldo, as mentioned, put it rather bluntly: "What is more important in the day-to-day, year-to-year, decade-to-decade operation of government than the ways in which politics and administration are conceptualized, rationalized, and related one to the other?"[51]

The public administration scholar Mark Rutgers[52] notes that the intricacies of public administration pivot on three pairs of concepts: politics and administration, private and public, and state and society. The three pairs may even be considered the founding dichotomies of the field. In all these areas, the classical-liberal perspective is of key relevance in illuminating issues and possible approaches to finding solutions.

First, the private-public tension—already familiar to our discussion—is essential. The specific interpretations and definitions, as well as the ways in which the differences and similarities are construed, have significant implications. Dichotomies of huge analytical and normative significance, such as state versus market or profit versus non-profit, pivot on the private-public dichotomy. The second grand dichotomy pointing to the interface that defines public administration is that of the relationship between state and society, that "positions public administration as something 'in between' the authority to make decisions (state) and the people that are to be administered (society)."[53] At the same time, the second dichotomy shows the complexity of links that connect governance to the rest of society. Once seen in this embedded context, the states become one of the many existing possible governance arrangements in a vast field of arrangements at different levels, with different functions, structures, and circumstances. The third pair of concepts is the politics-administration dichotomy, considered the major founding dichotomy in public administration:

> The perception of a distinction between politics and administration is not simply an accidental result of a certain period of American history, to be put aside as fiction or nonsense. The distinction is writ deep in several millennia of Western history.[54]

On the other hand, public administration scholar Frederick Mosher observes:

> The concept that policy should be determined by politically responsible officials, institutionally separated from the execution of policy—i.e., administration—and the arguments attendant upon it, [is] relatively recent in political and intellectual history. One finds little reference to them in the writings of many of the great political thinkers, and this perhaps reflects the general lack of concern they felt about administration.[55]

Patrick Overeem[56] notes both the centrality and controversial nature of the distinction, irrespective of the historical interpretation. "We see, then, that the politics–administration dichotomy (PAD) as a whole comprises two basic elements: a certain distinction between politics and administration (P/A) and a certain idea about their dichotomous relationship (D)."[57] Public administration scholar Mark Rutgers remarks that "this has consequences for almost every topic in the discourse on public administration: responsibility, recruitment, the policy-process, professionalism, democracy, bureaucracy." He warns that it is necessary "to be careful, however, because there is no unanimity about what the distinction precisely refers to, or if it is even tenable at closer examination."[58]

To sum up, a review of the defining dichotomies of the field reveals how public administration as a field and as a practice has to deal by its very nature with domains that are riddled with ambiguities and tensions and volatility. The territory on which public administration must build its foundation is constantly shifting in multiple and diverse interface areas. Simultaneously, there is a sense of familiarity with these issues of overlapping and shifting conceptual and socio-institutional boundaries and of dichotomies of great practical significance. Our discussion of the public choice approach and classical-liberal building blocks was precisely about these issues. We now see clearer how, by being at the core of the phenomena of interest in public administration (politics and administration, public and private, state and society) what we have called the "classical-liberal" perspective is dealing with the very essence of public administration. Regardless of whether one likes it or not, whether one wants to name it "classical liberal" or not, it is not a tangential, marginal view and it is not addressing marginal issues. Our discussion of the public administration has placed us in multiple ways and from many angles exactly in the same conceptual and thematic space that the discussion of the classical liberal–public choice perspective has outlined.

An Area of Convergence

The inherent link between public choice and public administration is now easier to grasp. The pivotal position of the Ostroms' work becomes salient. Indeed, there is one crucial moment in the evolution of the field of public administration when what we call a classical-liberal perspective, inspired with its normative individualism and its comparative institutional analysis, is explicitly advanced in the field. It is a moment when the public choice revolution converges with the debates in the re-evaluation of public administration already noted in this chapter. The result is the articulation of the democratic administration argument, an argument that clearly applies and expands the classical-liberal legacy. It is the moment when V. Ostrom's radical perspective emerges in the double context of the public administration and the public choice literature. The public choice approach was advocated as the vehicle of a systematic reassessment, reinterpretation, and reconstruction of public administration. The domain of public administration was presented as a natural ground for the applied public choice approach.

Our effort to identify and develop the classical-liberal perspective in public administration will turn now to this attempt to introduce public choice in public administration and an attempt to introduce public administration in public choice. That is to say to public choice as a foundational theory in public administration, and public administration as the applied level of public choice. The effort is done against a conceptual background that combines the Madisonian and Tocquevillian perspectives, updating them for the realities of the twentieth-century political and governance context.[59]

As this chapter shows, the rise of the field of public administration was long and delayed. It took place in the midst of a disciplinary milieu—political science—that from its inception had a structural bias against the core elements defining public administration. The break from political science came to fruition in the 1970s as a final stage in a process of the field's self-awareness and independent institutionalization. Its emergence required carving an identity and a territory in stiff competition with not only political science and business administration but also with an aggressive start-up—public policy studies. That led to public administration breaking apart as an independent, autonomous field with an agenda of even further specialization in the intellectual division of labor, with a strict focus on specific policy issues, areas, processes, and techniques. That was precisely the moment when the Ostroms came to the fore to advance the public choice perspective. Only when seen in this broader picture can the real dimensions and significance of their agenda for public administration be appreciated.

Vincent Ostrom advanced to the new old field going through, by that time, an identity crisis of growth, a possible solution with two facets. The first facet was theoretical and methodological, and its content was straightforward, although radical and controversial. Practitioners and students of public administration must rethink and reconstruct the theory underlying their field. The conceptual framework pivoting on bureaucracy theory that they adopted at its inception as an academic discipline was leading to a theoretical crisis and a practical dead end. Vincent Ostrom offered an alternative: public choice. public choice, he argued, should be in fact the foundational theoretical framework for public administration. In its belated emergence to self-awareness and disciplinary institutionalization, public administration should incorporate the new "no name field" developing in the confines of modern economics without hesitation. The accidents of disciplinary and intellectual history should be disregarded. The proper foundation of public administration is in public choice theory. The proper operational basis of public choice is public administration.

> Fashioning the architecture for a system of democratic administration will require different concepts and different solutions from those that can be derived from Wilson, Goodnow, W. F. Willoughby, White, and Gulick. Instead, a new theory of democratic administration will have to be fashioned from the works of Hamilton, Madison, Tocqueville, Dewey, Lindblom, Buchanan, Tullock, Olson, William Niskanen, and many others. . . . The theory of externalities, commons, and public goods; the logic of collective action and public enterprise; the concepts of public service industries; and fiscal federalism will have prominent places in that theory.[60]

The second facet was a normative vision. V. Ostrom saw public choice as being strongly connected to the intellectual tradition that had inspired America's founders with the radical idea that societies may be capable of establishing good government by reflection and choice. For Ostrom, the analytical core of public choice encapsulated two more layers: (a) a pure normative vision about the good society and good government, and (b) a series of constitutional, political, and administrative solutions for its implementation. In addition, Ostrom was hinting at an implicit narrative of the evolution of self-governance in which it is presumed that, at one point in history, a certain type of political system and its associated constitutional system created the conditions for the emergence of a new form of public administration: democratic administration. This special variety of administration is structurally different from the traditional, better-known bureaucratic adminis-tration.[61] The Ostrom confluence of public choice and public administration thus emerges naturally as crucial for our attempt to understand the nature and potential of a reconstructed and updated classical-liberal perspective on governance. The next part of our argument deals with those challenges.

5

Public Choice, Public Administration, and Self-Governance

The Ostromian Confluence

The previous chapter has shown that some of the preeminent pioneers of the public choice movement were in fact initially public administration scholars. Although today that fact is ignored or forgotten, the public choice revolution was from its beginning deeply conversant with the field of public administration. At the same time, we were also reminded that the field of public administration was built on a theoretical foundation that assumes and implies dichotomies and concepts that capture phenomena of shared interest with the field of political economy. Many of the phenomena have been technically elaborated in political economy terms by public choice theorizing. Furthermore, the founding dichotomies of public administration thinking are embedded in normative issues that emerge in the tensions between private and public, state and market, and individual and society dichotomies. But those are exactly the points where the methodological and normative individualist assumption induces the public choice perspective to take implicitly and sometimes explicitly an inexorable classical-liberal stance.

The present chapter uses Elinor and Vincent Ostroms' work as a vehicle, taking advantage of its special and unique nature. As we have already observed, the Ostroms' initial work deals with public administration not figuratively, in between the lines and by default, as all public choice work does, but literally. Moreover, and crucial for our arguments, during the initial decades of the public choice movement, the scholars of the Bloomington School were considered the main promoters of the public choice revolution in the field of public administration. They were also at the core of that field—outliers but not eccentrics. Their endeavors in the 1960s and 1970s were in many respects a systematic attempt not only to introduce into the discipline public choice insights that deal with the study of the administrative side of public affairs but also, and even more so, to revolutionize the field, to start a paradigm shift toward basic public choice principles and a normative ideal of democratic self-governance administration.

We now have an enhanced sense of the meaning and context of the Ostroms' work as an attempt to promote the public choice perspective in public administration and the public administration perspective in public choice. This chapter will further focus on this point of convergence between the two intellectual traditions, as illustrated by the Ostroms' perspective. It will take a closer look at the nature, significance, and reception of the Ostroms' work in the field of public administration. The chapter will substantiate the claim that the Ostroms were the main advocates of public choice in public administration studies and that they were recognized as such by the field. The evidence is overwhelming and the fact that this essential side of their contribution is largely neglected today requires explanation. Given the pivotal position at the junction of the two traditions, we also need to consider in a systematic way the reception of the Ostroms' public administration perspective in the context of public choice, or more precisely, the fiasco of that reception. We also look at what could be said about the mainstream theoretical and epistemological public choice evolution, from the viewpoint of the Ostroms and from what the insights gained that way may mean today. We then take a closer look at the social philosophy dimensions ingrained in their alternative perspective.

It is important to stress that we do not insist that this social philosophy should be labeled as exclusively classical liberal or that the Ostroms portray it as such. We do claim that it is compatible with the classical-liberal tradition, that it is in large part rooted in it, and—more important for our purposes—that it is an excellent vehicle or basic structure to use in updating and advancing a contemporary version of a governance theory in that tradition. We are confident the Ostroms would have not opposed the use of their work as a source of inspiration, benchmark, vehicle, or building block for the development of governance theories and approaches in any tradition compatible with the ideals and values of human self-governance. An important underlying point of our argument is that the Ostroms open the possibility of significant further elaboration. Using the social philosophy insights and concepts provided by their work, we demonstrate how those insights and concepts could function as the core structure of an approach that integrates a synthesis of the incentive-based public choice and the knowledge-based epistemic choice of Austrian theory inspiration. We illustrate the last point using the example of a remarkable author who kept alive this type of approach in the field of public administration long after the initial effect of the Ostroms' efforts had faded: Michael Spicer.

Public Administration and the Ostromian Perspective

From the field's beginning, public administration scholars recognized that, normatively speaking, what the Ostroms call "democratic administration" is part of a special formula of social organization. It is defined by fragmentation of authority and overlapping jurisdictions in constitutional limits "that sharply [curtail] public actions by promoting alternative, private nonprofit, or local options for collective action."[1] As opposed to the bureaucratic command-and-control, hierarchy-centered vision, the Ostromian perspective "puts a premium on competition, pluralism, open choices, and constitutional alternative modes of collective action that maximize personal liberties."[2] In such a system, the normative focal point will not be "preoccupied with simplicity, neatness, and symmetry but with diversity, variety, and responsiveness to the preferences of constituents."[3] Attention will shift from bureaucratic command-and-control structures to "the opportunities individuals can pursue in multi-organizational environments."[4] Finally, policy analysis will become more a form of comparative institutional assessment, thus concentrating on "problems of institutional weakness and failure inherent in any organizational structure or institutional arrangement" and on "the opportunity costs inherent in different organizational arrangements."[5]

The radicalness, profundity, and magnitude of Ostroms' proposition could hardly be exaggerated. To make things even more interesting and difficult to dismiss on grounds of improper radicalism, in the new Ostromian perspective, the traditional public administration theory with its focus on bureaucracies and hierarchies is not negated or abolished. It is relegated to be a subdivision, a part of a broader and more general theoretical and normative perspective. The new relationship was supposed to be one between a general theory of social order and governance and a particular theory, relevant for certain domains, facets, and historical moments. In brief, seen from the public choice standpoint, the Ostromian rendition of public choice in public administration is not a mere advocacy of an analytical method or of the application of a mode of reasoning to areas to which it had not previously applied. Rather, it is a vehicle for a vision of social order and governance, an essential ingredient of the science and art of association.

The fact that the challenge posed by the Ostroms' work to the field of public administration was recognized as such by the field itself is not at all difficult to document. It is true that for a while, starting sometime in the 1980s, the field exhibited some uneasiness with their work and its implications and legacy. Yet the John Gaus Award, which is conferred annually by the American Political Science Association (APSA) to honor "the recipient's lifetime of exemplary scholarship in the joint tradition of political science and public administration," was given to Vincent Ostrom in 2005, marking a new era of rapprochement. "In a lifetime of exemplary scholarship," states the letter nominating him, "Professor Ostrom has challenged and changed our understanding of American politics and administration involving metropolitan and municipal government, resource management, and educational policy, as well as federalism and constitutional analysis."[6] In the 1950s, "he achieved intellectual breakthroughs in the study and practice of water resource management and educational administration."[7] In the 1960s, "he made us think differently about metropolitan organization and public administration, while being at the same time editor in chief of the leading journal in the profession, *Public Administration Review*."[8] In the 1970s, "he offered novel interpretations of federalism and constitutional choice, serving also as co-founder and president of the Public Choice Society. The books and articles he wrote during this period—many translated in other languages—continue to be cited and used."[9]

Vincent Ostrom's role as a pivotal figure both as a participant in the initial public choice conferences, when public choice had not yet settled on an official name, and as its key promoter in public administration is recognized and reemphasized by Theo Toonen, a leading public administration scholar of the current generation. Toonen is fond of noting how in 1964, as an editor of *Public Administration Review*, Vincent Ostrom urged from the beginning that scholars "keep in touch with any newly emerging no-name fields that may represent important and exciting developments for the advancement of public administration."[10] The Ostromian public choice episode is now solidly entrenched in the history of the discipline.

The role the Ostroms had at the interface between public administration and public choice theory is well captured in *Public Choice Theory in Public Administration: An Annotated Bibliography* by Nicholas Lovrich and Max Neiman, published in 1984, with a foreword by Robert Golembiewski.[11] Their attempt to take stock of the developments at that interface is especially relevant for our discussion. Theirs is a comprehensive assessment based on a systematic bibliographical review of the first two decades of the public choice advancement in public administration, an assessment done at the critical moment when the gap between the public administration mainstream and the Ostroms began to increase. Lovrich and Neiman begin by noting that "public choice represents a new and rapidly growing influence in public administration." There are few graduate programs and textbooks in public administration "that do not include analytical and normative public choice approaches," and "it is quite safe to assume that there are precious few public administration instructors who have not read Vincent Ostrom's exposition of public choice theory in *The Intellectual Crisis in American Public Administration* (1973)." Moreover, "it is likewise a safe speculation that many such instructors and students have studied the exchange of views by Ostrom (in advocacy) and Golembiewski (in criticism) in the *American Political Science Review* [1977], an exchange by two eminent scholars which has done much to promote professional interest in this topic."[12]

Lovrich and Neiman's collection of two hundred abstracts of relevant works is divided into two groups: normative studies that deal with "the desirability of public choice orientations toward the proper design and operation of governmental programs and agencies"[13] and empirical studies. Vincent and Elinor Ostrom's contributions, as well as those of their collaborators, are heavily represented in both categories— Elinor's more in the empirical section; Vincent's more in the normative one. As with other literature reviews, the Ostroms' work is perceived both from the perspective of the big paradigmatic push it advocated and from the perspective of the various public administration subfields and issue areas to the study of which they contributed: intergovernmental relationships (federalism and polycentricism), co-production and provision of collective goods, public finance, measurement and evaluation, natural resources management, private-public governance arrangements, metropolitan administration, and public management.

Commenting on the spread of influence of the public choice approach beyond the confines of academia, Lovrich and Neiman point again toward Vincent Ostrom. In a moment when successful politicians and their appointees "promised new, innovative approaches" entailing "less regulation, lower taxes, more localized administration" and "a greater reliance upon both the private sector and volunteerism among the citizens," all these ideas and desiderata "found a comprehensive rationale in the works of public choice theorists."[14] Thus, "it is no accident of course, that Vincent Ostrom and a number of his associates were invited to formulate a plan for the reform of California governmental institutions by Ronald Reagan, then governor of the Golden State."[15]

The Ostroms' sustained public choice offensive was recognized as such over years, in an entire set of works that review and introduce the field, although the key paradigmatic challenge they advance is not always noted. For instance, Naomi Lynn and

Aaron Wildawsky's overview of *The State of the Discipline* of *Public Administration*, use Ostromian public choice as the typical example of approach, using objectivist assumptions and taking a political and structural perspective.[16] (As such, it occupies the fourth quadrant in a two-axis matrix: subjective–objective and political–organizational.) To explain that public choice "emphasis on a consumer perspective in decision making on the supply of services."[17] They use a reference to the Tibout model while they comment by editorializing rather inaccurately that "Ostrom's Democratic Administration sees bureaucracy as an absolute evil,"[18] They also remark on the Ostroms' influence on public budgeting analysis. In this respect, they note that public choice "provides a clearly demarcated theoretical reference point and philosophical criterion against which both budget processes and policies may be set," whereas "the normative level sets up standards for [the] design of systems of fiscal decision making, legitimizing decentralization and the decoupling of service provision and service delivery."[19]

A better-grounded view is given by the public administration historian and theorist H. George Frederickson and his coauthors in *The Public Administration Theory Primer: Essentials of Public Policy and Administration.*[20] They introduce rational choice as both the new orthodoxy and an ongoing "challenge to the prescriptive arguments taken from traditional public administration scholarship," explaining that some rational choice theory advocates argue that "it should be adopted as the core paradigm of the discipline."[21] That is, "these advocates present rational choice not simply as an economic framework that can be adopted to help understand bureaucratic behavior and the production of public services but also as a normative, democratic theory of administration in its own right."[22] With that, Frederickson et al. manage to pinpoint a major distinctive feature of the Ostromian approach to public choice and public administration. As we have seen, for Vincent Ostrom, public choice is, indeed, not a mere analytical method but the foundation of an entire normative political economy vision—a public organization paradigm, not a simple instrument among others in the toolkit of the social scientist or practitioner. "The most forceful and best-known articulation of this argument," explain the authors, "comes from Vincent Ostrom in his book *The Intellectual Crisis in American Public Administration* (1973). Ostrom argued that rational choice could not only provide an intellectual lifeboat but also provide the discipline with its theoretical ship of state."[23] Frederickson et al. note that the Ostroms' public choice democratic theory of administration is an alternative to the then-dominant bureaucratic and hierarchy theory, pointing to a tradition that goes back to Madison and the federalists.

Similar remarks could be found in *Preface to Public Administration: A Search for Themes and Direction* by Richard Joseph Stillman II: "The most popular, widely discussed, and controversial public administration scholarly treatise in the 1970s was probably Vincent Ostrom's *The Intellectual Crisis in American Public Administration*, [which] frontally assaulted the Wilson–Weber paradigm while proposing a replacement paradigm, which he called democratic administration."[24] Stillman thinks that the democratic administration paradigm attracted broad interest "because of its forceful attacks on traditional normative state-building and state-maintenance doctrines within twentieth-century public administration"[25] and contributed to and rode on the revival wave of Jeffersonian republicanism, grassroots democracy, and enthusiasm for a stateless society ideal. "The state dissolved as a recognizable entity in the Ostromian schema of 'public choice' (which in reality was 'private choice') where radical individualism replaced the state as the focal point for decision making."[26] Yet in the end, the impact was mixed and somewhat ironic. By the mid-1970s, many agreed with Vincent Ostrom's assessment of an intellectual crisis in public administration, as both an intellectual field and an activity, and found his diagnosis convincing. However, "few in public administration swallowed wholesale his prescription of 'public choice.'"[27]

In brief, Vincent Ostrom (and later Elinor) brought a bold, radical, and well-recognized public choice perspective to the field of public administration. Still, fifty years after the first advances, despite the interest and recognition their efforts have received, assessing their overall influence is an exercise riddled with ambiguities. In his recent *Public Administration Review* reassessment of the work of Elinor and Vincent Ostrom from a public administration perspective, Theo Toonen elegantly synthetizes the evolutions.[28] He notes "a somewhat distant and at times strained relationship with American public administration as an institutional field of teaching and research."[29] Thus, "in the United States, *The Intellectual Crisis* marked the beginning of a period in which the Ostroms were estranged from large parts of the establishment of the public administration discipline."[30] Toonen conjectures that the interdisciplinary nature of the Ostroms' work, as well as their eagerness to incorporate (or abandon) new theoretical and methodological ideas if their development proved not very productive, may have something to do with the uneasiness of the relationship. The fast pace at which they moved did not fit well with the overall pace of the discipline. At the same time, Toonen acknowledges that it was the tone of the Ostroms' stance that raised some ideologically driven reactions: "In many cases, the consolidation reforms were supported by liberal political forces and by many traditional public administration researchers searching to improve deteriorated regions and neighborhoods."[31] This context "gave the no-nonsense research attitude of the Ostroms an inadvertent but sustained ideological undertone."[32] The fact that large parts of the American public administration community "seemed to take *The Intellectual Crisis* more or less personally" did not help either.[33]

We are now at the root of a paradoxical situation. Although the "reinventing government" movement of the 1990s and the new public management or new public governance movement of recent vintage seem to be a natural extension of the pioneering ideas promoted in public administration by the Ostroms starting in the 1960s, their work is rarely quoted by leaders on the new wave. Laurence Lynn,[34] a major promoter of the new public management movement, barely recognizes the groundbreaking relevance of the Ostroms' contributions for the developments he advocates. Thus, as Toonen notes, the "Ostroms' approach and normative vision [have] materialized more in European than in American context,"[35] which has had a price. In the United States, reinventing government—an initiative that reflects an Ostromian propensity for "fragmentation, checks and balances, self-organizing and self-governing networks, competition for services and differentiation of demand [seems] only to have scratched the surface, whereas in the European context, various state systems went through fundamental changes, all amounting to a more differentiated, pluralistic and decentralized operation of government and public administration."[36]

In summary, we see how an overview of the field of public administration in the context of its disciplinary and historical evolution provides a better sense of its intrinsic relationship with the public choice program, as well as the crucial position it has for any attempt to move public choice from purely theoretical and academic research to practice. Also, our overview offers clearer insight into the inroads created by the Ostroms. However, the overview leaves us with a series of questions that are far from having only historical relevance. Why did the Ostroms' public choice perspective not have more success in public administration? Even if one protests the use of the notion of failure, it is clear that the Ostroms' success is not unqualified but is more a matter of interpretation. What should contemporary public choice scholars interested in policy and the applied side learn to avoid, or to do, from the Ostroms' experience of relative failure or relative success? Is there something consequential to learn here? These are important questions to ponder.

That being said, it is also important to recall that the Ostroms' work does not represent only an attempt to advance public choice in public administration. Their work may as well be seen as an attempt to advance the public administration universe of themes and perspectives in public choice. Hence, it is evident that the same question may be asked in reverse: Why was the Ostroms' public administration approach not more successful in public choice? What can be learned from a review of that experience?

Public Choice and the Ostroms

With respect to the public administration field's acceptance of the public choice perspective, it is easy to document the recognition given by the field itself to the significance and magnitude of the Ostroms' effort, as well as the limits and gaps of that recognition. Assessing overall success and failure is indeed a matter of criteria and their interpretation. Yet it is undeniable that public administration scholars at least understood what the Ostroms were about. Interestingly, that seems not to be the case when it comes to reception of the public administration perspective in the public choice program. It looks like the relevance and even the existence of the domain of public administration—as both an already established field and a social phenomenon in itself—were barely noticed and even less well understood in their unity and systemic nature.

Hence, the problems that the game theorist and political scientist Steven Brams identified in his presidential address to the Public Choice Society meeting in 2006 were dedicated to a direction "for the most part ignored in the scholarly literature on public choice"—the use of the theory and insights of this research program "to propose and to try to implement reforms that we deem desirable."[37] Central to Bram's address is the observation that what is largely missing from the public choice paradigm "are attempts to translate research findings into actions that might improve how individual and collective choices are made."[38]

Taking seriously the public administration perspective would have meant inducing from the beginning a different orientation to the evolution of the public choice program. Whether that was feasible or even desirable may be a matter of discussion. Yet it is clear that, if the applied level is the starting and the focal point, theoretical and empirical research efforts become an instrument for a problem- and practice-driven approach. That approach is focused on specific governance problems and dilemmas, as seen and interpreted through an explicitly articulated and explicitly assumed normative framework.

Furthermore, that approach is fundamentally different from an approach that starts with a positive social science ideal and that remains in the confines of its underlying logic that relegates the applied concerns to only a follow-up phase. That follow-up phase is a different enterprise in the intellectual division of labor, constantly praised but never taken seriously. We can easily see the roots of the current predicament. As described by Brams: a long series of efforts at analytical and empirical analyses for their own sake that, when it comes to their normative and practical relevance, "never tire of finding fault with a policy or program but do not propose constructive alternatives."[39] So the connection between the symptom and its cause is easy to establish, albeit indirectly and evoking a counterfactual argument.

That said, whereas the diagnosis is relatively uncomplicated and undemanding, the cure is less so. It appears that a real breakthrough on the applied front requires a mental shift as a precondition. The shift is from a concentration on theoretical puzzles and empirical generalizations (imagined more or less under the vague epistemological shadow of the notion of "covering law") to a preoccupation with institutional design and governance problems in a particular domain, pivoting on the public administration apparatus and its concrete operations. It may be a matter of debate whether this is anything other than a paradigm shift. For our discussion, it is sufficient to note that the Ostroms' public administration proposition to public choice entails a radical change of perspectives and mirrors their public choice proposition to public administration. Both propositions entail comparable foundational challenges that may well be called paradigm shifts.

But that is only part of the story. As the Bloomington program became more and more a "normal science" modeled on the neoclassical economics comfort zone, the Ostroms themselves were having their own assessment of the theoretical and analytical facet of the public choice program. A general sense of alienation resulted and spread among many of their associates and followers. In a remarkable piece on Vincent Ostrom and the legacy of his work, by Mike McGinnis and Elinor Ostrom,[40] there are thought-provoking clues regarding the theoretical reasons behind that attitude. An entire section of the paper is dedicated to Vincent Ostrom's concerns about the field's direction, explaining his departures from mainstream public choice scholarship. The authors note that Ostrom was eager to associate with the term *public choice* before "the term took on more specific connotations," but then he took strong exception "to many components of the public choice tradition as it subsequently developed."[41] The main points of their compiled list of issues in contention reveal a complex and thought-provoking picture that challenges the easy cohabitation with mainstream economics.

For instance, Vincent Ostrom wanted to push forward more radically the decision theory and rationality models to be used in nonmarket decision analysis. To understand decision-making in nonmarket settings, a question arises about exclusive use of the assumption that individuals "decide on the provision, production, and allocation of public goods using exactly the same decision-making processes they would use when exchanging private goods in a market setting."[42] With that, Ostrom was signaling a direction that is currently materializing with Vernon Smith's "ecological rationality" perspective[43] or psychologist Gerd Gigerenzer's research on heuristics and decision-making.[44] Also, Vincent Ostrom had serious reservations about the excessive and leveling use of efficiency in public policy. One of the benefits of polycentric systems of governance advocated by Vincent Ostrom, as McGinnis and Elinor Ostrom explain, is their capacity to capture economies of scale. Yet Vincent Ostrom never assumed that that is or should be the only goal under consideration. It may be the case that "in a polycentric order, individuals or communities might decide, for whatever reason, to sacrifice efficiency for the pursuit of other goals, such as accountability, fairness, or physical sustainability."[45] At the same time, Vincent Ostrom took seriously entrepreneurship as a phenomenon, an explanatory variable, and a normative factor. That, as we know, is always a problem for a hard-core, rational choice perspective. Crafting the institutional setting, the action area in which interactions and exchanges can take place, Ostrom writes, requires acts of institutional entrepreneurship. Public entrepreneurs are "artisans who creatively craft the institutional arrangements within which they live and act."[46] Therefore, "institutional analysts must learn to appreciate the skill associated with the establishment and the operation of institutional procedures."[47] An important corollary is that a "public enterprise system" coexist with a "private enterprise system," mutually reinforcing each other. Entrepreneurship fuels both, but entrepreneurial actions take different forms in the two different settings.[48]

Pursuing that logic to its implications, an approach that recognizes the importance of the entrepreneurial imagination, of the heterogeneity of individuals' preferences, and of the diversity of institutional performance criteria must be an approach that recognizes the importance of belief systems, framing effects, and causal and normative ideas: "No institution can be fully understood without taking into account the ways in which the participants themselves conceptualize the nature of their interaction."[49] Vincent Ostrom was convinced of the crucial importance of the epistemic, cognitive, and knowledge processes for institutional order and change, to the point where he coined the term *epistemic choice* to draw attention to the fact that most public choice phenomena are at least in part choices over images, ideas, expectations, and arguments. It is important to understand the role of deliberations, negotiations, and strategies for the rules of the game and their application, as well as the criteria and procedures used in those respects. Ultimately, conclude McGinnis and E. Ostrom, Vincent Ostrom "did not approve of the direction in which the public choice movement developed."[50] He was unhappy with its self-inflicted reductionism and constantly "reminded public choice scholars of the critical importance of ideas and of the complex and ever-changing patterns of compromise that is public administration."[51]

But as significant as those theoretical, epistemic, and methodological points are, it is the normative dimension that is crucial and that must be addressed. Even assuming that real or imaginary theoretical and methodological deficiencies are corrected (and, in fact, current public choice research methodically incorporates most such ideas), that does not guarantee a successful shift toward the applied-level policy frontier. There is little that would signal an escape from the current predicament. However, when the normative side is taken into account on its own terms, things change. A possible clue may be found in the line of argument reflected by Brams in encouraging efforts "to propose and to try to implement reforms that we deem desirable."[52] The key in reading his call should be the words *we deem desirable*. From where does that desirability come? And on what basis? Like it or not, prepared or not, here we enter deep normative territory. Desirability comes from an underlying normative vision. Any systematic effort to offer practical alternatives must be rooted in a normative vision. The choice is to articulate that vision and to try to strengthen it with feasibility and consistency arguments or to leave it implicit and tacit.

The problem is that, even if one shuns a big normative vision and claims that one is interested in only limited, precise suggestions regarding specifically contained public policy cases and situations, sooner or later it will be discovered that a policy problem leads to a public administration problem. A public administration problem leads to political system issues. And political system issues have inescapable constitutional-level implications of broad and deep normative ramifications. In brief, institutional structures of governance come embedded in complex networks of formal and informal relationships that all introduce numerous normative assumptions and implications into the picture. That is, Vincent Ostrom's normative political economy, in which democratic administration comes intertwined with a certain type of political and constitutional order, is not an act of intellectual whim or an accident. It is the result of following the logic of interdependence to its conclusion. Sooner or later, to adopt a policy stance means to tacitly operate with a systemic view and to embrace a series of normative principles that go beyond a particular level or issue that some may try to address in isolation. Like it or not, this is part and parcel of taking seriously the applied level and the policy ambitions of Brams.

That being said—and as a parenthesis within our argument—it is important to note that currently the dominant strategy adopted when it comes to the challenge of the normative dimension takes a different spin. So far, many public choice scholars tried to avoid this challenge by adopting an intermediate strategy—positioning as critics of the status quo but without a clear commitment to an alternative. Thus, per McGinnis and Ostrom, "Public Choice came to be associated with a deeply skeptical view of government" and remained limited to that initial attitude.[53] This is what Steven Brams noted too when he describes the efforts that "never tire of finding fault with a policy or program but do not propose constructive alternatives."[54]

Normatively speaking, skepticism is the cheap and easy version of having a normative position without making any serious effort to fully articulate it. Skepticism is one way of circumventing efforts to sort the following: (a) the concept of the normative ideal and its principles, (b) the institutional formula to materialize the ideal, (c) the feasibility analysis of the institutional formulas that are advanced, and (d) the implementation contextual strategies. Indeed, mounting a skeptical stance seems optimal in several respects. Not only does it require fewer intellectual efforts, it also generates fewer vulnerabilities. The anxiety caused by the potential vulnerability of exposing a normative construction that may be criticized and even labeled as ideological (a terrible word in social science circles) and the anxiety caused by the potential vulnerability of being considered a transgressor of the positive science and value-free science taboos and dogmas seem to play surprisingly important roles in the field. That is an ironic situation especially given Buchanan's explicit and repeated warning that economics itself, the mother discipline, is an enterprise that operates "between predictive science and moral philosophy."[55]

Social Philosophies of Self-Governance: An Ostromian Reconstruction of Governance Theorizing

We have identified the fact that Ostromian democratic administration stands at the confluence of public choice and public administration as the bearer of a deeper and broader social theory encapsulating both positive and normative elements. Again, we do not insist that this social philosophy should be labeled as "classical liberal" or that the Ostroms called it such. However we claim that it is not only compatible with the classical-liberal tradition and in large part demonstrability rooted in it, but also that it is an excellent vehicle for updating and advancing a contemporary version of a governance theory in the same tradition.

A close look at the Ostroms' perspective reveals that it is complex and profound enough to be considered what the literature calls a social theory or social philosophy. Both explicit and implicit in the Ostroms' work are attempts to understand, chart, evaluate, and articulate basic categories about how the social aspects of human life are considered, as well as a willingness to deal with philosophical questions about social order, governance, and social behavior. Encapsulated in the Ostroms' studies are views about the nature and desirability of alternative systems of social organization and an effort toward their philosophical understanding. Even more, their empirical and policy-relevant contributions could be positioned in a telling way at the intersection of several major trends in modern social thinking. To focus only on the more salient and publicly visible pieces of the research produced by the scholars of the Bloomington school, such as those on governance and commons, would be to miss an important part of the Ostroms' theoretical contribution.

Previously we discuss the social philosophy behind the Bloomington school's research agenda and the fact that two facets coexist with some uneasiness. The first is built around the basic insights and concepts regarding public choice's patterns of reasoning, as broadly defined. The second facet, already hinted by the list of points Vincent Ostrom uses to critically assesses mainstream public choice and its evolution—or the development of public choice along mainstream lines—as well as his advancement of epistemic choice, is built around a distinct view of social analysis. That view gives special attention to human action in conditions of uncertainty and social order seen as a knowledge-and-learning adaptation process. It builds on a series of observations about the human condition, fallibility, coercion, and error, as well as on the factors engendering institutional order as a response to the challenges posed by them. Irrespective of how the relationship between those is considered, one thing is clear and remains unchanged: both feature an unambiguous normative engagement on behalf of self-governance and a robust faith in human freedom and human ingenuity. Let us take a closer look at them and explore where they lead and what they suggest as a possible further elaboration on the directions outlined by them.

The Ostroms' initial work makes clear that the alternative theory of public administration they were in search of needed to combine a flexible conceptual framework with a robust analytical apparatus. That was found by the Ostroms in the work of "those political economists concerned with *institutional weaknesses* and *institutional failures* in non-market economies."[56] By comparing and contrasting the approach of those political economists with bureaucratic theorists of the Weber-Wilson school, the Ostroms conclude that the political economy or, more precisely, the public choice approach yielded the insights able to deliver. Public choice, they note, asked the right questions that pointed out the crucial issue of choice among forms of organization, institutional frameworks, or systems of rules. As Elinor Ostrom puts it, "Showing that one institutional arrangement leads to suboptimal performance is not equivalent, however, to showing that another institutional arrangement will perform better."[57] The crucial implication was that there is no single organization or institutional arrangement that is good in all circumstances. The goal of a wise policy is to search for an arrangement that "minimizes the cost associated with institutional weaknesses or institutional failure."[58] Public choice has the capacity to lead to a pluralistic theory of organizational life and of institutional arrangements. That, the Ostroms conclude, made it the best set of existing ideas that could also lead to reconstruction of a paradigm for democratic administration in the twentieth century.

The Ostroms did more than contribute to the ordinary public choice agenda. In fact, their contribution was entirely original, as it opened up a new horizon, not only in public choice but also in traditional political and policy sciences.[59] To see the ground-breaking dimension, it is necessary to return to the basic dichotomy of modern political science, states versus markets, and the corresponding market failure versus state failure theories. The Ostroms mounted a remarkable challenge to that dichotomy. As Elinor Ostrom[60] describes it, her work was a systematic attempt to transcend the basic dichotomy of modern political economy. On the one hand, there is the tradition defined by Adam Smith's theory of social order. Smith and his intellectual descendants focused on the pattern of order and the positive consequences that emerged from the independent actions of individuals pursuing their own interests in a given system of rules. That was the spontaneous order tradition wherein the study of markets— the competition among producers and consumers of pure private goods that leads to better allocation of resources—occupied a preeminent place. On the other hand, there is the tradition rooted in Thomas Hobbes's theory of social order. From that perspective, individuals, pursuing their own interests and trying to maximize their welfare, lead inevitably to chaos and conflict. From that possibility is derived the necessity of a single center of power that imposes order. In that view, social order is the creation of the unique Leviathan, which wields the monopoly power to make and enforce law. Self-organized and independent individuals thus have nothing to do with making order.

The Ostroms' view is that theorists in both traditions managed not only to keep the theories of market and state alienated from each other but also to keep separate the basic social philosophy visions of the two traditions. Smith's concept of market order was considered applicable for all private goods, whereas Hobbes's concept of a single center of power and decision applied for all collective goods. But what if the domains of modern political-economic life could not be understood or organized by relying only on the concepts of markets or states? What if a richer set of policy formulations is needed? Probably the best way to see the Ostroms' work is as an answer to that challenge—an attempt to build an alternative to the basic dichotomy of modern political economy and an effort to find an alternative to the concepts derived from Smith and Hobbes. "The presence of order in the world," Elinor Ostrom writes, "is largely dependent upon the theories used to understand the world. We should not be limited, however, to only the conceptions of order derived from the work of Smith and Hobbes."[61] A theory is needed that "offers an alternative that can be used to analyze and prescribe a variety of institutional arrangements to match the extensive variety of collective goods in the world."[62]

In both their theoretical and empirical work, the Ostroms and their collaborators demonstrate that, even regarding public goods and services that the market cannot supply (and the state pretends to supply efficiently), people can develop complex institutional arrangements to produce and distribute those goods and services. The notion of public economy was meant to accomplish two goals: to save the concept of public from the false notion that it meant the state and centralized systems of governance and to make clear the difference from market economy. In other words, the goal was to show that it is possible to have systems that are neither markets nor states and that preserve the autonomy and freedom of choice of the individual.[63] A new perspective on the institutional structures of that type opened. A complex system was revealed in which not only markets and hierarchies but also more hybrid and peculiar arrangements were combined to generate a special institutional architecture. Public economies, building blocks or areas of polycentrism, are different from state economies and are also different from market economies. That, by any standard, is a radical change of perspective. Public choice was gradually and profoundly converted in the Ostroms' hands into a brand of institutional theory of high relevance for governance theory and its applications.

We have shown so far why the Ostroms' research program, even if limited to the themes and perspectives inspired by public choice, would imply and engender a rich and challenging social philosophy. Let us move now to the other less well-known facet that yields resources and implications only explored up to a limit so far. A closer examination of the Ostroms' corpus of works reveals a second-level, underlying social philosophy of institutional order seen as a knowledge and information process. The fact that Vincent Ostrom nuances it with an almost existentialist concern for the human condition and its limitations makes it even more fascinating.[64]

To unveil the sources of the second dimension of the social theory behind the Bloomington agenda, it is necessary to examine a series of papers Vincent Ostrom wrote in the 1970s and early 1980s, wherein he attempts to crystallize his views on the problem of social order. From that second perspective, the starting point of the study of social order does not rest in a formal definition of rationality, as many fellow public choice and new institutionalist scholars suggest, but rather in an anthropological and historical understanding of "the human condition and what it is about that condition that disposes human beings to search out arrangements with one another that depend upon organization."[65] In the series of stylized facts reflecting that understanding, the first key element is choice. Nonetheless, this view of choice differs from the one advanced by the standard rational choice paradigm. Its basis is not formal or axiomatic but philosophical in the broad classical sense of the word. The argument is shaped by a bold ontological assertion that choice is the basic and defining element for humans and the social order they create. Because choice is a basic form of adaptive behavior, social organization could be seen as the expression of choice as a form of adaptive behavior. Organization solves problems but also creates new ones. Humans must adjust to them through learning and new choices. Solutions create new problems and challenges, and thus the cycle continues. Because it is the outcome of choice and because it engenders new choices, social organization is always fluid and vulnerable to ongoing challenges. Out of the many possible challenges, the most important are not external but could be traced back to human nature itself:

> Any creature that has unique capabilities for learning and generating new knowledge inevitably faces an uncertain future. Learning and the generation of new knowledge are themselves marks of fallibility. Infallible creatures would have no need to learn and generate new knowledge. Fallible creatures need to accommodate their plans to changing levels of information and knowledge.[66]

Fallibility, uncertainty, ignorance, learning, and adaptability thus become key concepts in such a stylized narrative of social order: "An appreciation of the tenuous nature of order in human society is the most important lesson to be learned about the human condition," writes Vincent Ostrom.[67] In the end, the source of vulnerability of humans' social arrangements can be found in the same forces that generate their dynamic resilience. This is a profound paradox and an inexhaustible source of social dilemmas.

Even an overview of the second dimension of the social philosophy of the Bloomington school reveals a departure from the standard political economy and public choice thinking that pivots on incentives and the rules of the game. Behind and beyond it, the argument leads to a problem of knowledge and to a theory of knowledge processes. The knowledge, both practical and theoretical (or the science and the art), to devise rules and meta-rules—institutions and institutional arrangements—and to support their operation by force, deliberation, and reason, is the pivotal element of the vision. Knowledge and learning are stabilizers of social order and drivers of social change. Social order, in the end, is a huge and complex knowledge process. The argument sounds Hayekian, and in many respects it is part of the same family, yet the nuances and differences are significant.

One example is given by the thesis that, as human capabilities for learning and communication increase, as new knowledge increases, the effect is to disrupt existing or established relationships and expectations about the future that are based on them. It is one thing to hope that more knowledge will reduce that uncertainty; it is something else to realize that, whereas new knowledge may reduce uncertainty in some areas, it may increase uncertainty in many others. It is necessary to know not only how to reduce uncertainty in specific domains but also how to manage it in the aggregate. In that respect, one way would be simply to block the growth of new knowledge in society. In such a case, routines based on specific and meticulous prescriptions for each activity become the norm. There is a second possibility, however, and it is the one of most interest to institutional theorists: designing rules and institutional arrangements that leave open to choice an entire range of learning and actions, while simultaneously trying to channel those actions and their knowledge base in the most beneficial way. The domain of learning should be understood in broad terms.

Learning takes place in markets through prices—that is, profits and losses—which signal the best direction for the use of resources. In a similar way, learning takes place through organizational experiments—failures and successes. Bankruptcy provisions in the legal system help deal with failed organizational experiments. The list of examples of rule systems that administer knowledge and implicitly manage uncertainty could continue. Our point is clear: the solution is not to try to block the knowledge process but to work with it through institutional means.

Another example of family resemblance but different emphasis is the thesis that there is a relationship between accepting a vision of the limits of individual and human knowledge and accepting the necessity of an open, pluralist, polycentric political system that functions on the basis of dispersed knowledge. There is, argues Vincent Ostrom, a relationship between assuming the perspective of an omniscient leader and believing in the viability of monocentrism, centralism, and comprehensive social planning. We thus start to see how the two facets of the Ostromian social theory may be linked or at least how they resonate with each other. Those who, as decision makers and advisers, assume "they can take the perspective of an omniscient observer," that they can "see" the "whole picture," are always a potential source of troubles. Their solutions or decisions will increase the predisposition to error, and their perception of their own capabilities may invite tyrannical behavior. In monocentric systems, this property is exponentially more dangerous; it is self-reinforcing.

> Those who have recourse to the perspectives of "omniscient" observers in assessing contemporary problems, also rely on political solutions which have recourse to some single center of authority where officials can exercise omnipotent decision-making capabilities and dealing with the aggregate problems of a society. . . . Somebody who takes the perspective of an omniscient observer will assume that he can "see" the "whole picture, "know" what is "good" for people, and plan or pre-determine the future course of events. Such a presumption is likely to increase proneness to error. Fallible men require reference to decision-making processes where diverse forms of analysis can be mobilized and where each form, of analysis can be subject to critical scrutiny of other analysts and decision-makers.[68]

Another insight regarding institutions and public governance comes to the fore. If a society accepts that all decision makers are fallible, it also recognizes the need to create institutional bulwarks against error. That is, society responds to the necessity of reducing error proneness by building "error-correcting procedures in the organization of decision-making processes."[69] Error-correcting procedures are organizational and institutional processes aimed at facilitating and speeding the rate of learning. Learning is the quintessence of error-fighting mechanisms. Correcting errors is part of any learning process. In this respect, systems of organization, including systems of government, can be viewed as arrangements that either facilitate or stifle opportunities for learning.[70]

This simple thesis has interesting implications for the ways in which we think of institutional performance. We are also pushed even further and deeper into the territory covered by knowledge process theory out of which the Austrian school is the preeminent representative. The Ostroms' approach thus seems to emerge as a pivotal convergence point: a theoretical construction combining traditional public administration themes and questions and public choice, bolstered by the knowledge process theory that is traditionally associated with the Austrian school's insights.

A Remarkable but Neglected Contribution

Our overview of the developments at the junction of public choice and public administration would not be complete without discussion of the remarkable but neglected work of Michael Spicer. For years, Spicer was one of the few scholars working in the mainstream of the field of public administration who was engaged at the interface of public administration, public choice, and the Austrian school's knowledge process theory. In a series of articles, some collected in Spicer's works,[71] he elaborates a set of new arguments that further develop the ideas of the Ostroms, Buchanan, and Hayek, and calibrates those ideas to the themes and debates of public administration. Spicer provides an impressive demonstration of the power of the alternative approach in public administration and governance analysis. In Chapter 2, we discuss Spicer's take on public administration, which focuses on disperse knowledge, discretion, constitutional political economy rules, and federalism. Here we use three more examples to illustrate Spicer's remarkable contribution: his elaboration of a contractarian approach to public administration, his interpretation of Hayek's take on public administration, and his public choice analysis of motivation in bureaucratic organizations.

Let us start with Spicer's contractarian approach to public administration.[72] One of the main conceptual tools public choice scholars use for performing normative comparative institutional analysis—for example, for the comparative analysis of voting systems,[73] tax policy,[74] and redistribution—is social contract theory.[75] According to that approach, it is assumed that risk-adverse individuals are placed behind a veil of ignorance with respect to their own positions in society and given the task of agreeing about the broad rules that will govern their society. If existing institutions cannot reasonably be justified from such an analysis, there is a strong case for reform, a strong case that existing institutions are unjust and deliberately discriminate against some groups for the benefit of others. Could the same theoretical apparatus be used to analyze public administration? Spicer argues that, although such a "methodology . . . is clearly outside the mainstream of public administration, most of the conclusions drawn from it are not."[76] The social contract approach provides a fresh perspective on existing debates in public administration, "helping scholars think through the normative implications of different systems of public administration."[77]

The main insight provided by Spicer's social contract approach concerns the problem of discretion in public administration. To what extent should public administration employees be constrained to be agents of the political sphere? A common assumption is that, ideally, politicians in democracies are perfect agents of the voters and public administration employees are perfect agents of politicians. However, what happens when, with an element of realism, two things are accepted: (a) owing to rational ignorance, voters cannot fully control politicians; and (b) as a result of Arrow's impossibility theorem, a coherent social welfare function might not emerge from voters' preferences? Spicer argues that a space is opened for administrative discretion as a tool for constraining politicians and preventing exploitation of the general public.[78]

Spicer also notes that there are two important sources of government exploitation. "First, public administration may be used as an instrument of exploitation by political leaders. . . . Second, public administrators themselves may exploit citizens in the exercise of bureaucratic discretion."[79] Private exploitation also exists, but "whereas the purpose of public organizations is, in part, to check private power, the purpose of designing constitutions is, in major part, to check public power."[80] Moreover, the focus on private exploitation is a distraction because, on the one hand, "competition among private organizations in many areas will often limit the exploitative power" and, on the other hand, "an important, if not the most important, way in which private organizations can exploit citizens is by gaining control of the coercive power of government."[81]

That focus on the two layers of possible government exploitation led Spicer to conclude that the optimal form of organization, on which people behind the veil of ignorance would probably focus, is what he calls the constrained discretion of the public administration:

> Such discretion makes it possible for public administrators to avoid being used by political leaders as an instrument of exploitation. . . . It is desirable that any one political leader or group of leaders should not have absolute authority over public bureaus. Absolute unity of command over public bureaus by any one group, while conducive to the effective and efficient achievement of its goals, increases significantly the risk that some citizens will be exploited by that group through public bureaus. Therefore, there is merit in having public bureaus accountable to more than one political master.[82]

That constrained discretion has two enabling conditions, one concerned with discretion and the other with the constraints on it.

How is bureaucratic discretion enabled? First, it cannot exist unless there is "some fragmentation of political authority or some separation of powers within government," such that bureaucratic discretion exists when the centers of political power are in conflict.[83] Here, Spicer builds on Tullock's work and obviously Vincent Ostrom's.[84] Second, bureaucratic discretion is impossible unless "administrative appointments [are] protected from political control so that the pressure which political leaders can exert on individual public administrators is limited."[85] Third, Spicer endorses Mainzer's idea of representative bureaucracy as a way of ensuring that bureaucrats are indeed motivated to oppose political attempts to exploit the public.[86] If public administrators are hired "from a broad range of economic, social, cultural and racial groups, . . . this increases the likelihood that significant numbers of bureaucrats as citizens will personally bear any costs which political leaders may seek to impose on any particular group through exploitative policies. As a result, there will be public administrators whose self-interest will influence them to block or subvert such policies."[87]

That argument does not lead, of course, to the conclusion that public administration should have unlimited discretion. How can public administration be limited? Spicer is skeptical of using only self-imposed moral constraints. He suggests, in a clear public choice vein, the use of a combination of rules and monitoring. The rules can limit budgets, require transparency with respect to spending, and specify hiring and firing practices. Spicer notes that, as a departure from standard arguments, "the purpose of such rules and procedures from a contractarian perspective should not be to force the administration to more closely follow the directives of political leaders. Rather, the purpose of rules and procedures should be to reduce the ability of administrators to use such discretion to enrich themselves at the expense of citizens."[88]

Finally, perhaps the most interesting conclusion Spicer draws from the contractarian perspective is that the "optimal type of public administration may vary between different levels of government."[89] Generally speaking, "the greater the fear of exploitation by political leaders, the greater the degree of constrained discretion which is desirable."[90] More specifically, Spicer notes that bureaucratic constrained discretion can act as a substitute for exit. Lower-cost exit makes political exploitation less likely, and it is generally easier to escape local governments than it is to escape central governments. This implies that "a greater degree of unity of command and political control than will be seen as acceptable in the administration of government in local and regional jurisdictions," whereas "in the case of central government, where exit from the jurisdiction is harder, a greater degree of constrained discretion in public administration will be seen as necessary to limit exploitation."[91]

Spicer's skillful elaboration and extension of public choice is further illustrated by his approach to motivating people in bureaucratic organizations.[92] Spicer elaborates the basic implications of Olson's logic of collective action,[93] and of public choice theory more broadly, for setting up efficient reward systems in private and public organizations. His approach builds on the team production model of the economists Armen Alchian and Harold Demsetz and differs from Tullock's 2005 book *Bureaucracy* in that he focuses mainly on collective action problems rather than diffusion of information problems in hierarchical systems.[94]

Spicer notes that there are three basic reward models: "rewards based on individual effort measured against some absolute standard, rewards based on individual effort compared to the effort of other subordinates, and rewards based on group effort."[95] The first type is commonly assumed in basic microeconomic models, and it is convenient for avoiding collective action issues, but it is highly unrealistic. Workers can alter their performance by choosing which activities to perform, as well as "the pace at which they perform them, and the quality of their performance."[96] These issues are often hard to monitor, and "in many cases, an absolute standard for measuring effort simply does not exist" because "the development of absolute standards that measure the full range of performance, rather than simply part of it, is difficult."[97] We are thus left to focus on the other two types of reward systems. Both are imperfect, as they reward individuals partly on the basis of how others are performing.

The main conclusion of Spicer's analysis is that which of the two reward systems works better for promoting organizational goals depends on a number of factors. He discusses in relative detail four interrelated factors: (a) the size of the group, (b) the jointness of production (that is, "the extent to which successful provision of the collective good requires contributions by all individuals in the group"[98]), (c) rates of personnel turnover, and (d) workers' altruism and loyalty. Small teams, with high jointness of production and low turnover, are better managed by group rewards. By contrast, large teams, with relatively independent workers and high turnovers, are better managed by relative rewards. That is because, in the first case, cooperation among workers is relatively easy to achieve and sustain, and hence a manager wants to avoid a situation in which workers collude to keep production efforts low. By rewarding individuals on the basis of group outcomes, the manager ensures that cooperation among workers is aligned with the organization's goals. By contrast, in the second case, cooperation among workers is relatively difficult, and free-riding is relatively easy. In this case, it is difficult for workers to reliably collude to keep efforts low. By rewarding relative individual efforts, the manager sets up a competitive environment for workers that benefits the organization's goals.

Such conclusions are important for both private and public organizations. For example, Spicer notes that "teachers and social workers exhibit such independence" of production.[99] They also form relatively large groups and, because of relatively high job security, have low turnover rates. The conclusion here is that teachers should be rewarded on the basis of relative individual efforts, rather than commonly shared pay rates. Because of teachers' unions, that is not the case in many countries, and, predictably, it leads to low quality of education (the organizational goal).

Thus, we see how a relatively simple application of public choice theory to public administration leads to a clear diagnosis of why some problems are pervasive and also suggests reforms that are possible, although perhaps politically difficult. As Spicer notes, sometimes a manager may have the capacity to alter either the reward system or the group size and the interdependency of workers' activities. As such, reforms of public administration need not necessarily focus solely on the faulty reward system. Public unions may make it extremely difficult to set up competitive reward systems for workers, but group sizes and interdependencies can perhaps be modified.

Furthermore, Spicer notes that departures from strict assumptions of self-interest do not significantly challenge those conclusions.[100] In fact, altruism and group loyalty can, under certain conditions, make things worse from the point of view of organizational goals. That is because they make worker collusion easier. Hence, if a mistaken reward system is adopted (given the size of the group, jointness of production, and turnover), altruism and group loyalty will compound the negative consequences of the error. Spicer notes that managers can, in principle, have some effect on worker-to-worker loyalty by rotating workers in different teams. But, ideally, the reward system itself would make this unnecessary. In the case of public administration, group loyalty is often encouraged and managed through large-scale public unions, usually to the detriment of the quality of service.

The third and last illustration of Spicer's contribution gives a sense of the broadness of his vision through his take on public administration, social science, and political association.[101] In Spicer's 1998 article, he adds another layer to his public choice and Hayekian interpretation of public administration by delving into political theorist Michael Oakeshott's distinction between understanding the state as a purposive organization versus a civil association[102] and by comparing how the convergent assumptions about the nature of the state lead to different ideas about the use of social science as a guide in public administration (see figure 5.1). Spicer argues, "Despite this continuing faith in the applicability of scientific techniques to the practice of public administration and public policy, the promises of the social sciences in these areas remain largely unfulfilled."[103] What is the explanation for the continuing failure?

Spicer amply documents that, in the past hundred years, most writers in public administration, including the most prominent figures, conceptualize the state as a "purposive association . . . in which individuals recognize themselves as bound together in terms of the joint pursuit of some common set of substantive purposes or ends."[104] According to that vision, states have a "coherent set of common purposes to which individuals are expected to subordinate their own particular purposes."[105] Furthermore, this "implies a particular vision of government" according to which "the role of government becomes one of identifying the common substantive purposes or ends for a political community and of managing the actions of various individuals and other resources in the community toward the attainment of those ends."[106] Such a vision of government is connected to a particularly optimistic and hopeful vision of the capacity of social science and reason to discover effective management techniques:

> Because of this faith in the powers of reason, those who tend to be optimistic about the ability of men and women to work cooperatively through government for common purposes or ends also tend to be optimistic about the ability of science and experts to provide guidance in this regard. . . . Many public administration writers have also explicitly expressed a belief that science can and should be harnessed toward the achievement of substantive state ends.[107]

However, argues Spicer, that is an illusion. Even setting aside the normative question of whether it would be desirable for states to become purposive organizations with goals "to which individuals are expected to subordinate their own personal ends," the fact is they virtually never are:

> The problem here is that this vision does not accurately describe the type of political association in which we live. It is only on rare occasions of

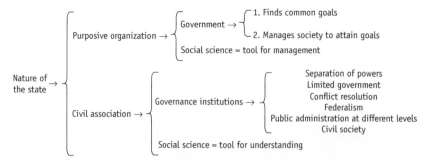

Figure 5.1 Two concepts of the nature of the state, government, and social science.

national consensus, such as during World War II, that our nation has really operated as a purposive association. For most of our history, we have not generally pursued a vision of the state as a purposive association but rather we have sought what Oakeshott . . . terms a *societas* or a "civil association."[108]

This point matters for several reasons. First, it provides a perspective on the connection between public administration and the American constitutional project, in particular James Madison's vision in which the function of civil association rules "is not to secure the achievement of any particular set of substantive purposes or objectives for the community."[109] Instead, the function "is solely to define the parameters by which individuals act and interact with each other as they pursue their own particular interests or purposes, either alone or in concert with others who happen to share those interests or purposes."[110] Spicer continues:

This vision of civil association provides the basis for our notion of a government that possesses limited powers over the actions and dealings of individuals and groups in society. . . . In a civil association, it is not necessary that individuals undertake particular actions that conform to certain substantive ends of the state because a civil association does not explicitly posit any such ends. Individuals in a civil association are permitted substantial discretion over their actions within a framework of rules that serve to limit the harm that their actions can impose on others.[111]

Second, this vision of a civil association does not require a social science of control and management. Social science has failed and will most likely continue to fail as a tool of control and management because a civil association "allows individuals to exercise a substantial degree of discretion in their actions and thereby to draw upon knowledge that is inaccessible to social scientists."[112] Consequently, "public administration writers who seek to inform practice need to be more modest and realistic with respect to what [social science] can contribute to practice." Also, other intellectual traditions can provide useful insight to the practice of public administration. In particular, "a sophisticated understanding of constitutionalism would seem essential to the practice of public administration in a civil association," and through "history and philosophy . . . we can come to a better understanding of how we, as human actors, have come to interpret the rules that govern our actions."[113]

To sum up, one could find in M. Spicer's multifaceted work an ingenious development of themes defining the program advanced by the Ostroms. The themes are further elaborated in a nuanced direction, and in many cases are reinvented and reinterpreted through the Hayekian and public choice insights. As such, that aspect of Spicer's work is an ongoing reference point and a source of inspiration for our effort here to advance the classical-liberal approach to governance analysis. This conceptual apparatus—as further elaborated in the next chapter—and the insights built on it will be our analytical and interpretive guidelines in Part III of the book.

6

Heterogeneity, Co-production, and Polycentric Governance

The Ostroms' Public Choice Institutionalism Revisited

Elinor and Vincent Ostrom have profoundly influenced our current understanding of the institutional order, of collective action, and of governance systems, and their achievements have been widely recognized. In 2009, Elinor, along with Oliver E. Williamson, was awarded the Nobel Prize in Economic Sciences, and Vincent received the American Political Science Association's John Gaus Award in 2005. Over time, their work was approached from different disciplinary and thematic angles and was considered a contribution to the study of many topics, including institutional diversity, common-pool resources, metropolitan governance, and institutional design. Yet as previous chapters establish, one aspect unites their many contributions and gives the Ostroms' work a special coherence and relevance for political sciences. That aspect is the attempt to build at the junction of the fields of public administration and public choice an approach that goes beyond the traditional dichotomies of market versus state or private versus public, which underlie not only the academic study of governance and politics but also public discourse and policy practice.

The Ostroms' work identifies a domain of complex social settings and institutional arrangements with features that elude the standard typologies framed by the private-public dualism. Such hybrid institutions, involving private-public mixed arrangements, quasi-markets, quasi-governments, and nonprofit and civil society organizations, are not adequately captured by the idealized models of a pure market or a pure government.[1] At the same time, it has become clearer that this complexity is an inescapable and defining component of what has traditionally been considered the realm of public affairs or public governance. Moreover, the existence of complexity is not of mere academic interest. In recent decades, recognition of its importance in public administration and public policy, as illustrated by the "Reinventing Government" task force of the Clinton administration and the New Public Management interest in private-public partnerships, quasi-markets, quasi-governments, and co-governance, has grown to the point that many authors speak about a paradigm change.[2]

The variety of possible institutional arrangements in this hybrid and heterogeneous space challenges our collective institutional imagination to go beyond existing theories in political science and economics. One of the Ostroms' main contributions was the development of a sophisticated framework for understanding and evaluating such arrangements. Yet despite their efforts in highlighting the importance of this domain, as well as in giving it one of the first conceptual articulations, their theoretical instruments are still not as widely appreciated as they should be. Instead, borrowing network theory or various disparate models from the microeconomics of industrial organization and pivoting on the principal agent problem seem to prevail. These instruments are not inappropriate or incorrect, but their relevance and usefulness can be fully grasped only when the Ostroms' alternative is introduced to the picture. The complexity of the subject matter requires not only a multitude of carefully chosen models but also a consolidated framework for putting all the pieces together.

This chapter is, first and foremost, an attempt to shed light on the Ostromian alternative and what it can deliver. The chapter elaborates the lines introduced in earlier chapters and the claims that the Ostroms crafted the basic building blocks for a systematic approach to the complex domain of governance in hybridity and heterogeneity and that they spelled out the logic that unites these blocks in a potential theoretical system that may be used in redefining the classical-liberal perspective on governance in the twenty-first century.[3] Nonetheless, this is still a work in progress, and various aspects of this project continue to be in intermediate stages of development. In this chapter we further develop two of Ostroms' claims. First, we identify one important and implicitly present but explicitly missing element of the system: a theory of value or, more precisely, a theory of the heterogeneous and ambiguous nature of social valuation. Second, we illustrate how the logical analysis of the problem of the conversion of heterogeneous private values into public value—a process essential for the construction of social order—leads naturally to the Ostroms' theme of co-production, a concept that emerges in our reconstruction as pivotal to their system in more than one way. We then demonstrate how, with the theory of co-production, we are now in a position to understand the nature and significance of polycentricity, which is the capstone of the Ostromian system introduced in Chapter 5. Finally, the present chapter shows how the analytical and theoretical pieces mentioned above fit together. The axis of value heterogeneity, co-production, and polycentricity is revealed as the backbone of a flexible and robust theoretical framework, well equipped to (a) organize empirical data, (b) generate theoretical conjectures, and (c) inspire normative and institutional design insights about phenomena emerging beyond conventional boundaries of the private and public sectors.

What Is at Stake?

The Problem of Value Heterogeneity and Conflicts of Vision

As Chapter 2 describes, a theory of value seems to be the natural complement of any governance approach based on a taxonomy or theory of private or public goods. That fact is recognized rather early in the public choice literature.[4] But once value theory is introduced to the picture, it changes in significant ways our understanding of the nature of goods and especially the private-public goods distinction. The fact that preferences about both private and public goods are heterogeneous and incommensurable is an implicit theme in much of the Bloomington school's work.[5] Yet, to date, it has not been fully articulated, although it is one of the defining features. While the study of social choice and public economics has focused on the problem of aggregating individual preferences into a single representative perspective—in most cases following the mechanics of formal voting systems or showing some interest for the informal cultural mechanisms that create focal points, the Bloomington school takes value heterogeneity for granted—without assuming that it can or, in most cases, should be aggregated away—and asks instead what the institutional arrangements are that make it possible for people with different values to peacefully coexist and self-govern. In Chapter 1 we see that this was also one of Buchanan's main concerns. Vincent Ostrom asks, given a world constituted by patterns of dominance, "Is it possible to conceive of binding and workable relationships being achieved by mutual agreement among colleagues working with one another?"[6] Furthermore, "Is it possible to use problem-solving modes of inquiry to achieve a more steady course, by using political processes to craft common knowledge and shared communities of understanding, establish patterns of social accountability, and maintain mutual trust?"[7]

The very idea of how a good political system looks is thus changed and redefined. The goal is not to look for the best way to aggregate values into a single coherent system but instead to seek the best way in which heterogeneous, incommensurable, and incomparable values can coexist and if not enrich at least not undermine each other. From the Bloomington school perspective, the systemic centripetal aggregation of values is more a tool of last resort for some values and some limited cases rather than for the main concern with most values, most of the time. Going beyond the ideal theory or the general social choice approach, the Ostroms and their collaborators identify one principle or institutional formula that creates the conditions for coping with that challenge: polycentricity.[8] Polycentricity is an institutional arrangement that involves a multiplicity of decision-making centers acting independently but under the constraints of an overarching set of norms and rules that restrict externalities and create the conditions for an emergent outcome to occur at the level of the entire system through a bottom-up competitive process. These overarching norms and rules are usually created and enforced by the decision centers themselves rather than by an outside third party, and they are responsible for how productive and resilient the emergent order within the polycentric system is. As revealed by Elinor Ostrom's research on common-pool resources management, when the social choice processes that create the overarching rules satisfy certain principles, the resulting rules tend to be better and the system more successful.[9]

The key of the Ostromian system is that polycentricity is the solution to the problems created by belief and value heterogeneity. Furthermore, it is the institutional arrangement that turns this heterogeneity into an asset. As previously noted by one of us (Aligica),[10] the research on the impact of heterogeneity upon outcomes is strangely contradictory: on one hand, it seems that heterogeneity undermines stability and social cohesion, but on the other hand, it is the very fuel for progress and resilience. The solution to this paradox is that only a subset of societies manages to deal with heterogeneity successfully. Those that do reap great benefits from it. Heterogeneity thus holds a great promise but also a great risk.

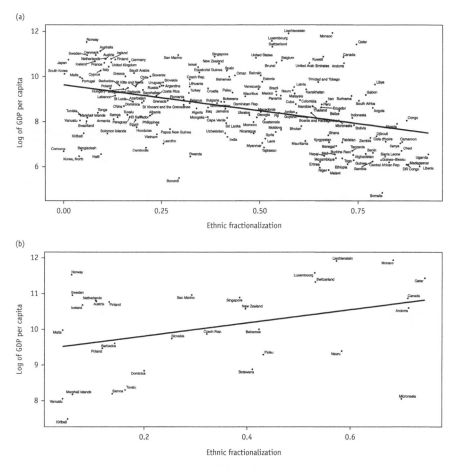

Figure 6.1 Relationship between ethnic fractionalization and GDP per capita.
(a) Including all countries. (b) Including only politically stable countries.
Source of data: Jan Teorell, Stefan Dahlberg, Sören Holmberg, Bo Rothstein, Anna Khomenko, and Richard Svensson, *The Quality of Government Standard Dataset, Version Jan16* (University of Gothenburg: The Quality of Government Institute, 2016).

A quick way to visualize this idea is by looking at the relationship between ethnic, linguistic, and religious fractionalization on the one hand, and GDP per capita on the other (figures 6.1–3). When we consider a sample of all countries, the relationship is clearly negative—higher levels of fractionalization corresponding to lower levels of development. However, when we consider only the subsample of *politically stable* countries, the relationship between ethnic-linguistic fractionalization and development reverses and becomes positive. In other words, for the countries that manage to achieve stability, ethnic-linguistic fractionalization turns into an asset. Interestingly, the same does not hold for religious fractionalization; its negative relationship to development becomes even stronger for the subset of politically stable countries.[11]

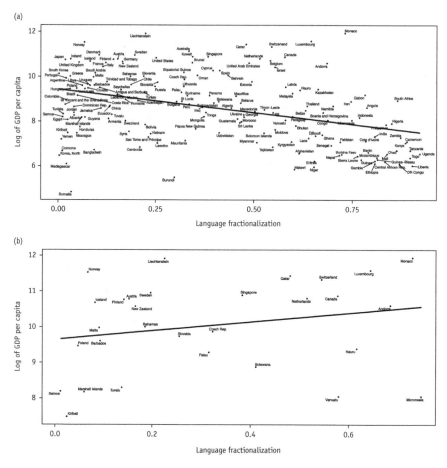

Figure 6.2 Relationship between language fractionalization and GDP per capita. (a) Including all countries. (b) Including only politically stable countries. *Source of data:* Teorell et al., *The Quality of Government Standard Dataset.*

Why is it that some societies manage to turn heterogeneity into an asset, while others are subverted by it? Why is religious fractionalization harder to turn into an asset than ethnic and linguistic fractionalization? To understand the operating principles of polycentricity and its normative significance becomes a critical task. As Vincent Ostrom elaborated in *The Meaning of Democracy and the Vulnerabilities of Democracies,*[12] a successful self-governing system provides its members the greatest possible opportunity for living under rules of their own choice, hence leading to complex federalist structures, while at the same time preserving a broad "shared community of understanding" such that political and social stability is not undermined. In other words, a successful self-governing system is polycentric: it allows institutional diversity within itself, capturing the benefits of such diversity in turns of dynamism, creativity, and resilience, while preserving a legitimate set of overarching rules and norms that are used to curtail negative externalities and solve conflicts.

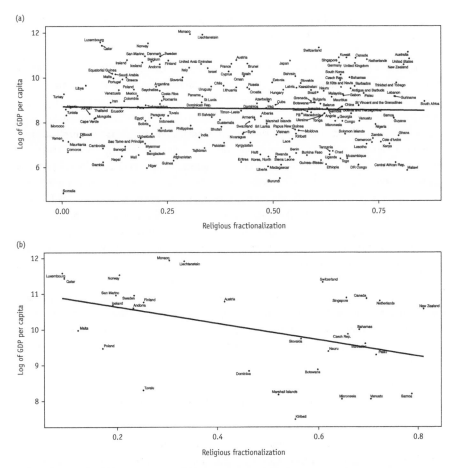

Figure 6.3 Relationship between religious fractionalization and GDP per capita.
(a) Including all countries. (b) Including only politically stable countries.
Source of data: Teorell et al., *The Quality of Government Standard Dataset.*

The biggest challenge entailed in building such polycentric systems is that externalities are often subjective and people often strongly disagree with respect to what counts as "public." For instance, is education simply a private good, helping individuals develop useful skills for which they are later compensated in the labor market, or is it more? How much more? What exactly are the public positive and negative spillovers of education, how important are they, and, if they are important, how would an education system be best managed to limit the negatives and enhance the positives? Such questions have no obvious, simple, and uncontroversial answers. And the answers are bound to depend on certain subjective value judgments as well as on uncertain estimates of various causal connections. Moreover, such issues are pervasive and concern not just education but many other quasi-public, quasi-private matters. We cannot simply just declare what "the best" solution is and go ahead and implement it. Instead, we need to think about the institutional arrangements that facilitate a peaceful and inclusive negotiation process between parties with different values and visions. As a first step, we need to better understand how preferences about other people's behaviors interact.

Polycentricity thus entails developing a descriptive theory of the nature of public values, of how they materialize in various states of affairs in the public realm, of how they interact and evolve over time, and of how they relate to the variety of private values and preferences. The theory of value heterogeneity looms in the background of the private-public distinction with all its normative and institutional implications.

Such a perspective combines positive and normative theorizing. One of the most neglected facets of the theory of collective goods is the crucial role subjectivity plays. The extent to which a good is deemed to be rivalrous and whether it generates externalities depend on the subjective value estimations of the agents involved, which is not something intrinsic to the good. As positive social scientists, we must accept, as a basic corollary of methodological individualism and of the subjectivity of values, that only the individual decides whether something is or is not of personal concern. This is a fact but one that has significant normative implications. In practice, certain values are imposed on individuals regardless of whether they think it is their concern. That is why an understanding is needed of the details of the social and political process by which some values, but not others, end up being generally enforced and embedded into practice. Hence, the first important matter at stake in this chapter is to bring into the open a certain type of subjective value theory as a key component of institutional theory and analysis.

Co-production and the Creation of Public Value

Co-production describes a situation in which the consumer's input is an essential part of the production process. In many respects, the microeconomic theory that completely separates the producer from the consumer, is an idealization. For instance, even something as simple as driving a car involves co-production. But this standard idealization is mostly harmless in typical microeconomic contexts. This is not the case when we deal with collective goods, and in particular with the problem of establishing the value of those goods, which involves potential conflicts. In a self-governing democratic system the rules satisfy the preferences of those subjected to those rules, and, for this to happen, citizens need to have some input into the creation of those rules (when exit and moving costs are non-trivial, Tiebout competition only takes you so far).[13] In other words, democracy can be understood as a co-production of rules.

A value-based approach positions us to reconsider the problem of the creation of public value in governance systems, especially with respect to co-production. It is necessary to understand not only the concept of public value but also how it is created, that is, to better understand the social, economic, and political processes by which groups and societies create a state of affairs deemed valuable by some (preferably many) of their members. The theory of co-production is one of many relatively well-developed attempts to delve into the "how" question.[14] Yet until recently,[15] the theory has contained a technical public choice ambiguity that has somehow escaped notice for the past thirty years: in its standard accounts, the theory assumes that agents work to maximize total output (i.e., they all altruistically work for the public good) but neglects the fact that agents may also maximize individual profit. It is unrealistic to assume that individuals only try to maximize total output or collective benefits while entirely ignoring their own individual profits. Once individual concerns are introduced, we obtain a novel type of market failure that the literature has otherwise neglected. This type of market failure is an important but ignored legacy of the Ostroms' work, and it helps us further articulate a distinctive approach to governance on normative individualist lines, thereby circumventing the synoptic delusion.

This market failure is related to the well-known team production problem, but it differs in a crucial regard.[16] Whereas team production involves cooperation for producing something for an outside consumer, in the case of co-production the good is consumed by members of the production team. For this reason, the problem of monitoring can be solved more easily because the agents have a vested interested in having the good produced in the appropriate quantities and qualities.

The comparison between team production and co-production gives us a new and more rigorous understanding of the synoptic illusion (discussed in Chapter 1). The synoptic illusion is basically the belief that co-production problems can be addressed by using a team-production solution, namely top-down management. In fact, the team-production approach makes matters worse for co-production because it further removes the capacity of beneficiaries/producers to control the process, and it actually adds a third party who may have less of a stake in the production process.

This reasoning brings us back to the problem of polycentricity. As Elinor Ostrom and the economist Peter Leeson note, an important feature of polycentric arrangements is the ability to solve monitoring and enforcement problems.[17] The economists Armen Alchian and Harold Demsetz argue that in team production the top-down organized firm is created to solve the monitoring problem; by contrast, in the case of co-production, the monitoring problem is more effectively solved by polycentric arrangements.[18] That is why recognition of the co-production aspect of the production (seen as the process of constructing a public good or service) and provision (seen as the process of selecting the bundle of public goods or services for a collective consumption unit) of many public goods undermines the case for an overly centralized public administration.[19] In effect, advocates of centralization confuse co-production with team production and consequently inappropriately apply the firm model to public administration.

These arguments bring a new light to the problem of choosing the optimal scale for the production or provision of various public goods and enhance the case for the separation of public goods provision and production. Features, such as hybridity and heterogeneity, that define the third sector (roughly the nonprofit sector in contrast to the public sector and the private sector) thus become more intelligible.

Finally, these and other analytical and theoretical insights, seen in their logical and theoretical conjunction on the axis of value heterogeneity, co-production, and polycentricity, provide a better sense of the analytical and normative potential of the Ostroms' theoretical framework. Those insights constitute a strong argument in support of efforts to theoretically capture and precisely apply that potential. Those insights also happen to be timely efforts, as the increasingly salient phenomena emerging in public administration and business at the boundary between the private and public sectors, far from trivial, is changing the contours and configurations of the political and public domains. As such, they increasingly capture the attention of both scholars and decision makers.

Values, Evaluation, and Normative Heterogeneity

The semantic ambiguity surrounding the concept of values is notorious: values as norms, values as intuitions, values as cultural ideals, values as beliefs, values as generalized attributes, values as transcendental, values naturalized. At first glance, our discussion seems destined to focus on abstract normative principles. However, a discussion about values is as much a discussion about possible states of affairs—that is, possible features or states of the world—as it is about principles.

Let us focus more precisely on public values creation, the process of generating something that is "publicly valuable." A society or community engages in a collective process by which a certain input of resources, time, energy, or ideas is transformed into an output of public relevance. The output may always be evaluated in light of basic values or normative principles. To say that "public values are created" is shorthand for saying that the output—goods, services, or a certain state of affairs produced by combining ideas and circumstances via exchange—meets certain normative criteria. If the criteria are not met, value has not been created. The better the output satisfies those criteria, the more value has been created.

That may sound too abstract and general, so let us illustrate with an example of a collective action problem. Before the mid-1970s, Washington state's Pacific salmon fisheries were centrally managed, and policymakers faced a typical knowledge problem: the "centrally regulated system had focused on aggregations of species and spent little time on the freshwater habitats that are essential to maintain the viability of salmon fisheries over the long term."[20] In the mid-1970s, the management system changed as a result of a court decision that granted to "Indian tribes that had signed treaties more than a century before" the right "to 50% of the fish that passed through the normal fishing areas of the tribes."[21] Consequently, the state was required "to develop a 'co-management' system that involves both the state of Washington and the 21 Indian tribes in diverse policy roles related to salmon."[22] A new system of incentives was created at the local level. On the one hand, the state's continued involvement assured individual tribes that free-riding by other tribes would not be tolerated and, therefore, that their conservation efforts were worthwhile. On the other hand, the co-management system gave individual tribes an important economic stake in the resource, which in turn prompted them to solve the knowledge problem.

Thus, a change in institutional structures successfully transformed the resource—salmon—into a valuable item. The pre-1970s state of affairs was inferior to the later state of affairs, as judged by both the Indian tribes and state officials. The concrete mechanism by which the change occurred involved the better incentive of the local actors to gather the relevant information and act on that information. This example also highlights the importance of a fruitful interaction between a higher-level governance authority (the state) and local actors. The volume edited by Michael McGinnis, *Polycentric Governance and Development*, provides numerous other similar examples.[23]

In brief, from this perspective, to create public value is to create a state of affairs in a social system that as many people as possible consider to be an improvement over the previous state. But such simplicity is deceptive. We start to understand why if we unpack the notion of public value in the logical components of its conceptual space.[24]

The process of evaluation may be conceptualized through a framework with four elements: V, the value; E, the evaluator; S, the observed system (interpreted by E as a "value bearer"); and A, the state of affairs of S.

V, the Value

When evaluating and designing institutional arrangements, Vincent Ostrom considers such values as efficiency, resilience, fairness, and participation rate.[25] Similarly, the scholars Torben Beck Jorgensen and Barry Bozeman suggest an entire list: stability, social cohesion, common good, responsiveness, adaptability, productivity, and effectiveness.[26]

We will not delve into the philosophical complexities of this discussion here. Nonetheless, given their implicit role in the discussion, it is useful to briefly focus on the distinction between personal preferences (values in the common economic sense) and social norms (values in the broader normative sense). When talking about *public* values in this context, we are by necessity placing ourselves in the realm of the discussion about social norms, rather than personal preferences. However, the distinction between personal preferences and moral values is often fuzzy and ever changing, given that preferences can become moralized or norms can devolve into mere personal preferences.[27] One way to make sense of this fuzziness is to see social norms as a subset of preferences, a special kind of preferences about other people's behavior. Namely, they are preferences about other people's behavior that an individual wants everyone else to have as well—that is, it is unacceptable for anyone not to have them. Thus, we can see how moral phenomena are intrinsically connected to individual preferences and that the two could be addressed in conjunction in various models of complementarity or trade-offs.[28] Our approach is to follow Buchanan's discussion of the matter, spanning from his *Calculus of Consent* to *Ethics and Economic Progress*, and to identify values as a special kind of preference for the purpose of being able to use the rational choice apparatus in understanding them.

Buchanan classifies values in three categories.[29] His first type of values corresponds to the rule-utilitarian perspective: because the world is complicated, we cannot predict every consequence of our actions; instead, we rely on various general heuristics. "The individual, in isolation, may find it advantageous, in his or her long-term interest, to impose binding constraints on his or her own behavior, quite apart from the actions of others."[30] For instance, it is personally advantageous to develop a reputation of honesty, and it is difficult to predict when a lie would not be caught—hence, one should, under most circumstances be honest and avoid the risk of tarnishing one's reputation for minor benefits.

A second type of values correspond to exchanges. Although one may benefit from engaging in act X, one benefits from living in a society where no one does X. Hence, one offers restraint in exchange for everyone else offering restraint. One may benefit from stealing something, but one will still support the laws against theft and accept the legitimacy of punishment if caught stealing. As such, "constraints are accepted as the 'price' that must be paid, the 'bad' that must be suffered, to secure the expected 'good' that is represented by the reciprocal constraints on their behavior that others accept as their part of the contractual exchange."[31]

Finally, a third type of value, and the one Buchanan considers to be the most interesting and important, is the case when one benefits from others being subjected to a given rule or norm. " 'How do I want others to behave, both in general and toward me in particular?' This question, rather than 'How do *I* want to behave?' becomes the starting point for ethical norms and percepts."[32] This is related to other people's *preferences*. Buchanan notes that, to the extent that preferences can be altered,

> each party will find it advantageous to invest resources in modifying the preferences of others so as to produce the desired behavioral changes. If the institutions of moral-ethical persuasion, which I have called "the preacher" in the title of this chapter, are even marginally effective, each party to a potential interaction will have the incentive to "pay the preacher", that is, to invest in bringing the ordering of others around to the directions that will generate the spillover or external benefits promised.[33]

As an example, Buchanan discusses at length "Puritan values" of hard work and thrift.[34] He notes that when people work harder or longer, this is mathematically equivalent to there being more workers. Following Adam Smith's remark that "division of labor is limited by the extent of the market," and that division of labor leads to higher productivity, we can conclude that hard work creates a positive externality to society as a whole. Similarly, saving has a positive externality thanks to providing funds for investment, which expand the size of the whole economy. Buchanan's point here is that wages and interest rates do not *fully* compensate individuals for the social value they provide when they are hard-working or when they save. A tragedy of the commons problem seems to be emerging here, with everyone preferring that others work hard while they take their leisure. However, many societies have escaped this tragedy of the commons by creating ethical norms supporting hard work and thrift, and they may have done this by, quite literally, "paying the preacher."

For our discussion, a deeper look into the ontological nature and epistemological status of values is irrelevant. What is important to note is that when we talk about value creation, we are not talking about creating or reinventing new foundational normative principles. We are talking about new states of affairs, A, which are induced by production, exchange, or mere reconfiguration, in the light of a value, V.

E, the Evaluator

The second element in the puzzle is the holder of values, the actor making the normative judgment. Buchanan's discussion in *Ethics and Economic Progress* generally assumes that a rough consensus emerges via a culturally evolutionary process with respect to which values should be promoted. This is a similar perspective to Hayek's and Elinor Ostrom's.[35] But we can easily expand this economic perspective to deal with heterogeneity as Buchanan emphasizes the methodologically individualistic nature of his theory. He notes that his argument

> is not one that sets up some external criterion, whether this be economic growth, economic efficiency, or anything else, with the view toward promoting the moral-ethical norms that would indirectly further the achievement of this objective. I am not to be interpreted as suggesting that ethical norms may assist in maximizing some social welfare function. As in my other works, the methodology here remains strictly individualistic. Hence, when I suggest that there are economic reasons for the transmission of ethical percepts (for paying the preacher), I refer to reasons that apply to each and every person in the inclusive economic nexus. We are all in this together, and each and every one of us faces essentially the same situation.[36]

To account for heterogeneity, and for building the theory of the cultural evolution of norms, we need to account for divergent views of the people who evaluate the situation. Which actor assesses and considers the state of affairs as valuable? The evaluator may be an individual or a collective actor—family, corporation, state, and so forth.

If the evaluator is a collective entity, the problem gains additional multiple dimensions. Moreover, what is at stake is rarely a good-or-bad, yes-or-no matter. There are different levels or degrees of realization of the favored state of affairs; that is, the evaluator has a certain aspiration level, L, relative to each value.[37] For example, if the value under consideration is equity, it may be asked how equitable an individual, an institution, or a policy must be for the evaluator to declare that the value has been instantiated. Similarly, if the value is universal education or the eradication of poverty, the aspiration level to which E subscribes is the level of education or affluence whose achievement by everyone would constitute realization of the state of affairs that E favors. Hence, the aspiration level of value V from evaluator E's perspective must be specified, because failure to do so may lead to unnecessary confusion. In brief, the evaluator element is a source of multiple heterogeneities.

A, the State of Affairs

Statements such as "This public service agency is responsive" or "This public policy advances the public good" or "This public transportation system is resilient" identify a public value and assert something about a state of the world in a specific domain. By action, individual and collective, the world or, more precisely, a specific aspect of it changes in such a way that those possible states are realized. That means, in the context of our analysis, the creation (or production) of value.

S, the Observed System

When talking about a relevant state of affairs, it is necessary to be precise about the type of entity whose features are constituted in a state of affairs favored by E, the evaluator. A, the state of affairs, is a feature of an observed system, S (state, municipality, individual, group, public service, organization). For instance, we may look at individuals not as evaluators but as the intended value bearers, as observed systems. They might be further identified by sex, age, education, or social role. The state of affairs, A, deemed valuable regarding them, is a certain mindset, feature, capability, or resource that reflects a certain value, V. We may also distinguish, as in the case of evaluators, between individual and collective actors. Also, institutions and policies may be seen as observed systems. The adjectives *individual, institutional,* and *policy* specify the nature of the value bearer, S. For instance, the evaluator, E, may have in mind the realization of a certain state of affairs in which certain individuals are acting fairly. On the other hand, equity as one of E's institutional values might mean that E favors a state of affairs constituted by certain institutions that generate fair outcomes in a systematic fashion. The first approach is an ethical perspective that focuses on changing the values that guide individual choices irrespective of the imposed structure of penalties and rewards, whereas the second approach is an institutional perspective that focuses on the incentives structure in which individuals act irrespective of the moral norms to which they adhere. Such a difference of approach can obviously lead to very different normative positions and evaluations, although they are partly complementary.

To make sense of such differences of nuance, we can describe the evaluator, E, having a certain perspective, P, on S, the observed system. Although different evaluators, E_1 and E_2, may agree about physical identification of an observed system (for instance, they may agree that the system consists of individuals in a certain geographical region), they may have different perspectives on them. The issue of perspectives can sometimes take more radical forms of framing. For instance, E_1 may see all individual value bearers as belonging to the same group, whereas E_2 may separate them into two categories, natives and immigrants, and may apply different value standards to the immigrants. A Marxist evaluator will perceive employers of various corporations as belonging to a single class and will focus on the presumed conflict between owners of capital and workers. To a liberal evaluator, defining the observed system in such a manner makes little sense.[38] Thus, the same reality can not only be perceived from slightly different perspectives but also can be organized in radically different ways.

Perspectives also matter with regard to institutional and policy values. Institutions can be of different types: governments, corporations, churches, clubs, universities. Here too the evaluator's perspective can be specified. For example, universal secret elections and respect for democratic procedures may be among E's institutional values, but E may apply them only to the sovereign state level and not for corporate management or for non-Western underdeveloped societies. The same observed systems, as value bearers, could simultaneously be citizens, employees, and members of churches. The perspective on them, and the values considered relevant, will obviously differ depending on the context.

Such considerations may seem pedantic, but they are essential for understanding the magnitude of the challenge posed by any attempt to collectively generate states of affairs that are considered publicly or collectively valuable. In summary, this process can be viewed as an interaction between the evaluator, E, and the observed system, S, with the evaluator having values, V, and a certain aspiration level, L, for each value, as well as a perspective, P, about the observed system and its state of affairs, A.

This illustrates the complexity of any discussion about values in general and public or collective values in particular. A large number of combinations is possible even under ceteris paribus. The following questions arise: What is private value and what is public value in situations that are structurally defined by a complex mesh of variables? How is the line drawn between private and public in deliberations, preference aggregation, and social action and construction?

Consider as an example the situation mentioned by the psychologist Paul Rozin, in which a certain value, V, such as an environmental concern or vegetarianism, has not gained universal acceptance.[39] Some people who adhere to either or both values do so strongly and in a moral fashion. To use Buchanan's metaphor, they are going to "pay the preacher," and "the preacher" may end up more or less successful in promoting that value and changing the preferences of others. Many such cases are at the borderline between private and public. Suppose that a bimodal distribution of values exists among the evaluators. Is a 51-percent acceptance sufficient to make it "public"? Consideration of different levels of aspirations, different perspectives, and even different observed systems makes the matter even more complicated. When does a private preference about the behavior of others become a public value that needs universal enforcement? Where is the threshold at which it can be decided that one or another state of affairs needs to be generated because it is of "public value"?

Similarly, when the observed system is a socioeconomic class or an ethnic group, it may be hard to decide whether a public value bearer or a private one is involved. By contrast, the distinction between a private or public *evaluator* seems more straightforward. However, even then the distinction is not perfect. Is a nongovernment organization a private or public entity? Using what criteria? The classic distinction between excludable and nonexcludable goods also seems straightforward. Yet even that distinction includes a certain gradualist quantitative aspect—that is, some goods are easier to exclude than others, rather than being purely excludable or nonexcludable. The availability or non-availability of so-called property rights technologies that are able to bring about exclusion may make the difference.[40] Moreover, as mentioned, whether something counts as an externality has a subjective element to it.

Our examples are basic, even simplistic. All point to one conclusion—that the answer to the question "What makes something 'public'?" may differ depending on whether the focus is on the value, V; the value bearer, S; its state of affairs, A; or the evaluator, E. Looking at various possible combinations and including perspectives and levels of aspirations, we can understand why the usual approaches based on game theory are good starting points for a discussion that must go well beyond the set boundaries.

These conjectures are not merely exploratory. Studies of preference formation, deliberation, aggregation, public interest, voting, and bureaucratic mechanisms in democratic systems[41] reveal that the line between private and public, or individual and collective, is actually much fuzzier. Using the stylized facts of game theory to define, identify, and disentangle public goods and public value production situations works only to a point. There are many consequential situations in which the private-public distinction is not easily discernible. In such cases, it is necessary to move beyond formal preset models to identify and unpack the variety of mechanisms and processes that always seem to be strongly driven by circumstantial details.

Public management scholar Barry Bozeman dedicates much of his study to the problem of public value. He writes that public interest "changes not only case by case but also with the same case as time advances and conditions change."[42] The idea of "public" and by extension of "private" is dynamic. Per Bozeman, this suggests "the relevance of learning and empiricism"[43] and of the ongoing processes of social discovery, construction, and reconstruction, out of which various particular formulas of the "the public" emerge. As a major philosophical reference point, he identifies the pragmatist philosophy of John Dewey, whose works Vincent Ostrom considers of defining importance as well. What both Ostrom and Bozeman note is precisely that "the public" is not something static, ex ante, and objectively defined but rather something that emerges as a result of an ongoing social-political process of inquiry and negotiation.

The intuition that values heterogeneity and ambiguity requires a matching type of institutional heterogeneity to accommodate them in a process in which social discovery, social choice, and social production of publicly valuable states of affairs are intertwined is plausible prima facie. Yet the case needs to be detailed, illustrated, and analytically articulated. The question, more precisely, is how that happens. What are the social and institutional forms that discovery, production, provision, and consumption take in specific circumstances? The types of channels, processes, and mechanisms connecting and forging the realm of subjective preferences and values and the realm of institutional polycentricity that constructs them as public need to be pinpointed and analyzed.

A good starting point is to say that there are multiple ways in which social actors and groups engage in the process of shaping and reconfiguring the state of affairs of their social environment. Along with the private-public values divide may be used a typology that distinguishes among four types of economic processes—production, provision, exchange, and consumption—and two levels at which those processes can occur—individual and collective. The divide with respect to values determines which services and goods should be available to all out of some normative consideration, whereas the typology describes the detailed ways in which the economic processes involved may work.[44] As may be seen, the combinatorial potential is huge. Each combination, including the variety of possible institutional arrangements involved in each basic type, has significant operational and institutional consequences. Many deserve to be isolated and analyzed in depth. In the Ostroms' research program, several such combinations emerge as highly salient. In the next section, we focus on one—the case of co-production. That is a phenomenon of major, but relatively neglected, importance and may be used as an excellent illustration for the broader class of phenomena linking the realm of the private and subjectivity, on the one hand, and that of the public and its institutional architecture, on the other.

Before moving ahead, note that we are getting closer to the domain of one of the most profound problems in social science: How does "the public" emerge from "the private"? How is "the private" grounded in "the public"? What is involved in the efforts of individuals and groups to create states of the world of "public value" out of the apparent chaos of heterogeneity? As Vincent Ostrom puts it, "The conduct of public affairs requires the pooling, rearranging, and compromising of existing interests—in the constitution of common knowledge, shared communities of understanding, patterns of social accountability, and mutual trust—that are subject to challenge and to being reestablished and reaffirmed through processes of conflict resolution."[45] Such questions bring us to the *fons et origo* of social order where, as Vincent Ostrom writes, social reality is constituted and "brute facts" make room for "institutional facts."[46] On the one hand, we have intentionality and subjectivity; on the other hand, there is the intersubjective realm that has given way to the objective facts of the world that are facts only by human agreement.[47] Such states of affairs are not matters of subjective values, preferences, or evaluations. Yet they are anchored in the subjectivity of values and preferences. The Ostroms' investigations prepared the path for one way to deal with the problem, one way to study how humans cross the bridge from the conceptual, mental, or psychological to the social and institutional. Exploring co-production brings us closer to understanding one possible path on that bridge.

Co-production

The Ostroms' extensive empirical studies of governance and public administration reveal a series of cases wherein collaboration between those who supplied a service and those who used it was the factor that determined effective delivery of the service. In many instances, the users of services also functioned as co-producers and as major sources of the service's value. Without the informed and "motivated efforts of service users, the service may deteriorate into an indifferent product with insignificant value."[48] In co-production, the consumer is a necessary part of the production process. Consumer input is essential "if there [is] to be any production at all."[49] Such cases are excellent vehicles for illustrating the processes that take place at the ambiguous interface between private and public.

Examples abound. The production of certain services—from education and health care to police and fire protection to the justice system—depend in an essential way on the inputs of beneficiaries. Police often cannot catch criminals if citizens are unwilling to provide any clues. The effectiveness of fire protection services depends on citizens' efforts to prevent fires. The justice system cannot function if no one is willing to be a witness. An unwilling or apathetic student will not learn, even though the professor teaches. A doctor often needs a patient's input for a diagnosis, and cooperation in treatment is needed on the part of the patient. It is obvious in such cases, as well as others, that the framework of standard consumer theory,[50] which assumes a radical separation between producer (usually conflated with the provider) and consumer, is deficient. The Bloomington scholars addressed this deficiency by building a theory of co-production,[51] which was later expanded and applied to a variety of cases and settings.[52]

The Co-production Model and Some of Its Consequences

The producer that standard consumer theory assumes to be fully responsible for production is now called a "regular producer," and the consumer's input in the production process is taken into consideration by means of the consumer-producer concept. The two can in principle be connected in two ways: they could be substitutes or complements. It is the second type that leads to the most interesting situations.

The simple model (figure 6.4) assumes that both the regular producer and the consumer producer are interested in generating the highest output (or quality). The only concern is how to split their responsibilities. Given the opportunity cost for the consumer relative to that of the regular producer in providing the good (which leads to a particular slope of the budget constraint in figure 6.4), a particular optimum is determined. If, for instance, the regular producer tries to do more, it will lead to a decline in the co-production contribution from the consumer, and the output is actually going to be lower.

This provides a simple explanation for the "service paradox," which describes a situation in which "the better services are, as defined by professional criteria, the less satisfied the citizens are with those services."[53] This paradox emerges when the evaluation of the production process focuses solely on the part provided by the regular producer, ignoring the part played by the consumer producer. Consequently, in such cases, the co-production trade-off is drifting away from its optimum and the

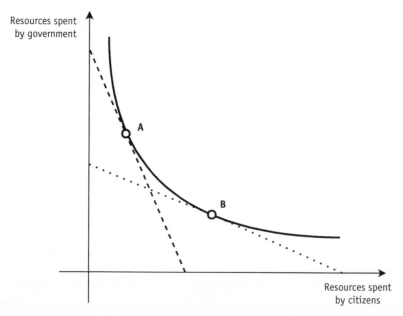

Figure 6.4 The simple co-production model of government provision of a service.

interaction between the two parts is becoming more and more defective despite the genuine efforts to improve the service.

This paradox and this blindness to the role of co-production plagues many public services. For example, in their studies of police services, Elinor Ostrom and collaborators have found that neither the "professionalization" of the police nor increased funding leads to better police services (as evaluated by surveys of citizens' satisfaction).[54] By contrast, when police departments are more decentralized and police-citizen relations are improved, the quality of police services also improves. This is because police activities often depend on gathering information from citizens. If citizens distrust the police and refuse to interact with them, the overall co-production output suffers even if the police are given large resources and are highly trained.

As Aligica and Boettke have noted, "the role of co-production came in many respects as a revelation," as it became obvious that the analysis of many public services was deficient because it ignored this issue. "Once it was clearly defined, co-production problems could be identified in many sub-domains of the service industries in both private and public sectors. . . . It was the standard assumption of the separation of production from consumption that blinded everybody from identifying the source of what was called the 'service paradox.'"[55]

A few other simple predictions follow: higher-income individuals are less likely to participate in co-production (because they have higher opportunity costs); technologies that make customer involvement easier increase the participation ratio (because the opportunity cost is decreased); and higher wage costs for regular production increase consumer participation (because regular production diminishes participation, and consumers compensate to some extent).

The Co-production Problems

A significant problem is that the exact shape of the co-production curve is unknown. This affects especially the public-private co-production, as governments have little means of evaluating costs.[56] With purely private co-production (such as concerts, customer service, websites, or health care services), the competition among different regular producers is bound to gradually structure the co-production process, via a trial-and-error process, somewhat close to its optimal form.[57]

However, the process is still not perfect, as regular producers maximize profit rather than output.[58] To put it differently, both parties to the co-production process tend to free-ride on the other's activities to some extent. This means that regular producers have an incentive to overinvolve their customers in the production process by underproducing themselves. This leads to an interesting insight that may well be interpreted as an unexplored type of market failure. In fact, here we are exploring a phenomenon that takes place at the boundary between a market failure and what Bozeman calls "public-value" failure,[59] and although the logic of model construction differs from that of Bozeman, who builds a list of "public-value" failure heuristic criteria by mirroring the logic of market failure, that type may well be considered an addition or a complement to Bozeman's list.

Figure 6.5 shows the difference between output produced under profit maximization (black line), and optimal production under output maximization (the gray line),

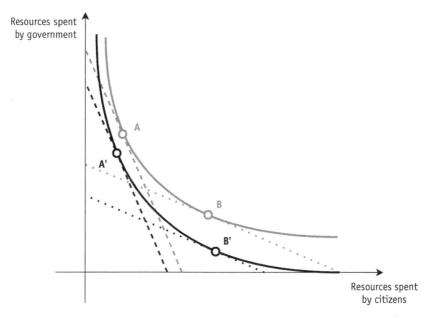

Figure 6.5 The co-production market failure: underproduction due to free-riding.

as calculated by Aligica and Tarko.[60] Lowering the opportunity cost pushes the actual output closer (but not identical) to the optimal output, because the regular producer can profit more by stimulating the co-production partner *and* the consumer, but the extent to which that can be done depends on the consumer's opportunity cost.

Another interesting result is that, for a given level of the consumer's opportunity cost, the effect of the budget reduction is smaller in the case of the profit maximization of regular-producer output than in the case of the total output maximization of the regular-producer output.[61] Consequently, this leads to a more optimistic view of what happens when government spending is reduced. Intuitively, it happens because under profit maximization the regular producers tend to overinvolve the consumer, and thus the budget reduction has less of an effect.

To give a concrete example, assuming realistically that professors are profit maximizers (rather than altruistically doing everything in their power to get the maximum education output out of their students, that is, professors are shirking to some extent), students must spend more time studying (and less time doing other things) than would be optimal. The effect is that if professors' wages are cut, the effect on education output is not as large as it would have been in a situation of idealized nonshirker professors. The same effect holds for all public services involving co-production—that is, police, health care, and so forth. That may sound like an obvious effect, but it is missing from other accounts of co-production because the other accounts assume that all agents are engaged in output maximization rather than profit maximization. That opens the door for more concrete studies. For example, how important is co-production inefficiency for explaining why in the past decades the quality of education in the United States has been stagnant despite a large increase in the budget for education?

Bearing in mind the co-production deadweight loss can also lead to a more nuanced view of privatization. A disadvantage of privatization, as we can see, is that profit maximization output may be lower than efficient output. So if government failures[62] are somehow avoided by various political mechanisms,[63] such as transparency and accountability, and a public interest focus is successfully pursued, it may be the case that the production or provision of certain services may be more efficient in a collective governance arrangement than a fully privatized arrangement.

How can the co-production failure be addressed? The similarity between team production and co-production is highly deceptive. The team production solution is intuitive: when something isn't working, put someone in charge to fix it—and the more disinterested and "objective" that person is, the better. As noted by Elinor Ostrom, this is quite wrong:

> Officials and policy analysts who presume that they have the right design can be dangerous. They are likely to assume that citizens are short-sighted and motivated only by extrinsic benefits and costs. Somehow, the officials and policy analysts assume that they have different motivations and can find optimal policy because they are not directly involved in the problem. . . . They are indeed isolated from the problems. This leaves them with little capability to adapt and learn in light of information about outcomes resulting from their policies. All too often, these "optimal" policies have Leviathan-like characteristics to them.[64]

The solution is not to search for a disinterested third party, who, almost by definition, will lack the knowledge and intrinsic motivation to solve the problem, but to properly channel the vested interests of the consumer producers. To use Buchanan's metaphor again, the solution is to "pay the preacher" and build a strong enough internal ethical motivation against free-riding. This is less feasible in the case of team production because the team (e.g., firm) is producing a good consumed by others. As such, the members of the team don't have a strong intrinsic stake in the good. But in the case of co-production, there is a strong vested interest in producing the good. For instance, thinking purely in term of extrinsic costs and benefits, it may follow that busy citizens will shirk their civic duties and, say, refuse to talk to the police. In practice, building a strong sense of community can in fact overcome the issue. Ignoring intrinsic motivation is indeed a significant error.[65] Similarly, thinking just in terms of extrinsic costs and benefits may lead to the conclusion that parents will undercontribute in the educational co-production process for their children. In practice, however, the fact that parents care about their children and are aware of the importance of education counterbalances this.

To put the question in more general terms, what bridges the gap between the individual profit-maximization equilibrium (which suffers from the free-riding underproduction problem) and the output-maximization optimum (of zero free-riding)? The answer is social norms. And social norms are not created by external third parties or by top-down management. Unfortunately, this lesson is far from being widely understood. For instance, as we note in the next chapter, the top-down involvement of the federal government in policing has effectively undermined the idea of "community policing" with predictable negative outcomes (as Elinor Ostrom and collaborators actually predicted in the 1970s).[66]

We have thus come to illuminate from a unique angle the contours and texture of the "third sector." Its position and significance become more evident. As public administration scholar Taco Brandsen and political scientist Victor Pestoff write, "The concept of co-production potentially offers a means of capturing a significant part of the quality of this dynamic [concerning] the role of the third sector in public service provision and the manner in which such services are produced."[67] Indeed, the third sector may be a means to elude government failures and pursue a public interest agenda, and our co-production analysis shows why it may be a more efficient form of provision and production of public services than either the state or profit-seeking firms.

Reframing the Decentralization Debate

As political scientists Ronald Oakerson and Roger Parks note in further developing and applying these notions, discussion about the third sector is related to the important distinction between *political* fragmentation and *functional* fragmentation.[68] Political fragmentation deals with the geographical separation of public administrative bodies, each of which "provides and produces all local services for its citizens."[69] Functional fragmentation deals with specialized profit or nonprofit enterprises, each of which "provides and produces each distinct service for all citizens."[70] As we discuss in the next section, functional fragmentation is often more efficient than political fragmentation. That is another reason why privatization often looks like a good idea, but it is also a reason for relying on the third sector, which is also compatible with functional fragmentation. The advantage of functional fragmentation is that it is more competitive. Political fragmentation has only "voting-with-your-feet" Tiebout competition *between* geographical areas, which often involves prohibitive transaction costs and cannot deal with the problem of bundling together many public services. Functional fragmentation, however, involves competition *inside* each geographical area. For example, the competition of nongovernment organizations for private donors is imperfect, owing to the "warm glow-giving" phenomenon,[71] but it is probably still a lot more effective than Tiebout competition. The situation of a government monopoly producer is probably the worst because the monopoly eliminates the incentive to find more efficient co-production structures and may also further reduce output.

If we compare co-production market failure to the better-known team production market failure,[72] which has opened the door for an entire literature on principal agent problems,[73] we see that much of the discussion about centralization or decentralization has been going on under an unstated assumption. That assumption is that the production of public goods by the public administration at various levels is a form of team production: the "team" is made up of various administrative units, and citizens are passive receivers of the services, rather than of co-production, in which the citizens are critical elements of the production processes. The arguments for centralization are similar in form to Alchian and Demsetz's theoretical explanation for why firms (i.e., islands of nonmarket centralized management) emerge as a result of the necessity for monitoring.[74] A centralized public administration is supposed to be more efficient for a similar reason, in that it would be able to stir and monitor the use of resources in a preferred direction, rather than allow them to be wasted by the decentralized administration, which supposedly duplicates efforts.[75]

Moreover, from a team production perspective, privatization, or functional fragmentation more generally, appears to make monitoring more difficult and thus decreases efficiency. From a co-production perspective, the opposite results. Rules need to be enforced to be considered *in use* rather than *in form*. In other words, rules need to really be guiding and shaping the practice as opposed to just being evoked but not applied. But for enforcement to be more than just in form, monitors also need monitoring. That seems to create a paradoxical infinite regress of monitors of monitors of monitors and so on. Co-production solves that problem by creating a "circle" of rules rather than a linear hierarchy. For instance, to use an example of common-pool resources management from Elinor Ostrom,[76] if a group of agents each take turns at being the monitor, the problem is diminished to manageable levels because the monitor will have a vested interest in making sure the rules are followed, and thus the monitor will not need outside monitoring. More generally, all systems of rules are ultimately built on a foundation of self-governing rules, and such self-governing rules exist as a result of agents' self-interest in having the rules enforced.[77]

Self-governing rules are important as the foundation, but they are not the only types of rules. Systems that depart at great lengths from self-governance tend to not only lack legitimacy but also to be rife with corruption, rent-seeking, and widespread inefficiencies because the monitors and enforcers have less of an intrinsic interest in doing their job properly. Thus, it becomes more costly to ensure the monitors are indeed doing their job. So it is always important to consider the incentives structure of those responsible for monitoring and enforcement, as well as for design of rules in general.[78] Considerations regarding economies of scale must be analyzed using realistic assumptions about the efficiency of the monitoring system at large scales. Furthermore, such considerations must also be analyzed under the co-production framework, rather than an assumption being made that the public producer can work independently of consumer input. Both considerations work in the direction of favoring more functional decentralization for production and of separating production and provision while also trying to find the appropriate balance or relationship in the production-provision- consumption triad.

The Ostroms link the problem of co-production to the observation that people can develop complex institutional arrangements to produce and distribute public goods and services, although no single center of authority is responsible for coordinating all relationships in such a public economy. The scholars of the Bloomington school extensively demonstrate the limits of having a single governing body at a certain fixed geographic scale and of assigning to that governing body a host of responsibilities about managing many different common-pool resources and public goods.[79] There is no one-size-fits-all solution. Depending on the exact nature of the good, the structure of the most effective co-production process—the process that creates the highest public value—can vary.

Democracy as a Rules Co-production Process

We are now in a position to approach from a fresh angle a rather peculiar but crucial type of "production"—the production of good rules. From such a perspective, representative democracy may be seen as an exemplary case of co-production. Representatives are in the position of regular producers, and citizens are in the position of consumer-producers. Democracy as an ideal is the view that the production of rules in all their aspects, including monitoring and enforcing, must involve the "customers" of those rules in various ways and capabilities. Political theorist Robert A. Dahl offers one way to formulate the problem when he writes that, ideally, democracy

> expands to maximum feasible limits the opportunity for persons to live under laws of their own choosing. . . . But to live in association with others necessarily requires that they must sometimes obey collective decisions that are binding on all members of the association. The problem, then, is to discover a way by which the members of an association may make decisions binding on all and still govern themselves. Because democracy maximizes the opportunities for self-determination among the members of an association, it is the best solution.[80]

We can adopt an even more specific form of articulating the problem by noting that a social system is a complex web of laws, contracts, and cultural norms that can be seen as emerging from a co-production process involving the state and civil society, with the quantities in the co-production diagrams (figures 6.4 and 6.5) now representing the quality of rules. The formal rules create constraints for contracts that can be enacted and may determine changes in the social norms. Conversely, social norms create constraints on the realm of formal rules by making certain laws difficult or impossible to enforce, or owing to legitimacy issues.[81]

Regardless of whether we consider the simple representative democracy model or the complex social system model, the co-production perspective leads to the same conclusion: to build a complex system of self-governing communities that coexist peacefully, we need to think of the social-political world as a large polycentric system. The critique of the use of the team production intuition in public administration leads to skepticism with respect to large-scale hierarchical systems of public administration. Instead, we need to think of a social order that has multiple rule creators acting as quasi-independent centers of power and authority in overlapping jurisdictions. This creates the conditions for improving the rules of the co-production process. On one hand, a diversity of viewpoints can be maintained and Tiebout competition puts additional pressure toward efficiency; on the other hand, mechanisms for conflict resolution are still available. We have thus reached the concept of polycentricity, the capstone of the Ostromian system.

Polycentricity

By considering the fact that different public goods, social dilemmas, and collective action situations are best managed at different scales, and the fact that private-public co-production is necessary for their effective management, we reach the concept of *polycentricity*, defined by Elinor Ostrom in the following way:

> By polycentric I mean a system where citizens are able to organize not just one but multiple governing authorities at differing scales. . . . Each unit exercises considerable independence to make and enforce rules within a circumscribed domain of authority for a specified geographical area. In a polycentric system, some units are general-purpose governments while others may be highly specialized. . . . In a polycentric system the users of each common-pool resource would have some authority to make at least some of the rules related to how that particular resource will be utilized.[82]

We have noted that heterogeneity may occur in all aspects of the evaluation process. There is a variety of values, often conflicting or involving trade-offs, with which the observed system can comply. As such, public value creation has a certain unavoidable subjective element that is instantiated by the fact that there always exist various evaluators that judge the same system or the same state of affairs. Moreover, even if different evaluators agree about a particular value, they can still have different aspiration levels regarding that value, or they can look at the same system from different perspectives. Such differences obviously have large consequences for the evaluation process and, consequently, for the proposed approaches to creating more public value. As such, we must face Dahl's dilemma about how to reconcile such deep heterogeneities with the inevitability of "collective decisions that are binding on all members of the association."[83] The better this dilemma is addressed, the better the system fares in creating public value from not just one single (often arbitrarily) privileged point of view but from as many different points of view as possible.

We can look at polycentricity as a structural solution to this dilemma. When people with different values and perspectives are allowed the freedom to follow those values and perspectives, they will gather and cooperate in particular co-production processes for the provision of public goods at different levels and in different circumstances. Aggregation continues to be a problem, yet now it is dispersed at multiple levels, segmented into a multitude of possible solutions.

The key challenge, of course, in contemplating the possibility of freedom to fashion a variety of arrangements at different levels is how to avoid having the entire system disintegrate into chaos. The theory of polycentricity addresses the issue of how to structure a variety of processes for public goods co-production. Figure 6.6 showcases the "logical structure of polycentricity" as systematized by Paul Aligica and Vlad Tarko,[84] highlighting the necessary and sufficient conditions for defining functional polycentricity patterns.

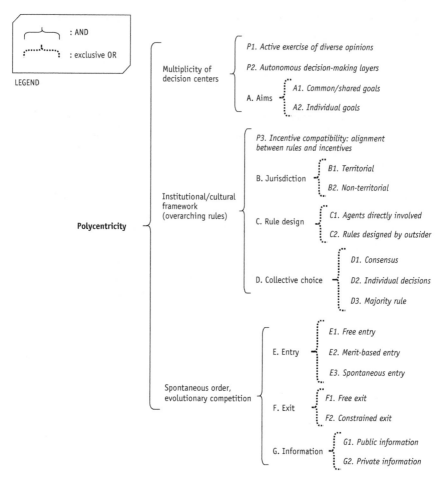

Figure 6.6 The logical structure of polycentricity. Adapted from Paul Dragos Aligica and Vlad Tarko, "Polycentricity: From Polanyi to Ostrom, and Beyond," *Governance* 25, no. 2 (2012).

The potential combinations demonstrate that various successful polycentric systems are possible. There are many ways in which freedom of organization can be successfully structured. What the systems have in common is the active exercise of diverse opinions, P_1; autonomous decision-making layers, P_2; and rules-incentives compatibility, P_3—that is, the members of the system do not see the rules as deliberately frustrating their goals. The first element avoids "institutional monocropping" and creates the conditions for a resilient and adaptable system.[85] The second element addresses the monitoring and enforcement problem; by allowing a certain amount of self-governance, the monitors have a vested interest in enforcing the rules. The third element addresses the co-production phenomenon head on. Whether users see the rules as compatible with their own interests is determined by their personal values and perspectives. When a variety of co-production systems coexist, the incentives compatibility is maximized.

As figure 6.6 shows, the other necessary conditions—the existence of an overarching system of rules (although not necessarily enforced by a single actor) and the conditions for evolutionary competition (spontaneous order)—can be achieved in practice in various ways. Structuring of the co-production diversity and avoidance of chaos are realized thanks to the overarching system of rules. That is the main difference between polycentricity and anarchy. As Oakerson and Parks write:

> Polycentric governance depends on two institutional conditions related to the design of governmental arrangements: the first is the existence of multiple independent centers of authority; the second is that their independence must not be absolute. All authority must be subjected to limits, and it must be possible to introduce new limits. Such limits exist in recognition of interdependencies among clustered and nested communities and serve to qualify the independence of various centers of authority.[86]

Apart from having an overarching system of rules that is not illegitimate in flagrant ways as a result of severe conflicts with members' interests, polycentricity also involves the following:

1. A clearly specified jurisdiction—Although that jurisdiction is not necessarily territorial, as in the scientific community or with the internal rules of multinational corporations.
2. A clear process of rules design—Although members are not always involved in rules design as in the common law justice system where many rules are created by an outside legislative body.
3. A clear process of collective choice—Depending on the case, it may or may not be possible for a variety of individual decisions to coexist. For example, in a market system they do coexist, but in democratic decisions about public goods, they cannot, and thus voting must be relied on.

Those conditions also allow mapping of the configurations that endanger a successful polycentric system—the breakdown of polycentricity giving way to either a monocentric system (authoritarian or not) or violent anarchy. Certain varieties of polycentricity are closer to breakdown conditions than others; Aligica and Tarko single out the following: A_1, B_1, C_2, D_3, E_2, F_2, and G_2.[87] Systems with those characteristics, although still polycentric, are more vulnerable.

In brief, the notion of polycentricity has a descriptive, heuristic, and analytical capacity. It helps us articulate a series of insights regarding the combinatorial structural conditions for an institutional order able to cope with the challenges of heterogeneity, collective action, and co-production. It also reframes the nature of the normative debates by challenging what exactly is to be debated. Elaborating a couple of implications pertaining to this normative facet will help fully articulate the applied level, the practical significance of the Ostromian system, and thus bring a final important point to our case for its superiority as a theoretical framework of governance. In Chapter 9 we offer one illustration of the use of this framework, for the purpose of analyzing and managing corporate social responsibility. Vlad Tarko has also used the framework for analyzing the institutional characteristics of the scientific commu-nity.[88] Most recently, Sergio Villamayor-Tomas has used the framework to analyze the water associations in Spain.[89]

Polycentricity and the Subjectivity and Heterogeneity of Values

Probably the most constructive way to address the normative angle is to ad-dress the problem of the "presumed conflict between private interests and public interests or the public good."[90] Political scientists John Jackson and David King map the realm of typical concerns about this nexus of normative themes, noting three major areas:

> The first is the concept of public, or collective, good and the accompanying *distribution* of individual preferences about the proper amount of that good. Second is the normative discussion about the public interest or the public good, which usually debates public decisions according to some singularly defined objective or outcome, such as larger defense expenditures, cleaner air, or a more progressive income distribution. Lastly, there are private, or particularistic, interests created by any governmental activity.[91]

The first section of this chapter addresses the first area of concern. The third area is the realm of public choice, which this chapter leaves in the background but which is an integral part of the Ostromian approach.[92] The second area of concern is the most interesting one for our purposes here. It is the one that best illuminates the spe-cific tones of the Ostromian perspective. For such authors as Jackson and King and many proponents of deliberative democracy models, the second area mainly involves a public debate or deliberation that establishes a certain normative consensus, con-vergence, or normalization with respect to the public values that should be of most concern.

By contrast, the polycentric approach is concerned with *the possibility of creating valued states of affairs from as many normative perspectives as possible.* Rather than asking only which voting system or deliberation and aggregation procedures leave the fewest people unsatisfied with the result, a more general question must be asked: Which *structure of political units*, each with its own collective choice system, leaves the fewest people unsatisfied with the production and provision of public goods, club goods, and common-pool resources?

Complicating the matter further is the fact that an optimal political structure cannot be fixed once and for all because technological changes and organizational innovations can severely alter the economies of scale with respect to some nonprivate goods. Thus, the more general question is which political structure is best able to adapt to such changes and remodel itself in a way that constantly approximates the optimal structure. Elinor Ostrom's arguments about the long-term resilience of polycentric systems must be seen in this light. The reason why polycentric systems are more resilient is that they are better at solving the adaptability problem, and they are good at solving it because they cope better with the knowledge and incentives problems.[93]

The polycentric approach thus no longer takes for granted that the existing heterogeneity of values (regarding the right, just, or efficient functioning of the social system) must be funneled into a single normative position at the collective level. Instead, it recognizes that the necessity for certain such centripetal dynamics is a consequence of the existing institutional structure, and if that structure is changed, some heterogeneity of values would persist at the collective level, in the form of a diversity of communities and sometimes overlapping communities and "clubs."[94] Thus, rather than taking the level of aggregation for granted and assuming that some mechanism of consensus generates the normative guidelines, the problem of finding the optimal aggregation levels now becomes a major concern. The way in which the level of preference aggregation is set in regard to different public issues and the way in which different levels of aggregation interact have significant consequences both in terms of efficiency and resilience and in terms of other social values such as fairness or autonomy. Thus, that is not something that can be easily separated from the other two areas.

There is another, perhaps simpler, way of describing this important normative insight. That is, the main focus is not on how to determine which values should be imposed on everyone but instead on the complementary question of how to decide about which matters we can agree to disagree. It is easier to decide the latter and let the fundamental values emerge implicitly than it is to decide what the fundamental values are and let the agreement to disagree be the subtext. That approach is also more in tune with how social dilemmas are actually solved in real life and how political compromises are reached. In a sense, it may be said that societies do not solve social choice problems so much as they solve polycentricity problems, and that social choice solutions operate in the space created by the existing polycentric arrangements.

Perhaps the clearest and most telling example of such an approach is the issue of religious freedom. Under an institutional system in which state and church are not separate, religious diversity must be funneled at the collective level into a single acceptable religion—that is, all citizens are members of the state church. The separation of church and state, with allowance for a multitude of churches to coexist in the same territory, is a type of institutional reform that eliminates the necessity for debate and processes that lead to homogenization; the heterogeneity of religious beliefs and values is preserved rather than "solved."

This can be seen as a paradigmatic example of the polycentric approach, and the claim is that other public issues—not all but more than are presently addressed this way—also can be addressed in a similar manner. What religious freedom has done is to switch an issue from the realm of political consolidation to functional fragmentation.

Thus, when thinking about the presumed conflict between private interests and public interests or about public good and public value creation failures, we must also consider the possibility that the conflict can be eliminated by maintaining diverse suppliers of nonprivate goods and diverse co-production processes, often overlapping on the same territory and creating redundancies. Sometimes the best solution to collective choice problems and the best way to achieve states of affairs that are publicly valuable from a variety of normative perspectives is to find not a better voting system but a better way to organize the aggregation levels. Existing governing bodies are often given too many responsibilities regarding the production of public goods, something that would most effectively be managed at different scales. Some collective action problems emerge simply as a result of the contradiction between the optimal levels of managing two different resources. When both are the responsibility of the same governing body that has an often far-from-optimal scale, public value is lost. It is lost regardless of how well the distribution problems (e.g., fairness) and the public choice problems (e.g., government transparency, limited rent-seeking) are addressed. It is for this reason that many Bloomington school scholars often emphasize the difference between the production and the provision of public goods.

Another effect of that approach is to change the emphasis from the procedural details of aggregation procedures (a discussion about *how*) to a discussion about *what* must be aggregated.[95] The crucial issue then becomes how to define the scope of what philosopher John Burnheim has called "legitimate material interest."[96] The basic classical-liberal intuition is that "nobody should have any input into decision making where they have no legitimate material interest" and avoidance of a situation in which "people are exercising authority over others, without warrant and without regard of their proper autonomy, by virtue of their political power."[97] More concretely, by "material" Burnheim means "to exclude interests that people have simply because of their intrusive desires about how others should fare" while by "legitimate" he means "to exclude material interests that are not based on entitlements that are morally sound."[98]

The great innovation of Burnheim's approach is that of moving the discussion from the purely normative (i.e., a debate about which entitlements are "morally sound") back to a discussion of which empirical and historical realities should take front stage. Polycentricity can be seen as a fundamental institutional mechanism for establishing Burnheim's "legitimate material interest" across many types of public issues, in an evolving and self-improving manner.

In a nutshell, what Vincent Ostrom meant by the "intellectual crisis in public administration"[99] is the fact that the field of public administration is yet to acknowledge and come to grips with the impossibility of identifying various "legitimate material interests" in an objective manner. To put it differently, the subjectivity of preferences affects not just the realm of simple private goods but also the realm of preferences about other people's behaviors. This involves not just the realm of controversial ethical judgments but also the controversies about how trade-offs between valuable social goals are to be made. This subjectivity undermines the legitimacy of numerous technocratic elements of public administration. The alternative is to embrace the polycentric point of view and always get back to self-governance as the key foundation.

Conclusion

In brief, taking co-production and polycentricity seriously results in a very different approach to the problem of the optimal political structure and leads to a truly institutionalist normative political economy. The optimal structure involves the following steps:

1. Separate the provision and the production of public goods. This is needed because the economies of scale of production and of provision often differ greatly.
2. Decentralize production on functional grounds rather than on political grounds by means of either privatization or the involvement of the third sector. This is needed because of the co-production aspect and of the fact that various goods are best produced at very different scales. Political units have a fixed scale, such that the bundling of services is inefficient.
3. Maintain a role for political units mainly in the provision rather than the production of public goods—except perhaps in the production of defense—such that the redistributive aspects of the welfare state can be maintained. These aspects can be maintained, for example, through voucher systems that secure provision but not production and that preserve the competitive framework for production.
4. Organize political units in a polycentric structure responsible for creating a resilient and adaptive ecosystem of rules and for settling debates about what should or should not be provided. An agree-to-disagree process would maintain the entire system's capacity to learn by trial and error.

In summary, in this chapter we try to reconstruct the underlying logic beginning with value heterogeneity, continuing with co-production, and concluding with polycentricity. In approaching this task, we assume that (a) the Ostroms craft the basic building blocks for a systematic approach to the domain of institutional hybridity, diversity, and quasi-markets and quasi-governments; and (b) they spell out the logic that unites those blocks in a comprehensive theoretical system. Recognizing that their system is still a work in progress and following that logic, this chapter tries to reinforce the emerging theoretical framework in three major ways: (a) explicitly articulating the elements of a theory of value heterogeneity as a component of the foundation of the entire Ostromian approach, (b) clarifying a technical ambiguity in the construction of the co-production model that connects the domain of individual subjective values with the domain of institutions and social order and elaborates the implications, and (c) reconsidering polycentricity—the capstone of the Ostromian system—and emphasizing several critical features that pertain to its positive analytical dimension and the normative dimension.

Overall, the chapter seeks to show how another step could be taken to integrate the three building blocks. Probably the most interesting result of these efforts is that public choice gains a new connotation. Seen from the Bloomington school's perspective, the discipline of public choice is about a truly public and collective social process, the essence of governance in applied terms. Public choice is not only a theory that applies the logic of individual decision-making in public or nonmarket settings. Nor is it concerned only with the collective deliberations and choices regarding public goods and social dilemmas in different social, bureaucratic, and political ecologies. It is also about the ways in which individual preferences, values, and decisions shaped by ecological rationality principles intertwine and evolve with the institutionally constructed environment and governance system. Public choice is about the phenomenon thus generated in which the public is not something ex ante but something that emerges as a result of an ongoing collective process of adjustment, inquiry, negotiation, discovery, learning, and coordination. It may be said that, in a sense, the Ostroms' contribution endogenizes public choice and naturalizes it with a strong dose of epistemic choice (as Vincent Ostrom identifies the entire domain of knowledge processes). Thus, what can be seen at work is the connection between public choice institutionalism and the intellectual tradition that has made a central focus of its attention the dynamics of learning, knowledge, and coordination processes in heterogeneous social settings. Simultaneously, we see how the idea of public governance is put in the fresh light of new theoretical lenses. Our next step is to take a closer look at the applied-level perspective revealed by the use of those concepts, theories, and frameworks.

PART III

FRAMING THE APPLIED LEVEL

Themes, Issue Areas, and Cases

It is tempting to associate the classical-liberal position in public policy with the case for privatization. Yet, as we have seen, classical liberalism means much more than that. A dogmatic stance, even with respect to privatization, is contrary to the classical-liberal spirit. Classical liberalism builds its system on individuals (as normative and analytical units), voluntary association, and self-governance. It is not about ideal types and end states but rather about social processes driven by individual preferences and the governance of emerging patterns of order. Classical liberalism is therefore about the decisions, institutions, and processes that take place at the dynamic interface between the private and the public. There are multiple forms of organization at the boundary between private and public. The power of the concepts and theories we have advanced so far is best revealed when we go beyond the simple cases. The complexities of the phenomena in different cases reveal the real potential of a nuancing and discerning apparatus that rejects formulaic analysis and solutions.

In Part III we make an exploratory effort to show how practical matters look through the lens of the classical-liberal perspective. Seen in conjunction, the cases explored in Part III show how governance problems can be thought of using the intellectual instruments introduced in the first two parts of the book.

The three issue areas discussed in Part III are metropolitan governance (Chapter 7), independent regulatory agencies (Chapter 8), and corporate social responsibility (Chapter 9). All three are positioned at the sensitive area of interface between the private and the public. Each illustrates a different facet and challenge of governance in conditions of complexity and hybridity. Each touches on different aspects of democratic governance and challenges some aspects of conventional wisdom. In all cases, we see the conceptual apparatus at work. The focus on polycentricity, public choice, knowledge processes, countervailing powers, and contractarianism allows us to frame, diagnose, and imagine solutions in specific areas of governance at the complex private-public interface. We hope these chapters show that the classical-liberal perspective is able to offer a coherent, imaginative, and constructive approach to a set of tangible governance challenges.

7

Metropolitan Governance

Polycentric Solutions for Complex Problems

To illustrate the applied-level prowess of the ideas introduced in the first two parts of this book, this chapter uses the case of metropolitan governance. In doing so, it builds on the Bloomington school's studies of police departments and the work of the scholars who advance that line of research.[1] This chapter uses the concept of polycentricity to understand how public administration in fact works, as well as to frame its problems and its appropriate domain of activity. From a descriptive point of view, it is important to properly account for the actual complexity of public administration and avoid the seduction of simple, but utterly impractical, idealizations. The metropolitan debate illustrates this problem clearly—showcasing the problem with "reformers" too infatuated with their models and too busy to check how the system they are trying to "improve" actually works. The first step in "reforming" metropolitan governance is to understand how metropolitan areas are in fact organized.

From a normative standpoint, the underlying thesis is that, even when government is involved in the production of public services, the most efficient form of organization is not hierarchical but polycentric. We use the example of police services to illustrate. This is also one of the first domains in which the polycentrism theoretical lens was applied. This chapter also revisits and presents new insights in the field of public administration and the literature, some fifty years after the Ostroms engaged in the metropolitan reform debate and launched their pioneering approach. The institutionalist, polycentricity-based, public choice perspective is applied, illustrated, and described at a concrete applied level.

The Complexity of Police Services

The provision of public safety and protection is the most basic of government services. How should police departments be organized to provide the best services at the lowest cost? Historically, metropolitan areas emerged in an unplanned fashion as neighboring small towns gradually grew to the point where their borders reached one another and combined into one de facto, but not de jure, large urban area. The administrative organization of metropolitan areas has remained decentralized because of their history. Should these legacy local governments be centralized as part of a larger hierarchical system which would govern the entire metropolitan area? The de facto organization is polycentric, reflecting the "multiplicity of political jurisdictions in a metropolitan area."[2] Should that be changed? Polycentricity is an important concept because it not only describes the de facto situation, but it can also be used to understand why the existing system works relatively well, in the sense that it has desirable emergent and unplanned properties. In the 1970s, as part of her first project at Indiana University, Elinor Ostrom coordinated a series of field studies of police department services in Indianapolis, Chicago, Grand Rapids, Nashville-Davidson, and St. Louis, followed by a more extensive national-level study covering eighty of the two hundred standard metropolitan statistical areas. That work is still the largest study of police departments performed to date. At the time, there were numerous calls to reform the organization of police departments by consolidating them. The consolidationists claimed that

> fragmentation of police services is extreme. . . . Wasted energies are lost motion due to overlapping, duplication, and noncooperation are not the worst consequences of this fragmentation. Large areas of the United States— particularly rural communities and the small jurisdictions in or near metropolitan areas—lack anything resembling modern, professional police protection.[3]

However, Elinor Ostrom, Roger Parks, and Gordon Whitaker discovered that "none of the major national recommendations for change cite empirical evidence to support their contentions" and, furthermore, that the recommendations were based on large misconceptions about how police departments were actually organized.[4] Every "fact" from the consolidationists' quote turned out to be a gross misconception. Ostrom, Parks, and Whitaker sought, first, to understand how police departments actually work and, second, to evaluate how well the departments were doing their job. They analyzed three types of direct services—patrol work, traffic control, and criminal investigations—and four types of auxiliary services—radio communications, adult pretrial detention, entry-level job training, and crime labs.

For example, although many police departments have their own crime labs, the researchers found that "state agencies supply lab services to police agencies in all but 1 of 80 standard metropolitan statistical areas. Seven states—California, Connecticut, Kentucky, Massachusetts, Oklahoma, Ohio, and South Carolina—have two different state agencies that supply lab services to direct service police agencies."[5] Despite the 1970s conventional wisdom that "having all services within the same department facilitates communication and coordination . . . in studying SMSAs [standard metropolitan statistical areas] with extensive division of services across agencies," E. Ostrom, Parks, and Whitaker "found considerable interdepartmental communication and coordination."[6] In other words, the arguments of consolidationists were shown to be based on a poorly informed perspective about how metropolitan areas actually operate. Different types of police activities have different economies of scale, and E. Ostrom and her colleagues have found that metropolitan police departments actually cooperated organically to take advantage of them. For instance, while patrol is usually done by the local departments (low economies of scale) and it is geographically circumscribed, homicide investigations are usually larger scale with local departments cooperating with the county sheriff and possibly the Federal Bureau of Investigation. By contrast, consolidating the small police departments as part of a larger metropolitan department led to lower quality patrols, as (a) fewer police were assigned to patrol and more were assigned to administrative overhead, and (b) the coproduction relationship between police and the community, based on more personal relationships, was undermined.

Police auxiliary services also showcased interesting examples of complex patterns of delivery.[7] For example, for adult pretrial detentions, the county sheriffs usually provide facilities used by many local police departments. Similarly, entry-level job training also has economies of scale. As such, few police departments train the new entrants themselves. Instead, they outsource this to state or federal agencies or to technical community colleges and institutes. Interestingly, some police departments use more than one single technical institute as providers of police training. Such competition among technical institutes is probably beneficial for keeping the quality of training high.[8]

As Vincent Ostrom, Charles Tiebout, and Robert Warren have intuited in their original theoretical paper published in 1961,[9] which started the polycentricity approach to public administration, such different services often have different optimal scales of production. Elinor Ostrom and her students have found that the organization of police departments indeed involves complex delivery patterns, including (a) autonomous local provision of some services; (b) cooperation across jurisdictions for large-scale problems; (c) alternate provision of the same service, based on predefined criteria, by more than one agency in the same jurisdiction; and (d) rare duplication of the provision of services by more than one agency without either cooperation or predefined criteria for alternation.[10]

Before exploring the general argument in more detail, we examine now the failure of hierarchical top-down interference in the realm of policing. After comparing "police departments serving similar neighborhoods within a metropolitan area," Elinor Ostrom "never found a large department policing numerous neighborhoods that outperformed smaller departments within the same metropolitan area in regard to direct services to citizens."[11] Furthermore, the "most efficient producers supply more output for given inputs in high multiplicity metropolitan areas than do the efficient producers in metropolitan areas with fewer producers."[12] As Elinor Ostrom recalled,

> The consistent finding from this series of studies is that small and medium-sized police departments perform more effectively than large police departments serving similar neighborhoods, and frequently at lower costs. . . . Instead of being a "problem" for the metropolitan area, small departments frequently contribute to the improvement of police services in the area.[13]

Figure 7.1 shows a comparison of residents' satisfaction with police performance for six neighborhoods in the Indianapolis, Indiana, area.[14] The cities of Beech Grove, Lawrence, and Speedway had small independent police departments,

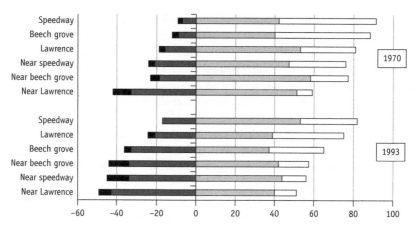

Figure 7.1 Performance of independent versus consolidated police departments for neighborhoods in Indianapolis, Indiana, 1970 and 1993, measured by surveyed citizens satisfaction. The colors indicate the levels of satisfaction from "Outstanding" to "Inadequate. Michael D. McGinnis, ed., *Polycentricity and Local Public Economies: Readings from the Workshop in Political Theory and Policy Analysis* (Ann Arbor: University of Michigan Press, 1999), 350.

whereas the nearby neighborhoods were covered by the Indianapolis Metropolitan Police Department. Across-the-board satisfaction with the police was greater for the smaller departments, which was indicative that smaller departments tended to be more responsive to residents' needs. Across-the-board satisfaction with the police departments decreased from 1970 to 1993, more so for the consolidated departments.

The Failure of Community Policing

Partly as a result of studies of police and local public economies in the 1970s, a reform movement took shape in the 1980s. Calls for a move toward community policing became more popular. As a result,

> police departments were advised to put police officers and community members in closer proximity by creating police "substations" and requiring police departments to have officers on foot patrol.[15]

At first glance, it seems that such reforms should have worked. But the results are generally mixed or negative, and the "reduction in crime [has been] primarily due to a trend towards larger police forces that has little to do with the adoption of any particular policing strategy."[16]

However, the move toward community policing has been largely illusory or superficial. Part of the problem is that community policing has been adopted as a top-down policy and in many ways has been a form without content—more of a populist slogan than a genuine reform. A bigger part of the problem is that police activities have actually been centralized, with the federal government having a greater influence on local police departments, especially because of the war on drugs and a move toward police militarization. In other words, further centralization has swamped whatever moves have been made toward genuine community policing: the top-down approach to the establishment of community policing and the increasing reach of federal interventions into local law enforcement have prevented the emergence of true community policing as understood by Ostrom and her colleagues at the workshop. Instead there has been a trend of centralization and militarization of the police, shifting the focus away from the needs of the community and toward the homogenous goals of federal policy.[17]

To make matters worse, the police-community meetings have gradually been bureaucratized. For example,

> Seattle's attempts at community policing were successful in the late 1970's and early 1980's when they were driven primarily by concerned citizen activists. However, over time, began to send fewer beat police and more bureaucrats to community meetings . . . participation waned as citizens began to feel that the purpose of the meetings had shifted from learning about citizen concerns to persuading the community to support traditional police action.[18]

The failure of community policing was not surprising to the Bloomington scholars. Elinor Ostrom and Whitaker warned of the possible distortion of the idea from the beginning:

> The problems in obtaining an adequate knowledge about local situations have led several large-scale police departments to experiment with local commander systems and other arrangements to decentralize administrative control of neighborhood patrol forces. While this reform may increase direct supervision of patrolmen in the field and may lead to more effective coordination of their efforts within neighborhoods, *it may be expected to decrease the responsiveness to citizens of patrolmen serving these areas* [emphasis added].[19]

In other words, properly understood, community policing involves not just a decentralized mechanism for knowledge aggregation but also—and this is critically important—allowance for the *goals* of the local government to be determined by its citizens. A decentralized police department that takes orders from the federal government and that is dependent for revenue and equipment on the central government is not going to be responsive to people's needs and will not perform well on most criteria of citizens' satisfaction.

The idea that local police departments should be financially independent of the central government and should be funded by the local community in order to be responsive to its citizens is known as fiscal equivalence.[20] That idea was familiar to E. Ostrom and Whitaker, and they recognized its importance in connection to the problem of political representation.[21]

The idea of fiscal equivalence is usually controversial because it implies that rich neighborhoods will have more resources than poor ones and hence better services. E. Ostrom and Whitaker's response to that is twofold. On the one hand, centralization of police departments and other local public services will not lead to improved outcomes for poor neighborhoods. On the contrary, those neighborhoods would be robbed of political representation. Centralized governments still respond more to richer constituencies; hence, absent local political representation, poorer neighborhoods are even more likely to be left behind.

On the other hand, E. Ostrom and Whitaker note that redistribution can, to some extent, be pursued as a distinct activity. There is no need to centralize the entire local public economy, with all its activities, to distribute money to poorer neighborhoods. That said, to avoid the Samaritan's dilemma—the perverse distortion of an aid recipient's incentives away from self-reliance—E. Ostrom and Whitaker argue that redistribution should be limited to emergency situations: "Citywide forces could be utilized to supplement the needs of any local area in times of emergency. Redistribution to the poorer neighborhood districts within the large city could be provided from citywide as well as state and federal sources."[22]

It is also important to bear in mind that performance depends to a large extent on how money is spent, rather than on how much is spent. Peter Boettke, Liya Palagashvili, and Jayme Lemke find that "Chicago police spent 14 times the dollar amount that the independent police departments did—but despite this differential in expenditure, citizens in the smaller communities received the same or higher level of service."[23]

That type of problem is most evident in black neighborhoods. In their study of police districts in Chicago, E. Ostrom and Whitaker find that "black citizens are among the constituents cited as least satisfied with the performance of local police and other public officials." Redistribution of resources does not help. On the contrary,

> redistribution of resources, itself, is not sufficient to bring about responsive police services. It appears that considerable resource redistribution is . . . occurring within the city of Chicago. More resources are probably being devoted to policing in the black neighborhoods studied than are derived revenue for such purposes from these areas. Residents of these neighborhoods, however, find police services no better and police somewhat less responsive than do village residents *despite* the much greater difference in resources devoted to policing.[24]

E. Ostrom and Whitaker found that because of so-called preventive policing there was, paradoxically, both too much policing and too little, as the use of the preventive patrolling by "some police forces simultaneously increases the resentment of residents and diverts police manpower from other activities such as answering calls and investigating the many crimes that do occur in the ghetto."[25] Interestingly, in this 1974 publication, the negative attitudes of black citizens toward the police were inversely related to their income: "Black respondents of higher income levels tended to be less likely to give high ratings to police than black respondents of lower income levels."[26] The bottom line was that in Chicago and elsewhere "police seem to be failing to serve the residents of many black neighborhoods in US cities,"[27] and the main reason was the subversion of genuinely local public economies by top-down control.

In the years after the Bloomington school conducted its studies, the situation deteriorated further. A 2016 study by Chicago's Police Accountability Task Force, with members appointed by the mayor, reveals a shocking situation.[28] The report finds that black residents were far more likely to be "stopped without justification, verbally and physically abused, and in some instances arrested, and then detained without counsel." Furthermore, of "404 police shootings between 2008 and 2015, . . . among the victims, 74% were black, even though black people make up just 33% of Chicago's population. . . . Of the 1,886 Taser uses between 2012 and 2015, 76% of those hit by stun guns were black." This decades-long history of police racism significantly worsened as a result of the war on drugs and police militarization,[29] and it is now even more difficult to change: "False arrests, coerced confessions and wrongful convictions are also a part of this history. Lives [have been] lost and countless more damaged. These events and others mark a long, sad history of death, false imprisonment, physical and verbal abuse, and general discontent about police actions in neighborhoods of color."[30]

In 1974, E. Ostrom and Whitaker analyzed a variety of reform proposals, including calls for increased professionalization of the police force and access to larger funding. "Police effectiveness depends, in part, on police understanding the nature of the community being served and police openness to suggestions, criticism, and complaints,"[31] they conclude. As a result, they find the following:

> Community control of police may, thus, provide an institutional framework for the effective expression of black citizen demands for impartial police service. . . . Professionalism alone does not appear to provide sufficient controls so that police will be responsive to their needs for protection and respect. Community control places that responsibility on the people themselves and provides them with the mechanisms by which to exercise it.[32]

Unfortunately, that advice was not taken, and instead the term *community policing* was distorted beyond recognition to mean almost the exact opposite of what the Bloomington school had recommended. As Vincent Ostrom would increasingly complain over the course of his life, the Orwellian distortion of language is a significant, understudied phenomenon in public choice.[33]

The Impossibility of Efficient Hierarchical Public Economies

The most important point made by Vincent Ostrom, Charles Tiebout, and Robert Warren is that analysis of the nature of public services that a metropolitan public department must solve leads to this conclusion: establishment of a consolidated hierarchical department unavoidably gives way to massive inefficiencies because administrative units operate at rigid scales. However, the scale of public issues varies and is always changing.[34]

The idea behind the impossibility theorem is fairly simple. All complex societies face numerous collective issues, which, by their nature, occur at various scales. To make matters more complicated, those scales change all the time as a result of new technologies and other social processes. By contrast, the public administration units are relatively few in number (compared to the overall number of issues) and have relatively rigid geographical scales. As such, a given administrative unit is always faced with challenges that do not properly fit its administrative scale. This is true for administrative units at all scales. In a hierarchical system, when the scale of a problem is larger than the scale of administrative unit A, responsibility for solving the problem goes to the larger administrative unit B, at a higher level. But B's scale can never accommodate all the problems that are larger than A's scale. As such, the hierarchical system is bound to be rife with inefficiencies because A has only one higher-level unit, B. Furthermore, the logic of bureaucracy leads all administrative units to expand beyond their proper scope.[35]

By contrast, polycentric governance assumes that small-scale administrative units can organize on a quasi ad hoc basis to address some larger-scale problems but not others. Different larger-scale problems are addressed by different configurations of smaller-scale units. As we have seen, E. Ostrom, Parks, and Whitaker find that police departments cooperated in precisely that diverse manner to take advantage of economies of scale with respect to criminal investigations, adult pretrial detentions, and auxiliary services (such as crime labs and entry-level job training).[36] As Ostrom, Tiebout, and Warren put it,

> The statement that a government is "too large (or too small) to deal with a problem" often overlooks the possibility that the scale of the public and the political community need not coincide with that of the formal boundaries of a public organization. Informal arrangements between public organizations may create a political community large enough to deal with any particular public's problem. Similarly, a public organization may be able to constitute political communities within its boundaries to deal with problems that affect only a subset of the population. It would be a mistake to conclude that public organizations are of an inappropriate size until the informal mechanisms, which might permit larger or smaller political communities, are investigated.[37]

Those informal mechanisms are the alternative to the rigid hierarchical organization. Ignoring polycentricity, partly because of misguided ideas about reform, can potentially generate huge costs. Such costs can arise especially with the logic of bureaucracy, which makes it exceedingly difficult to turn back from such reforms once they have failed. Elinor Ostrom highlights the issue by stating, "Failure, in many cases, leads to adoption of another program—one often based, as was the first, on inadequate analysis of the strategic behavior of the different actors. Failure seems to breed failure."[38]

That type of polycentric organization is, of course, not restricted to police departments. It covers all aspects of public economies. Vincent Ostrom stresses that the whole range of human affairs is polycentric.[39] The hierarchical arrangement of any complex public service will unavoidably be inefficient and slow to respond to changes. The only way to have a responsive system is to have a polycentric system that addresses various issues at different scales, which means that, to the extent governments are democratically accountable, citizens should expect them to create a polycentric organization of public administration. To the extent that politicians and other public entrepreneurs face constraints in delivering good governance, they will be guided by the inherent logic of the complexity of collective goods to create polycentric arrangements. It is thus not an accident that polycentric systems in which self-governance is allowed to operate as a guiding principle are observed across the world.

The Ostrom-Tiebout-Warren impossibility theorem can be reframed as an unavoidability theorem. Everywhere that politics works fairly well, that is, where the public sector is fairly responsive to citizens' needs and desires, polycentric governance, rather than hierarchical governance, is bound to be observed. Next, we look in more detail at the reasons why hierarchical public administration, unlike polycentric governance, is bound to be rife with inefficiencies.

Control over the Cause of the Problem

The cause of a problem must be under the control of the relevant administrative unit. For example, water pollution caused by a factory upriver that is outside the jurisdiction of the local authority cannot be solved by that authority. In the 1960s, when V. Ostrom, Tiebout, and Warren were writing, the following was happening: the city of Pasadena experienced severe smog, but the city's boundary did not "cover an area sufficient to assure effective control of the appropriate meteorological and social space that would include the essential variables constituting a 'smogisphere' of Southern California."[40] Individual cities in Southern California could not deal effectively with the problem, so county air pollution control districts were organized for the Los Angeles metropolitan area. Yet the districts failed, and the state government had "to assume an increasingly important role in smog control."[41]

The same holds for positive externalities. When an administrative unit provides a public good, there must be a way to prevent free-riding. If one group acts responsibly to avoid overfishing, for example, the problem is solved only if other groups are also prevented from overfishing. Mirroring what Buchanan and Tullock[42] would famously write a year later, V. Ostrom, Tiebout, and Warren summarize the situation as follows: "A function of government, then, is to internalize the externalities—positive and negative—for those goods which the producers and consumers are unable or unwilling to internalize for themselves."[43]

That idea is far more general than the concern with metropolitan governance. For example, in her studies of common-pool resources management problems, E. Ostrom encounters again and again the importance of polycentricity, and she urges

> readers to think more positively about complex, polycentric systems of governance that are created by individuals who have considerable autonomy to engage in self-governance. *Given the wide variety of ecological problems that*

individuals face at diverse scales, an important design principle is getting the boundaries of any one system to roughly fit the ecological boundaries of the problem it is designed to address [emphasis added]. Since most ecological problems are nested from very small local ecologies to those of global proportions, following this principle requires substantial investment in governance systems at multiple levels—each with some autonomy but each exposed to information, sanctioning, and actions from below and above.[44]

Notice the similarity to the challenges to metropolitan governance. And as there, the same intellectual difficulty is encountered here: "One of the important threats is the effort to impose uniform rules and large boundaries on systems so they are more comprehensible to academics and policymakers."[45]

Polycentricity is quite different from simple decentralization. Large-scale problems require large-scale solutions. The point is not to reduce the scale of all administrative units, but to fit the scale of the administrative unit to the scale of the issue. That said, the confusion between polycentricity and decentralization is somewhat understandable considering that overcentralization is far more common than undercentralization. As such, in practice, the concern for fitting an administrative unit to the scale of the problem often amounts to calling for decentralization, as in the example of community policing.

One simple way to understand the difference between polycentricity and decentralization (and thus fragmentation) is to think of the distinction proposed by the scholars Claudia Pahl-Wostl and Christian Knieper[46] and illustrated in figure 7.2.

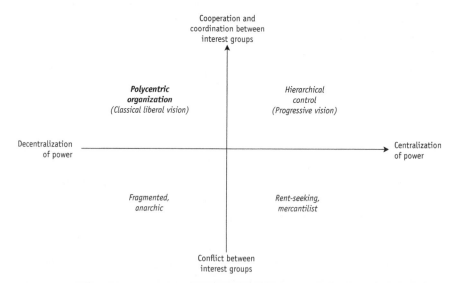

Figure 7.2 The distinction between polycentricity and fragmentation. Adapted from Claudia Pahl-Wostl and Christian Knieper, "The Capacity of Water Governance to Deal with the Climate Change Adaptation Challenge: Using Fuzzy Set Qualitative Comparative Analysis to Distinguish Between Polycentric, Fragmented and Centralized Regimes," *Global Environmental Change* 29 (2014): 139–54.

Accurately Measuring the Demand for Public Goods and the Opportunity Cost of Providing Them

When government tries to fix a problem, the cost of the problem must be properly evaluated; otherwise, government might spend either too many or too few resources to tackle the problem. But public goods are notoriously difficult to evaluate because everyone expects others to shoulder the costs. For example, surveys are a somewhat imperfect method of assessing costs because people might complain about everything—that is, far beyond the resources they are willing to contribute to address a given problem. To put it differently, when someone else is supposed to fix a problem, it is that person's job to find the resources to do it, and it is the job of others to complain.

According to the Ostroms, there is a more fundamental reason why the true demand for public goods is inherently difficult to evaluate:

> A decision to buy a particular good or service reflects willingness to forgo all other opportunities for which the money could have been used. An expression of demand in a market system always includes reference to what is forgone as well as what is purchased.
>
> The articulation of preferences in the public sector often fails to take account of forgone opportunities. . . . Because most public goods and services are financed through a process of taxation involving no choice, optimal levels of expenditure are difficult to establish.[47]

V. Ostrom, Tiebout, and Warren refer to this issue as the problem of "packageability" and note that "private goods, because they are easily packageable, are readily subject to measurement and quantification.[48] Public goods, by contrast, are generally not so measurable. With private goods each person gets his or her own separate, individual good, whereas with public goods everyone gets the same shared good. That may make coercion necessary to prevent free-riding, but

> whereas the income received for providing a private good conveys information about the demand for that good, payment of taxes under threat of coercion indicated only that taxpayers prefer paying taxes to going to jail. Little or no information is revealed about user preferences for goods procured with tax-supported expenditures.[49]

What is meant is that "alternative mechanisms to prices are needed to articulate and aggregate demands into collective choices that reflect individuals' preferences for a particular quantity and/or quality of public goods or services."[50] But all such alternative mechanisms suffer from serious problems. E. Ostrom and Whitaker note these problems with respect to rigorously evaluating the outputs of police departments: "Police departments characteristically provide all services without consumer charges, even though some similar services are provided privately. Thus, the market value of police output cannot be obtained."[51]

A standard result in public choice is that a person's decisions as part of a collective (e.g., when a person votes) are far less carefully made than are personal decisions because each individual has less control over the outcome.[52] For instance, regardless of the candidate for whom an individual votes, the candidate who wins the election, wins. There is no point for someone to regret his or her decision too much afterward. By contrast, if an individual buys what turns out to be the wrong car, that person does not have to live with that outcome and can justifiably regret not having made a different decision. This leads to troubling conclusions with respect to how much attention people pay to the costs of publicly provided goods.

Fiscal Equivalence and Redistribution

We have noted the importance of fiscal equivalence in the case of the failure of community policing. Again, the argument is far more general. Mirroring Buchanan and Wagner's concerns in *Democracy in Deficit*,[53] V. Ostrom and E. Ostrom note the following:

> Costs must be proportioned to benefits if people are to have any sense of economic reality. Otherwise beneficiaries may assume that public goods are free goods, that money in the public treasury is "the government's money," and that no opportunities are forgone in spending that money. When this happens, the foundations of a democratic society are threatened.[54]

The problem of populist politicians promising free goods, of course, occurs perpetually, and the voting public is more or less willing to let itself be swayed by illusions. The Ostroms note that an imperfect solution to this potentially large problem is the idea of "fiscal equivalence."[55] In addressing the problem of pressure groups, Buchanan and Tullock describe the possible solution as "requir[ing] that individuals and groups securing differential benefits also bear the differential costs."[56] The concept of fiscal equivalence is one of the major design principles for a sustainable social system, according to which proportionality between benefits and costs should exist.[57]

A problem with fiscal equivalence, as both Buchanan and Tullock and the Ostroms recognize, is that it cannot deal very well with "cases where over-all redistribution cannot be put aside."[58] Consider the example of a program that provides federal funds to aid depressed coal mining areas in West Virginia. Special taxes on the state's citizens "would be self-defeating." If such aid is to be financed out of general tax revenue, "a veritable Pandora's box may be opened." The reason is evident: depressed communities all over the United States—from old textile towns in New England to former mining areas in Colorado—"may all demand and receive federal assistance," and "excessive costs will be imposed on the whole population" as a result.[59]

The question, then, is one of how the system can be organized such that "genuinely depressed areas, considered as such by the whole population, would tend to be provided with assistance without at the same time opening up the whole set of grants to areas not considered to be deserving of assistance."[60] We can think of two possible solutions to that problem.

The first solution is to draw a lesson from how insurance companies deal with moral hazard. For example, to avoid having people indulge in too many unnecessary and expensive medical procedures, health insurance companies require copayments. By requiring members to pay a portion of costs, the companies introduce consideration of overall costs into a patient's decision about whether to have a particular procedure or service. The same type of approach can be used to address the problem of unnecessary and expensive medical procedures: the federal government can require a certain level of copayment from local governments.

That is how the European Union's structural funds program works. To access those funds, which are usually provided to poorer union members by the richer members for specific projects, the recipient is required to cosponsor the project. This can be understood as implicitly forcing fund recipients to rank the importance of various possible projects and to request structural funds only for the most important ones. Some of the more effective Eastern European governments, such as Poland's, have managed to organize in this fashion relatively well, and that has led to a high absorption rate of such funds. (Of the total funds available, principal recipient countries usually receive only a fraction, because they cannot organize to provide copayments.) The governments of those countries have used structural funds to help finance relatively important public goods, such as building roads. Less effective governments, such as Romania's, have been far less successful in obtaining structural funds, and this can be understood as a failure to organize collectively to rank the importance of various possible projects and then to cosponsor only the most important ones.

On the same grounds, Elinor Ostrom is critical of interventions that do not account for how an intervention ends up distorting the recipient developing country's incentives in perverse ways, a phenomenon known as the Samaritan's dilemma[61]:

> Showering a region with funds is a poor investment if that serves mainly to bolster political careers and builds little at the ground level. It makes more sense to invest modest levels of donor funds in local projects in which the recipients are willing to invest some of their own resources. If the level of external funding becomes very large without being strongly tied to a responsibility for repayment over time, local efforts at participation may be directed more at rent seeking than at productive investment activities.[62]

Another possible solution stems from analysis of the problem in terms of concentrated benefits and dispersed costs. Buchanan and Tullock's Pandora's box is opened because each special interest gets its concentrated benefit, while everyone gets stuck with the dispersed cost. For each case, the dispersed cost to one individual is very small, but it adds up. Paradoxically, everyone can end up worse off because the amount they end up paying in total, bit by bit, is lower than what they receive. That is the rent-seeking mechanism that Olson warns us that if left unchecked would gradually lead to stagnation, and it is one of the reasons why regulatory capitalism is not sustainable.[63]

Buchanan and Tullock think that one possible institutional solution to the problem would be to organize the aid relationship on an equal-size criterion. To ensure that recipients and providers have equal bargaining powers, their numbers should be roughly the same. "For example, if the designed aid to West Virginia were to be collected from special taxes levied on Oklahoma only, then we could be assured that roughly balancing political forces would determine the final outcome."[64] That sounds unusual and indeed does not reflect the hierarchical approach currently in use. Instead it would describe a polycentric mutual aid system in which providing assistance is paired with effective monitoring and assessment of genuine need. The civil or fraternal mutual aid societies that existed before the rise of the welfare state had just such a polycentric organization, but the system was largely replaced by the rise of the welfare state.[65] To some extent, such civil society organization still exists in faith-based initiatives.[66]

The Separation of Production and Provision of Goods

A recurring theme in the Bloomington school is that public services and goods that are consumed collectively can be produced by a variety of methods. Unlike the simplified perspective in most accounts of public economics, in which public services are assumed almost by definition to be produced by a government agency, the Ostroms and their collaborators document many hybrid institutions that do not fit well in either purely state or purely market categories. In contrast to the conflation between the public sphere and government,

> we need not think of "government" or "governance" as something provided by states alone. Families, voluntary associations, villages, and other forms of human association all involve some form of self-government. Rather than looking only to states, we need to give much more attention to building the kinds of basic institutional structures that enable people to find ways of relating constructively to one another and of resolving problems in their daily lives.[67]

One way to make sense of hybrid private-public arrangements is to think about the distinction between provision, or paying for a good, and production, creation of the good. As noted by Ronald Oakerson and Roger Parks, "One key insight of V. Ostrom, Tiebout, and Warren (1961) . . . was that public provision did not require public production by the same governmental unit. Indeed, all governments provide services to their citizenry that they do not produce in-house."[68] Oakerson and Parks also develop a more complex analysis of provision.[69] They note that, beyond just the decision to subsidize the production of a particular good, provision may include public decisions about "what quantities of each service to provide and what quality standards to apply, and how to arrange for and monitor production."[70] Whether "to contract out and what to produce in-house is a city-specific decision [that] requires careful attention to the nature of specific public goods and services and the local market for their procurement."[71]

The institutional complexity of hybrid systems can be even greater. The Ostroms note that a government may obtain the desired public goods by a variety of methods such as the following[72]:

- Operating its own production unit (e.g., a city with its own fire or police department).
- Contracting with a private firm (e.g., a city that contracts with a private firm for snow removal, street repair, or traffic light maintenance).
- Establishing standards of service and leaving it up to each consumer to select a private vendor and to purchase service (e.g., a city that licenses taxis to provide service or refuse collection firms to remove trash).
- Issuing vouchers to families and permitting them to purchase service from any authorized supplier (e.g., a jurisdiction that issues food stamps, rent vouchers, or education vouchers or that operates a Medicaid program).
- Contracting with another government unit (e.g., a city that purchases tax assessment and collection services from a county government unit, sewage treatment from a special sanitary district, or special vocational education services from a school board in an adjacent city).
- Producing some services with its own unit, and purchasing other services from other jurisdictions and from private firms (e.g., a city with its own police force that purchases laboratory services from the county sheriff's office, joins with several adjacent communities to pay for a joint dispatching service, or pays a private ambulance firm to provide emergency medical transportation).

Such arrangements, which are common, allow for a much more flexible public sector, but they do not fit very well into simple economic categories that assume clear distinctions between private and public, markets and governments. They lead to what the economist Richard Wagner calls an "entangled political economy."[73]

Conclusion

Using the case of metropolitan governance as an empirical reference point, V. Ostrom developed the concept of polycentricity by generalizing into the realm of public economics the concept of markets. At the same time, he avoided the unrealistic perfect competition assumption of Tiebout's first model of institutional competition.[74] As we have seen, when the mainstream of the public administration profession argued in favor of consolidating metropolitan administrations, the Ostroms dissented. They developed a competing intuition thanks to an ingenious analogy to markets, which highlights the potential efficiency of local public economies.[75] From the Ostroms' perspective, the most likely path to efficient public administration is not consolidation but rather the development of smart overarching rules that allow for productive arrangements between organizations that

> would manifest market-like characteristics and display both efficiency-inducing and error-correcting behavior. Coordination in the public sector need not, in those circumstances, rely exclusively upon bureaucratic command structures controlled by chief executives. Instead, the structure of interorganizational arrangements may create important economic opportunities and evoke self-regulating tendencies.[76]

The implications for the ways in which the problem of governance is understood are momentous. In her account of polycentricity, E. Ostrom observes that

> officials and policy analysts who presume that they have the right design can be dangerous. They are likely to assume that citizens are short-sighted and motivated only by extrinsic benefits and costs. Somehow, the officials and policy analysts assume that they have different motivations and can find optimal policy because they are not directly involved in the problem. . . . They are indeed isolated from the problems. This leaves them with little capability to adapt and learn in light of information about outcomes resulting from their policies. All too often, these "optimal" policies have Leviathan-like characteristics to them.[77]

Half a century later, there is a better grasp of the empirical evidence regarding the validity of the polycentric perspective with respect to local public economies, metropolitan governance, and common-pool resources management. But such examples may still seem relatively simple. Perhaps the system of police services in a metropolitan area is not large enough to create serious impediments to the creation of informal interorganizational arrangements. In his overview of different types of polycentric systems, V. Ostrom lays out several more challenging examples apart from markets and local public economies.[78] They all have the same features. They are decentralized systems in which coordination happens without hierarchical command and control, and they lack market prices for a coordination mechanism. How does coordination happen then? Such are the hard cases of emergent social orders, and the concept of polycentricity aims to provide a framework for analyzing under what conditions such emergent orders can be expected to coordinate in a productive fashion.

Beyond the purely scientific interest in building such a theory of productive emergent orders, more general than just the theory of markets, an understanding of the conditions under which departure from hierarchical organizations can be made without a descent into chaos is crucially important for building viable democratic societies in which citizens have as much control as possible over the rules they must follow. The notion of polycentricity has helped us frame and focus our approach here. As we have seen, complex governance problems such as those of metropolitan areas could be approached and reframed in novel and constructive ways, using the conceptual and theoretical apparatus advanced in the first two parts of this book. This chapter demonstrates that an alternative perspective is viable and fruitful not only in theory but also at the applied level of concrete governance domains and problems.

Independent Regulatory Agencies and Their Reform

An Exercise in Institutional Imagination

The growth of independent regulatory agencies (IRAs) is one of the biggest and yet largely neglected challenges to contemporary public governance. Such regulatory agencies have a longer history in the United States, but in recent decades they have also become increasingly important in Western Europe and other developed countries.[1] Their purpose is to regulate markets, while at the same time providing a credible commitment that they will not over-regulate them out of political expediency reasons. Due to the diversity of forms regulatory agencies may take, and due to the different ways they are connected to the political system, their "independence" is always a matter of context and degree. Thus the nature and degree of their independence varies from presidential to parliamentary systems in function of factors such as how the delegation of power is taking place, whether or not they are part of the executive branch, whether they are regulatory bodies exercising authority delegated by the government or the legislature, whether the hybrid regulator is having some degree of private ownership, and so on. Examples of federal-level regulatory agencies in the United States give a sense of this diversity (table 8.1).

Because IRAs are entities with great regulatory power but ambiguous accountability, they are even more vulnerable to regulatory capture than democratic legislatures. Furthermore, when they make errors their authority is rarely diminished. It is often expanded. For example, the errors made by the Federal Reserve have contributed to a financial crisis and a prolonged recession, but its authority has been expanded. Taking as a benchmark an ideal type model of IRAs, one may conjecture that the more independent the IRAs are, the more vulnerable they are to capture and the less accountable they are for their errors. Instead of *curbing* knowledge and incentive problems, IRAs *combine* and *amplify* them. Adding another administrative layer and endowing it with an aura of expert legitimacy makes the problems worse by obscuring the regulatory process even more.

Interestingly, Friedrich Hayek had been warning against the growth of IRAs as early as the *Road to Serfdom*, where he noted that "as planning extends, the delegation of legislative powers to diverse Boards and Authorities becomes increasingly common."[2] He worried that "the broadest powers are conferred on new authorities

Table 8.1 **US independent regulatory agencies**

Name	Year created	What the agency regulates
Interstate Commerce Commission/ Surface Transportation Board	1887	Commercial and passenger transportation across state borders; the commission was replaced by the board in 1995
Food and Drug Administration	1906	Consumer products (from food and drugs to toys); labeling for safety reasons; since 1969, also promotes public sanitation; since 1971, also radiation control
Federal Trade Commission	1914	Mergers, price discrimination, and deceptive labeling, packaging, and advertising
Federal Reserve System	1914	Banking and money supply
Federal Communications Commission	1934	All broadcasting: radio, TV, cable, telegraph, satellite
Securities and Exchange Commission	1934	Financial markets
National Labor Relations Board	1935	Labor practices
Federal Aviation Administration	1958	Air commerce, airports
Environmental Protection Agency	1970	Air pollution, waste disposal, radiation; since 1980s, also climate change and promotes education about the environment
Occupational Safety and Health Administration	1970	Work conditions
Consumer Product Safety Commission	1973	Consumer products to protect against fire hazards, poisonous substances; labeling for safety reasons
Nuclear Regulatory Commission	1975	Nuclear power plants; prevents theft of nuclear materials
Federal Energy Regulatory Commission	1977	Electricity prices, oil and gas transportation prices by pipelines

which, without being bound by fixed rules, have almost unlimited discretion in regulating this or that activity of the people."[3] This is indeed what has happened under the current system of delegating regulatory powers to IRAs. This process of increased delegation undermines the ideal of a rule of law society: "If the law says that such a

Board or Authority may do what it pleases, anything that Board or Authority does is legal—but its actions are certainly not subject to the Rule of Law. By giving the government unlimited powers, the most arbitrary rule can be made legal."[4] Since Hayek wrote this, regulatory agencies and especially regulatory agencies claiming "independence" have expanded enormously.

Looking across 16 sectors of the economy in 49 developed nations, Jacint Jordana, David Levi-Faur, and Xavier Fernández i Marán[5] have found that the rate by which new regulatory agencies were created grew from about 3 agencies a year in the 1970s, to 7 a year in the 1980s, to about 30 a year in the 1990s. The United States provides a fairly typical example of those trends. The increase in staffing at federal regulatory agencies in this country grew from about 50,000 staff members in the early 1960s, to a peak of 150,000 in the early 1980s, followed by a slight decline to about 100,000 during the Reagan administration. Regulatory agency staffing returned to a high level of about 170,000 employees annually throughout the 1990s and then a sharp increase to more than 250,000 in the 2000s.[6] Similarly, the growth of federal government spending on regulation grew from about $3 billion in the 1960s (in 2000 dollars adjusted for inflation), to about $15 billion in the early 1990s, to more than $40 billion in 2009 and 2010.[7]

The organizations that make up the traditional public sector have drastically evolved over the past fifty years. In the United States, a series of hybrid organizations have come to the fore, and Congress has been increasingly engaged in quasi-governmental issues ranging from the creation of nonprofit organizations to promote individual national parks to proposals to strengthen regulation of government-sponsored enterprises such as Fannie Mae.[8] Those hybrid organizations or quasi-governmental institutions (see figure 8.1) are entities that have "some legal relation or association, however tenuous, to the federal government."[9] Among those organizations, those claiming some sort of "independence" are of particular interest.

From a public choice perspective, let us consider what may be called the "independent regulatory agencies dilemma." On the one hand, if IRAs are independent of political control and shielded from democratic pressures, what creates the incentives for them to further the public interest? In our discussions of public choice, we have seen how the idea of simply putting experts in charge is naive. Technical expertise notwithstanding, such a system would be rife with problems regarding incentives. The incentives problem is indeed endemic in IRAs, as figure 8.2 illustrates. On the other hand, if IRAs attract rent-seeking away from the political sector, what is the incentive for the political sector to create genuinely independent IRAs? The rent-seeking problem may undermine the rationale for creating IRAs in the first place. That rationale was to further economic efficiency for which the political sector could then take credit. The sector could do so because of the general public's rational ignorance of who is genuinely responsible for what. At the same time, the rationale for creating IRAs would diminish the benefits that politicians can get from the rent-seeking firms and organizations. Thus, we do not expect politicians to create fully independent IRAs; indeed, this is what we see. Real-world IRAs are audited, and the nominations to leadership positions are under political control. Some may think that the trade-off leads to a happy outcome because it alleviates the first problem (see figure 8.2).

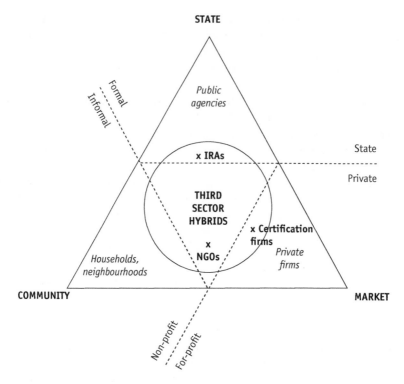

Figure 8.1 Third-sector hybrids and the approximate position of nongovernment organizations, independent regulatory agencies, and private certification companies. Adapted from Adalbert Evers and Jean-Louis Laville, *The Third Sector in Europe* (Cheltenham, UK: Edward Elgar, 2004), and Victor A. Pestoff, "Third Sector and Co-operative Services—An Alternative to Privatization," *Journal of Consumer Policy* 15, no. 1 (1992): 21–45.

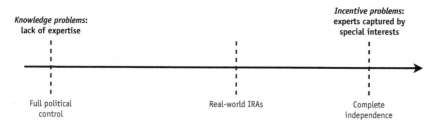

Figure 8.2 Independent regulatory agencies—between full political control and full independence.

The intellectual background behind the creation and control of IRAs is strangely hybrid. If we adopt an idealized view of democracy, ignoring the public choice causes of government failures, full political control in the areas covered by IRAs would only lead to knowledge problems because neither politicians nor the general public have the proper expertise. On the other hand, if we adopt a fairly realistic perspective on IRAs, we begin to understand the need to partially control and audit them. Thus, the rationale for the current organization of IRAs seems to be based on an idealized view of politics but a fairly realistic view of IRAs. By contrast, if we adopt a realistic perspective on politics as well, it may be the case that instead of curbing both knowledge and incentive problems, real-world IRAs combine and amplify them. If incentive problems in politics are ultimately caused by voters' rational ignorance and the problem of dispersed costs and concentrated benefits, adding another administrative layer, and endowing it with an aura of expert legitimacy, will only make the rational ignorance problem worse by further obscuring the regulatory process from the public.

This chapter applies to this theme some of the theoretical frameworks and insights introduced in the first two parts of the book. We take a concrete public governance issue characterized by hybridity to show how it looks in diagnosis and in potential solutions when seen from the perspective of public choice and comparative institutional analysis.

We indicate problems which are endemic for all IRAs, and that they are by no means accidental or easily corrected. There are deep structural reasons for why such problems appear. We also argue that there are no simple solutions here, as—contrary to the typical critics of IRAs—we believe that the attributes of IRAs cannot in fact be assumed by Congress or parliaments. Furthermore, for reasons that will become clear, politicians have very little incentive to assume the responsibility for the tasks currently performed by IRAs.

The Political Economy of Regulatory Hybridity and Independence

The first question we can ask is, "Why would politicians decide to create regulatory agencies with significant degrees of independence in the first place?" The answer is by no means obvious. At first glance, it looks rather paradoxical that the political class would voluntarily decide to reduce its own power. Every time we see someone apparently tying their own hand, something interesting must be going on.

As captured by the Congressional Research Service, there are a number of factors that influence the creation of agencies displaying hybridity and independence:[10] (a) current controls on the federal budget process that encourage agencies to develop new sources of revenue; (b) a desire by advocates of agencies and programs to be exempt from central management laws, especially statutory ceilings on personnel and compensation; (c) contemporary appeal of generic, business-focused values as the basis for a new public management; and (d) a belief that management flexibility requires entity-specific laws and regulations, even at the cost of less accountability to representative institutions. As mentioned, there is some disagreement over whether the new organizations are a step in the right direction.

Jonathan Koppell argues that such organizations are less likely to satisfy the management and time preferences of Congress but that they may deliver better results for citizens in terms of responsiveness and responsibility to the mission.[11] In truth,

Congress has a difficult time managing hybrids because their internal goals stand in conflict with those of traditional bureaucratic models, and they act more like intermediaries that require monitoring and regulation. Koppell notes that the hybrid organizations are far less likely than traditional agencies to satisfy congressional preferences but are also responsive to nonmission negative preferences, such as risk-based capital requirements for lenders. Accordingly, and with those organizations acting further removed or independent from direct congressional oversight, concerns exist about sacrificing sovereign control and being accountable to the general public. To that end, and because traditional forms of control will not help manage hybrids, more attention should be given to a hybrid's mission and strategic objectives at inception.[12]

The question remains: What are the drivers that have led Congress to create hybrid organizations if they are harder to manage and viewed as less accountable? Perry argues that establishment of a personnel staff ceiling, restrictive budgetary rules, and debt ceilings for agencies and the federal government have stimulated the use of organizations that occupy the border between public and private administration.[13] Those drivers create incentives to put wholly owned government organizations outside the scope of the federal budget. In thinking of those organizations as a form of public-sector innovation, it is easy to acknowledge the need for a diversity of government institutions that deliver services to citizens. However, the organizations and their services should meet a specific market demand rather than merely work around existing barriers that hamper or frustrate bureaucratic staff.

Along those lines, Massolf and Seldman argue that the underlying attraction of the quasi-governmental organization option can be traced to the inherent desire of organizational leadership, both governmental and private sector, to seek maximum autonomy in matters of policy and operations.[14] Hybrids provide flexibility to managers who seek to improve the performance of their agencies. In those organizations, performance is measured in outputs or results rather than in conformance to regulation, and managers are encouraged to take risks to achieve targets. Supporters of performance-based criteria for government management stress the need for flexibility, competition, and performance as desirable goals. The prominence of those values, in the view of supporters, provides critical elements in developing creative and successful management. Therefore, many believe that a quasi-government is where much of the future lies, away from what they characterize as the stultifying impact of alleged micromanagement, both congressional and executive; general management laws (e.g., personnel regulations); and budgetary constraints. In the quasi-government, some argue, management can do whatever is not forbidden by law, thus providing the basis for innovation and partnerships.

At fruition, hybrids provide an alluring option to policymakers and congressional staff members to deliver work in constrained environments. However, as mentioned, it could also be conjectured that such organizations may be harder to manage and may provide less accountability to the voting public. It may come down to personal philosophical views and preferences for the role that government should play in people's lives and to the analytical and interpretive framework used.

The idea is that the new regulatory order is defined by an increased role of governance through a more indirect system of representative democracy. The delegation of authority to elected officials is less central when agencies that have significant degrees of independence are created.[15] Experts formulate and administer policies in an autonomous fashion, and control and supervision occur through the audit but also through hearings and budgeting. The new division of labor in society is accompanied by "an increase in delegation, proliferation of new technologies of regulation, formalization of inter-institutional and intra-institutional relations, and the proliferation of mechanisms of self-regulation in the shadow of the state."[16] That type of dynamics for the private sector, IRAs, and the political sector generates an apparently paradoxical outcome of more regulation and freer markets.[17]

In a nutshell, once seen through the lens of public choice, as well as the lens of institutional analysis, the dynamic takes the following schematic form. As a consequence of democratic pressure, the political sector has a certain interest in generating economic growth. Consequently, it creates politically independent regulatory agencies to solve the problem of credible commitment and to attract businesses.[18] IRAs, however, complicate the issue of regulatory capture because lobbying activities can now sidetrack the political sector. Setting up IRAs creates a principal-agent problem on steroids. The political sector is thus in danger of losing control, and the economy as a whole is in danger of drifting toward mercantilism the more that IRAs diminish competition and promote business interests at the expense of consumer and taxpayer interests. In that situation, the political sector has three levers for retaining some level of control: defunding ill-behaved IRAs, auditing IRAs and businesses,[19] and enacting promarket legislation that increases competition and directly undermines IRAs' lobbyists.

IRAs from a Public Economics Perspective

Moe[20] describes two general normative perspectives on hybrid organizations. On the one hand, the constitutionalist school of thought opposes hybrid organizations. In that view, government and private organizations should be separated because hybrids raise accountability and management (fiduciary) concerns. On the other hand, the entrepreneur school of thought finds hybrid organizations an attractive option owing to the flexible nature of their organizational structures and their independence from the public. To a large extent, the debate is infused by philosophy but can still be framed in economic terms considering the trade-off between democratic accountability and efficiency. A natural approach has been to frame the issue as a principal-agent problem.[21]

Classifying Regulatory Problems

As discussed, we can classify the nature of goods based on their excludability and rivalry. We can now note that the same classification applies not only to physical goods and resources but also to regulations (see table 8.2). A particular issue can be more or less controversial, which corresponds to rivalry (i.e., the perceived negative spillover effects are low or high), and it can be more or less easy to approach by means of subsidiarity (i.e., it is more or less politically feasible to adopt a centralized decision on the issue or, on the contrary, to allow for a polycentric approach).

Table 8.2 **Types of regulations**

		Subsidiarity	
		Easy to decentralize	*Hard to decentralize*
Rivalry (how controversial the issue is)	High	Local governance and institutional competition	Independent regulatory agencies
	Low	Local governance and institutional diffusion	Centralized regulation by state agencies

Understanding the problem of regulation involves two steps. First, decision makers must decide what counts as a legitimate spillover effect, as opposed to an illegitimate attempt to intrude. Second, they must determine how difficult it is to prevent or compensate for these spillover effects. An issue is controversial or rivalrous if there is a wide divergence of opinions with respect to the answers to the first question, and a subsidiarity approach is unfeasible if those perceived illegitimate spillover effects are hard to prevent by private actions—that is, when the effects are due to various transaction costs; if it is hard for the offended private actors to seek compensation from the offending actors; or, in the case of positive spillovers, if it is difficult to prevent free-riding.

The simplest cases are when there is relatively wide consensus on the proper solution to a particular problem or when the spillover effects are easy to contain. When there is consensus but subsidiarity is hard, a centralized political decision on the issue is nonetheless possible. A normative case can also be made that in such cases the centralized political decision is indeed welfare enhancing. For instance, E. Ostrom gives the example of the US Geological Survey, which provides a useful service in gathering information in a cost-effective manner (to some extent, the information also has the aspect of a public good), and she notes that the central authority has the responsibility to curb "local tyrannies."[22] The example of local tyrannies is instructive because it highlights the following: when there is broad consensus about certain values, the divergence from those values is perceived as an unacceptable spillover cost to the others (if tolerated, such undesirable acts might spread) and the existence of a broad consensus makes it possible to adopt a centralized decision.

Consider now the other easy cases, corresponding to the first column in table 8.2, for which subsidiarity is easy to implement. In such cases, even when the solution to a particular problem is controversial, it is possible to allow for a divergence of approaches to persist. When there is controversy, there will be institutional competition, with various local regions adopting different policies. That leads to actual experimentation, as opposed to intellectual debate, and it may be the case that some solutions prove to be better than others and that public opinion eventually changes. It may also be the case that various solutions have different "cultural comparative advantages" and the variety persists.[23]

When there is little controversy but subsidiarity is nonetheless easy, there is often institutional diffusion rather than institutional competition. In other words, the same solution is adopted in a variety of jurisdictions, although there is no imposition from a central authority. Consider as an example the case of marriage licenses in the fifty states. In certain regards, such as the rejection of polygamy, a decision was imposed from the federal level. Similarly, the controversy regarding same-sex marriages involves the question of whether to allow different states to adopt different laws, or to consider this legal issue as of such importance that the same law must be imposed on all states (as the US Supreme Court has indeed decided in 2015). But for many other aspects, variety in marriage contracts persists across the states. Even so, the variety is not as large as it could be in principle, possibly because some diffusion is at play as well. For example, although the federal government does not regulate divorce, the diversity is not as large as it could be—for example, all states allow divorce.

Issues that have relatively uncontroversial solutions will thus be implemented either by centralized public agencies or by local authorities. Let us now turn to the most difficult case of common-pool regulatory problems—the case of highly controversial issues, which are hard to address by subsidiarity because of high perceived spillover effects.

Common-Pool Regulatory Problems

Our analysis is based on the recognition that, at the most general and abstract level, solutions to public issues are a special type of good that can be provided by private, public, or hybrid organizations. On the one hand, public issues can be more controversial or less controversial, which corresponds to the rivalry aspect. When an issue is controversial, people are more likely to see any imposed solution as infringing on their desires or rights. The more controversial the solution to a problem, which includes the possibility that numerous proposed solutions exist, the more likely it is that if A gets its way, B will not. On the other hand, when there is consensus for the proper solution, A gets its way and B does too; thus, the solution acts as a nonrivalrous good. By contrast, subsidiarity (i.e., a decentralized approach) can be more or less easy to implement because some issues involve more perceived external effects than do others. That is analogous to the excludability aspect of the good.

We define "common-pool regulatory problems" as problems that have controversial solutions (i.e., there is little consensus with respect to the proper solution) and high perceived external effects (i.e., subsidiarity is hard to implement). IRAs are designed to deal with such problems. They are analogous to the Ostromian hybrid private-public organizations that deal with common-pool resources.[24]

By contrast, when a solution is relatively uncontroversial, even if subsidiarity is not feasible, the issue tends to be approached by public non-independent regulatory agencies directly subordinated to and closely managed by the political authority. The other easy case involves situations when subsidiarity is feasible owing to low external effects, and the issue can be left to local regulatory bodies, regardless of how controversial it is.

The concept of "common-pool regulatory problems" explains the political need for something like IRAs, but it does not mean that the current organization of IRAs is effective. Numerous critiques of IRAs fail to understand that they do in fact respond to a genuine need, and they are created because the political sector tries to evade responsibility. Common-pool regulatory problems are political poison precisely because *any* proposal/solution is bound to be controversial, and to make matters worse, the difficulty of decentralized approaches means that the controversy is going to affect numerous people. Once we look at IRAs from this perspective it is less mysterious why politicians decide to create them. But many critiques of IRAs simply assume that parliaments could take over the activities of IRAs and bring democratic representativity back to these issues.

The Reform of IRAs: An Exercise in Institutional Imagination

This chapter highlights the need for a particular institutional arrangement for addressing common-pool regulatory problems—that is, controversial problems that are difficult to decentralize. IRAs might be such an arrangement, but the key question is whether they indeed succeed. The problem is that they seem to be rife with problems. The long list of concrete examples affecting virtually all agencies is daunting. To put it differently, IRAs seem not to be robust institutions, in the sense that they only work well under strong assumptions about their capacity to gather knowledge and their dedication to furthering the common good. In fact, IRAs seem to be poorly equipped to gather the relevant decentralized information necessary to make proper decisions, and they have very weak safeguards against corruption, bureaucratic problems, and capture by special interests.

We should recall that in the intellectual tradition that inspires our approach when assessing efficiency, the key question, as always, is *Compared to what?* We should note that IRAs may very well be an improvement on a situation when the decision is made by the political sector. But although it may be true that IRAs are preferable to centralized political control by Congress, it does not mean they are preferable to *any* other institutional alternative.

In the next section, we imagine two alternatives. First, we highlight the possible use of technology to improve democratic control, adapting some of our previous work on "virtual think tanks."[25] That is our way of asking, "What would V. Ostrom would do?," and of drawing inspiration from his work as a consultant to the Alaska Constitutional Convention in 1955–56. However, this alternative is not the only conceivable possibility. Second, we show examples of both successful and unsuccessful private certification, and we discuss a reform path that involves privatizing all existing IRAs and replacing them with private certification companies. We draw inspiration from economist Edward Stringham's work on private governance and Richard Wagner's work on privatized local administration.[26]

The Use of Technology to Revolutionize How IRAs Operate

Consider the idea that rent-seeking and regulatory capture exist because of dispersed costs and concentrated benefits. One way of diminishing their influence on the regulatory process is to lower the costs of broader participation, such that a wider range of interest groups can have their voices heard. Such diminished influence would bring closer to reality the idealized perspective on pressure groups put forward by Gary Becker and Donald Wittman.[27] In line with the calculus-of-consent logic, this can be done by lowering the decision-making transaction costs. Technology can be used for this purpose. As Adam Thierer's work has extensively demonstrated, technological innovation and change may be the decisive factor in inducing reforms in systems which otherwise are persistently resistant to change.

Our example here is inspired by the operation of open-source communities—notably, the way in which various versions of the Linux operating system are developed, drawing input from numerous users, and attracting numerous independent programmers to solve specific issues. We revisit the logic behind the idea of "virtual think tanks," which reflects the original idea of a think tank proposed by Herman Kahn, founder of the Hudson Institute.[28] We now note that existing IRAs could be similarly transformed.

Online communities for the development of open-source software have invented new modes of large-scale organization that could now be imported into other areas, currently organized in more traditionally bureaucratic and inefficient ways. We can draw inspiration from them and build far more comprehensive public policy solutions.

Kahn notes that, as far as knowledge is concerned, public policy faces trade-offs between scientific rigor and practical urgency, long-term predictions, and multidisciplinarity. Proper evaluation of the effects of alternative policies takes more time than is usually available. Public policy also has long-term effects, which can be difficult to evaluate objectively and rigorously. Furthermore, public policy often is necessarily multidisciplinary, having important consequences from a wide array of social concerns. That makes the matter even more complicated because specialized social scientists such as economists and sociologists will usually pay attention to only a relatively small subset of concerns. As a result of those constraints, the concerns of typical academic social scientists do not go hand in hand with the needs of policymakers.[29] Kahn's proposal is to address the problem by means of aggregating the views of a diverse group of experts. Today, the relevant technology has dramatically reduced the costs of actually implementing such expert systems.

Consider three knowledge aggregation mechanisms: consensus-building, voting (polling or averaging), and betting (prediction markets). And, consider two aggregation systems: those based on human facilitators (meta-experts) and automatic ones (computer algorithms).[30] For example, Vincent Ostrom was involved in drafting the Alaskan constitution as a facilitator, and he used consensus-building as the mechanism. He was initially hired as an expert, but he decided that a better outcome was likely if more people representing different interest groups were involved. Thus he switched to a position of facilitator of consensus-building.

Other mechanisms and aggregation systems can also give good results. When the number of people involved is too large, consensus-building becomes unfeasible, in which case voting or betting is more appropriate. Economist Robin Hanson makes a strong case that people should "vote on values, but bet on beliefs."[31] Hanson also notes that, although betting markets are far from perfect,

> the main robust and consistent finding is that it is usually quite hard, although not impossible, to find information not yet incorporated in speculative market prices. . . . My claim is *not* that betting prices are always more

accurate than other sources, but that they are a *robustly* accurate *public institution* estimating policy-relevant topics. When supported by similar resources and compared on the same topic, they are often substantially better, and only rarely substantially worse, than other info institutions with publicly visible estimates. Speculators provide a valuable service even when they just evaluate other public info institutions, and echo the most accurate of them.[32]

Betting markets work because of "incentive and selection effects: stronger accuracy incentives tend to reduce cognitive biases, those who think they know more tend to trade more, and specialists are paid to eliminate any biases they can find."[33] As a result, a betting market tends to aggregate the available knowledge in the best possible way.

Knowledge can also be aggregated by voting, making use of the "wisdom of the crowds" but this probably works less well because the voting mechanism does not create individualized penalties for those who make mistakes. For example, a rough idea can be had about the economics consensus on various issues by looking at the opinions expressed by the Initiative on Global Markets Economic Experts Panel. But those experts do not actually pay a price if they are wrong. As Hanson puts it, prediction markets work better than voting because "speculators tend to rely more on crowds when crowds know more, and on experts when experts know more."[34]

One way to improve existing IRAs is to redesign them by putting at the core mechanisms that aggregate the knowledge of numerous experts. Would that solve all IRA problems? No. But it may lead to important improvements by reducing the knowledge problems they face. As Hanson notes, such expert aggregation mechanisms still require an input with respect to values.[35] As such, the political sector may establish the goals that the regulatory agencies should follow, whereas the knowledge aggregation mechanisms would establish the best means for attaining those goals. By setting broad goals for regulatory agencies and by allowing an extensive range of experts to participate in the knowledge aggregation mechanism, rent-seeking and regulatory capture could also be significantly reduced.

Privatizing IRAs

Our experiment in institutional imagination could include an even more radical approach: privatizing some IRAs such that they are transformed into private certification companies (see figure 8.3). Obviously not all regulatory problems and regulatory arrangements are fitted for this type of solution. But the number of problems which may be dealt with via such solutions involving private or hybrid arrangements is far from negligible.

Note that such a reform does not involve "deregulation" but rather a switch from bureaucratic regulation by IRAs to market-based regulation. Market-based regulation is often stricter than state regulation because market-based regulation is subject to the threat of costly lawsuits and adverse reputational effects in the context of dynamic competition processes.[36] State regulation is often safe from lawsuits—as in the recent case of water poisoning in Flint, Michigan. Furthermore, when state regulation

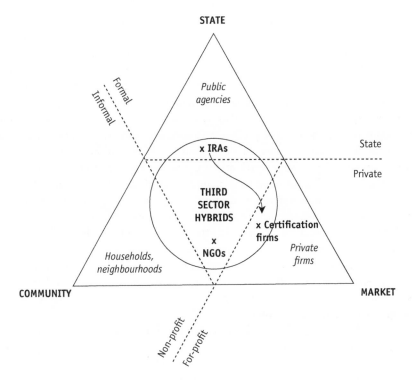

Figure 8.3 Privatizing all independent regulatory agencies. Adapted from Adalbert Evers and Jean-Louis Laville, *The Third Sector in Europe* (Cheltenham, UK: Edward Elgar, 2004), and Victor A. Pestoff, "Third Sector and Co-operative Services—An Alternative to Privatization," *Journal of Consumer Policy* 15, no. 1 (1992): 21–45.

is captured by private interests, the constraints are ever smaller. For example, the 2010 BP oil spill in the Gulf of Mexico—also known as the Deepwater Horizon oil spill—was made significantly more likely by captured state regulation (i.e., the fact that a cap on liabilities was in place). Those two problems—regulatory capture and bureaucratic unaccountability—often lead to weak regulations, distorted regulations, or both. We believe that giving the task of regulating markets to competing certification companies would lead to much-improved regulations.

Consider a simple example to illustrate the idea, as well as the possible problems. The industrial code of the American Society of Mechanical Engineers (ASME) is a private accreditation system. From the late nineteenth century into the early twentieth century, as a result of a series of accidents involving the explosion of pressure vessels, US states created a variety of regulations. Differences in those regulations from state to state made commerce difficult across state lines, with a producer of pressure vessels in one state needing to take into consideration the regulations in all other states where the producer would want to sell. As a result of the regulatory heterogeneity, ASME was formed with the purpose of providing uniform standards. ASME lobbied individual states to eliminate or harmonize their safety codes. Today, ASME's private code is far more comprehensive than any state's minimal regulations. State regulations are now only subsets of such previously developed private rules—the US industrial regulations that are a subset of ASME's code. Moreover, buyers of industrial equipment throughout the world often require that producers have ASME accreditation. According to ASME's website, "Over 100 countries accept the ASME Boiler and Pressure Vessel Code as a means of meeting their government safety regulations."[37]

The safety of industrial equipment is secured *not* by (relatively weak) state regulations but by the need of producers to secure private accreditation. Buyers of equipment do not demand only compliance with state regulations; they demand the more comprehensive private certification. Consequently, producers need to pay to obtain the private accreditation; that is, an organization such as ASME will inspect their production process before certification. The flip side is that private certification companies cannot be easily corrupted because if an unsafe product is certified, they risk losing their reputation. The value of their accreditation would go down significantly with each accident, and then the price the certification company could ask for its accreditation would go down. In other words, each error has an immediate effect. Unlike the bureaucratic system of IRAs, where there is no automatic mechanism for responding to errors, with private certification companies the price system operates as a general regulatory framework.

The Hayekian triangle[38] helps illustrate the structure of production relationships among buyers of consumption goods (e.g., energy), buyers of industrial equipment used for making such goods (e.g., power plants), producers of the equipment, and certification companies (see figure 8.4). The value that consumers attach to the end goods

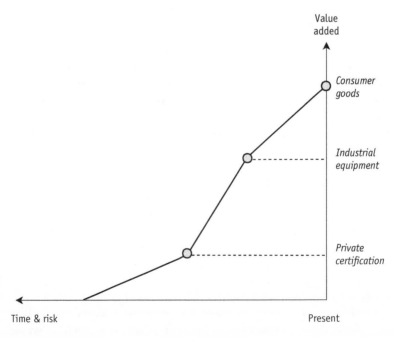

Figure 8.4 Private certification as a factor of production.

determines the overall value of the production chain. This constrains how much each actor in the production chain can charge. For example, private certification companies cannot overcharge the producers of industrial equipment, because they are limited by their revenues. From this perspective, it can be seen that certification is simply one of the factors of production. The regular market mechanism for allocating resources works as usual, and in this case it will determine *how strict* the regulations need to be. This is a key point.

Compare this mechanism to the case of an IRA such as the Food and Drug Administration (FDA). For a long time, there has been consensus among economists who have studied the FDA that it overregulates pharmaceuticals—that its requirements are too strict.[39] What does it mean for the drug approval process to be "too strict"? From a general welfare perspective, it means that the potential benefits of drugs that have not been approved outweigh the potential costs of the negative side effects of approved drugs. As the economist W. Kip Viscusi pointed out more than twenty years ago:

> There is a widespread consensus in the literature that the current FDA drug approval process establishes safety incentives that are excessive. The stringency of the process and the meticulous review of new pharmaceutical drugs are reflected in the substantial delays that U.S. consumers have experienced with respect to the introduction of new pharmaceutical products. . . . Studies have also shown that because of these delays Americans have been prevented from having access to new drugs with beneficial effects, as the agency places a greater weight on errors of commission rather than errors of omission. This imbalance in the emphasis for these two types of errors has led to excessive deterrence of new risks that may be created by pharmaceutical products and inadequate weight on reducing existing risks that patients now experience.[40]

This phenomenon is not an accident. The incentive structure in the FDA is such that the potential benefits of unapproved drugs are discarded and the fear of errors is exaggerated. The benefits of unapproved drugs are largely unseen, whereas an error is bound to garner a lot of attention. That kind of incentive problem exists to a lesser in private certification markets because private certification companies do not just face punishment when they make errors; they also are rewarded by getting paid for certifying good products. Furthermore, certification companies work on a subscription model. For instance, producers of industrial equipment need periodic ASME inspections of their production processes to maintain their certification.

If the FDA were privatized into several competing certification companies, we conjecture that a lot more drugs would be approved for the marketplace and also that the inspection process would be ongoing and subject to change if new information came to light. It is hard to say that privatizing the FDA would result in deregulation. It might result in stricter regulations on some margins and weaker ones on others. The important point is that the profit-and-loss mechanism in the pricing system would provide a much better foundation for making such trade-offs—that is, such trade-offs are more likely to be made in accordance with general welfare considerations.

By contrast, IRAs have virtually no basis on which to establish an efficient level of regulation or to strike the correct cost-and-benefits balance in terms of financing. As pointed out by the Ostroms on market relationships, "a decision to buy a particular good or service reflects a willingness to forgo all other opportunities for which that money could have been used. An expression of demand in a market system always includes reference to what is forgone as well as what is purchased."[41] By contrast,

> the articulation of preferences in the public sector often fails to take account of forgone opportunities. . . . Because most public goods and services are financed through a process of taxation involving no choice, optimal levels of expenditure are difficult to establish. The provision of public goods can be easily overfinanced or underfinanced. Public officials and professionals may have higher preferences for some public goods than the citizens they serve.[42]

Thus, there are good grounds for assuming that private certification would zero in on efficient solutions more often than IRAs do. Still, we do not want to imply that private certification markets work perfectly. We only claim that they would work better than the current system of IRAs. Let us consider two issues with private certification, as illustrated by ASME.

How Competitive Are Private Certification Markets?

Private certification can be done either by for-profit firms or by nonprofits. ASME, for example, is a nonprofit. At first glance, there is not much difference between for-profits and nonprofits. A nonprofit is simply a for-profit entity that reinvests all its profits back into the business. Although a nonprofit does not issue shares, it may provide large salaries to some of its employees. However, shares play an additional role. The price of shares of a for-profit entity that is badly managed tend to go down, hence making it easier for others to buy those shares and take control of the company. This is a simple market mechanism for allowing the change of bad management. By contrast, nonprofits do not have such a mechanism. A badly managed nonprofit is thus harder to reform because it is harder to change the management. Also, when employees are partially compensated with company shares, that instills an incentive to have a longer-term perspective. By contrast, nonprofits have no monetary mechanism for ensuring such a perspective and must rely on trust and organizational culture. (Given these problems, one may wonder why nonprofits exist at all. The answer is that they are a product of state laws, which provide differential tax benefits for nonprofits. For a long time, there was indeed no distinction between for-profits and nonprofits in the United States, and many civil society organizations used to be organized as regular corporations.)

A second problem is related to the fact that the private certification market may be far from competitive. For example, although ASME is not the only certification company, it is by far the largest. As a result, the large private certifier company may have large market power and engage in certain abuses or allow its agents to engage in abuses. Lawyer and scholar Mark R. Joelson notes the following:

In many industries, some degree of standardization is beneficial from the point of view of distributors, consumers, and other users of the product by reducing costs and facilitating purchasing decisions. Such standardization is generally achieved on a voluntary basis, by industry sponsored programs, rather than through government regulation. However, a product that is deemed "non-standard", as a result of such a process, tends to be excluded from the marketplace. The company making that product may justifiably believe that it has been the victim of an illegal group boycott and bring antitrust litigation or complain to the government.[43]

Indeed, ASME has been the first nonprofit to lose an antitrust lawsuit.[44] In 1972, the US Department of Justice successfully brought an antitrust claim arguing that ASME had enforced its code in a discriminatory and arbitrary fashion against non-US producers. In other words, the fact that ASME has formed an organization of American industry can have a certain effect as to how ASME implements regulatory decisions. In 1982, a manufacturer of heating boilers, Hydrolevel Corporation, successfully brought an antitrust lawsuit against ASME. The US Supreme Court decided that ASME had not properly controlled one of its agents. What happened was that the Hydrolevel Corporation was supposed to obtain the ASME certification from one of its direct competitors, a firm called M&M. That was an obvious example of a conflict of interest. Once the Hydrolevel Corporation realized that the market demand for its products plummeted without ASME certification, Hydrolevel sued.

> The Supreme Court affirmed, holding that ASME could be held liable in a private antitrust action, under the tort law principle of apparent authority, for the misdeeds of the standards committee officials. The Court considered that it was ASME's responsibility to prevent the persons acting on its behalf from exploiting its codes and procedures in such a manner as to injure [its] competitors in violation of the antitrust laws.[45]

Such an example shows that certification markets are not always perfect and that regular antitrust legislation may be enough to curb abuses. In other words, it is not clear that what is needed is a dedicated institution like an IRA. It is plausible that in many cases, regulation can be provided more efficiently by private certification, constrained by the legal system.

It is worth noting that the use of antitrust laws for such purposes is always tricky. Although our example concerning ASME seems unobjectionable, in other cases government intervention in private certification markets can severely undermine their efficiency. Stringham explains how the London Stock Exchange evolved in the eighteenth and nineteenth centuries working as a purely private organization and developing exclusion mechanisms for those seen as cheaters.[46] However, the cheaters appealed to the government to force their way into the exchange, hence lowering the efficiency of that market. The same kind of situation can occur in any private certification market. For example, suppose that the Hydrolevel Corporation had produced an unsafe product and that ASME had rightly refused to certify it. A successful antitrust lawsuit there would have harmed the market.

It is always difficult to see how best to make such trade-offs. For our purposes, it is sufficient to note that private certification markets work relatively well and, in conjunction with the legal system, do not tend to devolve into corruption. Notice also that, to the extent private certification has problems, the problems are due to monopoly issues. But IRAs are rife with monopoly issues by design. Furthermore, although it is easy to sue certification companies, it is harder (although not impossible) to sue IRAs.

In summary, the privatization proposal may seem radical at first glance. But our argument follows a very straightforward economic logic. It is hard to deny that the incentive structure faced by IRAs is significantly less consistent with broad public welfare than the incentive structure embedded in a certification market. All of certification markets' potential problems, such as monopoly power, are far worse in the case of IRAs. Furthermore, the empirical example of ASME, which can be seen as a paradigmatic case of how certification markets replacing IRAs would operate, shows that even nonprofits with large market power operate relatively well.

Conclusion

IRAs represent a serious challenge to democratic administration. They are government organizations that consist of unelected officials who often resist even the mild attempts to conduct an audit by the political sector. For example, the Federal Reserve System audit is highly controversial. IRAs are also vulnerable to corruption, rent-seeking, regulatory capture, and revolving-door problems. The standard critique of IRAs, highlighting their democratic unaccountability, identifies a real problem. But the solution usually advanced by such critics would probably make the problem even worse. The attributes of IRAs should not be assumed by Congress or parliaments.

This chapter notes, first, why IRAs respond to a genuine need because they are one way to address "common-pool regulatory problems" (i.e., controversial problems that are hard to decentralize). Second, the chapter uses the classical-liberal institutional imagination to present two possible improvements. One solution is to make use of the internet to massively broaden the pool of experts and the knowledge processes component of IRAs. That should both help address the knowledge problem faced by IRAs and ameliorate corruption problems. Another imaginable solution is to transform each IRA into several competing certification companies. As we argue, the polycentric order of a certification market may work relatively well, even when there are heavily oligopolistic features, and the polycentric method's largest failures can be rectified through the legal system (such as antitrust). Perhaps some IRAs are more amenable to the first solution and others to the second solution, but what is clear is that the existing arrangement, in which IRAs become more and more powerful and encompassing, is quite dangerous and badly in need of reform. In this chapter, we thus see one important instance of the classical-liberal perspective at work, leading to novel perspectives in a complex and difficult area of public governance. The next chapter addresses the growing and controversial debate on governance and corporate social responsibility.

9

Polycentric Stakeholder Analysis

Corporate Governance and Corporate Social Responsibility

One of the most sensitive issues in polycentric governance systems, systems that by their very nature imply hybrid forms of governance, is this: What are the responsibilities of the private sector in the public domain? As we have seen, sooner or later any classical-liberal approach to governance must confront the issue in a systematic way. This chapter offers an exploratory attempt to address private-sector responsibilities. Using the tools, perspectives, and insights articulated in previous chapters, this chapter engages with the corporate social responsibility (CSR) literature. CSR has emerged in the past several decades as a preeminent concept and subfield that deals with the public role of private business. An entire literature has grown around the notions of social responsibility and stakeholders and their theorizing and application. This chapter demonstrates how the ideas and theories discussed so far in this book combine, complement, and bolster that literature and the applied-level insights that are based on it.

The biggest challenge faced by a stakeholder analysis of CSR is to accommodate stakeholders' heterogeneity of preferences, beliefs, and values, as well as the institutional diversity and complex nested hierarchy of governance arrangements. A proper framework of analysis should be realistic in capturing problems of imperfect rationality, incomplete information, and potentially opportunistic behavior while preserving key elements of the normative democratic ethos characterizing the CSR literature. The theories on CSR and corporate governance start from the private corporate perspective of individual firms and their stakeholders but end up analyzing collective action problems. This converges with the concerns of traditional political economy and public choice literature discussed previously in this book.[1]

There should be no surprise that inspiration comes from the polycentric governance perspective developed by Vincent Ostrom in his public choice perspective on public administration to advance a possible response to the challenge of heterogeneity in the realm of CSR and corporate governance.[2] We want to give a sense of how a classical-liberal approach would look. The key task of the theory is to elaborate the idea of democratic governance systems that have overlapping and competing jurisdictions and are using diverse institutional arrangements but are operating under an overarching system of rules that constrains the interactions of social agents with heterogeneous values and preferences so that a productive social order emerges. Polycentricity can

189

be used as a purely descriptive tool of stakeholder analysis and a normative perspective for improving stakeholder-based governance systems, in line with the democratic bent and aspirations of the standard stakeholder analysis literature. The polycentric perspective provides another approach to the problem of accounting for the voices and interests of all stakeholders by means of procedures with a strong support from the theory of democratic governance. Along those lines, we propose a new framework of analysis that we call *polycentric stakeholder analysis*, which is based on what we define as the classical-liberal perspective. We also argue that current discussions regarding stakeholder governance systems may benefit from incorporating the Ostromian public choice perspective in multiple ways.

The Place of Polycentric Stakeholder Analysis in the Context of Corporate Social Responsibility Theories

In the early 1950s, economist Howard Rothmann Bowen asked: "What responsibilities to society may businessmen reasonably be expected to assume?" Since then, the field of CSR, as well as the diversity of views about it, has exploded.[3] In this chapter, we cannot hope to address the entirety of that wide diversity. We start by accepting that, as the David Baron succinctly puts it, CSR "involves going beyond what the letter of the law requires or the market demands."[4] More specifically, we adopt Jones's two main defining assumptions.[5]

First, we go along with the literature according to which CSR refers to responsibilities that corporations assume voluntarily—what is sometimes referred to as discretionary CSR—rather than as a result of following mandatory government regulations. Although that idea of discretionary CSR is not universally accepted, it seems to be the predominant point of view in the field[6] and has been explicitly emphasized from an early stage.[7] As Keith Davis puts it, "Social responsibility begins where the law ends. A firm is not socially responsible if it merely complies with the minimum required of the law."[8] Most authors on whose work we rely here accept that assumption. Bryan Husted and José Salazar distinguish between three types of CSR: strategic (as a means to increase profits), altruistic (genuinely concerned with social benefits), and coerced (influenced by taxes and subsidies).[9] We include the first two in our discussion.

Second, we adopt the view that CSR is more than just a rhetorical and largely empty public relations device by which corporations secure higher profits.[10] We take the view that altruistic CSR is real and hence that there is something missing in Milton Friedman's famous critique of CSR, according to which the social responsibility of corporate officials is only "to make as much money as possible for their shareholders."[11] Apart from its normative content, his perspective has problems as a purely positive description of actual corporate behavior. For example, even in the early 1970s, most firms were engaged in such activities as minority hiring and training, environmental concerns, contributing to education and the arts, urban renewal, and civil rights[12]; in the 1990s, the scope of CSR activities expanded even more.[13] As business ethicist Domènec Melé notes, "It is hard to affirm that all practices of CSR are profitable."[14]

Our proposal can still be seen as an example of a broader business case for CSR.[15] Although firms generally operate in a competitive environment, the environment does not force them into a strategy of profit maximization (computed on the basis of opportunity costs) but instead creates a weaker evolutionary pressure toward having positive accounting profits.[16] Scholars Abagail McWilliams and Donald Siegel, along with Husted and Salazar, note that firms engaged in CSR experience additional costs and hence should be at a competitive disadvantage.[17] As McWilliams and Siegel put it, "To maximize profit, [a] firm should offer precisely that level of CSR for which the increased revenue (from increased demand) equals the higher cost (of using resources to provide CSR)."[18] But taking Armen Alchian at face value, we can predict that McWilliams and Siegel's model underestimates the level of CSR that firms can provide[19] and, according to the evidence, do provide.[20] That leaves more room for firms (especially large corporations) to pursue additional values apart from simply maximizing shareholder profits. This explains why, even in pure free markets, it should not be expected that CSR activities that go beyond profit maximization will be entirely weeded out by competitive pressures. Thus, the observation that corporations engage in various CSR activities that do not help their bottom line should not be seen as a major theoretical and empirical puzzle. It is a consequence of the fact that real markets rarely fit the perfect competition model; moreover, it reflects empirical reality.

Although this chapter focuses on the analytical side, the normative issues in identifying the distinctiveness of that approach and placing it in the context of the literature are unavoidable. We use Friedman's well-known position as a foil. According to Friedman's critique, when a manager does anything that is not aimed at maximizing profits, "he is to act in some way that is not in the interest of his employers."[21] That idea, however, assumes that shareholders do not have other values and interests apart from profits. In fact, they do, and the Alchian-like manner in which economic competition works leaves room for additional values to be implemented and reflected in a firm's activities. Although it is true that principal-agent problems create difficulties for shareholders to fully control a firm's managers,[22] the narrow profit maximization goal does not follow even if we abstract from the issue. That means the business case for CSR needs to be understood in broader terms than merely that CSR helps increase monetary profit.[23]

According to the standard business case for CSR, firms engage in CSR for a variety of business reasons[24]:

- Shareholder business case theories of CSR focus on risk reduction by (a) avoiding costly public relations disasters[25]; (b) facilitating marketing activities,[26] including by means of reputation-enhancing philanthropy[27]; and (c) reducing the potential for costly managerial errors by getting managers out of their epistemic bubbles.[28]
- Stakeholder business case theories of CSR focus on enhancing a firm's reputation and legitimacy as a means to establish trust with potential customers and thus expand market share on the demand side[29] and to attract talent and increase workers' productivity[30] and secure supply chains on the supply side.[31]
- Social integration business case theories of CSR focus on the idea that a corporation's profits are the result of a win-win synergistic relationship with its broader social environment[32]—for example, as a result of social learning[33] and by discovering its

competitive advantage by engaging with the wider community. As Kurucz, Colbert, and Wheeler put it, "Stakeholder demands are viewed less as constraints on organization, and more as opportunities to be leveraged to the benefit of the firm"[34]—for example, discovering new opportunities for profit in developing countries.[35]

Building on Wilber and on Kurucz, Colbert, and Wheeler, we propose a general typology of business cases for CSR by means of a two-dimension graph. The graph plots the locus of value (ranging from individuals and firms to holistic value communities and integral commons) versus the world view or the type of social theory that is being used (ranging from simple individualistic and reductionist theories to integral theories of complex emergence).[36] Table 9.1 adapts this classification, thus illustrating the location in the typology of the three perspectives identified previously and placing the polycentric governance approach in the same context.

As discussed in previous chapters, a polycentric system of governance is a collection of competing and cooperating decision-making centers acting independently in overlapping jurisdictions under a common system of rules and norms that limit negative externalities and free-riding.[37] In our case, the decision-making centers are the group of stakeholders. The polycentric stakeholder analysis (PSA) accommodates stakeholders' heterogeneity of preferences, beliefs, and values, and the complex nestedness of stakeholder governance systems. It is realistic in capturing imperfect rationality, limited information, and potentially opportunistic behavior while also preserving key elements of the normative democratic ethos that drives CSR more broadly.

The aim of PSA is to capture insights about the broad meaning and social relevance of corporate activities (specific to social integration CSR theories) and to do so while using the conceptual tools of the political economist. In other words, properly understood, adoption of the conceptual foundation of shareholder theories in terms of assuming that only individuals have values does not necessarily lead to Friedman's extreme position. On the contrary, it leads to a deep appreciation of the broader business case for CSR. Unlike existing elaborate business case theories for CSR that rely on value communities and integral commons (i.e., unrealistic assumptions or aspirations

Table 9.1 **Typology of business case theories for corporate social responsibility**

Locus of value			
Worldview	Individuals	Value communities	Integral commons
Reductionist	*Shareholder theories*	---	---
Pluralistic	---	*Stakeholder theories*	---
Complex emergence	Polycentric stakeholder analysis (PSA)	---	*Social integration theories*

Note: Italic text in the table = existing theories; PSA = authors' proposal.

of value homogeneity at the level of communities, societies, or even the planet as a whole), PSA starts by acknowledging the existence of deep-value heterogeneity. But we can offer a better account of corporate social integration by adopting this realistic assumption and using the theory of co-production.

Yet another distinctive feature of PSA is that, consistent with its origins in the Ostroms' work, it advances a perspective that circumvents the state-market, private-public dichotomy. At the same time, questions form about what Freeman et al. call the "separation fallacy" regarding the chasm between ethics and business, between efficiency and morality.[38] As Friedman states, "The only one responsibility of business towards society is the maximization of profits to the shareholder within the legal framework and *the ethical custom of the country*" (emphasis added).[39] The last part has sometimes been interpreted as a de facto recognition of CSR.[40] However, when applying the idea to practice, Friedman leaves out the part about ethical customs.[41] For example, he states that a corporation should not "make expenditures on reducing pollution beyond the amount that is in the best interests of the corporation *or that is required by law* in order to contribute to the social objective of improving the environment" (emphasis added).[42] Melé pinpoints the assumption behind Friedman's perspective in that he assumes a "full separation of the functions of the public and private spheres" according to which "the public good is pursued exclusively by public servants and politicians, but not by private businesses."[43] That is the inflection point where PSA gets another of its distinguishing features: a business case for CSR that is not committed to this standard dichotomy.

Our proposal, following E. Ostrom's institutional theories and her emphasis on the realm "beyond markets and state," is naturally skeptical of such attempts at full separation.[44] Moreover, the now robust literature on private governance shows that private individuals and collective associations (such as clubs) often address public issues.[45] Private means, such as reputation and private certification, regulate large areas of activity, and most economic activity cannot properly be understood without taking into account that the acting agents operate not only under externally provided constraints but also under internally assumed morals.[46] Hence, even without the emphasis and self-awareness brought about by CSR, private actors have long been engaged in social activities beyond the strict pursuit of monetary profit. To give a simple and famous example, lighthouses were long held as an example of a public good that only government could deliver, but in looking more closely at how lighthouses were provided historically, Coase finds that private actors essentially engaged in CSR (earning benefits in reputation, rather than directly in money) often constructed them.[47]

In summary, the CSR literature has repeatedly discussed the theme. The PSA approach revisits and complements that discussion from a novel angle. To put it differently, Friedman's hypothesis regarding "full separation of private and public spheres" comes under attack not just from the communitarian perspective ("socialist," as Friedman labels it) but also from the direction of the literature on self-governance and private governance.[48] Although the communitarian critique makes the normative case that corporations should care more about the broader social environment, the literature on private governance makes the positive case that corporations can deal more effectively than governments with a wide range of social issues and that they do so when given the opportunity. As long as it is understood that CSR is voluntary, the larger the scope of viable CSR, the smaller the role of coercive government. In other words, opposite to Friedman's assumption that accepting a role for CSR beyond mere profit maximization leads to socialism, the better that voluntary CSR activities work, the weaker the case is for government intervention. PSA, while building on realistic assumptions about human behavior and institutional order, offers a theoretical apparatus to the alternative normative position. That is, needless to say, a robust and well-grounded position of a classical-liberal nature.

Heterogeneity: Assumptions and Implications of Stakeholders' Approaches

At the core of PSA is the issue of heterogeneity. Most of its distinctive features are a result of the fact that it starts from the simple observation that most cases of CSR, governance, or stakeholder analysis are placed somewhere in the middle of a continuum that has homogeneity at one extreme and radical heterogeneity at another. That is sufficient to raise questions regarding the widespread representative agent homogenization assumption so prevalent in the literature. One of the most important problems in generating human cooperation and a free, peaceful, and productive social order has always been that individuals have a diversity of beliefs, values, identities, preferences, and endowments.[49] The problem of agent heterogeneity is a key issue in the study of human cooperation, social action, and social dilemmas.

When dealing with the problem, most of the time the social sciences use by default a strategy of homogenization by assumption: one version or another of a representative agent approach is used, thus solving the challenge of the heterogeneity of beliefs, preferences, assumptions, and so forth. Hence, general solutions outdoing the differences are possible because diversity, at its most basic level, can be circumvented, uncovering a basic structure of social rules, patterns, and laws that generates unity in diversity (and could be the basis of the "common good").

For example, Thomas Donaldson and Thomas Dunfee, inspired by political theorist Michael Walzer's idea of cross-societal norms, propose a process by which business ethics "hypernorms" could be identified.[50] Donaldson and Dunfee's "integrative social contracts theory" is holistic and sociological with normative concerns operating in a top-down fashion from society to individuals and firms.[51] They write: "Relevant sociopolitical communities are a primary source of guidance concerning stakeholder obligations of organizations formed or operating within their boundaries,"[52] and "managers can obtain useful guidance concerning the resolution of difficult stakeholder questions [by] reference to community authentic norms."[53] That is a more elaborate version of Friedman's "ethical custom of the country" mentioned earlier.

By contrast, building on the work on value heterogeneity in the Ostroms' tradition, the PSA approach advanced here preserves individual-level heterogeneity and shifts the focus to the process by which sociopolitical communities are formed. That process, and the entire discussion about normative matters, operates in a bottom-up fashion, from individuals toward overlapping collectivities of values (rather than toward a homogenized society). Heterogeneity and homogeneity coexist in any special group, organization, or society. But coexistence raises questions about strategies that are based exclusively on homogeneity assumptions and procedures. A process or procedure is involved in which heterogeneity and homogeneity interact. Such communities cannot be presupposed. Complex issues of social entrepreneurship are often involved in building such communities out of the interplay.[54] Moreover, when it comes to the more normative aspect, it must be asked who will decide which community norms are authentic. It would be a mistake for managers to ignore salient stakeholders simply because they have been labeled inauthentic. To do so would open the door for a convenient rhetorical strategy by which rationalization is easy and whereby those with whom there is disagreement are ignored. What are the procedures, processes, rules, and heuristics by which basic norms emerge and are validated, legitimized, or applied and amended? Donaldson and Dunfee's analysis leaves out key problems that a robust theory of stakeholder analysis must address, because such processes obviously have something to do with stakeholders operating in an institutional collective choice environment that the stakeholders could at least partially change.

The empirical and practical presence of persistent and widespread heterogeneity is a reminder that the homogenization strategy has notable limitations with significant practical implications. What happens when consensus does not exist?[55] Are social cooperation and governance still possible for individuals who do not share the same beliefs, values, ideas, and identities?[56] How can broad social integration theories of CSR be accounted for without assuming away the diversity of normative perspectives? The key claim is that homogenization of various beliefs or objectives of the social actors is not always an important precondition to governance and institutional order. As Nicholas Rescher puts it, management "need not root in agreement—and not even in a second-order agreement in the processes for solving first-order conflicts—as long as the mechanisms in place are ones that people are prepared (for however variant and discordant reasons) to allow to operate in the resolution of communal problems."[57]

Such theoretical questions of political economy and institutional and governance theory are also important for any stakeholder theory. As Michael Jensen argues, managers cannot maximize more than one objective function.[58] That idea led Jensen to propose the "enlightened stakeholder theory," according to which "the objective function of [a] firm is to maximize the long-term firm value."[59] Jensen's view expands Friedman's perspective but not enough to clarify the ambiguities surrounding the term *value* or to fully account for how corporations behave.[60] Much hinges on the various (heterogeneous!) interpretations of key terms, in this case, *value*. As Dunfee notes, "A better way to view the Friedman–Jensen arguments is that they are just that, arguments about a way they would prefer to see the world structured. But that is not the world that we live in."[61] Friedman and Jensen would probably not disagree. "Nor is it likely a world that most citizens would prefer to live in."[62] This quote gets to the core of the issue: to a large extent, the debates about CSR have been conflicts of vision based on divergent moral viewpoints. But to provide a positive account of the world of CSR as a whole, it is necessary to go beyond a personal preferred point of view to acknowledge the full diversity of views. Hence, PSA may be seen as a move in a more realistic and constructive direction.

Most of the time stakeholders' governance is governance under conditions of heterogeneity. Even if each given manager has a preferred personal view about the proper scope of CSR, each must face the fact that their stakeholders may have widely divergent views and expectations. The divergence of expectations must be included in any analysis. The question, then, is as follows: What are the mechanisms and processes that should be highlighted and used in such circumstances? What are the collective meta-level rules, procedures, and patterns that govern the mechanisms and processes? As economist Joseph T. Mahoney notes, the "question of how the economic surplus generated by the firm is, or should be, allocated among the various *stakeholders* has been given little research attention."[63] The situation has not improved much since. In our view, a key reason for this state of affairs is that existing CSR theories, as table 9.1 highlights, cannot properly deal with the issue of heterogeneity. Hence, those theories cannot overcome the limitations of Jensen's single objective function maximization. By contrast and as expanded on in the next sections, PSA is designed to provide a possible solution by modeling CSR decisions as (democratic) co-production procedures in heterogeneity and polycentric circumstances, rather than as simple mathematical optimization problems.

In our approach, we follow Dunfee's suggestion.[64] (We agree with his diagnostic while obviously disagreeing with the homogenizing approach of Donaldson and Dunfee's "integrative social contracts theory" that we criticized earlier.[65]) Echoing Mahoney,[66] Dunfee notes that, although "managers are seen as having a large zone of discretion in designating stakeholders as beneficiaries of social investment. Ironically, stakeholder theory, at least in its current state of development, fails to provide fine-grained help concerning how managers should cope with the allocation problem when making social investments."[67] One of the main stumbling blocks is the absence of a proper procedure for determining "stakeholder salience."[68] Dunfee's suggestion is to frame the problem "as a market-like phenomenon involving needy stakeholders competing for assistance from potential suppliers of social goods, including corporations."[69]

The main difficulty in following Dunfee's suggestion is that market-like emergent orders without prices operating as the coordination catalyst are not guaranteed to produce efficient outcomes and lack an entrepreneurial (public or institutional entrepreneurship) driver toward the efficient allocation of resources. Dunfee notes that, as far as CSR is concerned, "there is no simple demand and supply mechanism."[70] Even with prices, well-known market failures exist, but without prices to facilitate productive coordination, the failures of emergent orders having public or collective goods or action features can be amplified and multiplied. Institutional entrepreneurship may emerge, but to put it differently, entrepreneurship in nonmarket settings is not always productive, but it can often be wasteful or even destructive.[71] Nonetheless, in close conjunction with Ostrom's institutionalism, we do have an incipient theory of productive entrepreneurship in nonmarket settings, known as "public entrepreneurship."[72] The theory of polycentricity has also developed as a direct attempt to answer the same challenge of understanding nonmarket (but market-like) mechanisms for building productive social orders.[73] Both the theory of public entrepreneurship and the theory of polycentricity deal with the same field of phenomena at the interface between the private and the public. In that respect, our proposal for PSA can also be understood as a public entrepreneurship CSR theory.

Dunfee's suggestion to search for a market-like phenomenon to coordinate CSR activities[74] is thus useful for laying out the agenda and highlighting the tasks that a theory of public entrepreneurship applied to the realm of CSR would have to perform. He poses a number of key questions:

- How can a corporation "align [its] social investments with [its] comparative advantages in providing social goods"?[75] Sometimes the answer is obvious. For example, for Walmart to provide help after Hurricane Katrina, by delivering "truckloads of supplies, including free prescription drugs," was an obvious extension of its usual comparative advantage.[76] But the answer to the question is less obvious on most occasions. Generally speaking, CSR "competencies may lie in intellectual property, or proximity, or ability to distribute, or in special knowledge of employees."[77]
- How can a corporation "treat social investments in a manner similar to their financial investments by specifying social goals and objectives and then evaluating their investments to make sure that the goals and objectives are realized"?[78] That is the challenge the theory of public entrepreneurship could be designed to address. How can such an evaluation occur in the absence of prices as mechanisms for social coordination?
- How can corporations "be completely transparent in all dimensions of CSR"?[79] Because CSR usually refers to the provision of various public goods, allowing "outsiders, including relevant stakeholders and their representatives, [to] render independent judgments concerning whether [a] firm is achieving its [CSR] goals" and providing "other potential corporate suppliers . . . the information to better inform their own decisions" can increase the system-level efficiency. But that goes against the regular practice of competitive economic activities when secrecy plays an important role. So, although two firms may be competitors in their regular activities, they may be natural cooperators in their CSR activities. How will they manage questions about secrecy and patents?

PSA will not provide a ready-made recipe for answering such questions—and the questions are genuinely hard, and some specific context can be expected for the answers. However, PSA charts the intrinsic logic of decision-making in such circumstances and offers a framework for mapping, analyzing, and understanding the contextual patterns and factors of specific cases. By implication, PSA helps the efficacy of CSR decision-making. Rather than providing a one-size-fits-all purported solution to CSR management, a tentative PSA framework provides a broader approach that can help both researchers and managers recognize the diversity of CSR problems and design specific solutions and different methods of stakeholder involvement.

Public Value: Its Nature and Creation

At the center of CSR, governance, and stakeholder situations is the problem of public value—or collective value creation. The challenge is such: How could one group collectively generate from the diversity of individual values, preferences, views, and beliefs a convergent common public or collective value? What are the mechanisms by which could be generated from the diversity of individual values, a state of nature, a social state, that embeds a common value that is desirable or at least acceptable to the multitudes of individuals for which the value is salient? That challenge is at the core of the governance studies tradition in political science and CSR. The two traditions converge in the domain defined and underlined by these problems. Accepting that CSR involves more than a roundabout method of increasing profits and that firms can aim to create value not only for shareholders but also for a wider range of stakeholders (as a result of shareholders' "altruism," to use Husted and Salazar's terminology[80]) leads to an inquiry about the nature of public value creation. In other words, we are led into an extensive literature that is almost a subfield of inquiry in political science.[81] In what follows, we rely on a simplified account specifically designed for the theory of polycentricity (see Chapter 6). As noted, that theory is by its nature based on that problem. A polycentric system is the institutional social description of the action area or context in which public or collective value is generated in conditions of heterogeneity. Our contribution here is less foundational or theoretical and more applied. We are now demonstrating how to apply the polycentric theory of public value creation to the problem of stakeholder analysis.

Recall that an economic analysis of public values starts with a somewhat peculiar meta ethics, namely the conceptualization of moral values as special cases of preferences. As noted, we understand moral values as preferences people have about other people's behavior and want everyone else to have as well. Such preferences are not the only kind of possible preferences about other people's behaviors. Voluntary agreements, such as contracts and clubs, also specify how others should behave. But, unlike moral values, if some people disagree or refuse to comply, the other people simply accept it and find other willing participants. By contrast, people view moral values as a code or standard that everyone else must comply with. Game theory analysis of how norms persist and spread provides the background explanation for this definition. As Robert Axelrod shows, for a norm to persist, agents need to (a) comply with it, (b) punish those who do not comply, and (c) punish those who do not punish.[82] In other words, norms reflect a preference about other people's behaviors, plus a meta preference that everyone has the same preference and acts on that preference.

That theory dovetails Walzer's account of "moral minimalism," which has influenced much of the social integration CSR literature.[83] Moral values can be seen as preference minimalism, reflecting a limit to matters of taste—or *de gustibus non est disputandum*—when it comes to other people's behaviors. Regarding other people's behaviors, not everything can be allowed; moral relativism has a limit. However, unlike the social integration accounts, the economic account of public values remains at the individual level, and it is compatible with the persistence of irreducible heterogeneity of values. That idea is important because, although Walzer's moral minimalism may be correct (it can be argued that it is indeed "a set of standards to which all societies can be held . . . rules against murder, deceit, torture, oppression, and tyranny"[84]), Donald and Dunfee's hypernorms for business ethics are much more evasive and controversial.[85] In our view, PSA should be performed under the working assumption that no such hypernorms exist.[86]

Once public values are understood as instances of preferences, an individual-level analysis can be pursued. As explained in Chapter 6, to account for value heterogeneity, it is necessary to examine the diversity of evaluators. Evaluators may have not only different values and different aspiration levels for those values (which determine their willingness to compromise) but also different epistemic perspectives on the observed system (e.g., using different categories to systematize and understand the world) and different evaluation criteria for the state of affairs (which variables are considered relevant and that are estimated or measured). Consequently, the activities of a firm may be understood in different ways by different stakeholders who attach different meanings to various acts, and evaluated on the basis of a variety of ethics criteria.

This understanding allows us to provide a different perspective to defining stakeholders and identifying their salience for a firm's CSR.[87] According to the PSA perspective, the stakeholders are the evaluators of a firm's activity (and only those evaluators), and the salience of the stakeholders is determined by the distance between the shareholders' own perspectives (both normative and epistemic) and the stakeholders' perspectives. Accordingly, someone who does not evaluate the firm's activity is not a stakeholder, even if that person is a beneficiary. Beneficiaries who are not evaluators can enter the CSR picture only because other stakeholders care about them. For example, a firm that provides relief for homeless people has a host of stakeholders who care about and evaluate the firm's activity in this regard (including those who are effectively involved in providing the relief), but many homeless people may simply be passive recipients. Many forms of aid and philanthropy are similar. The logic behind excluding passive beneficiaries from the set of stakeholders is that, by not being evaluators, their actions are never directed toward changing managerial decisions (either CSR decisions or routine business decisions). Managerial decisions may change as a result of information updates about such passive beneficiaries, but not as a result of their deliberate actions.

Furthermore, because PSA is a business case theory of CSR, albeit a broad one, the salience of stakeholders (i.e., how much their opinions matter for managerial decisions) is ultimately determined by their correspondence with the views and desires of managers and shareholders. Again, that statement is not normative but factual. The configuration of the decision-making process—the structure of authority and power—necessitates that the stakeholder and manager be placed at the center of the analytical framework. In the end, it is a measure of recognizing the heterogeneity of the situation in the asymmetries of decision-making power and responsibility of different classes of stakeholders. For example, anti-Walmart protesters are unlikely to be among Walmart's prominent stakeholders, even though they are clearly evaluating Walmart's activities. Stakeholders with perspectives that are very different from those of a firm's shareholders have an elevated salience. But that is the case only in an indirect manner because other shareholders—those who have high salience—care about not upsetting the stakeholders. This includes sheer monetary profit reasons, but there is no reason to limit it to monetary profit reasons.

Let us compare this to standard stakeholder theory, as synthesized by Dunfee.[88] According to Dunfee, a stakeholder is "(1) anyone whom relevant laws and norms require be recognized as a stakeholder, (2) anyone whom hypernorms require be recognized as a stakeholder, and (3) anyone whom the managers of the organization determine, acting consistently with organizational values, to have a legitimate need which can be ameliorated through the use of the core competencies of the corporation."[89] As we argue here, the first two identification criteria are problems. The first presupposes homogeneity of values, and the second refers to hypernorms that may not even exist. In a sense, the first two criteria put the cart before the horse because, in practice, communities united by certain norms emerge through dynamic processes that display many facets and that may involve a strong social entrepreneurial element.[90] Furthermore, that given firm's CSR may actually be one of the key factors helping the social entrepreneurship go through normative change and adjustment. In other words, social responsibilities are not necessarily externally imposed on a firm. They may arise from the firm itself, or the firm may be a necessary ingredient in the formation of various communities of interests. For example, in the absence of a firm's capacity to address certain needs (or a perception about presumed capacity), a community of people may not emerge to raise awareness about those needs.

Dunfee's third identification criterion is similar to the PSA criterion, and it includes a reference to the salience of stakeholders—to legitimate needs and to the ability to ameliorate them. There is, however, a subtle difference between the two perspectives. The PSA perspective does not determine stakeholders as a result of a conscious decision on the part of a firm's managers. Consequently, it allows for the possibility that managers make mistakes about properly or fully identifying the set of stakeholders. That is analogous to the ordinary case of a firm making errors about the demand for its products. Dunfee accounts for the possibility of managerial error by means of his first two criteria, but once a thorough individual perspective is adopted, those criteria are problems. Hence, PSA succeeds in capturing the individual perspective of concerns addressed by the reference to norms, and it also manages to preserve the heterogeneity of values. In the PSA perspective, managers try to identify all the salient stakeholders—that is, all those who will evaluate the firm's activities and who have a close enough affinity to the firm's shareholders that dismissing them would amount to failing to properly serve shareholders broad values (including their "altruistic" desires).

For example, although Chick-fil-A may not count pro-gay activists among its salient stakeholders, the Mozilla Foundation does—hence the foundation's diametrically opposed reactions to a very similar event. Chick-fil-A's charitable foundation had donated millions of dollars to political organizations that were considered hostile to LGBT rights, and in 2012, Chick-fil-A's chief operating officer and president Dan Cathy made public comments opposing same-sex marriage. Despite some public protests, Cathy kept his position. Later, he said he regretted drawing the company into the controversy, and the company stopped donating to organizations that were considered anti-gay. When Mozilla's co-founder Brendan Eich was named CEO in 2014, protests and boycotts ensued over Eich's 2008 support for an anti-gay marriage bill in California. Eich resigned two weeks after becoming CEO. Note that PSA allows analysis of this divergence and the behavior of the two organizations (and of their stakeholders) without assuming any particular prevailing ethical norm about acceptance or rejection of same-sex marriage. In fact, the existence of value heterogeneity here may have contributed to what may be seen as an error by Mozilla in properly managing its relationship with salient stakeholders. Indeed, as soon as Eich became CEO, three of Mozilla's directors resigned, and later a large-scale boycott against the Firefox browser determined Eich's resignation.

In summary, PSA suggests an approach in which different social actors (with different capabilities, endowments, preferences, and identities) play a polycentric game in an institutional landscape defined by fragmented and overlapping decision areas. Where the individual social actors' perceptions and strategies and the institutional setting meet, the interaction generates a dynamic process of both ethical and economic relevance. The Ostroms and their collaborators developed a method for dealing with such institutional decision configurations—the institutional analysis and development framework (IAD). For our purposes, it is important to reference IAD and to note that it captures the polycentric parameters; our focus is on a specific configuration of interest—the stylized facts of a modal CSR situation. The next section of this chapter delves into the issue of stakeholder salience—the pivotal element of the situation—and provides a systematic way by which CSR effectiveness can be conceptualized. Later, we present a fuller framework of analysis about how to consider salient stakeholders.

A Calculus-of-Consent Strategy for Charting and Estimating CSR Effectiveness

The usual unstated expectation that the stakeholders' system of relationships and governance should stay as close as possible to democratic standards is a key idea in the literature on stakeholder analysis and CSR and corporate governance more broadly. Hence, strong standard democratic theory assumptions and values support that literature. Ideally, it may be said that a stakeholders' governance system should be democratic. Its legitimacy and efficiency may hinge on that. Democracy may be seen as an attitude, culture, way of life, or set of values, but ultimately it is about collective decision-making and preference aggregation.[91] Usually, that insight is related to the twin notions of control and legitimacy. First, democracy is a mechanism for generating, operating, and controlling power and authority through a set of voting arrangements. Second, majoritarian control and preference aggregation together are the major source and determinant of legitimacy. The aggregative model of democracy thus links in a coherent framework the key themes of preference aggregation, control, authority, and legitimacy.

Seen in that light, the problem of democracy, including in stakeholders' systems, appears deceivingly simple. The simplicity evaporates in looking at the details, as noted in Chapter 1. First, there are multiple ways of determining preference revelation and multiple ways for a group to make decisions by voting—unanimity rule, first-preference majority rule, and so forth. Each method may lead to different results.[92] Outcomes are, at minimum, sensitive to the rules used to aggregate opinions. In other words, what constitutes a majority differs from one case to another and may depend on the relevant collective decision-making institutions as much as on the preferences of the group's members. Thus, "combining individual preferences into group choice, by majority rule or some other method, is not a straightforward undertaking"[93] because it is contingent on institutions. There is "no magic wand that transforms this individual clarity about preferences into a collective clarity."[94] And "when the group size is large, when individual preferences are heterogeneous, or when there is a large number of alternatives for group members to consider," things become even more problematic.[95]

The emergence of solutions in stakeholder systems centered in the business area must therefore confront problems similar to those of political systems if the mechanisms of preference aggregation are to be used with liberal democratic, not authoritarian, social dictatorship models. There is no escape from the social choice paradoxes[96] or public choice dilemmas.[97] PSA that operates in the classical-liberal tradition starts from a blunt recognition of that reality.

We cannot fully account for and counteract such problems here. Each problem can and should be treated separately and in conjunction with others in various configurations generated by the combinatorial logic of polycentric systems. In this book, we want to draw attention to the huge challenge and approach to CSR and corporate governance studies. In addition, we want to offer an approach that, in the larger framework of the polycentricity perspective, focuses on one specific issue and tries to advance a simplified model that alleviates some of the key challenges. A particular challenge is that of homogenizing a heterogeneous group of stakeholders. As may be expected, we propose that a particular model of democracy analysis, namely the calculus-of-consent model invoked and used repeatedly in the previous chapters,[98] can be adapted to the problem of CSR management. We propose that it be used to both identify the logic of stakeholders' decision-making landscape and assess the efficacy of their decisions. The model shows how CSR managers can give priority to some of their core salient stakeholders, even if they are a minority among the larger group of stakeholders.

Assume that, with the PSA identification criterion discussed earlier, CSR managers can create an ordered list of stakeholders from the highest salient ones to the lowest. (That ignores many of the challenges noted earlier, but we must adopt such a strategy to isolate and analytically process each major problem.) Ronald Mitchell, Bradley Agle, and Donna Wood's procedure, which looks at power, legitimacy, and urgency,[99] can be used to order the list of stakeholders. The question is how far should a corporation's CSR resources be spread and thinned out from addressing the needs of the most salient stakeholders to the needs of the least salient? As Dunfee points out, "The stakeholder literature . . . does not provide sufficient guidance for managers facing allocation issues."[100] Dunfee considers the allocation problem to be so difficult that he is deeply skeptical it can be addressed any time soon. His point is legitimate, as we have noted. The literature on democratic preferences aggregation and social choice gives us some hints about how difficult the problem with any aggregation method truly is. Despite Dunfee's skepticism, we argue that underlying the complex edifice and process of polycentric stakeholder systems is a discernable logic of effective choice that could establish some boundary conditions and signal that it is possible to avoid skepticism or nihilism in the design of such systems.

Once we order stakeholders from the most salient to the least salient, we can look at the CSR costs of satisfying them. (Again, we are looking at estimation and judgmental decision-making, not monetary calculations.) The more stakeholders that a corporation tries to consider, the bigger the cost. Hence, the CSR scope costs function, $S(n)$, monotonously increases as the number of stakeholders, n, increases. By contrast, we can also consider the CSR risk function, $R(n)$, which would cover all three types of business cases for CSR mentioned earlier, from simple risks associated with public relations disasters to more complex risks associated with reputation and legitimacy (e.g., the risk of failing to attract talent), and all the way to the most complex risks associated with social learning and the failure to pursue the CSR goals. That risk function monotonously decreases. The more stakeholders a corporation takes into consideration, the less likely the corporation is to miss something important.

Combining the two costs results in a graph like that in figure 9.1. The minimum of the total costs determines the optimal spread of CSR activities—that is, the set of salient stakeholders that the corporation should take into consideration. If the set of stakeholders is smaller, the CSR scope costs will be smaller, but the risk increase will disproportionately outweigh the reduction in scope costs. If, by contrast, the set of stakeholders is larger than that optimum, the risks will be even further diminished, but the increase in scope costs will make it not worth it. This optimal set of stakeholders determines whose opinions and values should matter for CSR managers. This logic (in marginal costs and marginal benefits) is similar to the one used by McWilliams and Siegel and Husted and Salazar, but it uses a theory of public economics.[101] McWilliams and Siegel and Husted and Salazar theorize CSR as if it were a private good, thus missing the democratic ethos at the heart of CSR.[102]

We have thus provided a simple theory of CSR effectiveness, which, at least in principle, solves the allocation problem and identifies a guideline logic to CSR managers in thinking about the range of stakeholders that need to be considered. Moreover, we have identified the existence of a centripetal point, an operational tendency in the basic logic of decision-making of CSR. We have identified that there are some limiting, boundary conditions. It is possible to pinpoint with more precision—an inside band of relative effectiveness and an outside region—that it is not the case that anything

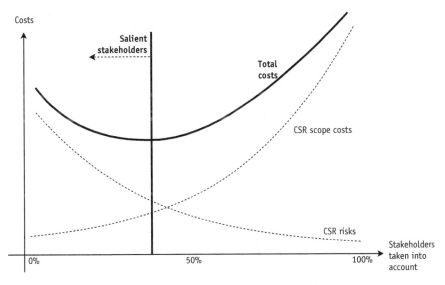

Figure 9.1 Calculus-of-consent model for determining CSR efficiency.

goes as long there is good will among the actors involved when it comes to CSR effectiveness in resource allocation and the trade-offs involved. This, however, is only the beginning of the problem. We have made the problem more manageable, at least conceptually, by pointing out the decision constraints of effectiveness. The more difficult part, after identifying the salient stakeholders, is determining the rules and criteria that will govern the CSR activities and the polycentric processes of which they are part. The theory of polycentricity, discussed in the next section, offers a further guideline for addressing that more difficult problem.

The PSA Framework: Polycentrism and Co-production as Analytical and Heuristic Instruments

At first glance, refusing to take the heterogeneity of evaluators off the table makes the problem of CSR management impossibly complex. There are multiple circles of decision-making—concentric and overlapping—that may have shareholders and managers at the center and other social actors and stakeholders with different stakes and different intensities at various salient distances. How can we map all the possible stakeholders, with their divergent perspectives on how to understand the world and how to judge a firm's activities in overlapping and competing areas of decision-making and issues? The homogenizing assumption has the advantage of simplifying the problem in that there would be only one frame of reference. The idea of business ethics hypernorms shared across industries would simplify matters even more, thereby offering the promise that firms could learn from each other's CSRs even across different spheres of activity. The downside, however, is one of losing realism.

The previous section showed how to delineate the set of relevant (salient) stakeholders, but the stakeholders still form a heterogeneous group. Fortunately, the theory of polycentricity has been better systematized in recent years, allowing us to better deal with heterogeneity. This section explains how it may be possible to turn that systematization into a tool for CSR analysis and possibly for decision-making.

We have seen that the diversity of possible polycentric systems can be understood as being the foundation of three key characteristics: (a) there is a multiplicity of autonomous decision-making centers; (b) the actions of those decision-making centers are circumscribed by an overarching system of rules and norms; and (c) the content of the system of rules and norms is such that it creates incentives compatibility—that is, it aligns the incentives of individual actions with desirable social outcomes, thus setting the stage for a productive emergent order.

The multiplicity of autonomous decision-making centers is essential for maintaining creativity and dynamism, as well as the resilience of the system.[103] The diversity avoids groupthink and one-size-fits-all solutions. It also provides insurance against unexpected shocks, thus avoiding the situation of having the system as a whole affected at the same time, because different centers have different vulnerabilities and, from case to case, can help each other. It is for such reasons that polycentric systems often outperform monocentric hierarchical systems, especially when the production of public goods is at stake. But it is the third aspect, which varies in its details from case to case, that connects the theory of polycentricity to the theory of public entrepreneurship mentioned earlier. What public entrepreneurs do is either discover and implement such overarching rules or act as focal points for promoting good norms that create broad incentive compatibility for all the actors involved and hence promote productive social orders.

For our discussion, it is possible to imagine the polycentric circles at various levels and of various configurations. They may be approached as centers of a firm's decision-making structure. Or the circles may be seen as the firm's stakeholders, who evaluate the firm as the autonomous decision-making centers, with the CSR managers playing the role of public entrepreneurs who must discover a system that promotes the desired social goal. The system can be understood as the set of overarching rules and norms. For example, the CSR management usually must decide which inclusion and exclusion rules to use—for example, the types of criteria someone should fulfill in order to qualify as a salient stakeholder. Furthermore, an important idea is that, because of the nature of most social goals, the best outcomes are usually achieved when the stakeholders are involved in various ways in the production. We have now reached a crucial element of the polycentric governance literature: the concept of co-production.

We have discussed the idea that the consumer may be a key part of production—co-production. In addition, we are familiar with its fundamental importance for understanding the production of public goods.[104] Typical examples are education and health (the student must contribute actively to learning and the patient to being healed). Yet, interestingly enough, governance is also a co-production good that has huge consequences, and we can see why a polycentrism-stakeholders-public value paradigm intrinsically implies a co-production element. In the context of our discussion, we can treat the concept of co-production as the political economy approach to the demands of social integration CSR theories. But the co-production theory is not holistic or sociological, yet it maintains individual-level perspective and preserves heterogeneity. Hence, we argue, it provides an improved perspective of realism.

We can also better understand now why CSR does not always come naturally to firms and sometimes requires important changes in perspective. The management system behind the delivery of most private goods can be understood as one of team production.[105] In team production, the consumer is not part of the production process, and workers are not (necessarily) consumers of the product. But team production and co-production systems do address the same managerial problem: they are both systems for preventing shirking and free-riding in the production process, and hence they are easily confused.[106] But depending on the nature of the good being produced, it is crucial to properly identify the correct system of production. A co-production problem often is found in social activities; if a hierarchical team production system is put in place, the result will be inefficient. That means those overseeing CSR practices often must change their management system and, in particular, involve stakeholders in making decisions to a much larger extent than managers are used to.

CSR activities can involve a wide variety of situations; hence, contrary to the idea of business ethics hypernorms, it is not advisable to propose one-size-fits-all recipes. The theory of polycentricity at the foundation of PSA is broad enough to cover numerous relationships between CSR management and stakeholders.

Figure 9.2 highlights the key elements that the decision-making process in CSR situations must take into account. Some elements are not directives about how to do CSR but rather guidelines about the type of problem that needs to be solved. Some elements are determined by the nature of the problem at hand. Specifically, are the stakeholders acting as disparate individuals or as organized collectives of individuals with shared goals (figure 9.2, 1c)? Is the problem territorially circumscribed (2b)? Are stakeholders' entry and exit as salient stakeholders matters of choice or necessity (3a and 3b)?

Most elements involve key decisions by CSR management. Depending on the importance of co-production, one matter that needs to be decided is the level of stakeholder involvement in the rules design process or, to put it differently, the level of

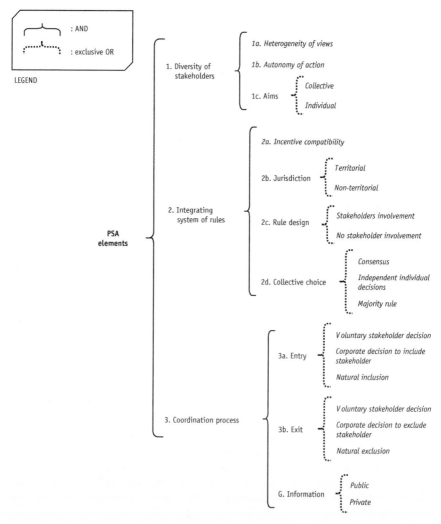

Figure 9.2 The PSA elements for CSR management.

paternalism of the CSR activity (2c). Considering that stakeholders' opinions and values may differ, is the achievement of CSR goals dependent on some form of aggregation (e.g., facilitating consensus or deciding by majority rule), or is it possible to achieve CSR goals while interacting with stakeholders on an individual basis (i.e., some CSR goals require dealing with stakeholders on an individual basis; 2d)? If entry and exit decisions are made by CSR managers, they need to decide (and face the possibility that they are mistaken) whether some stakeholders are not salient enough to be included (3a and 3b). As Dunfee puts it, "Because it is impossible for corporations to respond to all of the needs of their stakeholders . . . triage is required" (3c).[107] Finally, and again dovetailing Dunfee's account, can the relevant information be made public? As Dunfee notes, there are often good reasons why sharing information contributes to CSR goals, but that is not always the case, even when only CSR goals are considered.[108] For example, sometimes one might want to take precautions to avoid groupthink, especially if empirical evaluation is not easily available. This chapter extends the public choice institutional theory perspective by applying it to the domain of corporate governance and stakeholder analysis, illuminating how a framework based on it has the potential to satisfy the major descriptive and analytic criteria required by such a framework while attempting to preserve key elements of the normative democratic ethos that drives CSR more broadly.

Conclusion

What are the most effective ways to analyze corporate agency and responsibility as part of complex, overlapping, and competitive formal and informal governance arrangements at the interface of the private and the public, the market, the state and the civil society, and the for-profit and nonprofit sectors? What kind of theoretical frameworks should be used to best conceptualize, analyze, and design stakeholder-based governance systems? Such frameworks must satisfy at least three criteria: (a) they should capture and accommodate both descriptively and normatively the heterogeneity of preferences, objectives, beliefs, and values of the stakeholders as well as the institutional diversity and the complex nestedness of the various governance systems embedded in the stakeholders' system; (b) they should capture and analytically deal with the nature and implications of imperfect rationality, information, and potential opportunistic behavior by the agents on the ground; and (c) they should accommodate the normative democratic ethos that pervades much of the governance and CSR literature.

This chapter advances a possible response to those challenges. Building on the literature on institutional theory and political economy, the chapter identifies and introduces the polycentric governance perspective. We argue that contemporary discussions regarding stakeholder governance systems (more specifically, the institutional analysis of corporate governance and CSR) may benefit in multiple ways from incorporating the public choice institutionalism perspective. With that end in view, we articulate one possible approach to that task by showing how the concepts of polycentricity, polycentric systems of governance, and co-production (situations in which consumers of goods and services participate in the production process—in this case members of self-regulating communities coproducing, validating, and managing the rules and norms under which they operate) may be used to model and interpret the interactions between different stakeholders of a corporation and the parameters and processes constraining or directing its activities. We demonstrate the relevance, applicability, and viability of the theoretical apparatus and general perspective developed in the first two parts of the book. Irrespective of what one may call it (classical liberalism seems to us to best capture both the spirit and the intellectual genealogy), the perspective's distinctiveness and viability are proven. Moreover, the proof did not result from applying the perspective to easy, simple cases but rather to a set of issue areas of great institutional, social, and normative complexity. This chapter presents a case for the general viability of the classical-liberal perspective on governance at both the theoretical and the applied levels.

Conclusions

Governance and Public Management: A Vindication of the Classical-Liberal Perspective?

This book specifies and elaborates a particular perspective on the problem of public governance. It outlines a system of thought and the elements of a doctrine of governance with distinctive properties. Although, in the end, the label under which this system is presented is immaterial, we claim that both as a matter of intellectual genealogy and as a matter of logical consistency it makes sense to associate it with the classical-liberal tradition. Doing so leads not only to a distinctive view on the entire range of themes pertaining to the field and practice of public governance but also to a rather coherent paradigm, via the full elaboration of the underlying logic connecting all these themes. What we identify as "classical-liberal" basic beliefs and theoretical assumptions do make a difference. The public administration principles and frameworks that surface as a result of our exercise are sufficiently distinct to validate the notion that there is indeed *in nuce* a classical-liberal theory of public governance to be derived from the foundational liberal philosophical and theoretical writings and from the public rhetoric and positions they inspire. Further development of the theory and its translation into practice is, however, a more complicated task. Yet, a closer look at the developments in public governance since 1990s offers a fresh and intriguing view of the issue. We end our argument with an interpretation of those developments and their relevance for the perspective elaborated in this book.

In the beginning of our discussion in this book, we noted that public administration emerged as a field at the end of the nineteenth century, in the wake of the demise of classical liberalism as a reigning political and economic paradigm. As a consequence, participation by classical liberals in the intellectual development of public administration as a field was marginal.[1] When the revival of classical liberalism redefined the parameters of public debate and public policies in the second half of the twentieth century, classical-liberal scholars focused mainly criticizing existing statist policies and administrative structures and on the general theory of statism. Only limited attention was dedicated to the development of a positive doctrine of public governance. These are well established facts.

Yet, interestingly, in our discussion thus far, the more we advance in our exploration of classical-liberal public choice themes and approaches in the context of public administration, the more points of convergence and more affinities we discover between the public choice insights of the classical-liberal ethos and the ideas that fuel more recent reforms in the field of public administration. The more we advance in articulating, by using the intrinsic logic of the classical-liberal perspective, diagnoses and solutions to public governance problems, the more we can see that such diagnoses and solutions are far from alien to the contemporary field and practice of public administration.

Such affinities should not be a surprise. We have encountered an important moment in the evolution of the field, when a bold paradigmatic change proposition was put forward from a public choice perspective. And we have seen that in the field of public administration the ethos of classical liberalism was never totally exhausted. The arguments presented in this book enable us to identify an intriguing and interesting phenomenon. The clearer the articulation of the classical-liberal perspective on governance, the more we discover that there have already been attempts to define and implement akin approaches but without mentioning explicitly the "classical-liberal" label and conceptual underpinning. In brief, contemporary public administration, in both theory and practice, seems to have moved increasingly closer to some of the core ideas we have seen emerging as central to what we identify in this volume as the classical-liberal perspective on governance.

That is not speculation but rather a straightforward observation, and it can be substantiated by an overview of the literature. The main point is this: the current state of basic and applied theorizing in public administration invited us to seriously reconsider our understanding of the relationship between classical-liberal insights and public governance, as defined by the field and practice of public administration. The history and evolution of doctrines and practices of public governance seem to be working in more complex and less obvious ways than we expected. Arguably, from the perspective of our discussion, the most important developments in recent decades took place under the labels of "governance" and "new public management." Taking a closer look at them, we recognize elements unmistakable similar to the Ostromian democratic administration, the public choice insights and the contextualist institutionalism perspective that all played such a preeminent part in our study.

The changes in approach that have taken place in public administration in the past decades have been described in diverse ways. Probably the most well known such descriptions have been those done under the labels of "governance" and "new public administration." But irrespective of label and approach, all converge around several key observations. B. Guy Peters and John Pierre offer an informative synthetic evaluation.[2] Owing to global financial pressures and increased demands, they explain, governments have found themselves stretched thin and unable to administer as directly as before. The state is increasingly unable to exercise control and must be content with exercising influence. Hence, private actors and hybrid forms of organization have greater sway in traditionally public domains. Most government activity is increasingly thought of as bargaining with groups and networks of actors. That blurs the distinction between the private and public sectors. Private-public partnerships and other hybrid institutional forms have arisen. The result is a phenomenon that may be called "governance without government." Its concrete manifestation is a kind of outsourcing to, or partnership with, the private sector. Given those developments, as Peters and Pierre explain, "governance" has come to indicate the full gamut of semipublic mechanisms and institutions for implementing policy, as opposed to government. That opens up a wide array of policy instruments that, in more traditional circumstances, governments often overlook in favor of direct means. And it leads to a more complex way of understanding the nature and operation of public management and administration—"the new public management."

One cannot take a position here on the different interpretations of the relationship between the two facets of the phenomena—the new public management and governance. For our purposes, it is important to capture the phenomenon that the two ideas define. In that respect, we are well served by the complementary angles they offer. Again, Guy Peters and John Pierre's take on the matter regarding the transformations of the 1990s offers a good overview: the new public management pertains to the management of an organization (a management theory), whereas governance is more about relationships between organizations (a political theory). But both governance and the new public management each have a diminished view of the role of elected officials, putting emphasis instead on political entrepreneurship, the pooling of public and private resources, and a complex and dynamic model of setting priorities.

Governance and the new public management both stress output control rather than input control. Input control conceals inefficiency and does not relate performance to demand. In the "steering" versus "rowing" dichotomy, both focus on steering. (*Steering* stands for setting goals and priorities and *rowing* stands for hierarchical directing). The new public management is strictly about outcomes, while governance focuses on process and on setting goals, giving considerable discretion to subordinate agencies. Regarding accountability, the new public management relies on market or quasi-market discipline. "Both governance theories and NPM [new public management] consider that the public–private dichotomy is obsolete, though the reasons for reaching that conclusion are different." The new public management encourages adoption of management styles from the private sector under the assumption that the same problems exist regardless of context—private or public. In both the private- and public-sector, competition and internal markets are tools to increase efficiency. Hence, the new public management requires relaxation of political control over subsidiary agencies; it allows for more accurate assessment of costs, uses benchmarks more energetically, and induces more direct contact with customers and stakeholders. On the other hand, "governance is generally more concerned with blending public and private resources than with competition in the public sector."[3] Although not necessarily opposed to competition, governance is still very concerned about the question of market failure. Moreover, there is concern about the potential conflict between efficiency and norms of legality and equality.

The new public management, note Peters and Pierre, was more salient in Britain, while the governance approach seems to have taken hold more in Western Europe—specifically Austria, Belgium, Netherlands, and the Scandinavian countries—favored by those countries' corporatist governing style. In most cases, fiscal crises have led to market-driven administrative reforms. Apparently, the debate is less relevant for the United States, according to Peters and Pierre. With the "absence of a strong state tradition" in the United States, "the tradition of a strong civil society bears some of the brunt of governing."[4] Private-sector delivery of services has always characterized the United States, unlike its more recent appearance in Europe. That means the United

States has already been engaged in something like governance without government, so the shift has been less dramatic.

The developments we have just outlined have generated a robust literature. Probably the clearest indicators of the status and influence of that literature are *The Oxford Handbook of Governance* and *The Oxford Handbook of Public Management*.[5] Both volumes reconfirm that, far from being of eccentric or marginal relevance, the governance themes outlined above are at the core of both the academic and applied agenda.

The Oxford Handbook of Governance is built around the idea that since the 1990s, owing to a multifaceted process that changed the role of the state and the boundaries for the public, private, and voluntary sectors, a new reality has been created at both the national and the global levels. A shift has taken place from regimes centered on nation-states to pluralist, multilevel, polycentric arrangements; from politics, hierarchies, and communities to markets; from provision to regulation; from public authority to private authority; and from big government to small government.[6] The retreating reach of government control has led to an "expanding role of civil society in directing and regulating the uses of public resources," and decentralization and de-monopolization have encouraged a variety of formal and informal hybrid private-public organizational forms.[7] Those changes have led to a move from regulation based on command and control to flexible and diverse forms of regulation in which self-regulation is an important element. The overall result has been the growth of "governance without government."[8] Similarly, *The Oxford Handbook of Public Management* confirms the emergent salience of such themes as proactive administration, street-level bureaucracy, administrative responsiveness and responsibility, citizen participation, decentralization, private-public partnerships, contracting, and nongovernment organizations.

One of the most effective metaphors repeatedly used to describe those phenomena and developments is the distinction between rowing functions (tax collection, service provision, redistribution) and steering functions (rulemaking, monitoring, and enforcement). The idea is that a shift has occurred from command-and-direct provision by states—states that do both the rowing and the steering—to states that increasingly steer while markets and nonprofit civil society do the rowing. David Levi-Faur notes somewhat ironically in the opening chapter of *The Oxford Handbook of Governance* that in many respects the multiplicity of shifts from Weberian bureaucracy to "regulocracy" invites the emergence of "a science of shiftology," a systematic study of those changes.[9]

Readers familiar with the public choice tradition will recognize, even in a description as brief as the one above, an array of familiar themes. Since its beginnings in the early 1960s, the public choice literature has advanced arguments regarding the nature and desirability of such formulas and developments in public governance. For instance, Gordon Tullock's work on bureaucracy sums up the basic public choice theme by raising doubts that the high degree of coordination assumed by many governmental tasks is achievable through the mechanisms of bureaucratically organized hierarchies, while noting that society possesses relatively more effective alternative methods of achieving such coordination.[10] According to Gordon Tullock, although most traditional government functions are not suitable for market organization, it is still possible to create less bureaucratic (even nonbureaucratic) methods for coordinating such activities. Tullock was emblematic of the public choice advocacy of a shift to a more efficient mode of organizing the public system that would increase both "our liberties and our ability to control the future."[11] Among the solutions suggested is a "sizable reduction in the total amount of activities attempted by the governmental apparatus," as well as wider use of local governments as a means to reduce the number of problems the central government must deal with.[12]

As discussed in the present volume, James Buchanan, in his *What Should Economists Do?*, insisted that economic analysis should be "neutral to the proper private sector–public sector mix" because "people may decide to do things collectively or may not."[13] As a result, various forms of social organization may emerge. Buchanan even advances the idea of a general framework for the study of governance processes and arrangements: "symbiotics," defined as "the study of association between dissimilar organisms" in "unique relationships involving cooperative associations of individuals when interests are different."[14] Last but not least, as we have seen, the study of the variety of public governance forms is a domain marked by the pioneering efforts of the Ostroms. V. Ostrom's work with Tiebout and Warren formed the foundation of an alternative paradigm of democratic public administration, as opposed to a bureaucratic one.[15] They emphasize that authority and decision-making powers are institutionalized at different levels and domains and that functional governance systems may be organized around competition, cooperation, and bargaining between those domains and levels. The work of the Bloomington scholars on the commons, public economies, polycentricity, and the "neither market nor state" realm thus deals with the core of the governance agenda.

In brief, the phenomena and themes covered by the new public management and governance are also at the core of the intellectual tradition engaged by this book's topic and concerns. The themes include not only the variety of governance forms and areas but also the various facets and conceptualizations, including governance (a) as a structure, or architecture of institutions; (b) as a process, or the dynamics of functions; (c) as a mechanism, or procedures and decision rules; and (d) as a strategy, or actions related to control and institutional design that shape preferences and decisions. At the same time, they tellingly capture the tensions between alternative modes of understanding the new reality. For instance, on the one hand, there is the thesis of hollowing out the state, whereby authority either shifts up to markets and transnational institutions or down to local governments, business communities, and nongovernment organizations. On the other hand, there is the thesis that the state has reasserted its authority by shifting its focus at the meta level toward "regulating the mix of governing structures such as markets and networks and deploying indirect instruments of control," the notion of metagovernance.[16]

From the range of themes that point toward the confluence of ideas discussed here, let us focus on a final illustration. That illustration shows the convergence between on the one hand the constitutional and process views in the tradition explored in this book and the notion of public administration as metagovernance, on the other. One major theme strongly illuminated by the public choice revolution is that any discussion of public policies and policy initiatives—policy theory, policy design, policy implementation, policy evaluation—must, sooner or later, deal with the institutional and constitutional arrangements that set the stage for policy action. In other words, the discussion must factor in realistically the formal and informal rules of the game at the constitutive level. Then one should make the distinction between the provision of the framework—law, security, structure of governance responsibilities, and so on—and the policy decisions—particular acts of administration. In applied-level terms, that means that there are many situations in which implementation of a public policy requires a change in rules, incentives, and processes—something that goes beyond the basic operational-level implementation of a policy decision in a given setting. In fact, large parts of the reforms and policy implications drawn from the insights of the public choice research program are precisely about the institutional structure of the administrative state and its functioning at all levels, from the lowest (the operational one) to the highest (that of constitutional choice). We understand now that the public choice approach to public policy is by its nature mostly indirect: to go through institutional and incentive structures, to deal with the ecology of decision-making in different settings, and to analyze the various patterns of cooperation and coordination in specific architectures of choice. It is a meta-level approach, and after a closer look, that is the essence of the domain of public governance and administration: the institutional and organizational design of the architecture of public choice of collective decision-making on public issues with a view to both the incentive and the knowledge problems. Public administration is ultimately about building, maintaining, and operating in real-life structures and processes that function as preconditions, infrastructure, and determinants for real-life public policies and their management.

That sets the stage for better understanding of the roots of the idea of "metagovernance" as it has emerged in the field of public administration in conjunction to the newer developments. The concept captures and defines the same reality of the interplay of different levels in the architecture of public choice and governance, as identified by public choice scholars. The starting point is the already familiar observation that the context of public administration has changed from government (a unitary will that presides over a bureaucracy) to governance (multiplicity of self-regulating private or public institutions). Governments, writes Eva Sørensen, whose concise but comprehensive argument we use in presenting the basic features of the idea of metagovernance, "search for ways to exploit the self-regulating capacities of the wider society in order to meet the permanently growing demands for public governance."[17] Metagovernance is a way "to make authoritative hierarchical rule and self-regulating markets, civil societies, and networks compatible." This practice pivots on political and economic framing and the construction of institutions. It is governing by shaping the rules of the game that modify the rule structure as opposed to governing by modifying the results of the game.

Through the lens of metagovernance, we can see how the themes and ideas explored in this book emerge in a new light. The new public management may be treated as a metagovernance strategy whose goal is to enhance efficiency through the regulatory framework of self-regulating markets via the design of institutional rules. Informed by public choice and rational choice theories, the new public management aims to create optimal conditions for competition, both within public sector and between the private and public sectors. Metagovernance "to some extent undermines the traditional institutions of representative democracy [but] does not necessarily threaten democracy as such [so long as] all affected citizens are capable of influencing on-going processes of self-regulation."[18] In fact, by allowing officials to focus on broad goals rather than details of implementation, metagovernance may even enhance democracy. In a similar way, explains Sørensen, community participation may be interpreted as a metagovernance strategy. As such, community participation "seeks to enhance governance, not through the shaping of self-interested action, but through the promotion of community-based collective action."[19] By cajoling people into po-litical participation, the strategy aims for decentralization of political power to local communities, and a special emphasis is put on the self-regulating capacity of local communities, bolstered by the establishment of participatory bodies (neighborhood councils, etc.) that oblige affected actors to work together.[20] Sørensen summarizes by noting that "liberal societies have always aimed to govern through the regulation of a self-regulating market and civil society," and in that respect metagovernance is a strategy for doing so.[21] Hence, it is not to be considered a radical break with liberal forms of governance."[22] With metagovernance, "self-regulation, formerly a privilege of the private sector [is extended] into the public sphere,"[23] with the line between private and public becoming less important and the scope of public administration widening, deepening, and being made much more complex.

It goes without saying that there are many other available examples and references to the literature that advances the metagovernance perspective. Yet, the goal here is not to offer a comprehensive overview but to illustrate the observa-tion that, with a closer look, a confluence of views could be identified by looking at the ways in which public administration, as both a practice and a scholarly field, has evolved during the past decades. A striking similarity of viewpoints could be identified, by looking at the ideas that have fueled the reform proposals in public governance, as well as at the insights, concepts, and arguments identified in this book as pertaining to the intellectual tradition influenced by (or relevant for) the classical-liberal ethos.

To what extent this intriguing convergence be considered a vindication of the classical-liberal ethos captured by the democratic administration vision and to what extent a more compelling alternative interpretation may be offered, are fascinating topics in themselves. Have the recent crises and challenges to the liberal system of globalized freedom of movement and exchange undermined the trends discussed here? Is the pendulum now swinging back from democratic polycentric governance toward bureaucratic administration? Are our observations about the "convergence" built on mere inertial phenomena? These questions are for future projects to explore. But even more important for the subsequent agenda is the practical relevance, at the applied level, of approaching governance issues through the lenses identified and delineated in this book. Further elaboration of the applied-level implications of all of the above is the main task ahead and the next step of the intellectual program re-flected in the pages of this book. Above and beyond existing or possible trends and irrespective of historical circumstances, the idea of self-governance in polycentric, pluralistic systems that reflect the diversity of individual preferences and values, and that consist of the variety of institutional arrangements emerging as a result of that diversity, carries with it a vision of governance worth elaborating, advocating, and advancing.

NOTES

Introduction

1. The term *public administration* is used in this book in two ways. The first designates an activity, a form of social cooperation, and the real-life organization and management of public affairs. The literature usually refers to this as "public administration." The second meaning designates the discipline, the area of study and inquiry, a domain of academic and public discourse which explores both positively and normatively the processes and organization arrangements associated with the activity of public administration. The literature usually refers to this as "the field of public administration" or, alternatively, "Public Administration" (capitalized). Similarly, the literature usually refers to on one hand, "public choice" and, on the other hand, "the field of public choice" or "Public Choice." The first denotes the activities and institutions by which a society makes collective choices—how people make choices in groups as opposed to individually. The second denotes the academic field at the interface between economics and political science that studies how collective choices can be made efficiently. The field of public choice includes William Riker's Rochester school of political science, James Buchanan and Gordon Tullock's Virginia school of political economy, and Vincent and Elinor Ostrom's Bloomington school of political economy.

2. Woodrow Wilson, *Congressional Government: A Study in American Politics* (Baltimore: John Hopkins University, 1885 [1956]), available at https://archive.org/details/congressionalgov00wilsa. See also Woodrow Wilson, "The Study of Administration," *Political Science Quarterly* 2, no. 2 (1887): 197–222.

3. Paul Dragos Aligica and Peter J. Boettke, *Challenging Institutional Analysis and Development: The Bloomington School* (London and New York: Routledge, 2009).

4. Vlad Tarko, *Elinor Ostrom: An Intellectual Biography* (London: Rowman and Littlefield International, 2016).

5. Vincent Ostrom to James Buchanan, October 10, 1977. George Mason University, Buchanan Archives.

6. Ibid.

7. Ibid.

8. Elinor Ostrom, *Understanding Institutional Diversity* (Princeton, NJ: Princeton University Press, 2005), 284.

9. Vincent Ostrom, "Polycentricity," working paper presented at annual meeting of the American Political Science Association, Washington, DC, September 5–9, 1972.

10. Vincent Ostrom, *The Meaning of American Federalism: Constituting a Self-Governing Society* (San Francisco: ICS Press, 1991).

11. Ibid., 228.

12. Vincent Ostrom, *The Meaning of Democracy and the Vulnerability of Democracies: A Response to Tocqueville's Challenge* (Ann Arbor: University of Michigan Press, 1997), 1.

Chapter 1

1. See especially the following: Randy Barnett, *The Structure of Liberty: Justice and the Rule of Law* (New York: Oxford University Press, 1998); Jason Brennan and David Schmidtz, *A History of Liberty* (Malden, MA: Wiley-Blackwell, 2010); Edwin van de Haar, *Degrees of Freedom: Liberal Political Philosophy and Ideology* (New York: Routledge, 2015); Richard Epstein, *Skepticism and Freedom: A Modern Case for Classical Liberalism* (Chicago: University of Chicago Press, 2003); Gerald Gaus, *The Tyranny of the Ideal: Justice in a Diverse Society* (Princeton, NJ: Princeton University Press, 2016); Gerald Gaus, *The Order of Public Reason: A Theory of Freedom and Morality in a Diverse and Bounded World* (New York: Cambridge University Press, 2011); Jacob T. Levy, *Rationalism, Pluralism, and Freedom* (New York: Oxford University Press, 2015); David Schmidtz, *Rational Choice and Moral Agency* (Princeton, NJ: Princeton University Press, 1995); David Schmidtz, *Elements of Justice* (New York: Cambridge University Press, 2006); John Tomasi, *Free Market Fairness* (Princeton, NJ: Princeton University Press, 2012). Lawrence White, *The clash of economic ideas: the great policy debates and experiments of the last hundred years* (Cambridge: Cambridge University Press, 2012).
2. Chandran Kukathas, *The Liberal Archipelago: A Theory of Diversity and Freedom* (New York: Oxford University Press, 2003), 2.
3. Robert A. Dahl, *Democracy and Its Critics* (New Haven, CT: Yale University Press, 1989), 89.
4. James M. Buchanan, *The Collected Works of James M. Buchanan, Volume 7: The Limits of Liberty* (Indianapolis, IN: Liberty Fund, 2000), 24.
5. Vincent Ostrom, *The Meaning of Democracy and the Vulnerabilities of Democracies: A Response to Tocqueville's Challenge* (Ann Arbor: University of Michigan Press, 1997), 121.
6. James M. Buchanan, "Justification of the Compound Republic: The *Calculus* in Retrospect," *Cato Journal* 7, no. 2 (1987): 305–12.
7. Elinor Ostrom, *Governing the Commons: The Evolution of Institutions for Collective Action* (New York: Cambridge University Press, 1990).
8. Abram Bergson, "On the Concept of Social Welfare," *Quarterly Journal of Economics* 68, no. 2 (1954): 233–52.
9. James C. Scott, *Seeing Like a State: How Certain Schemes to Improve the Human Condition Have Failed* (New Haven, CT: Yale University Press, 1998), 2.
10. Ibid., 78.
11. Ibid., 79.
12. Friedrich A. Hayek, *Law, Legislation and Liberty, Volume 1: Rules and Order* (Chicago: University of Chicago Press, 1973), 14–15.
13. Friedrich A. Hayek, "The Use of Knowledge in Society," *American Economic Review* 35, no. 4 (1945): 519–30.
14. Ostrom, *The Meaning of Democracy*, 121.
15. Scott, *Seeing Like a State*.
16. James M. Buchanan, "The Foundations for Normative Individualism," in *The Collected Works of James M. Buchanan, Volume 1: The Logical Foundations of Constitutional Liberty* (Indianapolis, IN: Liberty Fund, 1999), 288.
17. Barnett, *The Structure of Liberty*, 2.
18. Ostrom, *The Meaning of Democracy*, 272–73.
19. Friedrich A. Hayek, "Individualism: True and False," in *Individualism and Economic Order* (Chicago: University of Chicago Press, 1948).
20. Christopher H. Achen and Larry M. Bartels, *Democracy for Realists: Why Elections Do Not Produce Responsive Government* (Princeton and Oxford: Princeton University Press, 2016)
21. Kenneth J. Arrow, *Social Choice and Individual Values* (New Haven, CT: Yale University Press, 1951).
22. Achen and Bartels, *Democracy for Realists*, 27.
23. Ibid., 30.
24. James M. Buchanan, "Politics without Romance: A Sketch of Positive Public Choice Theory and Its Normative Implications," in *The Collected Works of James M. Buchanan, Volume 1: The Logical Foundations of Constitutional Liberty* (Indianapolis, IN: Liberty Fund, 1999), 45–59.

25. James M. Buchanan, "Taxation in Fiscal Exchange," in *The Collected Works of James M. Buchanan, Volume 1: The Logical Foundations of Constitutional Liberty* (Indianapolis, IN: Liberty Fund, 1999), 146.

26. Ibid., 144.

27. Ibid., 145.

28. Vincent Ostrom, *The Intellectual Crisis in American Public Administration*, 3rd ed. (Tuscaloosa: University of Alabama Press, 2008 [1973]); Richard E. Wagner, *Mind, Society, and Human Action: Time and Knowledge in a Theory of Social Economy* (New York: Routledge, 2010); Adam Smith, Richard E. Wagner, and Bruce Yandle, "A Theory of Entangled Political Economy, with Application to TARP and NRA," *Public Choice* 148, no. 1/2 (2011): 45–66).

29. Buchanan, "Taxation in Fiscal Exchange," 146.

30. Ibid., 145.

31. Ibid., 145–46.

32. Elinor Ostrom and Vincent Ostrom, "The Quest for Meaning in Public Choice," *American Journal of Economics and Sociology* 63, no. 1 (2004): 105–47.

33. Buchanan, "Justification of the Compound Republic," 401.

34. Sandra Peart, and David M. Levy, *The "Vanity of the Philosopher": From Equality to Hierarchy in Post-Classical Economics* (University of Michigan Press, 2009). chap. 9

35. Richard E. Wagner, *Politics as a Peculiar Business: Insights from a Theory of Entangled Political Economy* (Cheltenham, UK, and Northampton, MA: Edward Elgar, 2016), 56.

36. Ibid., 59.

37. James M. Buchanan, *What Should Economists Do?* (Indianapolis, IN: Liberty Fund, 1979).

38. James Buchanan, "Public Choice: The Origins and Development of a Research Program" (Fairfax, VA: Center for Study of Public Choice, George Mason University, 2003)

39. Anthony Downs, *Inside Bureaucracy* (Boston: Little, Brown, 1967).

40. William A. Niskanen, *Bureaucracy—Servant or Master? Lessons from America* (London: Institute of Economic Affairs, 1973).

41. Adam Smith, *The Wealth of Nations*, Book I, Chapter X.

42. A. C. Pigou, *Wealth and Welfare* (London: Macmillan, 1912), 247–48.

43. A. C. Pigou, *The Economics of Welfare*, 4th ed. (London: Macmillan, 1932 [1920]), 331–32.

44. Scott, *Seeing Like a State*, 2–3.

45. Ronald H. Coase, "The Problem of Social Cost," *The Journal of Law & Economics* 3 (1960): 1–44; Peter J. Boettke, *Living Economics: Yesterday, Today, and Tomorrow* (Oakland, CA: Independent Institute, 2012).

46. Ronald H. Coase, "The Economics of Broadcasting and Government Policy," *The American Economic Review* 56, no. 1/2 (1966): 440–47.

47. James M. Buchanan, *The Collected Works of James M. Buchanan, Volume 6: Cost and Choice: An Inquiry in Economic Theory* (Indianapolis, IN: Liberty Fund, 1969 [1999]).

48. See also Karen I. Vaughn, "Does It Matter That Costs Are Subjective?," *Southern Economic Journal* 46, no. 3 (1980): 702–15.

49. Steven G. Medema, "Finding His Own Way: The Legacy of Ronald Coase in Economic Analysis," in *The Legacy of Ronald Coase in Economic Analysis, Vol. 1*, ed. Steven G. Medema (Aldershot, UK, and Brookfield, VT: Edward Elgar, 1995), ix–lxix.

50. James M. Buchanan and Roger D. Congleton, *Politics by Principle, Not Interest: Towards Nondiscriminatory Democracy* (New York: Cambridge University Press, 1998).

51. Steven G. Medema, *The Hesitant Hand: Taming Self-Interest in the History of Economic Ideas* (Princeton, NJ: Princeton University Press, 2009).

52. Ludwig von Mises, *Liberalism: The Classical Tradition*, trans. Ralph Raico, ed. Bettina Bien Greaves (Indianapolis, IN: Liberty Fund 2005 [1927]), xix.

Chapter 2

1. John Stuart Mill, *On Liberty and Utilitarianism* (New York: Knopf, 1992 [1859]), 14.

2. John Stuart Mill, *Principles of Political Economy with Some of Their Applications to Social Philosophy* (London: Longmans, Green, 1909 [1848]), 941–42.
3. Steven G. Medema, *The Hesitant Hand: Taming Self-Interest in the History of Economic Ideas* (Princeton, NJ: Princeton University Press, 2009).
4. Ibid., 71.
5. Arthur Cecil Pigou, *Economics in Practice: Six Lectures on Current Issues* (London: Macmillan, 1935), 127.
6. Medema, *The Hesitant Hand*, 71.
7. Ibid.
8. Antonio de Viti de Marco, *First Principles of Public Finance* (New York: Harcourt, Brace, 1936), 45.
9. Antonio de Viti de Marco, *First Principles of Public Finance* (New York: Harcourt, Brace, 1936), 45.
10. James M Buchanan, *The Collected Works of James M. Buchanan, Volume 5: The Demand and Supply of Public Goods* (Indianapolis, IN: Liberty Fund, 1999).
11. Ibid., ch. 9.
12. Friedrich A. Hayek, *Law, Legislation and Liberty, Volume 2: The Mirage of Social Justice* (Chicago: University of Chicago Press, 1976).
13. Friedrich A. Hayek, *The Constitution of Liberty* (Chicago: University of Chicago Press, 1960), 224–25.
14. Edward Peter Stringham and Todd J. Zywicki, "Hayekian Anarchism," *Journal of Economic Behavior and Organization* 78, no. 3 (2011): 290–301.
15. Hayek, *Law, Legislation and Liberty*, vol. 2, 88–89.
16. Friedrich A. Hayek, *Law, Legislation and Liberty, Volume 3: The Political Order of a Free People* (Chicago: University of Chicago Press, 1979), 43.
17. Ibid., 45.
18. Hayek, *The Constitution of Liberty*, 64, 92, 142.
19. Medema, *The Hesitant Hand*, 89–99.
20. Ibid., 98.
21. Ibid., 89–99.
22. Gary J. Miller, *Managerial Dilemmas: The Political Economy of Hierarchy* (Cambridge, UK: Cambridge University Press, 1992).
23. Elinor Ostrom, *Governing the Commons: The Evolution of Institutions for Collective Action* (Cambridge, UK: Cambridge University Press, 1990).
24. If players maximize their expected utility, in what is called "correlated equilibrium," one player will cooperate if the expected utility of cooperation is greater than the expected utility from defection. If one player subjectively thinks that the other player is more than 50 percent likely to cooperate, the first player will choose to cooperate; with other numerical payoffs, the probability threshold will of course be different. If both players think this, they will both choose to cooperate. If players are even imperfect Bayesian updaters, a history of cooperation will increase trust and thus make cooperation even more likely. See Robert J. Aumann, "Subjectivity and Correlation in Randomized Strategies," *Journal of Mathematical Economics* 1 (1974): 67–96, and Robert J. Aumann, "Correlated Equilibrium as an Expression of Bayesian Rationality," *Econometrica* 55, no. 1 (1987): 1–18.
25. The way in which this is usually demonstrated depends on the other player having a "trigger strategy." For example, the other player will start cooperating, but if a player defects once, that player will perpetually defect from there on. Obviously, under different assumptions about the other player's trigger strategy, with different numerical payoffs, or both, the result will be different, but the general idea holds, namely that there are cases under which cooperation can happen even in a prisoners' dilemma.
26. E. Ostrom, *Governing the Commons*, 6–7.
27. William J. Baumol, "Entrepreneurship: Productive, Unproductive, and Destructive," *Journal of Political Economy* 98, no. 5 (1990): 893–921.

28. Peter T. Leeson and Peter J. Boettke, "Two-Tiered Entrepreneurship and Economic Development," *International Review of Law and Economics* 29, no. 3 (2009): 252–59.

29. E. Ostrom, *Governing the Commons*, 7.

30. Fred E. Foldvary, "Urban Planning: The Government or the Market," in *Housing America: Building Out of a Crisis*, ed. Randall G. Holcombe and Benjamin Powell (Oakland, CA: The Independent Institute, 2009), 323–42.

31. See Wikipedia, "Maryland Route 200," for a good description, including a discussion of difficulties involved in the government decision-making process: https://en.wikipedia.org/wiki/Maryland_Route_200.

32. Fred E. Foldvary and Daniel B. Klein, "The Half-Life of Policy Rationales: How New Technology Affects Old Policy Issues," *Knowledge, Technology and Policy* 15, no. 3 (2002): 82–92.

33. James M. Buchanan and Gordon Tullock, *The Calculus of Consent: Logical Foundations of Constitutional Democracy* (Ann Arbor, MI: University of Michigan Press, 1962).

34. Elinor Ostrom and Vincent Ostrom, "The Quest for Meaning in Public Choice," *American Journal of Economics and Sociology* 63, no. 1 (2004): 106.

35. Ronald H. Coase, "The Nature of the Firm," *Economica* 4, no. 16 (1937): 386–405; Oliver E. Williamson, "Credible Commitments: Using Hostages to Support Exchange," *The American Economic Review* 73, no. 4 (1983): 519–40.

36. Benjamin Klein, Robert G. Crawford, and Armen A. Alchian, "Vertical Integration, Appropriable Rents, and the Competitive Contracting Process," *Journal of Law and Economics* 21, no. 2 (1978): 297–326.

37. Buchanan and Tullock, *The Calculus of Consent*.

38. See J. M. Guttman, "Unanimity and Majority Rule: The Calculus of Consent Reconsidered," *European Journal of Political Economy* 14, no. 2 (1998): 189–207, and Russell S. Sobel and Randall G. Holcombe, "The Unanimous Voting Rule Is Not the Political Equivalent to Market Exchange," *Public Choice* 106, no. 3/4 (2001): 233–42. Those authors challenge the idea that unanimity leads to minimal external costs. For example, when unanimity is approached, a holdout problem occurs. We gloss over such details, as they do not affect our main points.

39. Buchanan and Tullock, *The Calculus of Consent*, 97–116.

40. Vincent Ostrom, *The Political Theory of the Compound Republic: Designing the American Experiment*, 3rd ed., rev. (Lanham, MD: Lexington Books, 2008 [1987]).

41. Vincent Ostrom, Charles M. Tiebout, and Robert Warren, "The Organization of Government in Metropolitan Areas: A Theoretical Inquiry," *American Political Science Review* 55, no. 4 (December 1961): 831–42.

42. Buchanan and Tullock, *The Calculus of Consent*, 3–9.

43. E. Ostrom and V. Ostrom, "The Quest for Meaning in Public Choice," 105–47.

44. Vincent Ostrom, "Epistemic Choice and Public Choice," *Public Choice* 77, no. 1 (1993a): 163–76; Vincent Ostrom, "The Place of Languages in the Political Economy of Life in Human Societies," Working Paper No. W93-6, Workshop in Political Theory and Policy Analysis, Indiana University, 1993c; Paul H. Rubin, "Ideology," in *The Elgar Companion to Public Choice*, ed. William F. Shughart II and Laura Razzolini (Cheltenham, UK: Edward Elgar, 2001); Wayne A. Leighton and Edward J. Lopez, *Madmen, Intellectuals, and Academic Scribblers: The Economic Engine of Political Change* (Stanford, CA: Stanford University Press, 2012); Vlad Tarko, "The Role of Ideas in Political Economy," *The Review of Austrian Economics* 28, no. 1 (2015): 17–39.

45. Peter J. Boettke, *Living Economics: Yesterday, Today, and Tomorrow* (Oakland, CA: Independent Institute, 2012); Leighton and Lopez, *Madmen, Intellectuals, and Academic Scribblers*.

46. James M. Buchanan, "Is Economics the Science of Choice?," in *Roads to Freedom: Essays in Honour of Friedrich A. von Hayek*, ed. Erich Streissler (London: Routledge, 1969), 47–64.

47. Paul Dragos Aligica and Vlad Tarko, "Co-production, Polycentricity, and Value Heterogeneity: The Ostroms' Public Choice Institutionalism Revisited," *American Political Science Review* 107, no. 4 (2013): 726–41.

48. See chapter 5. Randall G. Holcombe, *The Economic Foundations of Government* (New York: New York University Press, 1994).

49. James C. Scott, *Seeing Like a State: How Certain Schemes to Improve the Human Condition Have Failed* (New Haven, CT: Yale University Press, 1998), 7.

50. Robert Sugden, *The Economics of Rights, Co-operation and Welfare*, 2nd Edition (New York: Palgrave Macmillan, 2005 [1986]), 3.

51. Vincent Ostrom, *The Meaning of Democracy and the Vulnerabilities of Democracies: A Response to Tocqueville's Challenge* (Ann Arbor: University of Michigan Press, 1997), 215–16.

52. Richard E. Wagner, *Fiscal Sociology and the Theory of Public Finance: An Exploratory Essay* (Cheltenham, UK: Edward Elgar, 2007); Richard E. Wagner, "Democracy and the Theory of Public Finance: A Polycentric, Invisible-Hand Framework," *Public Finance and Management* 12, no. 3 (2012): 298–315.

53. Gerald Gaus, *The Tyranny of the Ideal: Justice in a Diverse Society* (Princeton, NJ: Princeton University Press, 2016).

Chapter 3

1. Norman P. Barry, *The Invisible Hand in Economics and Politics: A Study in the Two Conflicting Explanations of Society: End-States and Processes* (London: Institute of Economic Affairs, 1988), 3–5.

2. Ibid.

3. Friedrich A. Hayek, *Studies in Philosophy, Politics and Economics* (Chicago: University of Chicago Press, 1967), 19.

4. Scott Gordon, *Constitutionalism from Ancient Athens to Today* (Cambridge, MA: Harvard University Press, 1999).

5. Ibid., 361.

6. M. J. C. Vile, *Constitutionalism and the Separation of Powers* (Indianapolis, IN: Liberty Fund, 1998).

7. Ibid., 409.

8. Ibid., 408–9.

9. Ibid., 408–9.

10. Ibid., 408–9.

11. Ibid., 408–9.

12. Ibid., 400.

13. Ibid., 405.

14. For situations of exceptional circumstances (disaster, crisis and recovery), see Nona Martin Storr, Emily Chamlee-Wright, and Virgil Henry Storr, *How We Came Back: Voices from Post-Katrina New Orleans* (Arlington, VA: Mercatus Center at George Mason University, 2015). V. Storr, S. Haeffele, and L. Grube, *Community Revival in the Wake of Disaster: Lessons in Local Entrepreneurship with Stefanie HaeffeleBalch and Laura E. Grube** (New York: Palgrave Macmillian, 2015); and Virgil Storr and Laura Grube, "The Capacity for Self-Governance and Post-Disaster Resiliency," *The Review of Austrian Economics* (2013): 1–24. Chamlee-Wright, Emily, and Virgil Henry Storr, "The Role of Social Entrepreneurship in Post-Katrina Community Recovery," *International Journal of Innovation and Regional Development* 2, no. 1 (2010): 149–64. Chamlee-Wright, Emily, and Virgil Henry Storr, "Club Goods and Post-Disaster Community Return," *Rationality and Society* 21, no. 4 (2009): 429–58.

15. Richard C. Cornuelle, *Healing America: What Can Be Done about the Continuing Economic Crisis* (New York: G. P. Putnam's, 1983), 174.

16. Ibid., 173.

17. Ibid., 173.

18. Ibid., 67.

19. Ibid., 68.

20. Ibid.

21. Kenneth Boulding, "The Grants Economy," *Michigan Academician* (Winter). Reprinted in Fred R. Glahe, ed., *Collected Papers of Kenneth Boulding: Vol. II: Economics* (Boulder, CO: Colorado Associated University Press, 1969 [1971]), 482.

22. Lester M. Salamon and Helmut K. Anheier, "The Civil Society Sector," *Society* 34, no. 2 (1997): 60–65.
23. Michael Polanyi, *The Logic of Liberty* (Indianapolis, IN: Liberty Fund, 1998 [1951]).
24. Ibid.; Vincent Ostrom, "Polycentricity," working paper presented at annual meeting of the American Political Science Association, Washington, DC, September 5–9, 1972, reprinted in *Polycentricity and Local Public Economies: Readings from the Workshop in Political Theory and Policy Analysis*, ed. Michael D. McGinnis (Ann Arbor: University of Michigan Press, 1999).
25. Vincent Ostrom, "Polycentricity (Part I)," in *Polycentricity and Local Public Economies: Readings from the Workshop in Political Theory and Policy Analysis*, ed. Michael D. McGinnis (Ann Arbor: University of Michigan Press, 1999), 55–56.
26. Vincent Ostrom, *The Intellectual Crisis in American Public Administration*, 3rd ed. (Tuscaloosa: University of Alabama Press, 2008 [1973]).
27. Elinor Ostrom, "Metropolitan Reform: Propositions Derived from Two Traditions," *Social Science Quarterly* 53, no. 3 (1972): 474–93; Vincent Ostrom, Robert Bish, and Elinor Ostrom, *Local Government in the United States* (San Francisco: ICS Press, 1988).
28. V. Ostrom, *The Intellectual Crisis in American Public Administration*.
29. Ibid., 20–23; Vincent Ostrom, *The Meaning of American Federalism: Constituting a Self-Governing Society* (San Francisco: ICS Press, 1991); Vincent Ostrom, "Some Ontological and Epistemological Puzzles in Policy Analysis," Working Paper No. W91-16, American Political Science Association Meeting, Washington, DC, August 30, 1991, p. 5.
30. Woodrow Wilson, *Congressional Government* (New York: Meridian Books, 1956 [1885]) 30.
31. Vincent Ostrom, "Polycentricity (Part I)," working paper presented at annual meeting of the American Political Science Association, Washington, DC, September 5–9, 1972 V; Ostrom, "Some Ontological and Epistemological Puzzles in Policy Analysis"; Vincent Ostrom, "The Place of Languages in the Political Economy of Life in Human Societies," Working Paper No. W93-6, Workshop in Political Theory and Policy Analysis, Indiana University, Bloomington, 1993.
32. V. Ostrom, "Polycentricity (Part I)," in *Polycentricity and Local Public Economies*, 53.
33. Joseph A. Schumpeter, *History of Economic Analysis* (London: Routledge, 1954), 41.
34. Vincent Ostrom, "The Human Condition," Workshop Archives, Workshop in Political Theory and Policy Analysis, Indiana University, Bloomington, 1982, 1–2; V. Ostrom, "Some Ontological and Epistemological Puzzles"; V. Ostrom, "The Place of Languages."
35. V. Ostrom, "Polycentricity (Part I)," in *Polycentricity and Local Public Economies*, 52–75; V. Ostrom, "Polycentricity (Part II)," in *Polycentricity and Local Public Economies*, 119–39.
36. Kenneth N. Bickers and John T. Williams, *Public Policy Analysis: A Political Economy Approach* (Boston: Houghton Mifflin, 2001), 94.
37. Elinor Ostrom, "The Comparative Study of Public Economies," *American Economist* 42, no. 1 (1998): 3–17.
38. Bickers and Williams, *Public Policy Analysis*, 94.
39. Richard E. Wagner, "Complexity, Governance and Constitutional Craftsmanship," *American Journal of Economics and Sociology* 61, no. 1 (2002): 105–22; Richard E. Wagner, "Democracy and Public Finance: A Polycentric, Invisible-Hand Framework," *Public Finance and Management* 12, no. 3 (2012): 298–315.
40. V. Ostrom, *The Intellectual Crisis in American Public Administration*, 10–11; Vincent Ostrom, "Artisanship and Artifact," *Public Administration Review* 40, no. 4 (1980): 309–17; Vincent Ostrom, "The Constitutional Level of Analysis: A Challenge," Working Paper No. 85-41, Workshop in Political Theory and Policy Analysis, Indiana University, Bloomington, 1986; Vincent Ostrom, "Problems of Cognition as a Challenge to Policy Analysts and Democratic Societies," Working Paper No. 90-5, Workshop in Political Theory and Policy Analysis, Indiana University, Bloomington, 1990; V. Ostrom, *The Meaning of American Federalism*; Vincent Ostrom, "Epistemic Choice and Public Choice," *Public Choice* 77, no. 1 (1993): 163–76; V. Ostrom, "The Place of Languages."
41. V. Ostrom, "Some Ontological and Epistemological Puzzles," 11.
42. Ibid.

43. Friedrich A. Hayek, *Individualism and Economic Order* (Chicago: University of Chicago Press, 1980 [1948]), 8–9.

44. Ibid., 33–56.

45. Ibid., 92–106; Friedrich A. Hayek, "Competition as a Discovery Procedure," *Quarterly Journal of Austrian Economics* 5, no. 3 (2002): 9–23.

46. Friedrich A. Hayek, "The Use of Knowledge in Society," *American Economic Review* 35, no. 4 (1945): 519–30.

47. Ibid., 78.

48. Ibid., 82.

49. Ibid., 83.

50. Ibid., 90–91.

51. Ibid., 91.

52. Vernon L. Smith, *Rationality in Economics: Constructivist and Ecological Forms* (New York: Cambridge University Press, 2008).

53. James M. Buchanan and Gordon Tullock, *The Calculus of Consent: Logical Foundations of Constitutional Democracy* (Ann Arbor, MI: The University of Michigan Press, 1962), 43–62; James M. Buchanan, *What Should Economists Do?* (Indianapolis, IN: Liberty Fund, 1979); James M. Buchanan, "Market Failure and Political Failure," in *The Collected Works of James M. Buchanan, Volume 18, Federalism, Liberty, and the Law* (Indianapolis, IN: Liberty Fund, 2001 [1988]), 276–88; Elinor Ostrom and Vincent Ostrom, "The Quest for Meaning in Public Choice," *American Journal of Economics and Sociology* 63, no. 1 (2004): 105–47.

54. William F. Shughart II and Laura Razzolini, eds., *The Elgar Companion to Public Choice* (London: Edward Elgar, 2001); Gordon Tullock, Arthur Seldon, and Gordon L. Brady, *Government Failure: A Primer in Public Choice* (Washington, DC: Cato Institute, 2002); Dennis C. Mueller, *Public Choice III* (Cambridge, UK: Cambridge University Press, 2003); Randy T. Simmons, *Beyond Politics: The Roots of Government Failure* (Oakland, CA: Independent Institute, 2011).

55. Paul H. Rubin, "Ideology," in *The Elgar Companion to Public Choice*, ed. William F. Shughart and Laura Razzolini (London: Edward Elgar, 2001 [1994]).

56. James M. Buchanan, "Is Economics the Science of Choice?," in *Roads to Freedom: Essays in Honour of Friedrich A. von Hayek*, ed. Erich Streissler (London: Routledge, 1969); James M. Buchanan, "On the Structure of an Economy: A Reemphasis of Some Classical Foundations," in *The Collected Works of James M. Buchanan, Volume 18, Federalism, Liberty, and the Law* (Indianapolis, IN: Liberty Fund, 2001 [1989]), 263–75; James M. Buchanan, "The Individual as Participant in Political Exchange," in *The Collected Works of James M. Buchanan, Volume 18, Federalism, Liberty, and the Law* (Indianapolis, IN: Liberty Fund, 2001 [1993]), 185–97.

57. E. Ostrom and V. Ostrom, "The Quest for Meaning in Public Choice"; Elinor Ostrom and Vincent Ostrom, *Choice, Rules and Collective Action: The Ostroms on the Study of Institutions of Governance*, ed. Filippo Sabetti and Paul Dragos Aligica (Colchester, UK: ECPR, 2014).

58. Elinor Ostrom, "A Behavioral Approach to the Rational Choice Theory of Collective Action: Presidential Address, American Political Science Association, 1997," *American Political Science Review* 92, no. 1 (1998): 1–22; Elinor Ostrom, *Understanding Institutional Diversity* (Princeton, NJ: Princeton University Press, 2005); Elinor Ostrom, "Do Institutions for Collective Action Evolve?," *Journal of Bioeconomics* 16, no. 1 (2014): 3–30; V. Ostrom, "Polycentricity (Part I)," in *Polycentricity and Local Public Economies*, 52–75; V. Ostrom, "Polycentricity (Part II)," in *Polycentricity and Local Public Economies*, 119–39; Elinor Ostrom, "Beyond Markets and States: Polycentric Governance of Complex Economic Systems," *American Economic Review* 100, no. 3 (2010): 641–72; Paul Dragos Aligica and Filippo Sabetti, eds., *Choice, Rules and Collective Action* (Colchester, UK: ECPR Press, 2014).

59. Buchanan, "On the Structure of an Economy," 268.

60. Ibid., 270.

61. Ibid., 270.

62. Vincent Ostrom, *The Meaning of Democracy and the Vulnerability of Democracies: A Response to Tocqueville's Challenge* (Ann Arbor: University of Michigan Press, 1997).

63. V. Ostrom, "Epistemic Choice and Public Choice."

64. Ibid.

65. James M. Buchanan, *Liberty, Market and State: Political Economy and the 1980s* (New York: New York University Press, 1986), 75–76.

66. Michael W. Spicer, "On Friedrich Hayek and Public Administration: An Argument for Discretion within Rules," *Administration and Society* 25, no. 1 (1993): 46–59.

67. Michael W. Spicer, "A Contractarian Approach to Public Administration," *Administration and Society* 22, no. 3 (1990): 303–16.

68. Frank Marini, ed., *Toward a New Public Administration: The Minnowbrook Perspective* (Scranton, PA: Chandler Publishing, 1971); Gary L. Wamsley, Robert N. Bacher, Charles T. Goodsell, Philip S. Kronenberg, et al., *Refounding Public Administration* (Thousand Oaks, CA: SAGE, 1990).

69. Spicer, "On Friedrich Hayek and Public Administration."

70. Ibid.

71. Hayek, "The Use of Knowledge in Society."

72. Israel M. Kirzner, *Competition and Entrepreneurship* (Chicago: University of Chicago Press, 1973); Israel M. Kirzner, *The Meaning of the Market Process: Essays in the Development of Modern Austrian Economics* (London: Routledge, 1992); Israel M. Kirzner, "Entrepreneurial Discovery and the Competitive Market Process: An Austrian Approach," *Journal of Economic Literature* 35, no. 1 (1997): 60–85.

73. Spicer, "On Friedrich Hayek and Public Administration," 49.

74. Ibid., 50.

75. Ibid., 50.

76. Michael M. Harmon, *Action Theory for Public Administration* (New York: Longman, 1981), 70.

77. Herbert A. Simon, *Administrative Behavior*, 4th ed. (New York: Free Press, 1997 [1945]).

78. Spicer, "On Friedrich Hayek and Public Administration."

79. Ibid., 51.

80. Barry R. Weingast, "The Economic Role of Political Institutions: Market-Preserving Federalism and Economic Development," *Journal of Law, Economics, and Organization* 11, no. 1 (1995): 1–31.

81. Spicer, "On Friedrich Hayek and Public Administration."

82. Spicer, "A Contractarian Approach to Public Administration."

83. Ostrom, *The Meaning of Democracy and the Vulnerabilities of Democracies.*

84. Spicer, "On Friedrich Hayek and Public Administration," 55.

85. Ibid., 55.

86. Friedrich A. Hayek, *The Constitution of Liberty* (Chicago: University of Chicago Press, 1960), chap. 7; Michael Wohlgemuth, "Democracy and Opinion Falsification: Towards a New Austrian Political Economy," *Constitutional Political Economy* 13, no. 3 (2002): 223–46.

87. Spicer, "On Friedrich Hayek and Public Administration," 56.

88. Ibid., 57.

89. Ibid., 57.

Chapter 4

1. Woodrow Wilson, "The Study of Administration," *Political Science Quarterly* 2, no. 2 (June 1887): 197–222.

2. Ibid.

3. Ibid.

4. Dwight Waldo, "Afterword: Thoughts in Retrospect—and Prospect," in *A Search for Public Administration: The Ideas and Career of Dwight Waldo*, ed. Brack Brown and Richard J. Stillman II (College Station: Texas A&M University Press, 1986).

5. Ibid.

6. Ibid.

7. Ibid., 166–67.

8. Ibid., 166–67.

9. Ibid., 166–67.

10. Ibid., 167.

11. Ibid., 167.

12. Ibid., 167.

13. Ibid., 167.

14. Ibid., 167.

15. Ibid., 167.

16. Ibid., 167.

17. Ibid., 167.

18. Ibid., 160–66.

19. Fry and Raadschelders, *Mastering Public Administration*, 11.

20. Vincent Ostrom, *The Intellectual Crisis in American Public Administration*, 3rd ed. (Tuscaloosa: University of Alabama Press, 2008 [1973]).

21. Wilson, "The Study of Administration."

22. Ibid.

23. Ibid., emphasis added.

24. Ibid.

25. See, for example, James Buchanan and Gordon Tullock, *Calculus of Consent*.

26. Fry and Raadschelders, *Mastering Public Administration*, 11.

27. Ibid.

28. Ibid.

29. Dwight Waldo, "Politics and Administration: On Thinking about a Complex Relationship," in *A centennial history of the American Administrative State*, ed. Ralph Clark Chandler (New York: The Free Press, 1987), 91.

30. Jos C. N. Raadschelders, *Public Administration: The Interdisciplinary Study of Government* (New York: Oxford University Press, 2013).

31. Howard E. McCurdy, *Public Administration: A Bibliographic Guide to the Literature* (New York: Marcel Dekker, 1986).

32. James Pfiffner, *Public Administration* (New York: The Ronald Press Company, 1967), 11–13.

33. Grover Starling, *Managing the Public Sector* (Boston: Wadsworth, 1998).

34. Gary L. Wamsley and Mayer N. Zald, *The Political Economy of Public Organizations: A Critique and Approach to the Study of Public Administration* (Lanham, MD: Lexington Books, 1973).

35. H. George Frederickson, Kevin B. Smith, Christopher W. Larimer, and Michael J. Licari, *The Public Administration Theory Primer*, 2nd ed. (Boulder, CO: Westview Press, 2012 [2003]).

36. Ibid., 100.

37. Ibid.

38. Ibid., 234.

39. Richard J. Stillman II, *Public Administration: Concepts and Cases*, 9th ed. (Boston: Cengage Learning, 2010), 27.

40. Raadschelders, *Public Administration*, 114.

41. Ibid., 122.

42. Ibid., 208.

43. Ibid., 104.

44. Ibid.

45. Ibid., 104.

46. Robert B. Denhardt, *Theories of Public Organization*, 6th ed. (Boston, MA: Wadsworth, 2004).

47. Ibid., 16.

48. Ibid.

49. Ibid.

50. Waldo, "Politics and Administration."

51. Ibid.

52. Mark R. Rutgers, "Theory and Scope of Public Administration: An Introduction to the Study's Epistemology," *Public Administration Review: Foundations of Public Administration Series*

(2010): 1–45, https://pdfs.semanticscholar.org/565c/2f428d4b1e5a8817ff986ed8067c96e4
a10b.pdf.

53. Ibid., 2.
54. Waldo, "Politics and Administration," 98.
55. Frederick C. Mosher, *Democracy and the Public Service* (Oxford: Oxford University Press, 1982), 91.
56. Patrick Overeem, *The Politics–Administration Dichotomy: Toward a Constitutional Perspective*, 2nd ed. (Boca Raton, FL: CRC Press, 2012), 12; Patrick Overeem, "The Value of the Dichotomy: Politics, Administration, and the Political Neutrality of Administrators," *Administrative Theory and Praxis* 27, no. 2 (2005): 311–29.
57. Overeem, *The Politics–Administration Dichotomy*, 12.
58. Rutgers, "Theory and Scope of Public Administration," 16.
59. Denhardt, *Theories of Public Organization*.
60. Vincent Ostrom, *The Intellectual Crisis in American Public Administration*, 114.
61. Ibid.

Chapter 5

1. Richard J. Stillman II, *Preface to Public Administration: A Search for Themes and Direction* (Burke, VA: Chatelaine Press, 1999 [1991]), 189.
2. Ibid.
3. Ibid.
4. Ibid.
5. Vincent Ostrom, *The Intellectual Crisis in American Public Administration*, 3rd ed. (Tuscaloosa: University of Alabama Press, 2008 [1973]).
6. Public Administration Section of American Political Science Association, "Gaus Awards," *Public Administration Section Newsletter* 4, no. 1 (2005).
7. Ibid.
8. Ibid.
9. Ibid.
10. Vincent Ostrom, "Editorial Comment: Developments in the 'No-Name' Fields of Public Administration," *Public Administration Review* 24, no. 1 (1964): 62–63.
11. Nicholas P. Lovrich and Max Neiman, *Public Choice Theory in Public Administration: An Annotated Bibliography* (New York: Garland, 1984).
12. Ibid., xxii.
13. Ibid.
14. Ibid., xxii–xxiii.
15. Ibid., xxii–xxiii.
16. Naomi B. Lynn and Aaron B. Wildavsky, eds., *Public Administration: The State of the Discipline* (Chatham, NJ: Chatham House, 1990).
17. Ibid., 233.
18. Ibid., 146.
19. Ibid., 246.
20. H. George Frederickson, Kevin B. Smith, Christopher W. Larimer, and Michael J. Licari, *The Public Administration Theory Primer*, 2nd ed. (Boulder, CO: Westview Press, 2012).
21. Ibid., 195, 209–12.
22. Ibid., 210–14.
23. Ibid., 210.
24. Stillman, *Preface to Public Administration*, 142.
25. Ibid., 142.
26. Ibid., 142–43.
27. Ibid., 143.

28. Theo Toonen, "Resilience in Public Administration: The Work of Elinor and Vincent Ostrom from a Public Administration Perspective," *Public Administration Review* 70, no. 2 (2010): 192–202.

29. Ibid., 197.

30. Ibid.

31. Ibid.

32. Ibid.

33. Ibid.

34. Laurence E. Lynn Jr., *Public Management: Old and New* (New York: Routledge, 2006).

35. Theo A. J. Toonen, "Networks, Management and Institutions: Public Administration as 'Normal Science,'" *Public Administration* 76, no. 2 (1998): 229–52.

36. Ibid., 230–32.

37. Steven Brams, "The Normative Turn in Public Choice," *Public Choice* 127, no. 3 (2006): 245–50.

38. Ibid., 246.

39. Ibid.

40. Michael D. McGinnis and Elinor Ostrom, "Reflections on Vincent Ostrom, Public Administration, and Polycentricity," *Public Administration Review* 72, no. 1 (2012): 15–25.

41. Ibid., 20–21.

42. Ibid., 20.

43. Vernon L. Smith, *Rationality in Economics: Constructivist and Ecological Forms* (New York: Cambridge University Press, 2008).

44. Gerd Gigerenzer, *Rationality for Mortals: How People Cope with Uncertainty* (New York: Oxford University Press, 2008).

45. McGinnis and Ostrom, "Reflections on Vincent Ostrom," 20.

46. Ibid.

47. Ibid.

48. Ibid.

49. Ibid.

50. Ibid.

51. Ibid.

52. Brams, "The Normative Turn in Public Choice," 245.

53. McGinnis and Ostrom, "Reflections on Vincent Ostrom," 20.

54. Brams, "The Normative Turn in Public Choice," 246.

55. James M. Buchanan, *Economics: Between Predictive Science and Moral Philosophy* (College Station: Texas A&M University Press, 1987).

56. Paul Dragos Aligica and Peter J. Boettke, *Challenging Institutional Analysis and Development: The Bloomington School* (London and New York: Routledge, 2009), 125.

57. Elinor Ostrom, "The Comparative Study of Public Economies," *American Economist* 42, no. 1 (1998): 4.

58. Aligica and Boettke, *Challenging Institutional Analysis and Development*, 125.

59. For an extended discussion, see Paul D. Aligica and Peter J. Boettke, "The Two Social Philosophies of Ostroms' Institutionalism," *Policy Studies Journal* 39, no 1 (2011): 29–49; 2012; and especially Paul D. Aligica and Peter J. Boettke, "Institutional Design and Ideas-Driven Social Change: Notes from an Ostromian Perspective," *The Good Society* 20, no. 1 (2011): 50–66, from which this section draws.

60. Elinor Ostrom, "Beyond Markets and States: Polycentric Governance of Complex Economic Systems," *American Economic Review* 100, no. 3 (2010): 641–72; E. Ostrom, "The Comparative Study of Public Economies," 3–17; Elinor Ostrom, "An Agenda for the Study of Institutions," *Public Choice* 48, no. 1 (1986): 3–25.

61. E. Ostrom, "The Comparative Study of Public Economies," 14.

62. Ibid.

63. Vincent Ostrom and Elinor Ostrom, "Legal and Political Conditions of Water Resource Development," in *Polycentric Governance and Development: Readings from the Workshop in Political Theory and Policy Analysis*, ed. Michael McGinnis (Ann Arbor: University of Michigan

Press, 1999), 42–59; Vincent Ostrom and Elinor Ostrom, "Public Goods and Public Choices," in *Alternatives for Delivering Public Services: Toward Improved Performance*, ed. E. S. Savas (Boulder, CO: Westview Press, 1977), 7–49.

64. For an extensive discussion, see Paul Dragos Aligica and Peter J. Boettke, *Challenging Institutional Analysis and Development: The Bloomington School* (New York: Routledge, 2009); Paul Dragos Aligica and Peter Boettke, "The Two Social Philosophies of Ostroms' Institutionalism," *Policy Studies Journal* 39, no. 1 (2011): 29–49.

65. Vincent Ostrom, "Why Governments Fail: An Inquiry into the Use of Instruments of Evil to Do Good," in *The Theory of Public Choice—II*, ed. James M. Buchanan and Robert D. Tollison (Ann Arbor: University of Michigan Press, 1984), 422–35; Vincent Ostrom, "The Human Condition," Workshop Archives, Workshop in Political Theory and Policy Analysis, Indiana University, Bloomington, 1993c.

66. Vincent Ostrom, "Artisanship and Artifact," *Public Administration Review* 40, no. 4 (1980): 311.

67. V. Ostrom, "The Human Condition," 3; Vincent Ostrom, "Order and Change Amid Increasing Relative Ignorance," Working Paper No. W73-1, Workshop in Political Theory and Policy Analysis, Indiana University, Bloomington, 1973; Vincent Ostrom, "The Constitutional Level of Analysis: A Challenge," Working Paper No. 85-41, Workshop in Political Theory and Policy Analysis, Indiana University, Bloomington, 1986.

68. V. Ostrom, "Order and Change."

69. V. Ostrom, "The Human Condition," 32; V. Ostrom, "Order and Change"; Vincent Ostrom, "Some Ontological and Epistemological Puzzles in Policy Analysis," Working Paper No. W82-16, Workshop in Political Theory and Policy Analysis, Indiana University, Bloomington, 1991b.

70. V. Ostrom, "The Human Condition," 31–32; V. Ostrom, "Order and Change"; Elinor Ostrom, Roy Gardner, and James Walker, *Rules, Games, and Common-Pool Resources* (Ann Arbor: University of Michigan Press, 1994).

71. Michael W. Spicer, *Public Administration and the State: A Postmodern Perspective* (Tuscaloosa: University of Alabama Press, 2001); Michael W. Spicer, *In Defense of Politics in Public Administration: A Value Pluralist Perspective* (Tuscaloosa: University of Alabama Press, 2010).

72. Michael W. Spicer, "A Contractarian Approach to Public Administration," *Administration and Society* 22, no. 3 (1990): 303–16.

73. James M. Buchanan and Gordon Tullock, *The Calculus of Consent: Logical Foundations of Constitutional Democracy* (Ann Arbor, MI: The University of Michigan Press, 1962).

74. Geoffrey Brennan and James M. Buchanan, *The Power to Tax: Analytical Foundations of a Fiscal Constitution* (New York: Cambridge University Press, 1980).

75. Geoffrey Brennan and James M. Buchanan, *The Collected Works of James M. Buchanan, Volume 10, The Reason of Rules: Constitutional Political Economy* (Indianapolis, IN: Liberty Fund, 2000); James M. Buchanan and Roger D. Congleton, *Politics by Principle, Not Interest: Towards Nondiscriminatory Democracy* (New York: Cambridge University Press, 1998); John Rawls, *A Theory of Justice, Revised Edition* (Cambridge, MA: Belknap Press, 1999 [1971]).

76. Spicer, "A Contractarian Approach to Public Administration," 303–16.

77. Ibid., 306, 313–14.

78. Ibid., 308.

79. Ibid., 307.

80. Ibid., 307.

81. Ibid., 307.

82. Ibid., 308.

83. Ibid., 308–9.

84. Gordon Tullock, *The Selected Works of Gordon Tullock, Volume 6: Bureaucracy*, ed. and intro by Charles K. Rowley (Indianapolis, IN: Liberty Fund, 2005); Vincent Ostrom, *The Political Theory of a Compound Republic: Designing the American Experiment*, 3rd rev. ed. (Lanham, MD: Lexington Books, 2008 [1987]).

85. Spicer, "A Contractarian Approach to Public Administration," 309.

86. Lewis C. Mainzer, *Political Bureaucracy* (Glenview, IL: Scott, Foresman, 1973).

87. Spicer, "A Contractarian Approach to Public Administration," 309.

88. Ibid., 311.

89. Ibid., 312.

90. Ibid., 312.

91. Ibid., 313.

92. Michael W. Spicer, "A Public Choice Approach to Motivating People in Bureaucratic Organizations," *Academy of Management Review* 10, no. 3 (1985): 518–26.

93. Mancur Olson, *The Logic of Collective Action: Public Goods and the Theory of Groups*, rev. ed. (Cambridge, MA: Harvard University Press, 1971 [1965]).

94. Armen A. Alchian and Harold Demsetz, "Production, Information Costs, and Economic Organization," *American Economic Review* 62, no. 5 (1972): 777–95; Tullock, *Bureaucracy*.

95. Spicer, "A Public Choice Approach," 521.

96. Spicer, "A Public Choice Approach," 520.

97. Ibid., 521.

98. Ibid., 522.

99. Ibid., 522.

100. Ibid., 519–20.

101. Michael W. Spicer, "Public Administration, Social Science, and Political Association," *Administration and Society* 30, no. 1 (1998): 35–52.

102. Michael Oakeshott, *Rationalism in Politics and Other Essays* (Indianapolis, IN: Liberty Fund, 1991).

103. Spicer, "Public Administration, Social Science, and Political Association," 35.

104. Ibid., 37.

105. Ibid.

106. Ibid., 38.

107. Spicer, *Public Administration and the State*, 24.

108. Spicer, "Public Administration, Social Science, and Political Association," 44.

109. Ibid., 45.

110. Ibid.

111. Ibid., 46.

112. Ibid., 48.

113. Ibid., 50.

Chapter 6

1. Vincent Ostrom and Elinor Ostrom, "Public Goods and Public Choices: The Emergence of Public Economies and Industry Structures," in *The Meaning of American Federalism*, 163–97 (San Francisco, Calif: ICS Press, 1991). (paper originally published in 1977).

2. Taco Brandsen and Victor Pestoff, "Co-production, the Third Sector and the Delivery of Public Services," *Public Management Review* 8, no. 4 (2006): 493–501; Victor Pestoff, Taco Brandsen, and Bram Verschuere, eds., *New Public Governance, the Third Sector and Co-production* (New York: Routledge, 2012); Laurence E. Lynn Jr., *Public Management: Old and New* (New York: Routledge, 2006); Theo Toonen, "Resilience in Public Administration: The Work of Elinor and Vincent Ostrom from a Public Administration Perspective," *Public Administration Review* 70, no. 2 (2010): 193–202.

3. Vincent Ostrom and Elinor Ostrom, "Public Goods and Public Choices," in *Polycentricity and Local Public Economies: Readings from the Workshop in Political Theory and Policy Analysis*, ed. Michael D. McGinnis (Ann Arbor: University of Michigan Press, 1999), 75–103; Elinor Ostrom, *Understanding Institutional Diversity* (Princeton, NJ: Princeton University Press, 2005); Elinor Ostrom and Roger B. Parks, "Neither Gargantua nor the Land of Lilliputs: Conjectures on Mixed Systems of Metropolitan Organization," in *Polycentricity and Local Public Economies: Readings from the Workshop in Political Theory and Policy Analysis*, ed. Michael D. McGinnis (Ann Arbor: University of Michigan Press, 1999), 284–305; Ronald J. Oakerson and Roger B. Parks, "The Study of Local Public Economies: Multi-organizational, Multi-level

Institutional Analysis and Development," *Policy Studies Journal* 39, no. 1 (2011): 147–67; Michael C. Munger, "Endless Forms Most Beautiful and Most Wonderful: Elinor Ostrom and the Diversity of Institutions," *Public Choice* 143, no. 3/4 (2010): 263–68; Paul Dragos Aligica and Peter Boettke, "The Two Social Philosophies of Ostroms' Institutionalism," *Policy Studies Journal* 39, no. 1 (2011): 29–49; Mark Sproule-Jones, Barbara Allen, and Filippo Sabetti, "Normative and Empirical Inquiries into Systems of Governance," in *The Struggle to Constitute and Sustain Productive Orders: Vincent Ostrom's Quest to Understand Human Affairs*, ed. Mark Sproule-Jones, Barbara Allen, and Filippo Sabetti (Lanham, MD: Lexington Books, 2008), 3–10; Richard E. Wagner, "Self-Governance, Polycentrism, and Federalism: Recurring Themes in Vincent Ostrom's Scholarly Oeuvre," *Journal of Economic Behavior and Organization* 57, no. 2 (2005): 173–88.

4. James M. Buchanan, *The Collected Works of James M. Buchanan, Volume 5: The Demand and Supply of Public Goods* (Indianapolis, IN: Liberty Fund, 1999 [1968]), 120.

5. Michael D. McGinnis and Elinor Ostrom, "Reflections on Vincent Ostrom, Public Administration, and Polycentricity," *Public Administration Review* 72, no. 1 (2012): 15–25.

6. Vincent Ostrom, *The Meaning of Democracy and the Vulnerabilities of Democracies: A Response to Tocqueville's Challenge* (Ann Arbor: University of Michigan Press, 1997), 4.

7. Ibid., 18–19.

8. Vincent Ostrom, "Polycentricity (Part 1 and 2)," in *Polycentricity and Local Public Economies*, ed. Michael D. McGinnis (Michigan: University of Michigan Press, 1999), 52–74 (paper originally published in 1972); Vincent Ostrom, "Polycentricity: The Structural Basis of Self-Governing Systems," in *The Meaning of American Federalism* (San Francisco: ICS Press, 1991), 223–48; Elinor Ostrom, "Polycentricity, Complexity, and the Commons," *The Good Society* 9, no. 2 (1999): 37–41; Robert L. Bish, "Federalist Theory and Polycentricity: Learning from Local Governments," in *Limiting Leviathan*, ed. Donald P. Racheter and Richard E. Wagner (Cheltenham, UK, and Northampton, MA: Edward Elgar, 1999). Paul Dragos Aligica and Vlad Tarko, "Polycentricity: From Polanyi to Ostrom, and Beyond," *Governance* 25, no. 2 (April 1, 2012): 237–62; Peter J. Boettke, Jayme S. Lemke, and Liya Palagashvili, "Polycentricity, Self-Governance, and the Art & Science of Association," *The Review of Austrian Economics* 28, no. 3 (June 10, 2014): 311–35; Peter J. Boettke and Rosolino A. Candela, "Rivalry, Polycentricism, and Institutional Evolution," *New Thinking in Austrian Political Economy* 19 (2015): 1–19; Vlad Tarko, *Elinor Ostrom: An Intellectual Biography* (London: Rowman & Littlefield International, 2016), ch. 2; Michael D. McGinnis, "Polycentric Governance in Theory and Practice: Dimensions of Aspirations and Practical Limitations," presentation at The Ostrom Workshop Polycentricity Workshop, Indiana University, Bloomington, 2016.

9. Elinor Ostrom, "Beyond Markets and States: Polycentric Governance of Complex Economic Systems," *American Economic Review* 100, no. 3 (June 2010): 641–72; Elinor Ostrom, *Governing the Commons: The Evolution of Institutions for Collective Action.* (Cambridge, UK, and New York: Cambridge University Press, 1990); Elinor Ostrom, *Crafting Institutions for Self-Governing Irrigation Systems* (San Francisco and Lanham, MD: ICS Press, 1992); Elinor Ostrom, Roy Gardner, and Jimmy Walker, *Rules, Games, and Common-Pool Resources* (Ann Arbor: University of Michigan Press, 1994); Elinor Ostrom, James Walker, and Roy Gardner, "Covenants with and without a Sword: Self-Governance Is Possible," *American Political Science Review* 86, no. 2 (June 1992): 404–417. Elinor Ostrom, *Understanding Institutional Diversity* (Princeton, NJ: Princeton University Press, 2005); David Sloan Wilson, Elinor Ostrom, and Michael E. Cox, "Generalizing the Core Design Principles for the Efficacy of Groups," *Journal of Economic Behavior & Organization* 90, Supplement (June 2013): S21–32; Paul Dragos Aligica and Vlad Tarko, "Institutional Resilience and Economic Systems: Lessons from Elinor Ostrom's Work," *Comparative Economic Studies* 56, no. 1 (March 2014): 52–76; Vlad Tarko, *Elinor Ostrom: An Intellectual Biography* (London: Rowman and Littlefield International, 2016).

10. Paul Dragos Aligica, *Institutional Diversity and Political Economy: The Ostroms and Beyond* (Oxford and New York: Oxford University Press, 2013), ch. 1.

11. Ethnic, linguistic, and religious fractionalization are measured by A. Alesina, A. Devleeschauwer, W. Easterly, S. Kurlat, and R. Wacziarg, "Fractionalization," *Journal of*

Economic Growth 8 (2003): 155–94. Fractionalization "reflects probability that two randomly selected people from a given country will not belong to the same ethnic/linguistic/religious group. The higher the number, the more fractionalized society" (Quality of Government Institute Standard Codebook 2018, p. 74). GDP per capita is taken from the UN data and measured in 2016 US dollars (UN Statistics 2015, "National accounts main aggregates database"). Political stability is measured by D. Kaufmann, A. Kraay, and M. Mastruzzi, "The Worldwide Governance Indicators: A Summary of Methodology, Data and Analytical Issues," World Bank Policy Research Working Paper, 5430. Political stability "combines several indicators which measure perceptions of the likelihood that the government in power will be destabilized or overthrown by possibly unconstitutional and/or violent means, including domestic violence and terrorism" (Quality of Government Institute Standard Codebook 2016, p. 618). We considered a country as "politically stable" if this index was above 1. All the above data has been aggregated into a single dataset by Jan Teorell, Stefan Dahlberg, Sören Holmberg, Bo Rothstein, Anna Khomenko, and Richard Svensson, "The Quality of Government Standard Dataset, Version Jan16" (University of Gothenburg: The Quality of Government Institute, 2016).

12. Vincent Ostrom, *The Meaning of Democracy and the Vulnerabilities of Democracies: A Response to Tocqueville's Challenge* (Ann Arbor: University of Michigan Press, 1997).

13. Albert O. Hirschman, *Exit, Voice, and Loyalty: Responses to Decline in Firms, Organizations, and States* (Cambridge, MA: Harvard University Press, 1970); Edward McPhail and Vlad Tarko, "The Evolution of Governance Structures in a Polycentric System," in *Handbook of Behavioral Economics and Smart Decision-Making: Rational Decision-Making within the Bounds of Reason*, ed. Morris Altman (Cheltenham, UK: Edward Elgar, 2017), 290–313.

14. Robert B. Parks, Paula C. Baker, Larry Kiser, Ronald Oakerson, Elinor Ostrom, Vincent Ostrom, Stephen L. Percy, Martha B. Vandivort, Gordon P. Whitacker, and Rick Wilson, "Consumers as Coproducers of Public Services: Some Economic and Institutional Considerations," *Policy Studies Journal* 9, no. 7 (1981): 1001–11; Taco Brandsen and Victor Pestoff, "Co-production, the Third Sector and the Delivery of Public Services," *Public Management Review* 8, no. 4 (2006): 493–501; Oakerson and Parks, "The Study of Local Public Economies: Multi-organizational, Multi-level Institutional Analysis and Development."

15. Paul Dragos, Aligica and Vlad Tarko, "Co-Production, Polycentricity, and Value Heterogeneity: The Ostroms' Public Choice Institutionalism Revisited," *American Political Science Review* 107, no. 4 (November 2013): 726–41.

16. Armen A. Alchian and Harold Demsetz, "Production, Information Costs, and Economic Organization," *American Economic Review* 62, no. 5 (1972): 777–95; Gary J. Miller, *Managerial Dilemmas: The Political Economy of Hierarchy* (New York: Cambridge University Press, 1992).

17. Ostrom, *Understanding Institutional Diversity*, 255–86; Peter T. Leeson, "Government, Clubs, and Constitutions," *Journal of Economic Behavior and Organization* 80, no. 2 (2011): 301–8.

18. Alchian and Demsetz, "Production, Information Costs, and Economic Organization."

19. Michael McGinnis, "An Introduction to IAD and the Language of the Ostrom Workshop: A Simple Guide to a Complex Framework," *Policy Studies Journal* 39, no. 1 (2011): 179.

20. Elinor Ostrom, "Polycentricity, Complexity, and the Commons," *The Good Society* 9, no. 2 (1999): 37–41.

21. Ibid.

22. Ibid.

23. Michael D. McGinnis, ed., *Polycentric Governance and Development: Readings from the Workshop in Political Theory and Policy Analysis* (Ann Arbor: University of Michigan Press, 1999).

24. Kurt Baier and Nicholas Rescher, *Values and the Future: The Impact of Technological Change on American Values* (New York: Free Press, 1969).

25. Vincent Ostrom, *The Political Theory of a Compound Republic: Designing the American Experiment* (Lanham, MD: Lexington Books, 2008).

26. Torben Beck Jorgensen and Barry Bozeman, "Public Values: An Inventory," *Administration and Society* 39, no. 3 (2007): 354–81.

27. Paul Rozin, "Moralization," in *Morality and Health*, ed. Allan M. Brandt and Paul Rozin (New York: Routledge, 1997), 379–402; Paul Rozin, "The Process of Moralization," *Psychological Science* 10, no. 3 (1999): 218–21.

28. James M. Buchanan and Gordon Tullock, *The Collected Works of James M. Buchanan, Volume 3: The Calculus of Consent: Logical Foundations of Constitutional Democracy* (Indianapolis, IN: Liberty Fund, 1999), 27–30.

29. James M. Buchanan, *Ethics and Economic Progress* (Norman: University of Oklahoma Press, 1994), ch. 3.

30. Ibid., 61.

31. Ibid., 66.

32. Ibid., 62.

33. Ibid., 70.

34. Ibid., ch. 1 and 2.

35. Peter J. Boettke, "The Theory of Spontaneous Order and Cultural Evolution in the Social Theory of FA Hayek," *Cultural Dynamics* 3, no. 1 (1990): 61–83; Luciano Andreozzi, "Hayek Reads the Literature on the Emergence of Norms," *Constitutional Political Economy* 16, no. 3 (September 2005): 227–47; Gerald F. Gaus, "Hayek on the Evolution of Society and Mind," in *Cambridge Companion to Hayek* (Cambridge, UK: Cambridge University Press, 2007), 232–58; Elinor Ostrom, "Collective Action and the Evolution of Social Norms," *Journal of Natural Resources Policy Research* 6, no. 4 (October 2, 2014): 235–52; Vlad Tarko, "The Role of Ideas in Political Economy," *The Review of Austrian Economics* 28, no. 1 (2015): 17–39.

36. James M. Buchanan, *Ethics and Economic Progress*, 87–88.

37. Baier and Rescher, *Values and the Future*.

38. Ibid.

39. Rozin, "Moralization"; Rozin, "The Process of Moralization."

40. Terry L. Anderson and Peter J. Hill, eds., *The Technology of Property Rights* (Lanham, MD: Rowman and Littlefield, 2001).

41. Gerald Gaus, *The Order of Public Reason: A Theory of Freedom and Morality in a Diverse and Bounded World* (New York: Cambridge University Press, 2011); Chandran Kukathas, *The Liberal Archipelago: A Theory of Diversity and Freedom* (New York: Oxford University Press, 1999); Barry Bozeman, *Public Values and Public Interest: Counterbalancing Economic Individualism* (Washington, DC: Georgetown University Press, 2007); Jack Knight and James Johnson, *The Priority of Democracy: Political Consequences of Pragmatism* (Princeton, NJ: Princeton University Press, 2011).

42. Bozeman, *Public Values and Public Interest*, 13; Barry Bozeman, "Public-Value Failure: When Efficient Markets May Not Do," *Public Administration Review* 62, no. 2 (2002): 145–61.

43. Bozeman, *Public Values and Public Interest*, 13.

44. Vincent Ostrom and Elinor Ostrom, "Public Goods and Public Choices: The Emergence of Public Economies and Industry Structures," in *The Meaning of American Federalism* (San Francisco: ICS Press, 1991), 163–97 (paper originally published in 1977).

45. V. Ostrom, *The Meaning of Democracy and the Vulnerabilities of Democracies*, 147.

46. Ibid., 25.

47. John R. Searle, *The Construction of Social Reality* (New York: Free Press, 1995), 1–2; John R. Searle, "Social Ontology: Some Basic Principles," *Anthropological Theory* 6, no. 1 (2006): 12–29.

48. Vincent and Elinor Ostrom, "Public Goods and Public Choices," in *Polycentricity and Local Public Economies: Readings from the Workshop in Political Theory and Policy Analysis*, ed. Michael D. McGinnis (Ann Arbor: University of Michigan, 1999), 94.

49. Parks et al., "Consumers as Coproducers of Public Services."

50. Geoffrey A. Jehle and Philip J. Reny, *Advanced Microeconomic Theory*, 3rd ed. (New York: Prentice Hallearson, 2011).

51. Parks et al., "Consumers as Coproducers of Public Services."

52. Brandsen and Pestoff, "Co-production, the Third Sector and the Delivery of Public Services"; Oakerson and Parks, "The Study of Local Public Economies"; Victor Pestoff, Taco

Brandsen, and Bruno Verschuere, *New Public Governance, the Third Sector and Co-production* (New York: Routledge, 2012).

53. V. Ostrom and and E. Ostrom. "Public Goods and Public Choices."

54. Elinor Ostrom, ed., *The Delivery of Urban Services: Outcomes of Change* (New York: Sage, 1976); Elinor Ostrom, Roger B. Parks, and Gordon P. Whitaker, *Patterns of Metropolitan Policing* (Cambridge, MA: Ballinger, 1978);. McGinnis, *Polycentricity and Local Public Economies*; Peter J. Boettke, Liya Palagashvili, and Jayme Lemke, "Riding in Cars with Boys: Elinor Ostrom's Adventures with the Police," *Journal of Institutional Economics* 9, no. 4 (December 2013): 407–25; Peter J. Boettke, Jayme S. Lemke, and Liya Palagashvili, "Re-Evaluating Community Policing in a Polycentric System," *Journal of Institutional Economics* 12, no. 2 (June 2016): 305–25.

55. Paul Dragos Aligica and Peter J. Boettke, *Challenging Institutional Analysis and Development: The Bloomington School* (London and New York: Routledge, 2009), 33.

56. V. Ostrom and E. Ostrom, "Public Goods and Public Choices."

57. Armen A. Alchian, "Uncertainty, Evolution, and Economic Theory," *Journal of Political Economy* 58, no. 3 (1950): 211–21.

58. Parks et al., "Consumers as Coproducers of Public Services."

59. Bozeman, "Public-Value Failure," 150–51.

60. Paul Dragos Aligica and Vlad Tarko, "Co-Production, Polycentricity, and Value Heterogeneity: The Ostroms' Public Choice Institutionalism Revisited," *American Political Science Review* 107, no. 4 (November 2013): 726–41.

61. Ibid.

62. Clifford Winston, *Market Failure versus. Government Failure: Microeconomics Policy Research and Government Performance* (Washington, DC: Brookings Institution Press, 2006).

63. Ibid.

64. Elinor Ostrom, *Understanding Institutional Diversity* (Princeton, NJ: Princeton University Press, 2005), 256.

65. Edward Peter Stringham, "Embracing Morals in Economics: The Role of Internal Moral Constraints in a Market Economy," *Journal of Economic Behavior & Organization* 78, no. 1 (April 1, 2011): 98–109.

66. E. Ostrom and Whitaker in McGinnis, *Polycentricity and Local Public Economies*, 225.

67. Brandsen and Pestoff, "Co-production, the Third Sector and the Delivery of Public Services," 492.

68. Oakerson and Parks, "The Study of Local Public Economies."

69. Ibid.

70. Ibid.

71. James Andreoni, "Impure Altruism and Donations to Public Goods: A Theory of Warm-Glow Giving," *Economic Journal* 100, no. 401 (1990): 464–77.

72. Armen A. Alchian and Harold Demsetz, "Production, Information Costs, and Economic Organization," *The American Economic Review* 62, no. 5 (1972): 777–95.

73. Gary J. Miller, *Managerial Dilemmas: The Political Economy of Hierarchy* (Cambridge, UK: Cambridge University Press, 1992).

74. Armen A. Alchian and Harold Demsetz, "Production, Information Costs, and Economic Organization," *The American Economic Review* 62, no. 5 (1972): 777–95.

75. Paul Dragos Aligica and Peter J. Boettke, *Challenging Institutional Analysis and Development: The Bloomington School* (New York: Routledge, 2009); Oakerson and Parks, "The Study of Local Public Economies."

76. E. Ostrom, *Understanding Institutional Diversity*, 265.

77. Leeson, "Government, Clubs, and Constitutions."

78. Elinor Ostrom and Vincent Ostrom, "The Quest for Meaning in Public Choice," *American Journal of Economics and Sociology* 63, no. 1 (2004): 105–47; E. Ostrom, *Understanding Institutional Diversity*, 260–61.

79. Vincent Ostrom, Robert Bish, and Elinor Ostrom, *Local Government in the United States* (San Francisco: ICS Press, 1989); Ronald J. Oakerson, *Governing Local Public Economies: Creating*

the Civic Metropolis (San Francisco: ICS Press, 1999); Oakerson and Parks, "The Study of Local Public Economies"; Boettke, Palagashvili, and Lemke, "Riding in Cars with Boys," 407–25.

80. Robert A. Dahl, *Democracy and Its Critics* (New Haven, CT: Yale University Press, 1989), 89.

81. Sue E. S. Crawford and Elinor Ostrom, "A Grammar of Institutions," *American Political Science Review* 89, no. 3 (1995): 582–600; Peter J. Boettke, "Why Culture Matters: Economics, Politics, and the Imprint of History," in *Calculation and Coordination: Essays on Socialism and Transitional Political Economy* (New York: Routledge, 2001), 248–265; Peter J. Boettke, Christopher J. Coyne, and Peter T. Leeson, "Institutional Stickiness and the New Development Economics," *American Journal of Economics and Sociology* 67, no. 2 (2008): 331–58.

82. E. Ostrom, *Understanding Institutional Diversity*, 283.

83. Robert A. Dahl, *A Preface to Economic Democracy* (Berkeley and Los Angeles: University of California Press, 1985), 57.

84. Paul D. Aligica and Vlad Tarko, "Polycentricity: From Polanyi to Ostrom, and Beyond," *Governance* 25, no. 2 (2012): 237–62.

85. Elinor Ostrom, "Developing a Method for Analyzing Institutional Change," in *Alternative Institutional Structures: Evolution and Impact*, ed. Sandra S. Batie and Nicholas Mercuro (New York: Routledge, 2008), 48–76.

86. Oakerson and Parks, "The Study of Local Public Economies," 154.

87. Aligica and Tarko, "Polycentricity."

88. Vlad Tarko, "Polycentric Structure and Informal Norms: Competition and Coordination within the Scientific Community," *Innovation: The European Journal of Social Science Research* 28, no. 1 (January 2, 2015): 63–80.

89. Sergio Villamayor-Tomas, "Polycentricity in the Water-Energy Nexus: A Comparison of Two Polycentricity Pathways and Implications for Adaptive Capacity of Water User Associations in Spain," Mimeo, 2017.

90. John E. Jackson and David C. King, "Public Goods, Private Interests, and Representation," *American Political Science Review* 83, no. 4 (1989): 1143–64.

91. Ibid., 1145.

92. E. Ostrom and V. Ostrom, "The Quest for Meaning in Public Choice"; V. Ostrom, "Public Goods and Public Choices."

93. Mark Pennington, *Robust Political Economy: Classical Liberalism and the Future of Public Policy* (Cheltenham, UK: Edward Elgar, 2011).

94. James M. Buchanan, "An Economic Theory of Clubs," *Economica* 32, no. 125 (1965): 1–14; Donald J. Boudreaux and Randall G. Holcombe, "Government by Contract," *Public Finance Review* 17, no. 3 (1989): 264–80; Leeson, "Government, Clubs, and Constitutions."

95. John Burnheim, *Is Democracy Possible? The Alternative to Electoral Politics*, 3rd ed. (Sydney, Australia: Jump Up Publishing, 2006 [1985]).

96. Ibid., 3–4.

97. Ibid.

98. Ibid.

99. Vincent Ostrom, *The Intellectual Crisis in American Public Administration* (Tuscaloosa: University Alabama Press, 1973).

Chapter 7

1. Peter J. Boettke, Jayme S. Lemke, and Liya Palagashvili, "Re-evaluating Community Policing in a Polycentric System," *Journal of Institutional Economics* 12, no. 2 (2016): 305–25; Peter Boettke, Liya Palagashvili, and Jayme Lemke, "Riding in Cars with Boys: Elinor Ostrom's Adventures with the Police," *Journal of Institutional Economics* 9, no. 4 (2013): 407–25; Michael D. McGinnis, ed., *Polycentricity and Local Public Economies: Readings from the Workshop in Political Theory and Policy Analysis* (Ann Arbor: University of Michigan Press, 1999). Also, this chapter includes adapted material from Vlad Tarko, *Elinor Ostrom: An Intellectual Biography* (London: Rowman and Littlefield International, 2017).

2. Vincent Ostrom, Charles M. Tiebout, and Robert Warren, "The Organization of Government in Metropolitan Areas: A Theoretical Inquiry," *American Political Science Review* 55, no. 4 (1961): 831–42.

3. Committee for Economic Development, cited by Elinor Ostrom, Roger B. Parks, and Gordon P. Whitaker, "Defining and Measuring Structural Variations in Interorganizational Arrangements," *Publius* 4, no. 4 (1974): 87–108.

4. Elinor Ostrom, Roger B. Parks, and Gordon P. Whitaker, *Patterns of Metropolitan Policing* (Cambridge, MA: Ballinger, 1978), xxii.

5. Ibid., 279.

6. Ibid., xxxv.

7. E. Ostrom, Parks, and Whitaker, "Defining and Measuring Structural Variations"; E. Ostrom, Parks, and Whitaker, *Patterns of Metropolitan Policing*, 50.

8. Ibid., 51–52.

9. Vincent Ostrom, Charles M. Tiebout, and Robert Warren, "The Organization of Government in Metropolitan Areas: A Theoretical Inquiry," *American Political Science Review* 55, no. 4 (1961): 831–42.

10. Ibid.

11. Elinor Ostrom, "Polycentric Systems for Coping with Collective Action and Global Environmental Change," *Global Environmental Change* 20, no, 4 (2010): 550–57.

12. Elinor Ostrom and Roger B. Parks, "Complex Models of Urban Service Systems" in McGinnis, *Polycentricity and Local Public Economies*, 287.

13. Elinor Ostrom, "The Danger of Self-Evident Truths," *PS: Political Science and Politics* 33, no. 1 (2000): 33–46.

14. E. Ostrom and Whitaker, "Does Local Community Control of Police Make a Difference? Some Preliminary Findings" in McGinnis, *Polycentricity and Local Public Economies*, ch. 8.

15. Boettke, Lemke, and Palagashvili, "Re-evaluating Community Policing in a Polycentric System."

16. Ibid.

17. Peter J. Boettke, Jayme Lemke, and Liya Palagashvili, "The Relevance of the Municipality Debate for the Solution of Collective Action Problems," Mercatus Working Paper, Mercatus Center at George Mason University, Arlington, VA.

18. Boettke, Lemke, and Palagashvili, "Re-evaluating Community Policing in a Polycentric System."

19. E. Ostrom and Whitaker, "Does Local Community Control of Police Make a Difference? Some Preliminary Findings" in McGinnis, *Polycentricity and Local Public Economies*, 225.

20. James M. Buchanan and Gordon Tullock, *The Collected Works of James M. Buchanan, Volume 3: The Calculus of Consent* (Indianapolis, IN: Liberty Fund, 1999), 292–93; Mancur Olson, "The Principle of 'Fiscal Equivalence': The Division of Responsibilities among Different Levels of Government," *American Economic Review* 59, no. 2 (1969): 479–87; Vincent Ostrom and Elinor Ostrom, "Public Goods and Public Choices: The Emergence of Public Economies and Industry Structures," in Vincent Ostrom, *The Meaning of American Federalism: Constituting a Self-Governing Society* (San Francisco: ICS Press, 1991), 163–97.

21. E. Ostrom and Whitaker, "Does Local Community Control of Police Make a Difference?" in McGinnis, *Polycentricity and Local Public Economies*, 225.

22. Ibid.

23. Boettke, Palagashvili, and Lemke, "Riding in Cars with Boys."

24. E. Ostrom and Whitaker, "Does Local Community Control of Police Make a Difference?" in McGinnis, *Polycentricity and Local Public Economies*, 224.

25. Ibid., 207.

26. Ibid., 206.

27. Ibid., 207.

28. German Lopez, "8 Shocking Findings from a City Task Force's Investigation into the Chicago Police Department," *Vox*, April 13, 2016, http://www.vox.com/2016/4/13/11424638/chicago-police-racism-report.

29. Boettke, Lemke, and Palagashvili, "The Relevance of the Municipality Debate for the Solution of Collective Action Problems"; Boettke, Lemke, and Palagashvili, "Re-evaluating Community Policing in a Polycentric System"; Christopher J. Coyne and Abigail R. Hall-Blanco, "Foreign Intervention, Police Militarization, and the Impact on Minority Groups, George Mason University Working Paper in Economics No. 16-09, February 8, 2016, available through SSRN at https://ssrn.com/abstract=2729295 or http://dx.doi.org/10.2139/ssrn.2729295.

30. Lopez, "8 Shocking Findings."

31. E. Ostrom and Whitaker, "Does Local Community Control" in McGinnis, *Polycentricity and Local Public Economies*, 224.

32. Ibid., 225–26.

33. V. Ostrom, *The Meaning of American Federalism*; Vincent Ostrom, *The Meaning of Democracy and the Vulnerabilities of Democracies: A Response to Tocqueville's Challenge* (Ann Arbor: University of Michigan Press, 1997).

34. V. Ostrom, Tiebout, and Warren, "The Organization of Government in Metropolitan Areas."

35. William A. Niskanen Jr., *Bureaucracy and Representative Government* (New Brunswick, NJ: Aldine Transaction, 1971).

36. E. Ostrom, Parks, and Whitaker, *Patterns of Metropolitan Policing*.

37. V. Ostrom, Tiebout, and Warren, "The Organization of Government in Metropolitan Areas."

38. Elinor Ostrom, ed., *The Delivery of Urban Services: Outcomes of Change* (Thousand Oaks, CA: Sage, 1976), 7.

39. Vincent Ostrom, "Polycentricity: The Structural Basis of Self-Governing Systems," in *The Meaning of American Federalism* (San Francisco: ICS Press, 1991), 223–48.

40. V. Ostrom, Tiebout, and Warren, "The Organization of Government in Metropolitan Areas," 74–75.

41. Ibid.

42. Buchanan and Tullock, *The Calculus of Consent*, ch. 5–6.

43. V. Ostrom, Tiebout, and Warren, "The Organization of Government in Metropolitan Areas."

44. Elinor Ostrom, *Understanding Institutional Diversity* (Princeton, NJ: Princeton University Press, 2005), 258.

45. Ibid., 257.

46. Claudia Pahl-Wostl and Christian Knieper, "The Capacity of Water Governance to Deal with the Climate Change Adaptation Challenge: Using Fuzzy Set Qualitative Comparative Analysis to Distinguish between Polycentric, Fragmented and Centralized Regimes," *Global Environmental Change* 29 (2014): 139–54.

47. Vincent Ostrom and Elinor Ostrom, "Public Goods and Public Choices: The Emergence of Public Economies and Industry Structures," in V. Ostrom, *The Meaning of American Federalism*, 163–97, 185.

48. Ostrom, Tiebout, and Warren, "The Organization of Government in Metropolitan Areas."

49. V. Ostrom and E. Ostrom, "Public Goods and Public Choices," 175.

50. Ibid.

51. E. Ostrom and Whitaker, "Does Local Community Control" in McGinnis, *Polycentricity and Local Public Economies*, 179.

52. James M. Buchanan, "Individual Choice in Voting and the Market," *Journal of Political Economy* 62, no. 4 (1954): 334–43; Mancur Olson, *The Logic of Collective Action: Public Goods and the Theory of Groups*, rev. ed. (Cambridge, MA: Harvard University Press, 1971 [1965]); Mancur Olson, *The Rise and Decline of Nations: Economic Growth, Stagflation, and Social Rigidities* (New Haven, CT: Yale University Press, 1982), 17–117; Bryan Caplan, *The Myth of the Rational Voter: Why Democracies Choose Bad Policies* (Princeton, NJ: Princeton University Press, 2008).

53. James M. Buchanan and Richard E. Wagner, *Democracy in Deficit: The Political Legacy of Lord Keynes* (Indianapolis, IN: Liberty Fund, 2000 [1977]).

54. V. Ostrom and E. Ostrom, "Public Goods and Public Choices," 186–87.

55. Olson, "The Principle of 'Fiscal Equivalence,'"

56. Buchanan and Tullock, *The Calculus of Consent*, 291.

57. E. Ostrom, *Understanding Institutional Diversity*.

58. Buchanan and Tullock, *The Calculus of Consent*, 292.

59. Ibid., 292–93.

60. Ibid.

61. James M. Buchanan, "The Samaritan's Dilemma," in *Altruism, Morality and Economic Theory*, ed. Edmund S. Phelps (New York: Russell Sage Foundation, 1975), 71–86; Clark C. Gibson, Krister Andersson, Elinor Ostrom, and Sujai Shivakumar, *The Samaritan's Dilemma: The Political Economy of Development Aid* (Oxford: Oxford University Press, 2005).

62. Elinor Ostrom, in discussion with Aligica, 2003.

63. Olson, *The Rise and Decline of Nations*.

64. Buchanan and Tullock, *The Calculus of Consent*, 293.

65. David T. Beito, *From Mutual Aid to the Welfare State: Fraternal Societies and Social Services, 1890–1967* (Chapel Hill: University of North Carolina Press, 2000).

66. Michael D. McGinnis, "Legal Pluralism, Polycentricity, and Faith-Based Organizations in Global Governance," in *The Struggle to Constitute and Sustain Productive Orders*, ed. Mark Sproule-Jones, Barbara Allen, and Filippo Sabetti (Lanham, MD: Lexington, 2008), 45–64; Michael D. McGinnis, "Religion Policy and the Faith-Based Initiative: Navigating the Shifting Boundaries between Church and State," *Forum on Public Policy* 4 (2010), and Indiana University-Bloomington School of Public and Environmental Affairs Research Paper No. 2011-02-02, available through SSRN at https://ssrn.com/abstract=1762689.

67. Vincent Ostrom, in discussion Aligica, 2003.

68. Ronald J. Oakerson and Roger B. Parks, "The Study of Local Public Economies: Multi-organizational, Multi-level Institutional Analysis and Development," *Policy Studies Journal* 39, no. 1 (2011): 147–67.

69. Ibid.

70. Ibid.

71. Ibid.

72. V. Ostrom and E. Ostrom, "Public Goods and Public Choices."

73. Richard E. Wagner, "Entangled Political Economy: A Keynote Address," in *Advances in Austrian Economics* (Bingley, UK: Emerald Group, 2014), 15–36.

74. Charles M. Tiebout, "A Pure Theory of Local Expenditures," *Journal of Political Economy* 64, no. 5 (1956): 416–24. Also, economist Robert L. Bish argues, "Vincent's work is very similar to that of the Austrian economists, especially Mises . . . and Hayek," who "are not focused on equilibrium and optimization; they focus on information, incentives, innovation, adjustments, and feedback." Boettke, Lemke, and Palagashvili elaborate a similar claim. Robert L. Bish, "Vincent Ostrom's Contributions to Political Economy," *Publius: The Journal of Federalism* 44, no. 2 (2014): 227–48; Peter J. Boettke, Jayme S. Lemke, and Liya Palagashvili, "Polycentricity, Self-Governance, and the Art and Science of Association," *Review of Austrian Economics* 28, no. 3 (2014): 311–35.

75. V. Ostrom and E. Ostrom, "Public Goods and Public Choices."

76. Ibid.

77. E. Ostrom, *Understanding Institutional Diversity*, 256.

78. Vincent Ostrom, "Polycentricity: The Structural Basis of Self-Governing Systems," in V. Ostrom, *The Meaning of American Federalism*, 223–48.

Chapter 8

1. Mark Bevir and R. A. W. Rhodes, *Interpreting British Governance* (London and New York: Routledge, 2003); Adalbert Evers and Jean-Louis Laville, *The Third Sector in Europe* (Cheltenham, UK and Northampton, MA: Edward Elgar, 2004); Fabrizio Gilardi, *Delegation in the Regulatory State: Independent Regulatory Agencies in Western Europe* (Cheltenham, UK and Northampton, MA: Edward Elgar, 2009); Gilardi, Fabrizio, "Institutional Change in Regulatory Policies: Regulation through Independent Agencies and the Three New Institutionalisms," in *The Politics of Regulation: Institutions and Regulatory Reforms for the Age of Governance* (Cheltenham, UK: Edward Elgar, 2004), 67–89; Fabrizio Gilardi, "The Institutional Foundations of Regulatory Capitalism: The Diffusion of Independent Regulatory Agencies in Western Europe," *The Annals of the American Academy of Political and Social Science* 598, no. 1

(2005): 84–101; Peter Miller and Nikolas Rose, *Governing the Present: Administering Economic, Social and Personal Life* (Cambridge, UK and Malden, MA: Polity, 2008);

2. Friedrich A. Hayek, *The Road to Serfdom* (Chicago: University of Chicago Press, 1944), 86.

3. Ibid., 86–87.

4. Ibid., 86.

5. Jacint Jordana, David Levi-Faur, Xavier Fernández i Marán, "The Global Diffusion of Regulatory Agencies: Channels of Transfer and Stages of Diffusion," *Comparative Political Studies* 44, no. 10 (2011): 1343–69.

6. Veronique de Rugy and Melinda Warren, "Regulatory Agency Spending Reaches New Height: An Analysis of the U.S. Budget for Fiscal Years 2008 and 2009," Regulators' Budget Report 30, Mercatus Center at George Mason University, Arlington, VA, October 2009.

7. Ibid.

8. L. Massolf and H. Seldman, "The Blurred Boundaries of Public Administration," *Public Administrative Review* 40, no. 2 (1980): 124–30; Jonathan G. S. Koppell, *The Politics of Quasi-Government: Hybrid Organizations and the Dynamics of Bureaucratic Control* (Cambridge, UK: Cambridge University Press, 2003).

9. Ronald C. Moe, "The Emerging Federal Quasi Government: Issues of Management and Accountability," *Public Administration Review* 61, no. 3 (2001): 290–312.

10. Ibid.

11. Koppell, *The Politics of Quasi-Government: Hybrid Organizations and the Dynamics of Bureaucratic Control.*

12. Perry, J. L., "Should Quasi-Government Make Democrats Queasy?" *Public Administration Review* 64, no. 6 (2004): 744–46.

13. Ibid.

14. Massolf and Seldman, "Blurred Boundaries," 124–30.

15. Fabrizio Gilardi, "The Institutional Foundations of Regulatory Capitalism: The Diffusion of Independent Regulatory Agencies in Western Europe," *The Annals of the American Academy of Political and Social Science* 598, no. 1 (2005): 84–101.

16. David Levi-Faur and Jacint Jordana, "The Rise of Regulatory Capitalism: The Global Diffusion of Regulatory Capitalism," *Annals of the American Academy of Political and Social Science* 598, no. 1 (2005): 12–32; Massolf and Seldman, "Blurred Boundaries," 124–30; Gilardi, "The Institutional Foundations of Regulatory Capitalism," 84–101.

17. Steven K. Vogel, *Freer Markets, More Rules: Regulatory Reform in Advanced Industrial Countries* (Ithaca, NY, and London: Cornell University Press, 1996).

18. Gilardi, "Institutional Change in Regulatory Policies," 67–89; Gilardi, "The Institutional Foundations of Regulatory Capitalism"; Levi-Faur and Jordana, "The Rise of Regulatory Capitalism"; Jacint Jordana and David Levi-Faur, eds., *The Politics of Regulation: Institutions and Regulatory Reforms for the Age of Governance* (Cheltenham, UK: Edward Elgar, 2004).

19. Michael Power, *The Audit Society: Rituals of Verification* (Oxford and New York: Oxford University Press, 1997).

20. Moe, "The Emerging Federal Quasi Government."

21. Majone Giandomencio, "The Regulatory State and Its Legitimacy Problems," *Western European Politics* 22, no. 1 (1999): 1–24.

22. Elinor Ostrom, *Understanding Institutional Diversity* (Princeton, NJ: Princeton University Press, 2005), ch. 9.

23. Emily Chamlee-Wright and Don Lavoie, *Culture and Enterprise: The Development, Representation and Morality of Business* (Washington, DC: Cato Institute, 2000)

24. Elinor Ostrom, "Beyond Markets and States: Polycentric Governance of Complex Economic Systems," *American Economic Review* 100, no. 3 (2010), 641–72; Elinor Ostrom, *Governing the Commons: The Evolution of Institutions for Collective Action* (Cambridge and New York: Cambridge University Press, 1990).

25. Vlad Tarko and Paul Dragos Aligica, "From 'Broad Studies' to Internet-Based 'Expert Knowledge Aggregation'. Notes on the Methodology and Technology of Knowledge Integration," *Futures*, Special Issue: Flexible infrastructures, 43, no. 9 (November 2011): 986–95.

26. Edward Stringham, *Private Governance: Creating Order in Economic and Social Life* (New York and Oxford: Oxford University Press, 2015); Richard E. Wagner, "American Federalism: How Well Does It Support Liberty?," Mercatus Center, George Mason University, 2014.

27. Gary S. Becker, "A Theory of Competition among Pressure Groups for Political Influence," *The Quarterly Journal of Economics* 98, no. 3 (August 1, 1983): 371–400; Donald A. Wittman, *The Myth of Democratic Failure: Why Political Institutions Are Efficient* (Chicago: University of Chicago Press, 1995).

28. Vlad Tarko and Paul Dragos Aligica, "From 'Broad Studies' to Internet-Based 'Expert Knowledge Aggregation.'"

29. Herman Kahn, "The Alternative World Futures Approach," in *Search for Alternatives: Public Policy and the Study of the Future*, ed. Tugwell Franklin (Cambridge, MA: Winthrop, 1973), 107.

30. Vlad Tarko and Paul Dragos Aligica, "From 'Broad Studies' to Internet-Based 'Expert Knowledge Aggregation.'"

31. Robin Hanson, "Shall We Vote on Values, But Bet on Beliefs?," *Journal of Political Philosophy* 21, no. 2 (June 1, 2013): 151–78.

32. Ibid.

33. Ibid.

34. Ibid.

35. Ibid.

36. Jerry Ellig, *Dynamic Copetition and Public Policy: Technology, Innovation, and Antitrust Issues* (New York: Cambridge University Press, 2001).

37. "Organizational Overview," American Society of Mechanical Engineers website, accessed February 23, 2017, https://www.standardsportal.org/usa_en/sdo/asme.aspx.

38. Andrew Young, "Austrian Business Cycle Theory: A Modern Appraisal," in *Oxford Handbook of Austrian Economics*, ed. Peter J. Boettke and Christopher J. Coyne (Oxford: Oxford University Press, 2015).

39. W. Kip Viscusi, Joseph E. Harrington Jr., and John M. Vernon, *Economics of Regulation and Antitrust*, 4th ed. (Cambridge, MA: MIT Press, 2005); W. Kip Viscusi, "Regulatory Reform and Liability for Pharmaceuticals and Medical Devices," in *Advancing Medical Innovation: Health, Safety and the Role of Government in the 21st Century* (Washington, DC: Progress and Freedom Foundation, 1996), 79–102.

40. Viscusi, "Regulatory Reform and Liability," 90.

41. Vincent Ostrom and Elinor Ostrom, "Public Goods and Public Choices," in *The Meaning of American Federalism: Constituting a Self-Governing Society*, ed. Vincent Ostrom (San Francisco: ICS Press, 1991 [1977]), 185.

42. Ibid.

43. Mark R. Joelson, *An International Antitrust Primer: A Guide to the Operation of United States, European Union and Other Key Competition Laws in the Global Economy*, 3rd ed. (Alphen aan den Rijn, Netherlands: Kluwer Law International, 2006), 138.

44. Ibid., 139–40.

45. Ibid., 140.

46. Stringham, *Private Governance*, ch. 5.

Chapter 9

1. Ostrom, Vincent, and Elinor Ostrom, "Public Goods and Public Choices: The Emergence of Public Economies and Industry Structures," in *The Meaning of American Federalism* (San Francisco: ICS Press, 1991 [1977]), 163–97.

2. Vincent Ostrom, Charles M. Tiebout, and Robert Warren, "The Organization of Government in Metropolitan Areas: A Theoretical Inquiry," *American Political Science Review* 55, no. 4 (1961): 831–42; Vincent Ostrom, *The Intellectual Crisis in American Public Administration* (Tuscaloosa: University of Alabama Press, 1973); Vincent Ostrom, *The Political Theory of a Compound Republic: Designing the American Experiment* (Lincoln: University of Nebraska Press, 1987); Vincent Ostrom, "Polycentricity: The Structural Basis of Self-Governing Systems," in

Choice, Rules and Collective Action: The Ostroms on the Study of Institutions and Governance, ed. Filippo Sabetti and Paul Dragos Aligica (Colchester, UK: European Consortium for Political Research Press, 2014 [1991]), 45–60; Richard E. Wagner, "Self-Governance, Polycentrism, and Federalism: Recurring Themes in Vincent Ostrom's Scholarly Oeuvre," *Journal of Economic Behavior and Organization* 57, no. 2 (2005): 173–88; Theo Toonen, "Resilience in Public Administration: The Work of Elinor and Vincent Ostrom from a Public Administration Perspective," *Public Administration Review* 70, no. 2 (2010): 193–202; Michael D. McGinnis and Elinor Ostrom, "Reflections on Vincent Ostrom, Public Administration, and Polycentricity," *Public Administration Review* 72, no. 1 (2012): 15–25; Michael C. Munger, "Endless Forms Most Beautiful and Most Wonderful: Elinor Ostrom and the Diversity of Institutions," *Public Choice* 143, no. 3/4 (2010): 263–68.

3. Howard Rothmann Bowen, *Social Responsibilities of the Businessman* (New York: Harper, 1953), xi; Ronald K. Mitchell, Bradley R. Agle, and Donna J. Wood, "Toward a Theory of Stakeholder Identification and Salience: Defining the Principle of Who and What Really Counts," *Academy of Management Review* 22, no. 4 (1997): 853–86; Elisabet Garriga and Domènec Melé, "Corporate Social Responsibility Theories: Mapping the Territory," *Journal of Business Ethics* 53, no. 1 (2004): 51–71; André Habisch, Jan Jonker, Martina Wegner, and René Schmidpeter, eds., *Corporate Social Responsibility across Europe: Discovering National Perspectives of Corporate Citizenship* (Berlin: Springer, 2005); Duane Windsor, "Corporate Social Responsibility: Three Key Approaches," *Journal of Management Studies* 43, no. 1 (2006): 93–114; Andrew Crane, Abagail McWilliams, Dirk Matten, Jeremy Moon, and Donald S. Siegel, eds., *The Oxford Handbook of Corporate Social Responsibility* (New York: Oxford University Press, 2008).

4. David P. Baron, "Private Politics, Corporate Social Responsibility, and Integrated Strategy," *Journal of Economics and Management Strategy* 10, no. 1 (2001): 12.

5. M. Jones and Gerald D. Keim, "Corporate Social Responsibility: An Assessment of the Enlightened Self-Interest Model," *Academy of Management Review* 3, no. 1 (1978): 32–39.

6. See Tom Fox, Halina Ward, and Bruce Howard, *Public Sector Roles in Strengthening Corporate Social Responsibility: A Baseline Study* (Washington, DC: World Bank, 2002); Steven Lydenberg, *Corporations and the Public Interest: Guiding the Invisible Hand* (San Francisco: Berrett-Koehler, 2005); Jeremy Moon and David Vogel, "Corporate Social Responsibility, Government, and Civil Society," in *The Oxford Handbook of Corporate Social Responsibility*, ed. Andrew Crane, Abagail McWilliams, Dirk Matten, Jeremy Moon, and Donald S. Siegel (New York: Oxford University Press, 2008), 303–23.

7. For example, Clarence C. Walton, *Corporate Social Responsibilities* (Belmont, CA: Wadsworth, 1967).

8. Keith Davis, "The Case for and against Business Assumption of Social Responsibilities," *Academy of Management Journal* 16, no. 2 (1973): 312–22.

9. Bryan W. Husted and José De Jesus Salazar, "Taking Friedman Seriously: Maximizing Profits and Social Performance," *Journal of Management Studies* 43, no. 1 (2006): 75–91.

10. Richard Eells and Clarence C. Walton, *Conceptual Foundations of Business*, 3rd ed. (Homewood, IL: Richard D. Irwin, 1974); Archie B. Carroll, "A Three-Dimensional Conceptual Model of Corporate Performance," *Academy of Management Review* 4, no. 4 (1979): 497–505; Donna J. Wood, "Corporate Social Performance Revisited," *Academy of Management Review* 16, no. 4 (1991): 691–718; Diane L. Swanson, "Addressing a Theoretical Problem by Reorienting the Corporate Social Performance Model," *Academy of Management Review* 20, no. 1 (1995): 43–64; Jeffrey S. Harrison and R. Edward Freeman, "Stakeholders, Social Responsibility, and Performance: Empirical Evidence and Theoretical Perspectives," *Academy of Management Review* 42, no. 5 (1999): 479–87; Archie B. Carroll and Ann K. Buchholtz, *Business and Society: Ethics, Sustainability, and Stakeholder Management*, 9th ed. (Stamford, CT: Cengage Learning, 2015 [2008]).

11. Milton Friedman, *Capitalism and Freedom* (Chicago: University of Chicago Press, 1962), 133.

12. Henry Eilbirt and I. Robert Parket, "The Practice of Business: The Current Status of Corporate Social Responsibility," *Business Horizons* 16, no. 4 (1973): 11.

13. John Elkington, *Cannibals with Forks: The Triple Bottom Line of 21st Century Business* (Oxford: Capstone, 1997); Sophia A. Muirhead, *Corporate Contributions: The View from Fifty Years* (New York: Conference Board, 1999).
14. Domènec Melé, "Corporate Social Responsibility Theories," in *The Oxford Handbook of Corporate Social Responsibility*, ed. Andrew Crane, Abagail McWilliams, Dirk Matten, Jeremy Moon, and Donald S. Siegel (New York: Oxford University Press, 2008), 57.
15. Elizabeth C. Kurucz, Barry A. Colbert, and David Wheeler, "The Business Case for Corporate Social Responsibility," in *The Oxford Handbook of Corporate Social Responsibility*, ed. Andrew Crane, Abagail McWilliams, Dirk Matten, Jeremy Moon, and Donald S. Siegel (New York: Oxford University Press, 2008), 83–112.
16. Armen A. Alchian, "Uncertainty, Evolution, and Economic Theory," *Journal of Political Economy* 58, no. 3 (1950): 211–21.
17. Abagail McWilliams and Donald Siegel, "Corporate Social Responsibility: A Theory of the Firm Perspective," *Academy of Management Review* 26, no. 1 (2001):117–27; Husted and Salazar, "Taking Friedman Seriously."
18. McWilliams and Siegel, "Corporate Social Responsibility," 124.
19. Alchian, "Uncertainty, Evolution, and Economic Theory"; McWilliams and Siegel, "Corporate Social Responsibility."
20. Melé, "Corporate Social Responsibility Theories."
21. Milton Friedman, "The Social Responsibility of Business Is to Increase Its Profits," *New York Times Magazine*, September 13, 1970.
22. Gary J. Miller, *Managerial Dilemmas: The Political Economy of Hierarchy* (New York: Cambridge University Press, 1992); José Salazar and Bryan W. Husted, "Principals and Agents: Further Thoughts on the Fiedmanite Critique of Corporate Social Responsibility," in *The Oxford Handbook of Corporate Social Responsibility*, ed. Andrew Crane, Abagail McWilliams, Dirk Matten, Jeremy Moon, and Donald S. Siegel (New York: Oxford University Press, 2008).
23. Husted and Salazar, "Taking Friedman Seriously."
24. This classification was inspired by Kurucz, Colbert, and Wheeler, "The Business Case for Corporate Social Responsibility."
25. Norman E. Bowie and Thomas W. Dunfee, "Confronting Morality in Markets," *Journal of Business Ethics* 38, no. 4 (2002): 381–93.
26. Bradford Cornell and Alan C. Shapiro, "Corporate Stakeholders and Corporate Finance," *Financial Management* 16, no. 1 (1987): 5–14; Moses L. Pava and Joshua Krausz, "The Association between Corporate Social-Responsibility and Financial Performance: The Paradox of Social Cost," *Journal of Business Ethics* 15, no. 3 (1996): 321–57; Lee E. Preston and Douglas P. O'Bannon, "The Corporate Social-Financial Performance Relationship: A Typology and Analysis," *Business and Society* 36, no. 4 (1997): 419–29.
27. Carl Frankel, *In Earth's Company: Business, Environment and the Challenge of Sustainability* (Gabriola Island, BC, Canada: New Society Publishers, 1998); Ken Peattie, "Golden Goose or Wild Goose? The Hunt for the Green Consumer," *Business Strategy and the Environment* 10, no. 4 (2001): 187–99; Andrew Crane, "Unpacking the Ethical Product," *Journal of Business Ethics* 30, no. 4 (2001): 361–73.
28. B. L. Kedia and E. C. Kuntz, "The Context of Social Performance: An Empirical Study of Texas Banks," in *Research in Corporate Social Performance and Policy*, vol. 3, ed. L. E. Preston (Greenwich, CT: JAI, 1981), 133–54; Linda D. Lerner and Gerald E. Fryxell, "An Empirical Study of the Predictors of Corporate Social Performance: A Multi-dimensional Analysis," *Journal of Business Ethics* 7, no. 12 (1988): 951–59; Leena Lankoski, "Determinants of Environmental Profit: An Analysis of the Firm-Level Relationship between Environmental Performance and Economic Performance," (PhD diss., Helsinki University of Technology, 2000); Oliver Salzmann, Aileen Ionescu-Somers, and Ulrich Steger, "The Business Case for Corporate Sustainability: Literature Review and Research Options," *European Management Journal* 23, no. 1 (2005): 27–36.
29. David P. Baron, "Private Politics, Corporate Social Responsibility, and Integrated Strategy," *Journal of Economics and Management Strategy* 10, no. 1 (2001): 7–45; Charles W. L. Hill,

"National Institutional Structures, Transaction Cost Economizing and Competitive Advantage: The Case of Japan," *Organization Science* 6, no. 1 (1995): 119–31; Thomas M. Jones, "Instrumental Stakeholder Theory: A Synthesis of Ethics and Economics," *Academy of Management Review* 20, no. 2 (1995): 404–37; Andrew C. Wicks, Shawn L. Berman, and Thomas M. Jones, "The Structure of Optimal Trust: Moral and Strategic Implications," *Academy of Management Review* 24, no. 1 (1999): 99–116; Peter Kok, Ton van der Wiele, Richard McKenna, and Alan Brown, "A Corporate Social Responsibility Audit within a Quality Management Framework," *Journal of Business Ethics* 31, no. 4 (2001): 285–97; Paul C. Godfrey, "The Relationship between Corporate Philanthropy and Shareholder Wealth: A Risk Management Perspective," *Academy of Management Review* 30, no. 4 (2005): 777–98; Dawn Story and Trevor J. Price, "Corporate Social Responsibility and Risk Management," *Journal of Corporate Citizenship* 22 (2006): 39–51; André Habisch and Jeremy Moon, "Social Capital and Corporate Social Responsibility," in *The Challenge of Organizing and Implementing Corporate Social Responsibility*, ed. Jan Jonker and Marco de Witte (Basingstoke and Hampshire, UK: Palgrave, 2006), 63–77.

30. George J. Stigler, "Information in the Labor Market," *Journal of Political Economy* 70, no. 5 (1962): 94–105; Christian M. Riordan, Robert D. Gatewood, and Jodi Barnes Bill, "Corporate Image: Employee Reactions and Implications for Managing Corporate Social Performance," *Journal of Business Ethics* 16, no. 4 (1997): 401–12; Daniel B. Turban and Daniel W. Greening, "Corporate Social Performance and Organizational Attractiveness to Prospective Employees," *Academy of Management Journal* 40, no. 3 (1997): 658–72; Heather Schmidt Albinger and Sarah J. Freeman, "Corporate Social Performance and Attractiveness as an Employer to Different Job Seeking Populations," *Journal of Business Ethics* 28, no. 3 (2000): 243–53; Sandra A. Waddock, Charles Bodwell, and Samuel B. Graves, "Responsibility: The New Business Imperative," *Academy of Management Executive* 16, no. 2 (2002): 132–48.

31. Benjamin Cashore, "Legitimacy and the Privatization of Environmental Governance: How Non-State Market-Driven (NSMD) Governance Systems Gain Rule-Making Authority," *Governance* 15, no. 4 (2002): 503–29.

32. Wheeler et al., 2003

33. Steven J. Waddell, "Six Societal Learning Concepts for a New Era of Engagement," *Reflections* 3, no. 4 (2002): 19–27.

34. Kurucz, Colbert, and Wheeler, "The Business Case for Corporate Social Responsibility," 89.

35. C. K. Prahalad and Allen Hammond, "Serving the World's Poor, Profitably," *Harvard Business Review* 80, no. 9 (2002): 48–57; C. K. Prahalad, *The Fortune at the Bottom of the Pyramid: Eradicating Poverty through Profits*, 5th ed. (Upper Saddle River, NJ: Wharton School Publishing, 2014 [2009]).

36. Ken Wilber, *The Essential Ken Wilber: An Introductory Reader* (Boston: Shambhala, 1998); Ken Wilber, *A Theory of Everything: An Integral Vision of Business, Politics, Science, and Spirituality* (Boston: Shambhala, 2001); Kurucz, Colbert, and Wheeler, "The Business Case for Corporate Social Responsibility," 103.

37. Vincent Ostrom, Polycentricity,1972, Part II; Michael D. McGinnis and Elinor Ostrom, "Reflections on Vincent Ostrom, Public Administration, and Polycentricity," *Public Administration Review* 72, no. 1 (2012): 15–25; Paul D. Aligica and Vlad Tarko, "Polycentricity: From Polanyi to Ostrom, and Beyond," *Governance* 25, no. 2 (2012): 237–62; Paul Dragos Aligica and Vlad Tarko, "Co-production, Polycentricity and Value Heterogeneity: The Ostroms' Public Choice Institutionalism Revisited," *American Political Science Review* 107, no. 4 (2013): 726–41.

38. R. Edward Freeman, Jeffrey S. Harrison, Andrew C. Wicks, Bidhan L. Parmar, and Simone de Colle, *Stakeholder Theory: The State of the Art* (Cambridge: Cambridge University Press, 2010).

39. Friedman, *Capitalism and Freedom*, 133.

40. Husted and Salazar, "Taking Friedman Seriously."

41. Friedman, "The Social Responsibility of Business."

42. Ibid.

43. Melé, "Corporate Social Responsibility Theories," 59.

44. Elinor Ostrom, "Beyond Markets and States: Polycentric Governance of Complex Economic Systems," *American Economic Review* 100, no. 3 (2010): 641–72;Elinor Ostrom, Christina Chang, Mark Pennington, and Vlad Tarko, *The Future of the Commons: Beyond Market Failure and Government Regulation* (London: Institute of Economic Affairs, 2012).

45. Elinor Ostrom, *Governing the Commons*; Elinor Ostrom, *Understanding Institutional Diversity* (Princeton, NJ: Princeton University Press, 2005); Cashore, "Legitimacy and the Privatization of Environmental Governance"; Peter T. Leeson, *Anarchy Unbound: Why Self-Governance Works Better Than You Think* (Cambridge and New York: Cambridge University Press, 2014); Edward Stringham, *Private Governance: Creating Order in Economic and Social Life* (New York and Oxford: Oxford University Press, 2015).

46. Edward Peter Stringham, "Embracing Morals in Economics: The Role of Internal Moral Constraints in a Market Economy," *Journal of Economic Behavior and Organization* 78, no. 1–2 (2011): 98–109.

47. R. H. Coase, "The Lighthouse in Economics," *Journal of Law and Economics* 17, no. 2 (1974): 357–76.

48. Melé, "Corporate Social Responsibility Theories," 59.

49. Mark Sproule-Jones, Barbara Allen, and Filippo Sabetti, eds., *The Struggle to Constitute and Sustain Productive Orders: Vincent Ostrom's Quest to Understand Human Affairs* (Lanham, MD: Lexington Books, 2008); Paul Dragos Aligica, *Institutional Diversity and Political Economy: The Ostroms and Beyond* (New York: Oxford University Press, 2014); Elinor Ostrom and Vincent Ostrom, *Choice, Rules and Collective Action*, ed. Paul Dragos Aligica and Filippo Sabetti (Colchester, UK: European Consortium for Political Research Press, 2014).

50. Thomas Donaldson and Thomas W. Dunfee, *Ties That Bind: A Social Contracts Approach to Business Ethics* (Boston: Harvard Business School Press, 1999), ch. 3 and 5; Michael Walzer, *Interpretation and Social Criticism* (Cambridge, MA: Harvard University Press, 1987); Michael Walzer, "Moral Minimalism," in *From the Twilight of Probability: Ethics and Politics*, ed. William R. Shea and Antonio Spadafora (Sagamore Beach, MA: Science History Publications, 1992).

51. Thomas Donaldson and Thomas W. Dunfee, "Toward a Unified Conception of Business Ethics: Integrative Social Contracts Theory," *Academy of Management Review* 19, no. 2 (1994): 252–84; Donaldson and Dunfee, *Ties That Bind*.

52. Donaldson and Dunfee, "Toward a Unified Conception of Business Ethics."

53. Ibid., 252.

54. Peter J. Boettke and Christopher J. Coyne, "An Entrepreneurial Theory of Social and Cultural Change," in *Markets and Civil Society: The European Experience in Comparative Perspective*, ed. Víctor Pérez-Díaz (New York: Berghahn Books, 2009), 77–103; Peter J. Boettke and Christopher J. Coyne, "Context Matters: Institutions and Entrepreneurship," *Foundations and Trends in Entrepreneurship* 5, no. 3 (2009): 135–209.

55. William H. Riker, *Liberalism against Populism: A Confrontation between the Theory of Democracy and the Theory of Social Choice* (New York: Freeman, 1982).

56. Vincent Ostrom, *The Meaning of Democracy and the Vulnerabilities of Democracies: A Response to Tocqueville's Challenge* (Ann Arbor: University of Michigan Press, 1997); Aligica and Tarko, "Co-production, Polycentricity and Value Heterogeneity."

57. Nicholas Rescher, *Pluralism: Against the Demand for Consensus* (Oxford University Press, 1993).

58. Michael C. Jensen, "Value Maximization, Stakeholder Theory, and the Corporate Objective Function," *Business Ethics Quarterly* 12, no. 2 (2002): 235–56.

59. Ibid., 246.

60. Joseph T. Mahoney, "Towards a Stakeholder Theory of Strategic Management" (unpublished paper, Department of Business Administration, College of Business, University of Illinois at Urbana-Champaign, n.d.), https://www.utdallas.edu/negcent/seminars/mahoney/Towards%20a%20Stakeholder%20Theory%20of%20Strategic%20Management_Mahoney.pdf; Thomas W. Dunfee, "Stakeholder Theory: Managing Corporate Social Responsibility in a Multiple Actor Context," in *The Oxford Handbook of Corporate Social Responsibility*, ed. Andrew Crane, Abagail McWilliams, Dirk Matten, Jeremy Moon, and Donald S. Siegel (New York: Oxford University Press, 2008), 346–62.

61. Dunfee, "Stakeholder Theory," 352.
62. Mahoney, "Towards a Stakeholder Theory"; Dunfee, "Stakeholder Theory," 352.
63. Mahoney, "Towards a Stakeholder Theory," 4.
64. Dunfee, "Stakeholder Theory."
65. Donaldson and Dunfee, "Towards a Unified Conception of Business Ethics"; Donaldson and Dunfee, *Ties That Bind*.
66. Mahoney, "Towards a Stakeholder Theory."
67. Dunfee, "Stakeholder Theory," 361.
68. Ronald K. Mitchell, Bradley R. Agle, and Donna J. Wood, "Toward a Theory of Stakeholder Identification and Salience: Defining the Principle of Who and What Really Counts," *Academy of Management Review* 22, no. 4 (1994): 853–86.
69. Dunfee, "Stakeholder Theory," 361.
70. Ibid., 359.
71. Israel M. Kirzner, "The Perils of Regulation," in *Discovery and the Capitalist Process* (Chicago: University of Chicago Press, 1985); William J. Baumol, "Entrepreneurship: Productive, Unproductive, and Destructive," *Journal of Business Venturing* 11, no. 1 (1996): 3–22; Peter T. Leeson and Peter J. Boettke, "Two-Tiered Entrepreneurship and Economic Development," *International Review of Law and Economics* 29, no. 3 (2009): 252–59; Boettke and Coyne, "An Entrepreneurial Theory of Social and Cultural Change"; Boettke and Coyne, "Context Matters."
72. Ronald J. Oakerson and Roger B. Parks, "Citizen Voice and Public Entrepreneurship: The Organizational Dynamic of a Complex Metropolitan County," *Publius* 18, no. 4 (1988): 91–112; Peter G. Klein, Joseph T. Mahoney, Anita M. McGahan, and Christos N. Pitelis, "Toward a Theory of Public Entrepreneurship," *European Management Review* 7, no. 1 (2010): 1–15.
73. Vincent Ostrom, "Polycentricity: The Structural Basis of Self-Governing Systems," in *Choice, Rules, and Collective Action: The Ostroms on the Study of Institutions and Governance*, ed. Filippo Sabetti and Paul Dragos Aligica (Colchester, UK: European Consortium for Political Research Press, 2014), 45–60; Vincent Ostrom, "Polycentricity (Parts 1 and 2)," in *Polycentricity and Local Public Economies: Readings from the Workshop in Political Theory and Policy Analysis*, ed. Michael D. McGinnis (Ann Arbor: University of Michigan Press, 1999), 52–74 and 119–38
74. Dunfee, "Stakeholder Theory."
75. Ibid., 361.
76. Steven G. Horwitz, "Wal-Mart to the Rescue: Private Enterprise's Response to Hurricane Katrina," *Independent Review* 13, no. 4 (2009), 511–28; E. Chamlee-Wright and V. H. Storr, "'There's No Place Like New Orleans': Sense of Place and Community Recovery in the Ninth Ward after Hurricane Katrina," *Journal of Urban Affairs* 31, no. 5 (2009): 615–34.
77. Dunfee, "Stakeholder Theory," 355.
78. Ibid., 361.
79. Ibid.
80. Husted and Salazar, "Taking Friedman Seriously."
81. Barry Bozeman, "Public-Value Failure: When Efficient Markets May Not Do," *Public Administration Review* 62, no. 2 (2002): 145–61; Barry Bozeman, *Public Values and Public Interest: Counterbalancing Economic Individualism* (Washington, DC: Georgetown University Press, 2007); Torben B. Jorgensen and Barry Bozeman, "Public Values: An Inventory," *Administration and Society* 39, no. 3 (2007): 354–81.
82. Robert Axelrod, "An Evolutionary Approach to Norms," *American Political Science Review* 80, no. 4 (1986): 1095–111.
83. Walzer, *Interpretation and Social Criticism*; Walzer, "Moral Minimalism."
84. Michael Walzer, *Thick and Thin: Moral Argument at Home and Abroad* (Notre Dame, IN: University of Notre Dame Press, 1994), 10.
85. Walzer, *Interpretation and Social Criticism*; Walzer, "Moral Minimalism"; Donaldson and Dunfee, *Ties That Bind*.

86. For another critique of hypernorms and integrative theory, see Mark Douglas, "Integrative Social Contracts Theory: Hype over Hypernorms," *Journal of Business Ethics* 26, no. 2 (2000): 101–10.
87. Mitchell, Agle, and Wood, "Toward a Theory of Stakeholder Identification"; Dunfee, "Stakeholder Theory."
88. Dunfee, "Stakeholder Theory."
89. Ibid., 355.
90. Boettke and Coyne, "An Entrepreneurial Theory."
91. Karl R. Popper, *The Logic of Scientific Discovery* (London: Hutchinson of London, 1960); James M. Buchanan and Gordon Tullock, *The Calculus of Consent: Logical Foundations of Constitutional Democracy* (Indianapolis, IN: Liberty Fund, 1999 [1962]); John S. Dryzek, *Deliberative Democracy and Beyond: Liberals, Critics, Contestations* (Oxford and New York: Oxford University Press); Jack Knight and James Johnson, "The Priority of Democracy: A Pragmatist Approach to Political-Economic Institutions and the Burden of Justification," *American Political Science Review* 101, no. 1 (2007): 47–61; Jack Knight and James Johnson, *The Priority of Democracy: Political Consequences of Pragmatism* (Princeton, NJ: Princeton University Press, 2011)
92. Kenneth J. Arrow, *Social Choice and Individual Values* (New Haven, CT: Yale University Press, 1951); Riker, *Liberalism against Populism*; Shaun Hargreaves Heap, Martin Hollis, Bruce Lyons, Robert Sugden, and Albert Weale, *The Theory of Choice: A Critical Guide* (Oxford and Cambridge, MA: Wiley-Blackwell, 1992); Kenneth A. Shepsle and Mark S. Bonchek, *Analyzing Politics: Rationality, Behavior, and Institutions* (New York and London: W. W. Norton, 1997); Amartya Sen, "The Possibility of Social Choice," *American Economic Review* 89, no. 3 (1999): 349–78
93. Shepsle and Bonchek, *Analyzing Politics*, ch. 4.
94. Ibid.
95. Ibid.
96. Arrow, *Social Choice and Individual Values*.
97. Buchanan and Tullock, *The Calculus of Consent*.
98. Ibid.
99. Mitchell, Agle, and Wood, "Toward a Theory of Stakeholder Identification."
100. Dunfee, "Stakeholder Theory," 357.
101. McWilliams and Siegel, "Corporate Social Responsibility"; Husted and Salazar, "Taking Friedman Seriously."
102. McWilliams and Siegel, "Corporate Social Responsibility"; Husted and Salazar, "Taking Friedman Seriously."
103. E. Ostrom, "Beyond Markets and States"; Toonen, "Resilience in Public Administration."
104. Roger B. Parks, Paula C. Baker, Larry Kiser, Ronald Oakerson, Elinor Ostrom, Vincent Ostrom, Stephen L. Percy, Martha B. Vandivort, Gordon P. Whitaker, and Rick Wilson, "Consumers as Coproducers of Public Services: Some Economic and Institutional Considerations," *Policy Studies Journal* 9, no. 7 (1981): 1001–11; Taco Brandsen and Victor Pestoff, "Co-production, the Third Sector and the Delivery of Public Services," *Public Management Review* 8, no. 4 (2006): 493–501; Ronald J. Oakerson and Roger B. Parks, "The Study of Local Public Economies: Multi-organizational, Multi-level Institutional Analysis and Development," *Policy Studies Journal* 39, no. 1 (2011): 147–67; Victor Pestoff, Taco Brandsen, and Bram Verschuere, eds., *New Public Governance, the Third Sector and Co-production* (New York: Routledge, 2012); Aligica and Tarko, "Co-production, Polycentricity and Value Heterogeneity."
105. Armen A. Alchian and Harold Demsetz, "Production, Information Costs, and Economic Organization," *American Economic Review* 62, no. 5 (1972): 777–95; Gary J. Miller, *Managerial Dilemmas: The Political Economy of Hierarchy* (Cambridge, UK: Cambridge University Press, 1992).
106. Aligica and Tarko, "Co-production, Polycentricity and Value Heterogeneity."
107. Dunfee, "Stakeholder Theory."
108. Ibid.

Conclusions

1. Laurence E. Lynn Jr., "Public Management: A Concise History of the Field," in *The Oxford Handbook of Public Management*, ed. Ewan Ferlie, Laurence E. Lynn Jr., and Christopher Pollitt (New York: Oxford University Press, 2007), 27–50; Dwight Waldo, *The Administrative State: A Study of the Political Theory of American Public Administration* (Piscataway, NJ: Transaction Publishers, 2006 [1948]); Vincent Ostrom, *The Intellectual Crisis in American Public Administration*, 3rd ed. (Tuscaloosa: University of Alabama Press, 2008 [1973]); Jos. C. N. Raadschelders, *Public Administration: The Interdisciplinary Study of Government* (New York: Oxford University Press, 2012).

2. B. Guy Peters and John Pierre, "Governance without Government? Rethinking Public Administration," *Journal of Public Administration Research and Theory* 8, no. 2 (1998): 223–43.

3. Ibid.

4. Ibid.

5. David Levi-Faur, ed., *The Oxford Handbook of Governance* (New York: Oxford University Press, 2012); Ewan Ferlie, Laurence E. Lynn Jr., and Christopher Pollitt, eds., *The Oxford Handbook of Public Management* (New York: Oxford University Press, 2005).

6. Ferlie, Lynn, and Pollitt, *The Oxford Handbook of Public Management*, 7.

7. David Levi-Faur, ed., *The Oxford Handbook of Governance*.

8. Ibid., 7–9.

9. Levi-Faur, "From 'Big Government' to 'Big Governance'?," in *The Oxford Handbook of Governance*, 7.

10. Gordon Tullock, *Bureaucracy: The Selected Works of Gordon Tullock*, vol. 6, ed. Charles K. Rowley (Indianapolis, IN: Liberty Press, 2005 [1965]).

11. Ibid., 175.

12. Ibid., 235.

13. James M. Buchanan, *What Should Economists Do?* (Indianapolis, IN: Liberty Press, 1979 [1964]), 42.

14. Ibid., 35.

15. Vincent Ostrom, Charles M. Tiebout, and Robert Warren, "The Organization of Government in Metropolitan Areas: A Theoretical Inquiry," *American Political Science Review* 55, no. 4 (1961): 831–42.

16. Levi-Faur, *The Oxford Handbook of Governance*, 36.

17. Eva Sørensen, "Public Administration as Metagovernance," in *Public Administration in Transition: Theory, Practice, Methodology*, ed. Gunnar Gjelstrup and Eva Sørensen (Copenhagen: DJØF Publishing, 2007), 111–12.

18. Ibid., 112.

19. Ibid., 116–17.

20. Ibid.

21. Ibid., 122.

22. Ibid.

23. Ibid.

REFERENCES

Achen, Christopher H., and Larry M. Bartels. 2016. *Democracy for Realists: Why Elections Do Not Produce Responsive Government.* Princeton, NJ, and Oxford: Princeton University Press.

Albinger, Heather Schmidt, and Sarah J. Freeman. 2000. "Corporate Social Performance and Attractiveness as an Employer to Different Job Seeking Populations." *Journal of Business Ethics* 28 (3): 243–53.

Alchian, Armen A. 1950. "Uncertainty, Evolution, and Economic Theory." *Journal of Political Economy* 58 (3): 211–21.

Alchian, Armen A., and Harold Demsetz. 1972. "Production, Information Costs, and Economic Organization." *American Economic Review* 62 (5): 777–795.

Alesina, A., A. Devleeschauwer, W. Easterly, S. Kurlat, and R. Wacziarg. 2003. "Fractionalization." *Journal of Economic Growth* 8: 155–94.

Aligica, Paul Dragos. 2013. *Institutional Diversity and Political Economy: The Ostroms and Beyond.* Oxford and New York: Oxford University Press.

Aligica, Paul Dragos, and Peter J. Boettke. 2011. "Institutional Design and Ideas-Driven Social Change: Notes from an Ostromian Perspective." *The Good Society* 20 (1): 50–66.

Aligica, Paul Dragos, and Peter J. Boettke. 2011. "The Two Social Philosophies of Ostroms' Institutionalism." *Policy Studies Journal* 39 (1): 29–49.

Aligica, Paul Dragos, and Peter J. Boettke. 2009. *Challenging Institutional Analysis and Development: The Bloomington School.* London and New York: Routledge.

Aligica, Paul Dragos, and Filippo Sabetti, eds. 2014. *Choice, Rules and Collective Action.* Colchester, UK: ECPR Press.

Aligica, Paul Dragos, and Vlad Tarko. 2014. "Institutional Resilience and Economic Systems: Lessons from Elinor Ostrom's Work." Comparative Economic Studies 56 (1): 52–76.

Aligica, Paul Dragos, and Vlad Tarko. 2013. "Co-production, Polycentricity, and Value Heterogeneity: The Ostroms' Public Choice Institutionalism Revisited." *American Political Science Review* 107 (4): 726–41.

Aligica, Paul Dragos, and Vlad Tarko. 2012. "Polycentricity: From Polanyi to Ostrom, and Beyond." *Governance* 25 (2): 237–62.

Anderson, Terry L., and Peter J. Hill, eds. 2001. *The Technology of Property Rights.* Lanham, MD: Rowman and Littlefield.

Andreoni, James. 1990. "Impure Altruism and Donations to Public Goods: A Theory of Warm-Glow Giving." *Economic Journal* 100 (401): 464–77.

Andreozzi, Luciano. 2005. "Hayek Reads the Literature on the Emergence of Norms." *Constitutional Political Economy* 16 (3): 227–47.

Arrow, Kenneth J. 1951. *Social Choice and Individual Values.* New Haven, CT: Yale University Press.

Aumann, Robert J. 1987. "Correlated Equilibrium as an Expression of Bayesian Rationality." *Econometrica* 55 (1): 1–18.

Aumann, Robert J. 1974. "Subjectivity and Correlation in Randomized Strategies." *Journal of Mathematical Economics* 1: 67–96.

Axelrod, Robert 1986. "An Evolutionary Approach to Norms." *American Political Science Review* 80 (4): 1095–1111.

Baier, Kurt, and Nicholas Rescher. 1969. *Values and the Future: The Impact of Technological Change on American Values.* New York: Free Press.

Barnett, Randy. 1998. *The Structure of Liberty: Justice and the Rule of Law.* New York: Oxford University Press.

Baron, David P. 2001. "Private Politics, Corporate Social Responsibility, and Integrated Strategy." *Journal of Economics and Management Strategy* 10 (1): 12.

Barry, Norman P. 1988. *The Invisible Hand in Economics and Politics: A Study in the Two Conflicting Explanations of Society: End-States and Processes.* London: Institute of Economic Affairs.

Baumol, William J. 1990. "Entrepreneurship: Productive, Unproductive, and Destructive." *Journal of Political Economy* 98 (5): 893–921.

Becker, Gary S. 1983. "A Theory of Competition among Pressure Groups for Political Influence." *Quarterly Journal of Economics* 98 (3): 371–400.

Beito, David T. 2000. *From Mutual Aid to the Welfare State: Fraternal Societies and Social Services, 1890–1967.* Chapel Hill: University of North Carolina Press.

Bergson, Adam. 1954. "On the Concept of Social Welfare." *Quarterly Journal of Economics* 68 (2): 233–52.

Bevir, Mark, and R. A. W. Rhodes. 2003. *Interpreting British Governance.* London and New York: Routledge.

Bickers, Kenneth N., and John T. Williams. 2001. *Public Policy Analysis: A Political Economy Approach.* Boston, MA: Houghton Mifflin.

Bish, Robert L. 1999. "Federalist Theory and Polycentricity: Learning from Local Governments." In *Limiting Leviathan*, edited by Donald P. Racheter and Richard E. Wagner. Cheltenham, UK, and Northampton, MA: Edward Elgar.

Bish, Robert L. 2014. "Vincent Ostrom's Contributions to Political Economy." *Publius: The Journal of Federalism* 44 (2): 227–48.

Boettke, Peter J. 2012. *Living Economics: Yesterday, Today, and Tomorrow.* Oakland, CA: Independent Institute.

Boettke, Peter J. 2001. "Why Culture Matters: Economics, Politics, and the Imprint of History." In *Calculation and Coordination: Essays on Socialism and Transitional Political Economy*, 248–65. New York: Routledge.

Boettke, Peter J. 1990. "The Theory of Spontaneous Order and Cultural Evolution in the Social Theory of FA Hayek." *Cultural Dynamics* 3 (1): 61–83.

Boettke, Peter J., and Rosolino A. Candela. 2015. "Rivalry, Polycentricism, and Institutional Evolution." *New Thinking in Austrian Political Economy* 19::1–19.

Boettke, Peter J., and Christopher J. Coyne. 2009. "Context Matters: Institutions and Entrepreneurship." *Foundations and Trends in Entrepreneurship* 5 (3): 135–209.

Boettke, Peter J., and Christopher J. Coyne. 2009. "An Entrepreneurial Theory of Social and Cultural Change." In *Markets and Civil Society: The European Experience in Comparative Perspective*, ed. Víctor Pérez-Díaz, 77–103. New York: Berghahn Books.

Boettke, Peter J., Christopher J. Coyne, and Peter T. Leeson, 2008. "Institutional Stickiness and the New Development Economics." *American Journal of Economics and Sociology* 67 (2): 331–58.

Boettke, Peter J., Jayme S. Lemke, and Liya Palagashvili. 2016. "Re-Evaluating Community Policing in a Polycentric System." *Journal of Institutional Economics* 12 (2): 305–25.

Boettke, Peter J., Jayme S. Lemke, and Liya Palagashvili. 2014. "Polycentricity, Self-Governance, and the Art & Science of Association." *Review of Austrian Economics* 28 (3): 311–35.

Boettke, Peter J., Liya Palagashvili, and Jayme Lemke. 2013. "Riding in Cars with Boys: Elinor Ostrom's Adventures with the Police." *Journal of Institutional Economics* 9 (4): 407–25.

Boudreaux, Donald J., and Randall G. Holcombe. 1989. "Government by Contract." *Public Finance Review* 17 (3): 264–80.

Boulding, Kenneth E. 1969 (1971). "The Grants Economy." *Michigan Academician* (Winter). Reprinted in Fred R. Glahe, ed. *Collected Papers of Kenneth Boulding: Vol. II: Economics.* Boulder: Colorado Associated University Press.

Bowen, Howard Rothmann. 1953. *Social Responsibilities of the Businessman*. New York: Harper.

Bowie, Norman E., and Thomas W. Dunfee. 2002. "Confronting Morality in Markets." *Journal of Business Ethics* 38 (4): 381–93.

Bozeman, Barry. 2007. *Public Values and Public Interest: Counterbalancing Economic Individualism*. Washington, DC: Georgetown University Press.

Bozeman, Barry. 2002. "Public-Value Failure: When Efficient Markets May Not Do." *Public Administration Review* 62 (2): 145–61.

Brams, Steven. 2006. "The Normative Turn in Public Choice." *Public Choice* 127 (3): 245–50.

Brandsen, Taco, and Victor Pestoff. 2006. "Co-production, the Third Sector and the Delivery of Public Services." *Public Management Review* 8 (4): 493–501.

Brennan, Geoffrey, and James M. Buchanan. 1985 (2000). *The Collected Works of James M. Buchanan, Volume 10: The Reason of Rules: Constitutional Political Economy*. Indianapolis, IN: Liberty Fund.

Brennan, Geoffrey, and James M. Buchanan. 1980. *The Power to Tax: Analytical Foundations of a Fiscal Constitution*. New York: Cambridge University Press.

Brennan, Jason, and David Schmidtz. 2010. *A History of Liberty*. Malden, MA: Wiley-Blackwell.

Buchanan, James M. 2003. "Public Choice: The Origins and Development of a Research Program." Fairfax, VA: Center for Study of Public Choice, George Mason University.

Buchanan, James M. 1994. *Ethics and Economic Progress*. Norman: University of Oklahoma Press.

Buchanan, James M. 1993 (2001). "The Individual as Participant in Political Exchange." In *The Collected Works of James M. Buchanan, Volume 18: Federalism, Liberty, and the Law*. Indianapolis, IN: Liberty Fund.

Buchanan, James M. 1991 (1999). "The Foundations for Normative Individualism." In *The Collected Works of James M. Buchanan, Volume 1: The Logical Foundations of Constitutional Liberty*. Indianapolis, IN: Liberty Fund.

Buchanan, James M. 1989 (2001). "On the Structure of an Economy: A Reemphasis of Some Classical Foundations." In *The Collected Works of James M. Buchanan, Volume 18: Federalism, Liberty, and the Law*. Indianapolis, IN: Liberty Fund.

Buchanan, James M. 1988 (2001). "Market Failure and Political Failure." In *The Collected Works of James M. Buchanan, Volume 18: Federalism, Liberty, and the Law*. Indianapolis, IN: Liberty Fund.

Buchanan, James M. 1987. *Economics: Between Predictive Science and Moral Philosophy*. College Station, TX: Texas A&M University Press.

Buchanan, James M. 1987. "Justification of the Compound Republic: The *Calculus* in Retrospect." *Cato Journal* 7 (2): 305–12.

Buchanan, James M. 1986. *Liberty, Market and State: Political Economy and the 1980s*. New York: New York University Press.

Buchanan, James M. 1979 (1999). "Politics without Romance: A Sketch of Positive Public Choice Theory and Its Normative Implications." In *The Collected Works of James M. Buchanan, Volume 1: The Logical Foundations of Constitutional Liberty*. Indianapolis, IN: Liberty Fund.

Buchanan, James M. 1979. *What Should Economists Do?* Indianapolis, IN: Liberty Fund.

Buchanan, James M. 1976 (1999). "Taxation in Fiscal Exchange." In *The Collected Works of James M. Buchanan, Volume 1: The Logical Foundations of Constitutional Liberty*. Indianapolis, IN: Liberty Fund.

Buchanan, James M. 1975 (2000). *The Collected Works of James M. Buchanan, Volume 7: The Limits of Liberty*. Indianapolis, IN: Liberty Fund.

Buchanan, James M. 1975. "The Samaritan's Dilemma." In *Altruism, Morality and Economic Theory*, edited by Edmund S. Phelps. New York: Russell Sage Foundation.

Buchanan, James M. 1969 (1999). *The Collected Works of James M. Buchanan, Volume 6: Cost and Choice: An Inquiry in Economic Theory*. Indianapolis, IN: Liberty Fund.

Buchanan, James M. 1969. "Is Economics the Science of Choice?" In *Roads to Freedom: Essays in Honour of Friedrich A. von Hayek*, edited by Erich Streissler. London: Routledge.

Buchanan, James M. 1968 (1999). *The Collected Works of James M. Buchanan, Volume 5: The Demand and Supply of Public Goods*. Indianapolis, IN: Liberty Fund.

Buchanan, James M. 1965. "An Economic Theory of Clubs." *Economica* 32 (125): 1–14.

Buchanan, James M. 1954. "Individual Choice in Voting and the Market." *Journal of Political Economy* 62 (4): 334–43.

Buchanan, James M., and Roger D. Congleton. 1998. *Politics by Principle, Not Interest: Towards Nondiscriminatory Democracy*. New York: Cambridge University Press.

Buchanan, James M., and Gordon Tullock. 1962. *The Calculus of Consent: Logical Foundations of Constitutional Democracy*. Ann Arbor: University of Michigan Press.

Burnheim, John. 2006 [1985]. *Is Democracy Possible? The Alternative to Electoral Politics*, 3rd ed. Sydney, Australia: Jump Up Publishing.

Cashore, Benjamin. 2002. "Legitimacy and the Privatization of Environmental Governance: How Non-State Market-Driven (NSMD) Governance Systems Gain Rule-Making Authority." *Governance* 15 (4): 503–29.

Caplan, Bryan. 2008. *The Myth of the Rational Voter: Why Democracies Choose Bad Policies*. Princeton, NJ: Princeton University Press.

Carroll, Archie B. 1979. "A Three-Dimensional Conceptual Model of Corporate Performance." *Academy of Management Review* 4 (4): 497–505.

Carroll, Archie B., and Ann K. Buchholtz. 2015 (2008). *Business and Society: Ethics, Sustainability, and Stakeholder Management*, 9th ed. Stamford, CT: Cengage Learning.

Chamlee-Wright, Emily, and Don Lavoi. 2001. *Culture and Enterprise: The Development, Representation and Morality of Business*. London and New York: Routledge.

Chamlee-Wright, Emily, and Virgil Henry Storr., eds. 2010. *The Political Economy of Hurricane Katrina and Community Rebound.* Cheltenham, UK: Edward Elgar.

Chamlee-Wright, Emily, and Virgil Henry Storr. 2010. "The Role of Social Entrepreneurship in Post-Katrina Community Recovery." *International Journal of Innovation and Regional Development* 2 (1): 149–64.

Chamlee-Wright, Emily, and Virgil Henry Storr. 2009. "Club Goods and Post-Disaster Community Return." *Rationality and Society* 21 (4): 429–58.

Chamlee-Wright, Emily, and Virgil Henry Storr. 2009. "'There's No Place Like New Orleans': Sense of Place and Community Recovery in the Ninth Ward after Hurricane Katrina." *Journal of Urban Affairs* 31 (5): 615–34.

Coase, Ronald H. 1974. "The Lighthouse in Economics." *Journal of Law and Economics* 17 (2): 357–76.

Coase, Ronald H. 1966. "The Economics of Broadcasting and Government Policy." *The American Economic Review* 56 (1/2): 440–47.

Coase, Ronald H. 1960. "The Problem of Social Cost." *The Journal of Law & Economics* 3: 1–44.

Coase, Ronald H. 1937. "The Nature of the Firm." *Economica* 4 (16): 386–405.

Cornell, Bradford, and Alan C. Shapiro. 1987. "Corporate Stakeholders and Corporate Finance." *Financial Management* 16 (1): 5–14.

Cornuelle, Richard C. 1983. *Healing America: What Can Be Done about the Continuing Economic Crisis*. New York: G. P. Putnam's.

Coyne, Christopher J., and Abigail R. Hall-Blanco. 2016. "Foreign Intervention, Police Militarization, and the Impact on Minority Groups." *Peace Review* 28 (2): 165–70.

Crane, Andrew. 2001. "Unpacking the Ethical Product." *Journal of Business Ethics* 30 (4): 361–73.

Crane, Andrew, Abagail McWilliams, Dirk Matten, Jeremy Moon, and Donald S. Siegel, eds. 2008. *The Oxford Handbook of Corporate Social Responsibility.* New York: Oxford University Press.

Crawford, Sue E. S., and Elinor Ostrom. 1995. "A Grammar of Institutions." *American Political Science Review* 89(3): 582–600.

Dahl, Robert A. 1989. *Democracy and Its Critics*. New Haven, CT: Yale University Press.

Dahl, Robert A. 1985. *A Preface to Economic Democracy.* Berkeley and Los Angeles: University of California Press.

Davis, Keith. 1973. "The Case for and against Business Assumption of Social Responsibilities." *Academy of Management Journal* 16 (2): 312–22.

Downs, Anthony. 1967. *Inside Bureaucracy*. Boston, MA: Little, Brown .

de Harr, Edwin van. 2015. *Degrees of Freedom: Liberal Political Philosophy and Ideology*. New Brunswick, NJ: Transaction Publishers.

de Rugy, Veronique, and Melinda Warren. 2009. "Regulatory Agency Spending Reaches New Height: An Analysis of the U.S. Budget for Fiscal Years 2008 and 2009." Regulators' Budget Report 30, Mercatus Center at George Mason University, Arlington, VA, October.

de Viti de Marco, Antonio. 1936. *First Principles of Public Finance*. New York: Harcourt Brace.

Denhardt, Robert B. 2004. *Theories of Public Organization*, 6th ed. Boston: Wadsworth.

Donaldson, Thomas, and Thomas W. Dunfee. 1999. *Ties That Bind: A Social Contracts Approach to Business Ethics*. Boston: Harvard Business School Press.

Donaldson, Thomas, and Thomas W. Dunfee. 1994. "Toward a Unified Conception of Business Ethics: Integrative Social Contracts Theory." *Academy of Management Review* 19 (2): 252–84.

Douglas, Mark. 2000. "Integrative Social Contracts Theory: Hype over Hypernorms." *Journal of Business Ethics* 26 (2): 101–10.

Dryzek, John S. 2000. *Deliberative Democracy and Beyond: Liberals, Critics, Contestations*. Oxford and New York: Oxford University Press.

Dunfee, Thomas W. 2008. "Stakeholder Theory: Managing Corporate Social Responsibility in a Multiple Actor Context." In *The Oxford Handbook of Corporate Social Responsibility*, edited by Andrew Crane, Abagail McWilliams, Dirk Matten, Jeremy Moon, and Donald S. Siegel, 346–62. New York: Oxford University Press.

Eells, Richard, and Clarence C. Walton. 1974. *Conceptual Foundations of Business*, 3rd ed. Homewood, IL: Richard D. Irwin.

Eilbirt, Henry, and I. Robert Parket. 1973. "The Practice of Business: The Current Status of Corporate Social Responsibility." *Business Horizons* 16 (4): 11.

Ellig, Jerry. 2001. *Dynamic Competition and Public Policy: Technology, Innovation, and Antitrust Issues*. New York: Cambridge University Press.

Elkington, John, 1997. *Cannibals with Forks: The Triple Bottom Line of 21st Century Business*. Oxford: Capstone.

Epstein, Richard. 2003. *Skepticism and Freedom: A Modern Case for Classical Liberalism*. Chicago: University of Chicago Press.

Evers, Adalbert, and Jean-Louis Laville. 2004. *The Third Sector in Europe*. Cheltenham, UK, and Northampton, MA: Edward Elgar.

Levi-Faur, David, ed. 2012. *The Oxford Handbook of Governance*. New York: Oxford University Press.

Levi-Faur, David, and Jacint Jordana. 2005. "The Rise of Regulatory Capitalism: The Global Diffusion of Regulatory Capitalism." *Annals of the American Academy of Political and Social Science* 598 (1): 12–32.

Ferlie, Ewan, Laurence E. Lynn Jr., and Christopher Pollitt, eds. 2005. *The Oxford Handbook of Public Management*. New York: Oxford University Press.

Frankel, Carl, 1998. *In Earth's Company: Business, Environment and the Challenge of Sustainability*. Gabriola Island, Canada: New Society Publishers.

Freeman, Edward, Jeffrey S. Harrison, Andrew C. Wicks, Bidhan L. Parmar, and Simone de Colle. 2010. *Stakeholder Theory: The State of the Art*. Cambridge, UK: Cambridge University Press.

Friedman, Milton. 1970. "The Social Responsibility of Business Is to Increase Its Profits." *New York Times Magazine*, September 13.

Friedman, Milton. 1962. *Capitalism and Freedom*. Chicago: University of Chicago Press.

Foldvary, Fred E. 2009. "Urban Planning: The Government or the Market." In *Housing America: Building Out of a Crisis*, edited by Randall G. Holcombe and Benjamin Powell. Oakland, CA: The Independent Institute.

Foldvary, Fred E., and Daniel B. Klein. 2002. "The Half-Life of Policy Rationales: How New Technology Affects Old Policy Issues." *Knowledge, Technology and Policy* 15 (3): 82–92.

Fox, Tom, Halina Ward, and Bruce Howard. 2002. *Public Sector Roles in Strengthening Corporate Social Responsibility: A Baseline Study*. Washington, DC: World Bank.

Frederickson, George H., Kevin B. Smith, Christopher W. Larimer, and Michael J. Licari. 2003 (2012). *The Public Administration Theory Primer*, 2nd ed. Boulder, CO: Westview Press.

Garriga, Elisabet, and Domènec Melé. 2004. "Corporate Social Responsibility Theories: Mapping the Territory." *Journal of Business Ethics* 53 (1): 51–71.

Gaus, Gaus. 2016. *The Tyranny of the Ideal: Justice in a Diverse Society*. Princeton, NJ: Princeton University Press.

Gaus, Gerald. 2011. *The Order of Public Reason: A Theory of Freedom and Morality in a Diverse and Bounded World*. New York: Cambridge University Press.

Gaus, Gerald F. 2007. "Hayek on the Evolution of Society and Mind." In *Cambridge Companion to Hayek*, 232–58. Cambridge: Cambridge University Press.

Gibson, Clark C., Krister Andersson, Elinor Ostrom, and Sujai Shivakumar. 2005. *The Samaritan's Dilemma: The Political Economy of Development Aid*. Oxford: Oxford University Press.

Gigerenzer, Gerd. 2008. *Rationality for Mortals: How People Cope with Uncertainty*. New York: Oxford University Press.

Gilardi, Fabrizio. 2009. *Delegation in the Regulatory State: Independent Regulatory Agencies in Western Europe*. Cheltenham, UK, and Northampton, MA: Edward Elgar.

Gilardi, Fabrizio. 2005. "The Institutional Foundations of Regulatory Capitalism: The Diffusion of Independent Regulatory Agencies in Western Europe." *The Annals of the American Academy of Political and Social Science* 598 (1): 84–101.

Gilardi, Fabrizio. 2004. "Institutional Change in Regulatory Policies: Regulation through Independent Agencies and the Three New Institutionalisms." In *The Politics of Regulation: Institutions and Regulatory Reforms for the Age of Governance*, 67–89. Cheltenham, UK: Edward Elgar.

Godfrey, Paul C. 2005. "The Relationship between Corporate Philanthropy and Shareholder Wealth: A Risk Management Perspective." *Academy of Management Review* 30 (4): 777–98.

Gordon, Scott. 1999. *Controlling the State: Constitutionalism from Ancient Athens to Today*. Cambridge, MA: Harvard University Press.

Guttman, J. M. 1998. "Unanimity and Majority Rule: The Calculus of Consent Reconsidered." *European Journal of Political Economy* 14 (2): 189–207.

Habisch, André, Jan Jonker, Martina Wegner, and René Schmidpeter, eds. 2005. *Corporate Social Responsibility across Europe: Discovering National Perspectives of Corporate Citizenship*. Berlin: Springer.

Habisch, André, and Jeremy Moon. 2006. "Social Capital and Corporate Social Responsibility." In *The Challenge of Organizing and Implementing Corporate Social Responsibility*, edited by Jan Jonker and Marco de Witte, 63–77. Basingstoke, Hampshire, UK: Palgrave.

Harmon, Michael M. 1981. *Action Theory for Public Administration*. New York: Longman.

Hanson, Robin. 2013. "Shall We Vote on Values, But Bet on Beliefs?" *Journal of Political Philosophy* 21 (2): 151–78.

Harrison, Jeffrey S., and R. Edward Freeman. 1999. "Stakeholders, Social Responsibility, and Performance: Empirical Evidence and Theoretical Perspectives." *Academy of Management Review* 42 (5): 479–87.

Hayek, Friedrich A. 2002. "Competition as a Discovery Procedure." *Quarterly Journal of Austrian Economics* 5 (3): 9–23.

Hayek, Friedrich A. 1976. *Law, Legislation and Liberty, Volume 2: The Mirage of Social Justice*. Chicago: University of Chicago Press.

Hayek, Friedrich A. 1973. *Law, Legislation and Liberty, Volume 1: Rules and Order*. Chicago: University of Chicago Press.

Hayek, Friedrich A. 1967. *Studies in Philosophy, Politics and Economics*. Chicago: University of Chicago Press.

Hayek, Friedrich A. 1960. *The Constitution of Liberty*. Chicago: University of Chicago Press.

Hayek, Friedrich A. 1948. "Individualism: True and False." In *Individualism and Economic Order*, 1–32. Chicago: University of Chicago Press.

Hayek, Friedrich A. 1945. "The Use of Knowledge in Society." *American Economic Review* 35 (4): 519–30.

Hayek, Friedrich A. 1944. *The Road to Serfdom*. Chicago: University of Chicago Press.

Heap, Shaun Hargreaves, Martin Hollis, Bruce Lyons, Robert Sugden, and Albert Weale. 1992. *The Theory of Choice: A Critical Guide*. Oxford and Cambridge, MA: Wiley-Blackwell.

Hill, Charles W. L. 1995. "National Institutional Structures, Transaction Cost Economizing and Competitive Advantage: The Case of Japan." *Organization Science* 6 (1): 119–31.

Hirschman, Albert O. 1970. *Exit, Voice, and Loyalty: Responses to Decline in Firms, Organizations, and States.* Cambridge, MA: Harvard University Press.

Holcombe, Randall G. 1994. *The Economic Foundations of Government.* New York: New York University Press.

Horwitz, Steven G. 2009. "Wal-Mart to the Rescue: Private Enterprise's Response to Hurricane Katrina." *Independent Review* 13 (4): 511–28.

Husted, Bryan W., and José De Jesus Salazar. 2006. "Taking Friedman Seriously: Maximizing Profits and Social Performance." *Journal of Management Studies* 43 (1): 75–91.

Jackson, John E., and David C. King. 1989. "Public Goods, Private Interests, and Representation." *American Political Science Review* 83 (4): 1143–64.

Jensen, Michael C. 2002. "Value Maximization, Stakeholder Theory, and the Corporate Objective Function." *Business Ethics Quarterly* 12 (2): 235–56.

Joelson, Mark R. 2006. *An International Antitrust Primer: A Guide to the Operation of United States, European Union and Other Key Competition Laws in the Global Economy*, 3rd ed. Alphen aan den Rijn, Netherlands: Kluwer Law International.

Jones, Thomas M. 1995. "Instrumental Stakeholder Theory: A Synthesis of Ethics and Economics." *Academy of Management Review* 20 (2): 404–37.

Jordana, Jacint, and David Levi-Faur, eds. 2004. *The Politics of Regulation: Institutions and Regulatory Reforms for the Age of Governance.* Cheltenham, UK, and Northampton, MA: Edward Elgar.

Jordana, Jacint, David Levi-Faur, and Xavier Fernández i Marán. 2011. "The Global Diffusion of Regulatory Agencies: Channels of Transfer and Stages of Diffusion." *Comparative Political Studies* 44 (10): 1343–69.

Jorgensen, Torben Beck, and Barry Bozeman. 2007. "Public Values: An Inventory." *Administration and Society* 39 (3): 354–81.

Kahn, Herman. 1973. "The Alternative World Futures Approach." In *Search for Alternatives: Public Policy and the Study of the Future*, edited by Tugwell Franklin. Cambridge, MA: Winthrop.

Kedia, B. L., and E. C. Kuntz. 1981. "The Context of Social Performance: An Empirical Study of Texas Banks." In *Research in Corporate Social Performance and Policy*, vol. 3, edited by L. E. Preston, 133–54. Greenwich, CT: JAI.

Kirzner, Israel M. 1997. "Entrepreneurial Discovery and the Competitive Market Process: An Austrian Approach." *Journal of Economic Literature* 35 (1): 60–85.

Kirzner, Israel M. 1992. *The Meaning of the Market Process: Essays in the Development of Modern Austrian Economics.* London: Routledge.

Kirzner, Israel M. 1985. "The Perils of Regulation." In *Discovery and the Capitalist Process.* Chicago: University of Chicago Press.

Kirzner, Israel M. 1973. *Competition and Entrepreneurship.* Chicago: University of Chicago Press.

Klein, Benjamin, Robert G. Crawford, and Armen A. Alchian. 1978. "Vertical Integration, Appropriable Rents, and the Competitive Contracting Process." *Journal of Law and Economics* 21 (2): 297–326.

Klein, Peter G., Joseph T. Mahoney, Anita M. McGahan, and Christos N. Pitelis. 2010. "Toward a Theory of Public Entrepreneurship." *European Management Review* 7 (1): 1–15.

Knight, Jack, and James Johnson. 2007. "The Priority of Democracy: A Pragmatist Approach to Political-Economic Institutions and the Burden of Justification." *American Political Science Review* 101 (1): 47–61.

Knight, Jack, and James Johnson. 2011. *The Priority of Democracy: Political Consequences of Pragmatism.* Princeton, NJ: Princeton University Press.

Kok, Peter, Ton van der Wiele, Richard McKenna, and Alan Brown. 2001. "A Corporate Social Responsibility Audit within a Quality Management Framework." *Journal of Business Ethics* 31 (4): 285–97.

Koppell, Jonathan G. S. 2003. *The Politics of Quasi-Government: Hybrid Organizations and the Dynamics of Bureaucratic Control.* Cambridge, UK: Cambridge University Press.

Kukathas, Chandran. 2003. *The Liberal Archipelago: A Theory of Diversity and Freedom.* New York: Oxford University Press.

Kurucz, Elizabeth C., Barry A. Colbert, and David Wheeler. 2008. "The Business Case for Corporate Social Responsibility." In *The Oxford Handbook of Corporate Social Responsibility*, edited by Andrew Crane, Abagail McWilliams, Dirk Matten, Jeremy Moon, and Donald S. Siegel, 83–112. New York: Oxford University Press.

Lankoski, Leena. 2000. "Determinants of Environmental Profit: An Analysis of the Firm-Level Relationship between Environmental Performance and Economic Performance." PhD diss. Helsinki University of Technology.

Leeson, Peter T. 2014. *Anarchy Unbound: Why Self-Governance Works Better Than You Think*. Cambridge and New York: Cambridge University Press.

Leeson, Peter T. 2011. "Government, Clubs, and Constitutions." *Journal of Economic Behavior and Organization* 80 (2): 301–8.

Leeson, Peter T., and Peter J. Boettke. 2009. "Two-Tiered Entrepreneurship and Economic Development." *International Review of Law and Economics* 29 (3): 252–59.

Leighton, Wayne A., and Edward J. Lopez. 2012. *Madmen, Intellectuals, and Academic Scribblers: The Economic Engine of Political Change*. Stanford, CA: Stanford University Press.

Lerner, Linda D., and Gerald E. Fryxell. 1988. "An Empirical Study of the Predictors of Corporate Social Performance: A Multi-dimensional Analysis." *Journal of Business Ethics* 7 (12): 951–59.

Levy, Jacob T. 2015. *Rationalism, Pluralism, and Freedom*. New York: Oxford University Press.

Lopez, German. 2016. "8 Shocking Findings from a City Task Force's Investigation into the Chicago Police Department." *Vox*, April 13, http://www.vox.com/2016/4/13/11424638/chicago-police-racism-report.

Lovrich, Nicholas P., and Max Neiman. 1984. *Public Choice Theory in Public Administration: An Annotated Bibliography*. New York: Garland.

Lydenberg, Steven. 2005. *Corporations and the Public Interest: Guiding the Invisible Hand*. San Francisco: Berrett-Koehler.

Lynn Jr., Laurence E. 2007. "Public Management: A Concise History of the Field." In *The Oxford Handbook of Public Management*, edited by Ewan Ferlie, Laurence E. Lynn Jr., and Christopher Pollitt, 27–50. New York: Oxford University Press.

Lynn Jr., Laurence E. 2006. *Public Management: Old and New*. New York: Routledge.

Lynn, Naomi B., and Aaron B. Wildavsky, eds. 1990. *Public Administration: The State of the Discipline*. Chatham, NJ: Chatham House.

Mahoney, Joseph T. 2006. "Towards a Stakeholder Theory of Strategic Management." Department of Business Administration, College of Business, University of Illinois at Urbana-Champaign.

Mainzer, Lewis C. 1973. *Political Bureaucracy*. Glenview, IL: Scott, Foresman.

Majone, Giandomencio. 1999. "The Regulatory State and Its Legitimacy Problems." *Western European Politics* 22 (1): 1–24.

Marini, Frank, ed. 1971. *Toward a New Public Administration: The Minnowbrook Perspective*. Scranton, PA: Chandler.

Massolf, L., and H. Seldman. 1980. "The Blurred Boundaries of Public Administration." *Public Administrative Review* 40 (2): 124–30.

McCurdy, Howard E. 1986. *Public Administration: A Bibliographic Guide to the Literature*. New York: Marcel Dekker.

McPhail, Edward, and Vlad Tarko. 2017. "The Evolution of Governance Structures in a Polycentric System." In *Handbook of Behavioral Economics and Smart Decision-Making: Rational Decision-Making within the Bounds of Reason*, edited by Morris Altman, 290–313. Cheltenham, UK: Edward Elgar.

McGinnis, Michael D. 2016. "Polycentric Governance in Theory and Practice: Dimensions of Aspirations and Practical Limitations." The Ostrom Workshop Polycentricity Workshop, Indiana University, Bloomington.

McGinnis, Michael D. 2011. "An Introduction to IAD and the Language of the Ostrom Workshop: A Simple Guide to a Complex Framework." *Policy Studies Journal* 39 (1): 179.

McGinnis, Michael D. 2010. "Religion Policy and the Faith-Based Initiative: Navigating the Shifting Boundaries between Church and State." *Forum on Public Policy* 4 and Indiana University-Bloomington: School of Public and Environmental Affairs Research Paper No. 2011-02-02.

McGinnis, Michael D. 2008. "Legal Pluralism, Polycentricity, and Faith-Based Organizations in Global Governance." In *The Struggle to Constitute and Sustain Productive Orders*, edited by Mark Sproule-Jones, Barbara Allen, and Filippo Sabetti, 45–64. Lanham, MD: Lexington.

McGinnis, Michael D., ed. 1999. *Polycentric Governance and Development: Readings from the Workshop in Political Theory and Policy Analysis*. Ann Arbor: University of Michigan Press.

McGinnis, Michael D., and Elinor Ostrom. 2012. "Reflections on Vincent Ostrom, Public Administration, and Polycentricity." *Public Administration Review* 72 (1): 15–25.

McWilliams, Abagail, and Donald Siegel. 2001. "Corporate Social Responsibility: A Theory of the Firm Perspective." *Academy of Management Review* 26 (1): 117–27.

Medema, Steven G. 2009. *The Hesitant Hand: Taming Self-Interest in the History of Economic Ideas*. Princeton, NJ: Princeton University Press.

Medema, Steven G. 1995. "Finding His Own Way: The Legacy of Ronald Coase in Economic Analysis." In *The Legacy of Ronald Coase in Economic Analysis, Vol. 1*, edited by Steven G. Medema, iix–lxix. Aldershot, UK, and Brookfield, VT: Edward Elgar.

Melé, Domènec. 2008. "Corporate Social Responsibility Theories." In *The Oxford Handbook of Corporate Social Responsibility*, edited by Andrew Crane, Abagail McWilliams, Dirk Matten, Jeremy Moon, and Donald S. Siegel. New York: Oxford University Press.

Mill, John Stuart. 1859 (1992). *On Liberty and Utilitarianism*. New York: Knopf.

Mill, John Stuart. 1848 (1909). *Principles of Political Economy with Some of Their Applications to Social Philosophy*. London: Longmans Green.

Miller, Gary J. 1992. *Managerial Dilemmas: The Political Economy of Hierarchy*. Cambridge: Cambridge University Press.

Miller, Peter, and Nikolas Rose. 2008. *Governing the Present: Administering Economic, Social and Personal Life*. Cambridge, UK, and Malden, MA: Polity.

Mises, Ludwig von. 1927 (2005). *Liberalism: The Classical Tradition.* Translated by Ralph Raico. Edited by Bettina Bien Greaves. Indianapolis, IN: Liberty Fund.

Mitchell, Ronald K., Bradley R. Agle, and Donna J. Wood. 1997. "Toward a Theory of Stakeholder Identification and Salience: Defining the Principle of Who and What Really Counts." *Academy of Management Review* 22 (4): 853–86.

Moe, Ronald C. 2001. "The Emerging Federal Quasi Government: Issues of Management and Accountability." *Public Administration Review* 61(3): 290–312.

Moon, Jeremy, and David Vogel. 2008. "Corporate Social Responsibility, Government, and Civil Society." In *The Oxford Handbook of Corporate Social Responsibility*, edited by Andrew Crane, Abagail McWilliams, Dirk Matten, Jeremy Moon, and Donald S. Siegel, 303–23. New York: Oxford University Press.

Mosher, Frederick C. 1982. *Democracy and the Public Service*. Oxford: Oxford University Press.

Mueller, Dennis C. 2003. *Public Choice III*. Cambridge: Cambridge University Press.

Muirhead, Sophia A. 1999. *Corporate Contributions: The View from Fifty Years.* New York: Conference Board.

Munger, Michael C. 2010. "Endless Forms Most Beautiful and Most Wonderful: Elinor Ostrom and the Diversity of Institutions." *Public Choice* 143 (3/4): 263–68.

Niskanen, William A. 1973. *Bureaucracy—Servant or Master? Lessons from America*. London: Institute of Economic Affairs.

Oakerson, Ronald J. 1999. *Governing Local Public Economies: Creating the Civic Metropolis*. San Francisco: ICS Press.

Oakerson, Ronald J., and Roger B. Parks. 2011. "The Study of Local Public Economies: Multi-organizational, Multi-level Institutional Analysis and Development." *Policy Studies Journal* 39 (1): 147–67.

Oakerson, Ronald J., and Roger B. Parks, 1988. "Citizen Voice and Public Entrepreneurship: The Organizational Dynamic of a Complex Metropolitan County." *Publius* 18 (4): 91–112.

Oakeshott, Michael 1991. *Rationalism in Politics and Other Essays*. Indianapolis, IN: Liberty Fund.

Olson, Mancur. 1969. "The Principle of 'Fiscal Equivalence': The Division of Responsibilities among Different Levels of Government." *American Economic Review* 59 (2): 479–87.

Olson, Mancur. 1982. *The Rise and Decline of Nations: Economic Growth, Stagflation, and Social Rigidities*. New Haven, CT: Yale University Press.

Olson, Mancur. 1971 (1965). *The Logic of Collective Action: Public Goods and the Theory of Groups*, rev. ed. Cambridge, MA: Harvard University Press.

&Ostrom, Elinor. 2014. "Do Institutions for Collective Action Evolve?" *Journal of Bioeconomics* 16 (1): 3–30.

Ostrom, Elinor. 2010. "Beyond Markets and States: Polycentric Governance of Complex Economic Systems." *American Economic Review* 100 (3): 641–672.

Ostrom, Elinor, 2010. "Polycentric Systems for Coping with Collective Action and Global Environmental Change." *Global Environmental Change* 20 (4): 550–57.

Ostrom, Elinor. 2008. "Developing a Method for Analyzing Institutional Change." In *Alternative Institutional Structures: Evolution and Impact*, edited by Sandra S. Batie and Nicholas Mercuro. New York: Routledge.

Ostrom, Elinor. 2005. *Understanding Institutional Diversity*. Princeton, NJ: Princeton University Press.

Ostrom, Elinor. 2000. "The Danger of Self-Evident Truths." *PS: Political Science and Politics* 33 (1): 33–46.

Ostrom, Elinor. 1999. "Polycentricity, Complexity, and the Commons." *The Good Society* 9 (2): 37–41.

Ostrom, Elinor. 1998. "The Comparative Study of Public Economies." *American Economist* 42 (1): 3–17.

Ostrom, Elinor. 1998. "A Behavioral Approach to the Rational Choice Theory of Collective Action." *American Political Science Review* 92 (1): 1–22.

Ostrom, Elinor. 1992. *Crafting Institutions for Self-Governing Irrigation Systems*. San Francisco and Lanham, MD: ICS Press.

Ostrom, Elinor. 1990. *Governing the Commons: The Evolution of Institutions for Collective Action*. New York: Cambridge University Press.

Ostrom, Elinor. 1986. "An Agenda for the Study of Institutions." *Public Choice* 48 (1): 3–25.

Ostrom, Elinor, ed. 1976. *The Delivery of Urban Services: Outcomes of Change*. Thousand Oaks, CA: Sage Publications.

Ostrom, Elinor. 1972. "Metropolitan Reform: Propositions Derived from Two Traditions." *Social Science Quarterly* 53 (3): 474–493.

Ostrom, Elinor, Christina Chang, Mark Pennington, and Vlad Tarko. 2012. *The Future of the Commons: Beyond Market Failure and Government Regulation*. London: Institute of Economic Affairs.

Ostrom, Elinor, Roy Gardner, and James Walker. 1994. *Rules, Games, and Common-Pool Resources*. Ann Arbor: University of Michigan Press.

Ostrom, Elinor, and Roger B. Parks. 1999. "Neither Gargantua nor the Land of Lilliputs: Conjectures on Mixed Systems of Metropolitan Organization." In *Polycentricity and Local Public Economies: Readings from the Workshop in Political Theory and Policy Analysis*, edited by Michael D. McGinnis, 284–305. Ann Arbor: University of Michigan Press.

Ostrom, Elinor, Roger B. Parks, and Gordon P. Whitaker. 1978. *Patterns of Metropolitan Policing*. Cambridge, MA: Ballinger.

Ostrom, Elinor, Roger B. Parks, and Gordon P. Whitaker. 1974. "Defining and Measuring Structural Variations in Interorganizational Arrangements." *Publius* 4 (4): 87–108.

Ostrom, Elinor, James Walker, and Roy Gardner. 1992. "Covenants with and without a Sword: Self-Governance Is Possible." *American Political Science Review* 86 (2): 404–17.

Ostrom, Vincent. 1997. *The Meaning of Democracy and the Vulnerability of Democracies: A Response to Tocqueville's Challenge*. Ann Arbor: University of Michigan Press.

Ostrom, Vincent. 1993. "Epistemic Choice and Public Choice." *Public Choice* 77 (1): 163–76.

Ostrom, Vincent. 1993. "The Human Condition (Preliminary Draft)." *Workshop in Political Theory and Policy Analysis*. Bloomington: Indiana University.

Ostrom, Vincent. 1993c. "The Place of Languages in the Political Economy of Life in Human Societies." *Working Paper No. W93-6, Workshop in Political Theory and Policy Analysis*. Indiana University.

Ostrom, Vincent. 1991. *The Meaning of American Federalism: Constituting a Self-Governing Society.* San Francisco: ICS Press.

Ostrom, Vincent. 1991. "Polycentricity: The Structural Basis of Self-Governing Systems." In *The Meaning of American Federalism*, 223–48. San Francisco: ICS Press.

Ostrom, Vincent. 1991. "Some Ontological and Epistemological Puzzles in Policy Analysis." *Working Paper No. W91-16, Workshop in Political Theory and Policy Analysis*. Indiana University.

Ostrom, Vincent. 1990. "Problems of Cognition as a Challenge to Policy Analysts and Democratic Societies." *Working Paper No. 90-5, Workshop in Political Theory and Policy Analysis*. Indiana University.

Ostrom, Vincent. 1987 (2008). *The Political Theory of the Compound Republic: Designing the American Experiment*, 3rd rev. edition. Lanham, MD: Lexington Books.

Ostrom, Vincent. 1986. "The Constitutional Level of Analysis: A Challenge." *Working Paper No. 85-41, Workshop in Political Theory and Policy Analysis.* Indiana University.

Ostrom, Vincent. 1984. "Why Governments Fail: An Inquiry into the Use of Instruments of Evil to Do Good." In *The Theory of Public Choice—II*, edited by James M. Buchanan and Robert D. Tollison. Ann Arbor: University of Michigan Press.

Ostrom, Vincent. 1980. "Artisanship and Artifact." *Public Administration Review* 40 (4): 309–17.

Ostrom, Vincent. 1973 (2008). *The Intellectual Crisis in American Public Administration*, 3rd ed. Tuscaloosa: University of Alabama Press.

Ostrom, Vincent. 1973. "Order and Change Amid Increasing Relative Ignorance." *Working Paper No. W73-1, Workshop in Political Theory and Policy Analysis*. Indiana University.

Ostrom, Vincent. 1972 (1999). "Polycentricity (Part I)." In *Polycentricity and Local Public Economies: Readings from the Workshop in Political Theory and Policy Analysis*, edited by Michael D. McGinnis. Ann Arbor: University of Michigan Press.

Ostrom, Vincent. 1972 (1999). "Polycentricity (Part II)." In *Polycentricity and Local Public Economies: Readings from the Workshop in Political Theory and Policy Analysis*, edited by Michael D. McGinnis. Ann Arbor: University of Michigan Press.

Ostrom, Vincent. 1964. "Editorial Comment: Developments in the 'No-Name' Fields of Public Administration." *Public Administration Review* 24 (1): 62–63.

Ostrom, Elinor, and Vincent Ostrom. 2004. "The Quest for Meaning in Public Choice." *American Journal of Economics and Sociology* 63 (1): 105–47.

Ostrom, Vincent, and Elinor Ostrom. 1999. "Legal and Political Conditions of Water Resource Development." In *Polycentric Governance and Development: Readings from the Workshop in Political Theory and Policy Analysis*, edited by Michael McGinnis. Ann Arbor: University of Michigan Press.

Ostrom, Vincent, and Elinor Ostrom. 1991 (1977). "Public Goods and Public Choices." In *The Meaning of American Federalism*, 163–97. San Francisco: ICS Press. Originally published in E.S. Savas, ed. *Alternatives for Delivering Public Services: Toward Improved Performance*. Boulder, CO: Westview Press, 1977. Also included in *Polycentricity and Local Public Economies: Readings from the Workshop in Political Theory and Policy Analysis*, edited by Michael D. McGinnis, 75–103. Ann Arbor: University of Michigan Press, 1999.

Ostrom, Vincent, Robert Bish, and Elinor Ostrom. 1988. *Local Government in the United States.* San Francisco, CA: ICS Press.

Ostrom, Vincent, Charles M. Tiebout, and Robert Warren. 1961. "The Organization of Government in Metropolitan Areas: A Theoretical Inquiry." *American Political Science Review* 55 (4): 831–42.

Overeem, Patrick. 2012. *The Politics–Administration Dichotomy: Toward a Constitutional Perspective*, 2nd ed. Boca Raton, FL: CRC Press.

Overeem, Patrick. 2005. "The Value of the Dichotomy: Politics, Administration, and the Political Neutrality of Administrators." *Administrative Theory and Praxis* 27 (2): 311–29.

Pahl-Wostl, Claudia and Christian Knieper, 2014. "The Capacity of Water Governance to Deal with the Climate Change Adaptation Challenge: Using Fuzzy Set Qualitative Comparative Analysis to Distinguish between Polycentric, Fragmented and Centralized Regimes." *Global Environmental Change* 29: 139–54.

Parks, Robert B., Paula C. Baker, Larry Kiser, Ronald Oakerson, Elinor Ostrom, Vincent Ostrom, Stephen L. Percy, Martha B. Vandivort, Gordon P. Whitacker, and Rick Wilson. 1981. "Consumers as Coproducers of Public Services: Some Economic and Institutional Considerations." *Policy Studies Journal* 9 (7): 1001–11.

Pava, Moses L., and Joshua Krausz. 1996. "The Association between Corporate Social-Responsibility and Financial Performance: The Paradox of Social Cost." *Journal of Business Ethics* 15 (3): 321–57.

Peattie, Ken. 2001. "Golden Goose or Wild Goose? The Hunt for the Green Consumer." *Business Strategy and the Environment* 10 (4): 187–99.

Pennington, Mark. 2011. *Robust Political Economy: Classical Liberalism and the Future of Public Policy.* Cheltenham, UK: Edward Elgar.

Pestoff, Victor, Taco Brandsen, and Bram Verschuere, eds. 2012. *New Public Governance, the Third Sector and Co-production.* New York: Routledge.

Peters, B. Guy, and John Pierre. 1998. "Governance without Government? Rethinking Public Administration." *Journal of Public Administration Research and Theory* 8 (2): 223–43.

Pfiffner, James. 1967. *Public Administration.* New York: The Ronald Press Company.

Pigou, A. C. 1935. *Economics in Practice: Six Lectures on Current Issues.* London: Macmillan.

Pigou, A. C. 1920 (1932). *The Economics of Welfare,* 4th ed. London: Macmillan.

Pigou, A. C. 1912. *Wealth and Welfare.* London: Macmillan.

Polanyi, Michael. 1951 (1998). *The Logic of Liberty.* Indianapolis, IN: Liberty Fund.

Popper, Karl R. 1960. *The Logic of Scientific Discovery.* London: Hutchinson of London.

Power, Michael. 1997. *The Audit Society: Rituals of Verification.* Oxford and New York: Oxford University Press.

Prahalad, C. K., and Allen Hammond. 2002. "Serving the World's Poor, Profitably." *Harvard Business Review* 80 (9): 48–57.

Prahalad, C. K. 2009 (2014). *The Fortune at the Bottom of the Pyramid: Eradicating Poverty Through Profits,* 5th ed. Upper Saddle River, NJ: Wharton School Publishing.

Preston, Lee E., and Douglas P. O'Bannon. 1997. "The Corporate Social-Financial Performance Relationship: A Typology and Analysis." *Business and Society* 36 (4): 419–29.

Public Administration Section of APSA. 2005. "Gaus Awards." *Public Administration Section Newsletter* 4 (1): 1–2.

Raadschelders, Jos C. N. 2013. *Public Administration: The Interdisciplinary Study of Government.* New York: Oxford University Press.

Rawls, John. 1971 (1999). *A Theory of Justice, Revised Edition.* Cambridge, MA: Belknap Press.

Rescher, N. 1993. *Pluralism: Against the Demand for Consensus.* Oxford: Oxford University Press.

Riker, William H. 1982. *Liberalism against Populism: A Confrontation between the Theory of Democracy and the Theory of Social Choice.* New York: Freeman.

Riordan, Christian M., Robert D. Gatewood, and Jodi Barnes Bill. 1997. "Corporate Image: Employee Reactions and Implications for Managing Corporate Social Performance." *Journal of Business Ethics* 16 (4): 401–12.

Rozin, Paul. 1999. "The Process of Moralization." *Psychological Science* 10 (3): 218–21.

Rozin, Paul 1997. "Moralization." In *Morality and Health,* ed. Allan M. Brandt and Paul Rozin, 379–402. New York: Routledge.

Rubin, Paul H. 1994 (2001). "Ideology." In *The Elgar Companion to Public Choice,* edited by William F. Shughart II and Laura Razzolini. Cheltenham, UK: Edward Elgar.

Rutgers, Mark R. 2010. "Theory and Scope of Public Administration: An Introduction to the Study's Epistemology." *Public Administration Review: Foundations of Public Administration Series.*

Salamon, Lester M., and Helmut K. Anheier. 1997. "The Civil Society Sector." *Society* 34 (2): 60–65.

Salazar, José, and Bryan W. Husted. 2008. "Principals and Agents: Further Thoughts on the Fiedmanite Critique of Corporate Social Responsibility." In *The Oxford Handbook of Corporate Social Responsibility,* edited by Andrew Crane, Abagail McWilliams, Dirk Matten, Jeremy Moon, and Donald S. Siegel. New York: Oxford University Press.

Salzmann, Oliver, Aileen Ionescu-Somers, and Ulrich Steger. 2005. "The Business Case for Corporate Sustainability: Literature Review and Research Options." *European Management Journal* 23 (1): 27–36.

Schmidtz, David. 1995. *Rational Choice and Moral Agency*. Princeton, NJ: Princeton University Press.

Schmidtz, David. 2006. *Elements of Justice*. New York: Cambridge University Press.

Schumpeter, Joseph A. 1954. *History of Economic Analysis*. New York: Oxford University Press.

Scott, James C. 1998. *Seeing Like a State: How Certain Schemes to Improve the Human Condition Have Failed*. New Haven, CT: Yale University Press.

Searle, John R. 2006. "Social Ontology: Some Basic Principles." *Anthropological Theory* 6 (1): 12–29.

Searle, John R. 1995. *The Construction of Social Reality*. New York: Free Press. Sen, Amartya. 1999. "The Possibility of Social Choice." *American Economic Review* 89 (3): 349–78.

Simmons, Randy T. 2011. *Beyond Politics: The Roots of Government Failure*. Oakland, CA: Independent Institute.

Simon, Herbert A. 1945 (1997). *Administrative Behavior*, 4th ed. New York: Free Press.

Shepsle, Kenneth A., and Mark S. Bonchek. 1997. *Analyzing Politics: Rationality, Behavior, and Institutions* New York and London: W. W. Norton.

Smith, Adam, Richard E. Wagner, and Bruce Yandle. 2011. "A Theory of Entangled Political Economy, with Application to TARP and NRA." *Public Choice* 148 (1/2): 45–66.

Smith, Vernon L. 2008. *Rationality in Economics: Constructivist and Ecological Forms*. New York: Cambridge University Press.

Sobel, Russell S., and Randall G. Holcombe. 2001. "The Unanimous Voting Rule Is Not the Political Equivalent to Market Exchange." *Public Choice* 106 (3/4): 233–242.

Sørensen, Eva. 2007. "Public Administration as Metagovernance." In *Public Administration in Transition: Theory, Practice, Methodology*, edited by Gunnar Gjelstrup and Eva Sørensen, 111–12. Copenhagen: DJØF Publishing.

Spicer, Michael W. 2010. *In Defense of Politics in Public Administration: A Value Pluralist Perspective*. Tuscaloosa: University of Alabama Press.

Spicer, Michael W. 2001. *Public Administration and the State: A Postmodern Perspective*. Tuscaloosa: University of Alabama Press.

Spicer, Michael W. 1998. "Public Administration, Social Science, and Political Association." *Administration and Society* 30 (1): 35–52.

Spicer, Michael W. 1993. "On Friedrich Hayek and Public Administration: An Argument for Discretion Within Rules." *Administration and Society* 25 (1): 46–59.

Spicer, Michael W. 1990. "A Contractarian Approach to Public Administration." *Administration and Society* 22 (3): 303–316.

Spicer, Michael W. 1985. "A Public Choice Approach to Motivating People in Bureaucratic Organizations." *Academy of Management Review* 10 (3): 518–526.

Sproule-Jones, Mark, Barbara Allen, and Filippo Sabetti. 2008. "Normative and Empirical Inquiries into Systems of Governance." In *The Struggle to Constitute and Sustain Productive Orders: Vincent Ostrom's Quest to Understand Human Affairs*, edited by Mark Sproule-Jones, Barbara Allen, and Filippo Sabetti, 3–10. Lanham, MD: Lexington Books.

Sproule-Jones, Mark, Barbara Allen, and Filippo Sabetti, eds. 2008. *The Struggle to Constitute and Sustain Productive Orders: Vincent Ostrom's Quest to Understand Human Affairs*. Lanham, MD: Lexington Books.

Starling, Grover. 1998. *Managing the Public Sector*. Boston: Wadsworth.

Stigler, George J. 1962. "Information in the Labor Market." *Journal of Political Economy* 70 (5): 94–105.

Stillman II, Richard J. 2010. *Public Administration: Concepts and Cases*, 9th ed. Boston: Cengage Learning.

Stillman II, Richard J. 1991 (1999). *Preface to Public Administration: A Search for Themes and Direction*. Burke, VA: Chatelaine Press.

Stringham, Edward Peter, and Todd J Zywicki. 2011. "Hayekian Anarchism." *Journal of Economic Behavior and Organization* 78 (3): 290–301.

Stringham, Edward Peter. 2011. "Embracing Morals in Economics: The Role of Internal Moral Constraints in a Market Economy." *Journal of Economic Behavior and Organization* 78 (1): 98–109.

Stringham, Edward Peter. 2015. *Private Governance: Creating Order in Economic and Social Life.* New York and Oxford: Oxford University Press.

Storr, Nona Martin, Emily Chamlee-Wright, and Virgil Henry Storr. 2015. *How We Came Back: Voices from Post-Katrina New Orleans.* Arlington, VA: Mercatus Center at George Mason University.

Storr, Virgil Henry, Stephanie Haeffele, and Laura Grube. 2015. *Community Revival in the Wake of Disaster: Lessons in Local Entrepreneurship with Stefanie HaeffeleBalch and Laura E. Grube*.* New York: Palgrave Macmillian.

Storr, Virgil Henry, and Laura Grube. 2013. The Capacity for Self-Governance and Post-disaster Resiliency. *The Review of Austrian Economics*, 1–24.

Story, Dawn, and Trevor J. Price. 2006. "Corporate Social Responsibility and Risk Management." *Journal of Corporate Citizenship* 22: 39–51.

Sugden, Robert. 1986 (2005). *The Economics of Rights, Co-operation and Welfare*, 2nd ed. New York: Palgrave Macmillan.

Swanson, Diane L. 1995. "Addressing a Theoretical Problem by Reorienting the Corporate Social Performance Model." *Academy of Management Review* 20 (1): 43–64.

Tarko, Vlad. 2016. *Elinor Ostrom: An Intellectual Biography.* London: Rowman and Littlefield International.

Tarko, Vlad. 2015. "Polycentric Structure and Informal Norms: Competition and Coordination within the Scientific Community." *Innovation: The European Journal of Social Science Research* 28 (1): 63–80.

Tarko, Vlad. 2015. "The Role of Ideas in Political Economy." *The Review of Austrian Economics* 28 (1): 17–39.

Tarko, Vlad, and Paul Dragos Aligica. 2011. "From 'Broad Studies' to Internet-Based 'Expert Knowledge Aggregation'. Notes on the Methodology and Technology of Knowledge Integration." *Futures* 43 (9): 986–95.

Thierer, Adam. 2016. Permissionless *Innovation*: The *Continuing Case* for *Comprehensive Technological Freedom*. Mercatus Center at George Mason University.

Tiebout, Charles M. 1956. "A Pure Theory of Local Expenditures." *Journal of Political Economy* 64 (5): 416–24.

Toonen, Theo. 2010. "Resilience in Public Administration: The Work of Elinor and Vincent Ostrom from a Public Administration Perspective." *Public Administration Review* 70 (2): 192–202.

Toonen, Theo. 1998. "Networks, Management and Institutions: Public Administration as 'Normal Science.'" *Public Administration* 76 (2): 229–52.

Tomasi, John. 2012. *Free Market Fairness.* Princeton, NJ: Princeton University Press.

Tullock, Gordon. 1965 (2005). *The Selected Works of Gordon Tullock, Volume 6: Bureaucracy.* Edited and with an introduction by Charles K. Rowley. Indianapolis, IN: Liberty Fund.

Tullock, Gordon, Arthur Seldon, and Gordon L. Brady. 2002. *Government Failure: A Primer in Public Choice.* Washington, DC: Cato Institute.

Turban, Daniel B., and Daniel W. Greening. 1997. "Corporate Social Performance and Organizational Attractiveness to Prospective Employees." *Academy of Management Journal* 40 (3): 658–72.

Vaughn, Karen I. 1980. "Does It Matter That Costs Are Subjective?" *Southern Economic Journal* 46 (3): 702–15.

Vile, M. J. C. 1998. *Constitutionalism and the Separation of Powers.* Indianapolis, IN: Liberty Fund.

Viscusi, W. Kip, Joseph E. Harrington Jr., and John M. Vernon. 2005. *Economics of Regulation and Antitrust*, 4th ed. Cambridge, MA: MIT Press.

Viscusi, W. Kip. 1996. "Regulatory Reform and Liability for Pharmaceuticals and Medical Devices." In *Advancing Medical Innovation: Health, Safety and the Role of Government in the 21st Century*, 79–102. Washington, DC: Progress and Freedom Foundation.

Vogel, Steven K. 1996. *Freer Markets, More Rules: Regulatory Reform in Advanced Industrial Countries.* Ithaca, NY, and London: Cornell University Press.

Villamayor-Tomas, Sergio. 2017. "Polycentricity in the Water-Energy Nexus: a comparison of two polycentricity pathways and implications for adaptive capacity of water user associations in Spain." Mimeo.

Waddell, Steven J. 2002. "Six Societal Learning Concepts for a New Era of Engagement." *Reflections* 3 (4): 19–27.

Waddock, Sandra A., Charles Bodwell, and Samuel B. Graves. 2002. "Responsibility: The New Business Imperative." *Academy of Management Executive* 16 (2): 132–48.

Wagner, Richard E. 2016. *Politics as a Peculiar Business: Insights from a Theory of Entangled Political Economy*. Cheltenham, UK, and Northampton, MA: Edward Elgar.

Wagner, Richard E. 2014. "Entangled Political Economy: A Keynote Address." In *Advances in Austrian Economics*, 15–36. Bingley, UK: Emerald Group.

Wagner, Richard E. 2014. "American Federalism: How Well Does It Support Liberty." Mercatus Center, George Mason University.

Wagner, Richard E. 2012. "Democracy and the Theory of Public Finance: A Polycentric, Invisible-Hand Framework." *Public Finance and Management* 12 (3): 298–315.

Wagner, Richard E. 2010. *Mind, Society, and Human Action: Time and Knowledge in a Theory of Social Economy*. New York: Routledge.

Wagner, Richard E. 2007. *Fiscal Sociology and the Theory of Public Finance: An Exploratory Essay*. Cheltenham, UK: Edward Elgar.

Wagner, Richard E. 2005. "Self-Governance, Polycentrism, and Federalism: Recurring Themes in Vincent Ostrom's Scholarly Oeuvre." *Journal of Economic Behavior and Organization* 57 (2): 173–88.

Wagner, Richard E. 2002. "Complexity, Governance and Constitutional Craftsmanship."*American Journal of Economics and Sociology* 61 (1): 105–122.

Waldo, Dwight. 2006 (1948). *The Administrative State: A Study of the Political Theory of American Public Administration*. Piscataway, NJ: Transaction.

Waldo, Dwight. 1987. "Politics and Administration: On Thinking about a Complex Relationship." In *A centennial history of the American Administrative State*, edited by Ralph Clark Chandler. New York: The Free Press.

Waldo, Dwight. 1986. "Afterword: Thoughts in Retrospect—and Prospect." In *A Search for Public Administration: The Ideas and Career of Dwight Waldo*, edited by Brack Brown and Richard J. Stillman II. College Station: Texas A&M University Press.

Walton, Clarence C. 1967. *Corporate Social Responsibilities*. Belmont, CA: Wadsworth.

Walzer, Michael. 1992. "Moral Minimalism." In *From the Twilight of Probability: Ethics and Politics*, edited by William R. Shea and Antonio Spadafora. Sagamore Beach, MA: Science History Publications.

Walzer, Michael. 1994. *Thick and Thin: Moral Argument at Home andAbroad*. Notre Dame, IN: University of Notre Dame Press.

Walzer, Michael. 1987. *Interpretation andSocial Criticism*. Cambridge, MA: Harvard University Press.

Wamsley, Gary L., Robert N. Bacher, Charles T. Goodsell, Philip S. Kronenberg, John A. Rohr, Camilla M. Stivers, Orion F. White, and James F. Wolf. 1990. *Refounding Public Administration*. Thousand Oaks, CA: Sage.

Wamsley, Gary L., and Mayer N. Zald. 1973. *The Political Economy of Public Organizations: A Critique and Approach to the Study of Public Administration*. Lanham, MD: Lexington Books.

Weingast, Barry R. 1995. "The Economic Role of Political Institutions: Market-Preserving Federalism and Economic Development." *Journal of Law, Economics, and Organization* 11 (1): 1–31.

White, Lawrence H. 2012. *The Clash of Economic Ideas: The Great Policy Debates and Experiments of the Last Hundred Years*. Cambridge University Press.

White, Lawrence H. 2005. "The Federal Reserve System's Influence on Research in Monetary Economics." *Econ Journal Watch* 2 (2): 325–54.

Wicks, Andrew C., Shawn L. Berman, and Thomas M. Jones. 1999. "The Structure of Optimal Trust: Moral and Strategic Implications." *Academy of Management Review* 24 (1): 99–116.

Windsor, Duane. 2006. "Corporate Social Responsibility: Three Key Approaches." *Journal of Management Studies* 43 (1): 93–114.

Wilber, Ken. 2001. *A Theory of Everything: An Integral Vision of Business, Politics, Science, and Spirituality*. Boston: Shambhala.

Wilber, Wilber. 1998. *The Essential Ken Wilber: An Introductory Reader*. Boston: Shambhala.

Williamson, Oliver E. 1983. "Credible Commitments: Using Hostages to Support Exchange." *The American Economic Review* 73 (4): 519–40.

Wilson, David Sloan, Elinor Ostrom, and Michael E. Cox. 2013. "Generalizing the Core Design Principles for the Efficacy of Groups." *Journal of Economic Behavior & Organization* 90 (Supplement): S21–32.

Wilson, Woodrow. 1887. "The Study of Administration." *Political Science Quarterly* 2 (2): 197–222.

Wilson, Woodrow. 1885 (1956). *Congressional Government*. New York: Meridian Books.

Winston, Clifford. 2006. *Market Failure versus Government Failure: Microeconomics Policy Research and Government Performance*. Washington, DC: Brookings Institution Press.

Wittman, Donald A. 1995. *The Myth of Democratic Failure: Why Political Institutions Are Efficient*. Chicago: University of Chicago Press.

Wheeler, D., B. Colbert, and R. E. Freeman. 2003. "Focusing on Value: Reconciling Corporate Social Responsibility, Sustainability and Stakeholder Approach in a Network World." *Journal of General Management* 28 (3): 1–28.

Wohlgemuth, Michael. 2002. "Democracy and Opinion Falsification: Towards a New Austrian Political Economy." *Constitutional Political Economy* 13 (3): 223–246.

Wood, Donna J. 1991. "Corporate Social Performance Revisited." *Academy of Management Review* 16 (4): 691–718.

Young, Andrew 2015. "Austrian Business Cycle Theory: A Modern Appraisal." In *Oxford Handbook of Austrian Economics*, edited by Peter J. Boettke and Christopher J. Coyne. Oxford: Oxford University Press.

INDEX OF AUTHORS

INDEX OF CONCEPTS